Camera and Action

Camera and Action

American Film as Agent of Social Change, 1965–1975

Elaine M. Bapis

McFarland & Company, Inc., Publishers
Jefferson, North Carolina, and London

LIBRARY OF CONGRESS CATALOGUING-IN-PUBLICATION DATA

Bapis, Elaine M., 1949–
Camera and action : American film as agent of
social change, 1965–1975 / Elaine M. Bapis.
p.   cm.
Includes bibliographical references and index.

ISBN 978-0-7864-3341-4
softcover : 50# alkaline paper ∞

1. Motion pictures — United States — History.   2. Motion
pictures — Social aspects — United States.   I. Title.
PN1993.5.U6B294   2008   791.430973 — dc22   2008016019

British Library cataloguing data are available

On the cover: Ann-Margret and Jack Nicholson in Mike Nichols'
Carnal Knowledge (1971); Clapper ©2008 Shutterstock

Manufactured in the United States of America

McFarland & Company, Inc., Publishers
Box 611, Jefferson, North Carolina 28640
www.mcfarlandpub.com

For Nick and my precious family:
Often neglected but never forgotten during
these last months of cure and creation.

Acknowledgments

It takes a team to continue on difficult journeys. Thank you Bob Goldberg at the University of Utah Department of History for your consistent, critical commentary and unwavering enthusiasm for this project, despite the often tedious and overwritten drafts. Your experienced eye contributed to improvements at every stage in the process. I am grateful to Mary Strine, Eric Hinderaker, William Siska, and Rebecca Horn whose support and encouragement came unfailingly through many provocative questions and suggestions. Thank you Christine Pickett at the University for your diligence, your enthusiasm, and your excellent reading talent. Thank you Margaret Herrick and North Baker libraries. Madeleine at the Library of Congress made my research delightful.

Part of chapter V was originally published as "Easy Rider: Landscaping the Modern Western" in *The Landscape of Hollywood Westerns: Ecocriticism in an American Film Genre*, edited by Deborah A. Carmichael, published in 2006 by the University of Utah Press, and is used with permission.

As in every written project, there is a group of people that fills in the trail to publishing. For me it is the professors in the English Department at the University of Utah whose encouragement in my literary development is responsible for the beginnings of my professional life. I would like to thank Meg Brady, Steve Tatum, and Kathryn Stockton for giving me confidence in my early years. My friends and relatives offered endless encouragement; thank you for loving film with me. A special thanks to Sean Mooney for helping me keep my perspective, to Tom Harvey and Liza Nicholas for the provocative happy hours and the critical commentary, to Markie Fair for the special conversations, to Maria Mastakas and Alethia for saving me at the eleventh hour. My love of ideas began with my parents' faith in education. I am grateful for their insistence on academic learning. A special recognition goes to my father who was not able to see this completed. My deepest and heartfelt gratitude goes to my children for their patience during the most trying tasks and for their happiness over the finished product. In particular, thank you Nick, Michael, Eleni, Alethia, and Chris for always checking in and for your unwavering belief in me. Maria and Georgia, thank you for bringing such love into the world.

Table of Contents

Preface

This study examines the changes in the American film industry, audiences, and feature films during the years 1965–1975. With transformations in production codes, new adjustments in national narratives, a rise in independent filmmaking, and a new generation of directors and producers addressing controversial issues on the mainstream screen, film was part of the processes of social change that defined these years. Filmmakers advanced a new mantra in the business of Hollywood. Anything that was "new, now, and real" would be material for the lens and any story that went through the camera had to "tell it like it is."

Many baby boomers thought of film as an agent for social activism concerning such issues as the generation gap, the counterculture, masculinity, women's liberation, and multi-culturalism. Rather than comparing history to film and correcting data, *Camera and Action* places film inside historical processes. Using generation, gender, and ethnicity as categories of analysis, this work adds to the history of film as well as to the literature on representation, identity construction, and cinema as a visual site of debate.

Ten motion pictures stand out as representations of the important role that film played for many Americans from the mid–1960s to the mid–1970s. *The Graduate, Alice's Restaurant, Easy Rider, Midnight Cowboy, M*A*S*H, McCabe and Mrs. Miller, Carnal Knowledge, Little Big Man, The Godfather,* and *The Godfather: Part II* have become cinematic records of the cultural forces shaping American society during these turbulent years. Nine of the ten films have maintained an enduring legacy as icons in popular culture. The single film *McCabe and Mrs. Miller,* a box office flop, is included because it has maintained a critical status in academic studies and allows an important statement about the parameters of discourse at the time. These pictures memorialized a period when adversarial and unsettling narratives were a popular form of advocacy. In their success and qualified survival, each film helped define our relationship to the meaning of the late sixties and early seventies as historical reference points.

With transformations in the American film industry and the changing composition of audiences, viewer expectations became a necessary part of the story. *The Graduate* (1967) staked claims of generational authority. Two years after its release, Arthur Penn turned to the counterculture to show splits within the younger generation. Penn's *Alice's Restaurant* (1969) exemplified the Americanness of the hippie phenomenon and its use as a site of liberation. That same year, *Easy Rider* (1969) arrived front and center in America to meld new counter-culture men with the men of Westerns past. This experimental film registered the new taste in cinematic pleasure with its box office success and subsequent iconic status.

When a faux cowboy and a street hustler in *Midnight Cowboy* (1969) entered the cinematic conversation, audiences learned of the impact of movies on male identity. The anti-establishment men in Robert Altman's *M*A*S*H* (1970) introduced a new image of the war hero in film. Altman returned to look at the Western's role in the construction of gender identity and authority in *McCabe and Mrs. Miller* (1971). This film critiqued the genre and tested the possibility for women's equal opportunity and treatment in formula narratives. Mike Nichols turned the tables on the gender debates in *Carnal Knowledge* (1971) to show that not much had changed between men and women.

Arthur Penn, in *Little Big Man* (1970), considered what the impact of Hollywood has been on Native American identity. His groundbreaker tried to "tell it like it was" in the old West. American cinema came full circle to the return of the genre with Francis Ford Coppola's *The Godfather* (1972). His "family affair" constructed Italian ethnicity as a quintessential American identity and included the European ethnic in the multicultural debates of the 1970s. *The Godfather: Part II* (1974) both questioned and participated in the ethnic resurgence in the larger society.

Steven Spielberg's cinematic triumph with *Jaws* in 1975 showed that the boomer generation could double and triple film's potential to make money. Using mainstream film as an agent in social change and experiment gave way to reformulating national narratives. *Jaws*, *Star Wars*, *Rocky* and others absorbed the experimental approach into classical formulas and imprinted new myths and images onto the screen for the next generation. Film as entertainment-art spoke less about telling it like it was and more about how we wanted it to be. The big-draw picture had returned.

From 1965 to 1975, film became a culture, complete with its own beliefs about how, who, and what should dominate visual reality. Viewers and critics alike talked about, thought about, and studied cinema with true faith in its sanctity. They passionately made new claims about what it could do. This book intends to show how poignant the effects of those risks were. Filmmakers and audiences documented their convictions in the lively afterlife of most of these films. The story of these ten groundbreaking films takes us through the lens and into the theaters of daily life.

Introduction

For the Love of Film

It is the nature of the claims made for the images considered as evidence that determines both the discursive function of the events and the criteria to be employed in the assessment of their veracity as predicative utterances.

— Hayden White, "AHR Forum"

American popular film from 1965 to 1975 underwent significant changes in infrastructure and in what mainstream motion pictures came to mean. To use Hayden White's argument about the historical in images, "the nature of the claims" viewers and filmmakers made because of these transformations had something to do with the "criteria ... employed" in assessing a historical moment when a "sixties" mentality — that is, an antiestablishment sensibility — made its way into the hearts and minds of Americans. Of the several hundred releases from 1965 to 1975, ten films in particular stand out for their discursive function and criteria in social, cultural, and industry changes. *The Graduate* (1967), *Alice's Restaurant* (1969), *Midnight Cowboy* (1969), *Easy Rider* (1969), *M*A*S*H* (1970), *McCabe and Mrs. Miller* (1971), *Carnal Knowledge* (1971), *Little Big Man* (1970), *The Godfather* (1972), and *The Godfather: Part II* (1974) set, rejected, accommodated, and negotiated social trends. The first five pictures engaged in a sixties' generational discourse of antiestablishment. The last five joined the conversation about constructing something new in a 1970s environment of gender and multicultural debates. All ten, in one way or another, were recognized as important agents of cinematic, if not social, change through either Academy Award status or critical acclaim in academic circles, or as icons of popular culture recycled in later years. In the way viewers identified with their images, narratives, and subject matters, these pictures helped show the particular function of cinema in the production of meaning about the state of American society and culture during these years. Three discursive categories — generation, gender, and ethnicity — stand as the most prominent "utterances," articulating what film helped to imagine as socially possible then. These categories of analysis frame what was understood as vital to communicate with and therefore to live in American society.

From 1965 to 1975, the industry's importance as a place of cultural influence, with its capital, aesthetics, and public ceremony, deepened with filmmakers and spectators worldwide.

3

Film immersed itself in a new kind of cultural production with the Code break-up, a reconfiguration of audiences, a strong belief in film's agency to change society, and the shift of creative authority from the producer to the director. Filmmakers interested in combining experimental and expressive technique coincided with audience interest in new subject matter. The rise of independents changed the shape of Hollywood and broadened its thematic reach. Consequently, the contemporary context of the late 1960s gave filmmakers a new opportunity for success at theaters across the country.

Where Hollywood experienced an experimental boost from 1965, the industry found its big-budget confidence by 1975. The years of transition evolved into a 1970s industry renaissance. Isolating a few films during these years highlights the "nature of the claims" produced not only in the images circulated on screens but also in the cultural survival of those films. The life of their reception has influenced the "discursive function" of these years. As one historian explains, "bombarding the public with particular images does raise eyebrows and creates many opportunities for people to think in depth about particular issues affecting modern America."[1]

If film speaks to us in the present about issues in the past, it operates as a repository and a historical force, imparting the diverse ways people come to terms with the pressing concerns in everyday life. Film's "literary" quality offers an obvious chance to examine meaning, but its form, its framework of communication, is part of social processes that produce consequences. American cinema acted as an agent in the dissemination of values, beliefs, attitudes, social codes, and identity. Rather than highlighting the aesthetics, this study turns to the discursive interaction between film and its historical context. The films in this study reveal how patterns of social relations and assumptions about who we are were communicated and passed on from one generation to the next. Drawing on theories of representation and discourse, this project emphasizes film's contribution to the construction of a sixties narrative and the shaping of a seventies culture.[2]

Since its entrance into twentieth-century American society, the film of Hollywood has represented the real world, taken audiences into the realm of fantasy, and challenged thought through visual inquiry. Hollywood has dominated film worldwide as an economic power and a creator of master narratives, a distributor of discourse, a negotiator of boundaries, a measure of cinematic standard, and an employer of large numbers of people. One film historian goes so far as to claim it is "one of the most visible institutions in the United States, indeed the world." This industry made itself evident in every major downtown in the 1930s movie palace days and later in every local town with the modern shopping mall multiplexes.[3] Entertainment has been traded for money in newspapers, magazines, fan clubs, and radio gossip, not to mention critical reviews and television talk shows.[4] Filmmakers have modeled after Hollywood, resisted it, or at least have become part of the conversation of film dominated by the industry.[5] As one of the most powerful entities of the commercial market, American cinema produced a cultural environment measured in box office success and in the push and pull of the latter 1960s. Mainstream pictures provided a site for producing something new, something beyond the artistic innovations of previous cinematic periods and beyond the realm of film for film's sake. College-aged audiences and their professors drew an aura of mystery around the potential for film. It would be the individual medium that captured the full reality of a historical moment.

Film, more than literature, became a communal site of liberation from establishment sensibility for many college-aged Americans. Popular motion pictures, it was hoped, would be nothing less than a tool for creating a new social "environment." As one professor told *Saturday Review*, "film is freed to work as ... something which does not simply contain, but shapes people, tilting the balance of their faculties, radically altering their perceptions, and ultimately their views of self and all reality."[6] Movies were to be a site of intellectual inquiry, a place to reimagine the world according to the 1960s spirit of revolution, and thus a valuable social tool in change.

Intent on breaking boundaries, with the help of new camera technology, filmmakers literally and figuratively went into the streets. Everything was a subject for cinema. American mainstream cinema would be artistic, intellectual, and profitable. In one film historian's words, the popular coincided with the intellectual to make film the "preferred arena for dissident social activity."[7] By the seventies, classical narratives dominated — but with a twist. Steamy sex scenes, new levels of graphic violence, and on-site camera work mixed with convention. A film-school generation spoke a new language on screen by the seventies and modified the previous era's idea of America itself. Instead of assuming a nation solid and unified, it was a country diverse and multicultural. A tapestry, a mosaic, a montage — these logical motifs patterned a new idea of American culture. A paradigm of diversity represented what was perceived as a purer, more authentic America.

Such expectations of film as a social environment required a gritty realism that mirrored behavior of everyday life rather than mimicked its ideals. Like poetry for the Beats a generation earlier, film at this time became a preferred site of dissension and innovation. Youth audiences had been marketed prior to 1966 with the beach party narrative, but following the censorship changes after 1965, lines between acceptability and legality created a new category: the R-rated film, which brought a newly defined market into the cinematic fold — the under-thirty young-adult group. Film now explored sensitive social issues previously reserved for avant-garde, underground, or European stock.

The new Hollywood could not have made its way into the popular market without a new taste for the improvisation style of acting. Unknown actors and actresses such as Dustin Hoffman, Katharine Ross, Julie Christie, Al Pacino, and Robert De Niro turned the tables on the "bankable star" era. The grittier look of this new talent fostered realism more than glitz and glamour. In an atmosphere of student protest and political demonstration, sixties film challenged American accord and changed the American persona forever. The turning point in several ways was Mike Nichols' *Who's Afraid of Virginia Woolf?* in 1966. The Academy endorsed Nichol's raw portrait of family dysfunction and brought the iconoclastic art film officially into the mainstream theater.[8]

It is difficult to say for sure what makes a film popular, but defining these films as such indicates something more was going on than just entertainment. Popular features belonged to a general if diverse public and one broader than the art film group because of the tie to maximum profit and dependence on large amounts of capital, even for independent projects. Hence, a film that made it to the top could echo the voice of the viewers, not merely display the vision of the director. Box-office hits, therefore, performed cultural work by speaking a popular "language" that included contentious perspectives. By virtue of their historical context, these popular films constructed America and protested at the same time. [9]

Prior to the mid–1960s, for example, big draws generally reinforced mainstream cultural values and attitudes while critiquing excessive power. *High Noon* (1952) condemned Cold War mentality but sanctioned typical individualist idealism. During the later sixties, with changes in the studio system and censorship protocol, mainstream film asked about the idealism itself.

The feature film was a forum for both debating and reproducing identity within a range of circulating questions about Americanness and a space for negotiating new relations of power to press for wider margins of possibility.[10]

On one level, cinema transmits and secures meaning. On another level, once viewers pronounce a popular film a phenomenon, they identify with it socially, emotionally, and intellectually. Films on this plane become part of a collective cultural exchange[11] and facilitate what one film critic calls the "constitutive condition for national or even personal identity" to emerge. Features in that sense enjoy an educational function but if, as theorists claim today, people's "relationship to meaning is never entirely fixed and predetermined but can be open, unpredictable, and changeable [over time and circumstances] and is a matter of struggle and contention," then film's fate after its initial release is part of the contentious process of meaning, of assessing the veracity of events.[12] Asking cinema to provide evidence for social and cultural processes is not a simple question of sorting out the truth or fiction of any picture but recognizing how representations render ideas "intelligible." As one critic puts it, cinema is about "the allowable limits of difference."[13] These ten films were part of cultural passages by virtue of the historical situation and edifying context at the time of the films' release.[14]

As Hollywood transitioned into experiment, it also paralleled larger patterns of change in American beliefs, attitudes, and values. Pairing the decades by splitting them in the middle shows the relationship between a volatile restructuring of convention and a hopeful remaking of meaning. Where popular notions of reform guided civil rights and politics in the early part of the decade, calls for revolution within middle-class America preoccupied cultural and political protestors by the end. Before mid-decade, social roles did not deviate much from men as breadwinners and women as housewives. Policemen, teachers, managers, doctors, and other figures of authority could still expect a measure of deference. The national government was still portrayed as an instrument of defense and the provider of security. Protesting war was still unpopular. Male students wore shirts and ties on college campuses and women wore dresses or skirts.[15]

The 1965 escalation of troops in Vietnam increased draftee numbers, which resulted in heightened antiwar protests. A counterculture developed in San Francisco and spread in sensibility throughout American cities. Racial tension turned into riots and American youth rebelled differently than their predecessors. Casual and immodest dress, demands for sexual freedom, and a more violent form of dissent than previous years characterized youthful disapproval of American society. By fall 1965, reformers became revolutionaries; by the March on the Pentagon in 1967, anyone over thirty was suspect; and by the 1968 Chicago Democratic convention, police were pigs. College campus protests inundated campus buildings, and the National Guard entered state colleges to control antiwar demonstrators by the 1970s. Youth organizations such as Students for Non-violence Coordinating Committee and Students for a Democratic Society split internally and dispersed into scattered coalitions.

History still debates what exactly changed during this time. Some, for example, credit political radicals and the counterculture for being the primary agents of social and political change and challengers of status quo. Historian Douglas T. Miller summarizes the argument:

> Movement members ... transformed society and politics. They helped to liberalize racial and sexual attitudes, hastened the demise of the liberal consensus, and inadvertently fostered a conservative revival. Thus the New Left and the counterculture, though transitory and directly involving only a fraction of the population, shook the very foundations of American life.[16]

William O'Neill describes the 1960s as a period of America's "coming apart" in his book by the same title (1971). Others such as Godfrey Hodgson built on O'Neill's premise. Hodgson's *America in Our Time* begins the period with President Kennedy's promise of Camelot in 1960 and Nixon's resignation in 1974. The presidencies, as Hodgson writes, became "the master symbol of the public mood and national aspirations." Within that frame, Dallas and Watergate bookended the changes in American society during the two decades.[17] Alan Matusow concluded in *The Unraveling of America* (1984) that "optimism vanished" by 1968 when "fundamental differences in values emerged to divide the country."[18]

In the "unraveling" model, the seventies are highlighted as a loss of hope. Looking back in 1970, for example, David Halberstam wrote in *McCall's* magazine, "Good-by to the Sixties, to all that hope and expectation. It started so well." Like him, many believed "that ... all the pieces would come together for a golden era of American social and cultural progress, victory over the darker side of our nature, victory over injustice."[19]

The ongoing narrative about the sixties as a golden moment set the seventies up as a loss of "hope and expectation," as Halberstam claimed. Yet, the women's movement began its most hopeful and progressive period in the early 1970s. Rejuvenation of women's rights met with reconstruction of gender roles and social relationships between men and women. At the same time, new questions were asked of everyone. Who or what is American? Multicultural, ethnic, and diverse, many answered. The golden moment of hope for a social and political revolution that gave the sixties an iconic life of its own resulted in none other than a complete cultural revolution. By 1970, the American film industry was fully immersed in the accommodation of change and the negotiation of new possibilities.

Key issues of political and social rights traditionally negotiated in the home or in the local church or school were fought in popular culture. Men's and women's social roles, young people's social behavior, interracial relationships, drug habits, speech, and other aspects of values and beliefs became part of a national project reshaping America. These new notions of identity, mixed with calls for legitimacy and political authority, changed American culture in permanent ways. Film popularized the ideals of autonomy, the pursuit of pleasure, the myth of personal freedom, and then returned to the value of heritage, family, and group identity. Middle-class youth imprinted their historical significance and their "predicative utterances," giving the sixties a value, a discourse, and a lasting power into the 1970s. The body of films in this study shows how filmmakers used the far-reaching opportunities of the sixties and seventies in the remaking of their art.[20] Through those lenses, the sixties were both golden and chaotic, the seventies disappointing and rejuvenating.

Lamenting the loss of the golden moment is typical of sixties narratives, which measured victory as a political revolution, but what followed was a liberation on the popular front. It was culture more than class that defined the most pronounced sites of debate during these years. Filmmakers brought cultural disputes such as changing attitudes toward authority, new expressions of sexual roles, and changing American identity to the screen by popularizing the generation gap, women's liberation, and multiculturalism, making it possible to imagine a new society behaving differently than their parents. Seeing social change as a matter of culture measures the weight of the paradigm shift in beliefs about American ideals through film. If cinema is both reflective and affective, the films in this study glow with historical moments of new conflicts arising out of changing attitudes toward sex, workplace protocol, individual rights, and identity. How people worked through new ideas of generation, gender, and ethnicity in the larger society are both mirrored and constructed in these films.

The battleground of age identifies a general split between the younger and older generation. Three films in this category — *The Graduate*, *Alice's Restaurant*, and *Easy Rider* — became cultural icons speaking for a sixties generation gap. These films, released in the last few years of the 1960s, attempted to sort out the chaos of political and cultural rebellion as youth indulged in generational politics of age and the hippie counterculture. Popular dissent also turned into a commodity. RCA Victor ran an ad in the *Village Voice* for their record album *Hair*. "Bridge the generation gap," the ad read. "Buy this album and explain it to your folks. They'll be surprised how much they can learn," the ad continued.[21] In the "gap" discourse, the young were imagined as a group with privileged knowledge and new power in shaping American society. RCA's adult generation appeared naïve and uneducated, but both generations profited. A notion of the generation gap helped galvanize a new national sense of the cultural revolution and adversarial sentiment toward America to show that speaking out against conventional ideals by purchasing representative products was not only acceptable but obligatory.

The sixties idea of the generation gap defining hip youth filtered through the streets and onto college campuses and set the stage for deeper, longer lasting issues than age. Filmmakers had at hand different subject matter based more specifically on power relations. Anti-Vietnam demonstrations brought the most enduring sixties icons and images to life and opened avenues for deeper divides over men's identity and women's social roles. Women became more visible by publicly declaring equal opportunity rights, indelibly marking the 1970s as the gender years. The gender debates during the first part of the decade eclipsed the attention on the generation gap and the counterculture. Calls for equality from women forged divisions along different lines. Ranging from radical politics of feminism to a nationwide struggle over women's liberation, women's call to action reshaped social authority and personalized female legitimacy.

Men in popular film joined women in the conversation about the meaning of gender roles and integrated sixties rebellion into new narratives about identity and relationships. Films recorded the challenges to traditional male and female identities in a lasting way. In a cultural environment where advocates valued multiculturalism more than assimilation, American filmmakers tapped in and brought "ethnic activism" in line with changes in the value of heritage. Sharing previous civil rights' models, multiculturalism became a national project and viewers engaged in the importance of revising American history and popular culture narratives.

In an attempt to address the one-sided history of the West known to most Americans through Westerns, filmmakers revised the historical record and added another dimension to the debate about Americanness and activism. Many ethnics during the early 1970s asked if they were victims of the American melting pot. Americans called for consciousness raising and the pursuit of new forms of "group solidarity." Ethnics actively turned the new decade's rights agenda into a form of self-assertion and a way to "restructure America's public and political culture," as some historians explained.[22]

To set the context of film's discursive practices from 1965 to 1975, chapters I and II focus on the American film industry and audiences in transition. With production codes essentially dissolved and censorship bans lifted by the mid–1960s, Hollywood entered an era of experimentation and general restructuring. Directors replaced studio heads as the leading figures in the industry, and filmmakers experimented with new narratives, characterizations, and ways to symbolize America. Demographics affected the exhibition arm of the film industry and forced theaters to reconfigure their interior space and regional locations.

Since transformation in the production end of the industry is limited without a willing audience, Chapter II shows how the changing composition of viewer expectations is a vital part of the story of American cinema. If this was indeed a time of rising generational authority, then the college campus as a space where attitudes and power were debated and reconfigured cannot be ignored. Universities instituted film education programs and production centers, graduating a new kind of film consumer and producer. Education programs added to the cultivation of new patterns of reception.

Chapter III begins the discussion on discourse. More than any other film of its time, *The Graduate* (1967) struck a chord with a broad middle-class audience because the film reflected baby boomers, grown up. Voyeurs imagined themselves exposing the older generation's material success as idle luxury and pretense. A box-office magnet, *The Graduate* helped pull independents into mainstream cinema and circulate generational authority.

Chapter IV focuses on intragenerational splits. Arthur Penn's *Alice's Restaurant* (1969) provides one example of the way feature films defined a new everyman — the folk singer and hippie commune member, the youthful free spirit who would not live by example but by doing his own thing. The counterculture highlighted both a subterranean reality and an impossible idea. The general message that identified hippies' good works was needless persecution of those who were different. Being different was suddenly hip, and all restraints against excess — excessive sex, excessive leisure, excessive language, excessive color, and excessive displays of love — were ignored. Exaggeration defined what hippies were and ultimately could never be. *Alice's Restaurant* advocated counterculture intervention through love, friendship, and an exemplary reconsideration of the material world. In *Alice*, the new "folk" of the counterculture displaced "the people" of the 1930s and 1940s. The hippie commune served as a measure of the changing regard for middle-class ideals and the stake young people had in counterculture sensibility. Arlo Guthrie played himself and helped iconize the most ubiquitous image of liberation, if not revolution — long hair.

Chapter V explores the meaning of the counterculture as a general forum for change in *Easy Rider* (1969). The film updated the autonomous individual and reemphasized appearance as liberation. Chapter V compares the American ritual of freedom on the road to American values of responsibility, patriotism, and individualism. *Easy Rider* debates the role of material success and luxury in the face of the older generation's failing social reform. This film's popularity among young audiences stemmed from its perception of antiestablishment discourse and as an active response to the discriminatory practices in America, particularly imagined as in the South. Still one of the most popular icons from that era in popular culture, the image of Peter Fonda and Dennis Hopper riding across America on their Harley-Davidsons represents sixties nostalgia for a time when sensitivity to social problems lay in these specific antiestablishment attitudes. A new ride for the new man, *Easy Rider* set masculinity, formerly the territory of the Western, in the contemporary landscape.

Chapter VI introduces the complex nature of gender debates with John Schlesinger's *Midnight Cowboy* (1969). Schlesinger brought Dustin Hoffman back as Forty-Second Street hustler Ratso Rizzo and introduced Jon Voight to American audiences as the Texan who goes to Manhattan to make money off rich women. This film asked serious questions about the production of male identity through traditional Westerns. Similarly, it was time to question the traditional construction of masculinity in other areas. Chapter VII extends the discussion about the discourse of antiestablishment in Robert Altman's *M*A*S*H* (1970). The film mocks just about every traditional, iconic institution in America and rebuffs the conventional war film. The chapter points out the limitations to the new realism of "telling it like it is" in a film about men gone wild with antiestablishment rebellion.

Along with the sexual revolution, women's call for equality provided compelling opportunity to create roles for women as active agents in traditional genres. For its attempt to rewrite the Western from a woman's perspective, *McCabe and Mrs. Miller* (1971), discussed in Chapter VIII, showed the parameters and criteria in the assessment of the women's movement. It was one of the few films that self-consciously placed women squarely in the center of traditional narratives about men but did not depend on making her a sex object to do so. It is worth looking at for the method and technique of imagining women as resourceful and independent. While *McCabe* did not develop into a legend and icon like the other nine films, it is notable for its critical achievements and continued life in academic debates about gender and the Western during the 1970s. This film measures the extent to which American movies could embed gender issues and the experimental trend in mainstream film. This film's relative box office failure invites assumptions about the possibilities of altering time-honored genres from a feminist perspective.

Chapter IX returns to Mike Nichols to address the "battle of the sexes" and ask men and women the raw truth about their relationships. Nichols' *Carnal Knowledge* (1971) critiqued the women's movement during a relaxed censorship period with new visualizations of men's and women's relations. Jack Nicholson returns as the picture's male chauvinist to whom the rise of feminism, with its challenges to traditional notions of sexual identity, presented a threat and also a predicament for his self-image. Like Altman, Nichols reveals more contradictions than conclusions.

In the spirit of diversity, Chapter X addresses the move toward multiculturalism as a model for contemporary America. Arthur Penn's *Little Big Man* takes Dustin Hoffman back to the year 1876 where his character was the only white witness to the Battle of Little Big Horn. This film frames the debate about the production of Americanness and its many contradictions. Penn places "telling it like it is" at the center of his project to revise the ubiquitous image of the Indian as vicious savage in American cinema. As it newly represents Native Americans with focus on multicultural identity during the seventies, the film provides a chance to question the repercussions of the multicultural paradigm.

The last chapter shows American cinema's return to genre. Coppola's *The Godfather* (1972) incorporates the experimental trend into classical cinema and the antiestablishment sentiment with the need for heritage. The heart of the chapter rests on the construction of ethnicity as a way to broaden Americanness and include the European ethnic in the multicultural debates of the 1970s. *The Godfather: Part II* (1974) both questions and exploits romantic representation of ethnic identity during this time. These films comment on the exploitation of Italians in Hollywood tradition and gives voice to ethnic resurgence in the larger society. Paying attention to the popularity of film in any era means recognizing what is being exchanged through images. It also means being aware of social codes, legalities, and the general historical context in which those visuals form.

The Conclusion brings film to 1975 because at this time the film industry settled into its contemporary zone. Stephen Spielberg's cinematic triumph, *Jaws*, ensured that the big-draw picture had returned. The film industry experienced widespread changes in infrastructure and made particularly important inroads to secure its future. With Code break-ups, exhibition realignment, a new ratings system, and audiences willing to stand in line for something new and different, filmmakers adjusted what would be possible on screen. At the same time, popular advocacy was limited by popular discourse. In filmmaking's most liberal period of change, iconic films were largely composed of white experience and perspective. Critiques of race and class in these films remained undeniably minor. Social ills, it was perceived, were results of failed governments, families, churches, and convention. This is not to say that race and class were not part of the films' subtext during the period in focus. Rather, the films that saw culture as the means to social change show what discourses dominated. For the most part, race relations were held at a distance until Spike Lee popularized blacks' perspectives and experiences.

Within the margins of feature-length film, then, the ten pictures in this study helped establish the value of social change as they resolved questions of Americanness through the frameworks of generation, gender, and ethnicity. By virtue of their popular status and box office revenues (or lack of), these feature films helped determine "the discursive function of events" as produced and received. Judging from the films that won audience favor at the box office, in the classroom, or at the Academy Awards, one could make claims about what it meant to think of film as a social agent. Whereas traditional genres such as the Western portrayed ideal Americans overcoming forces beyond their control, these films deconstructed the power of those ideals. Hence, Benjamin of *The Graduate* and Captain America of *Easy Rider* refused to be hero and champion. That job was reserved for the film itself; when cinema after 1966 could do what it never was allowed before, the popular feature redefined itself considerably.

Almost a separate culture, like "a secular religion," during these years, film, in the words of one critic, "permeated American life in a way that it never had before and never has since." Susan Sontag chimed in, "It was at this specific moment in the 100-year history of cinema that going to movies, thinking about movies, talking about movies became a passion among university students and other young people. You fell in love not just with actors but with cinema itself."[23] Filmmakers found new commercial value for a grittier America between 1965 and 1975. The thriving, critical, feature-length film market made it possible for the Peter Fondas and Dennis Hoppers to experiment with success. A film-school generation followed up with changes of its own, creating new claims for what film could do. The industry reoriented itself toward big business and recentralized production dominance by 1975. The new filmmakers were ready to reinvent classic heroes in time for the upcoming bicentennial celebrations of America and the promotion of its ideals. Until then, a little dose of new, now, and real mixed well with the hope that "telling it like it is" could change things and with the love of film itself.

INDUSTRY
AND AUDIENCES

CHAPTER I

As Hollywood Turned

Expansion, Exhibition, Codes, and Directors at Mid-Decade

> The corporate criss-crossing, the dollar-lined ... indulgence ... of a plethora of new parent companies, the proliferation of independent production, the mushrooming of packaging from all points of the compass all combined to sweep aside ancient barriers and hallowed taboos. Now people were getting a chance to try as never before, and established people were trying new things as never before.
>
> — William Tusher, *Film Daily Yearbook*

On Oscar night, April 5, 1965, at the Santa Monica Civic Auditorium, two musical ladies, Mary Poppins and Eliza Dolittle, shared the spotlight when the Academy named Warner Brothers' *My Fair Lady* as the Best Picture and Julie Andrews as Best Actress in *Mary Poppins*. A year later at the thirty-eighth Awards ceremony, Twentieth-Century-Fox received Best Picture for *The Sound of Music*, which honored another singing lady, Maria von Trapp. Musicals and melodious voices were celebrated as the symbol of the industry's glamour on those nights, but this time it was with a difference — 30,000,000 television sets aired the special for the first time in Technicolor. Hollywood actors in tuxedos and actresses in red dresses, silvery shoes, and red lipstick received awards, gave speeches, and told jokes. In the midst, Oscar's gold shone brilliantly, making the 1966 audience the largest for a single-network program.

Yet, Hollywood's dramatically charged image that night dimmed in comparison to the transformation taking place in the industry. At mid-decade, Hollywood was in the process of reinventing itself in other ways. Essential to this transformation was the eclipse of the studio-era moguls. William Tusher, West Coast editor of trade publication *The Film Daily*, pronounced 1965 as "the year of the death of the Titans, the passing of dynasties, the changing of palace guards, and the birth of paradoxes. Jack Warner cashed in his chips.... Y. Frank Freeman resigned from Paramount," *Gone with the Wind* creator David O. Selznick and Production Code chief Joseph I. Breen died and the founder of Disney productions and Disneyland, Walt Disney, lay on his deathbed. Only one of the guards, Darryl Zanuck, remained active. With the moguls went the studio system that allowed five major companies to dictate all aspects of the industry. Production, distribution, and exhibition of films spun off in new directions, nurturing innovation and industrial revival. Searching for new survival strategies, industry leaders enlisted expansion and merchandizing programs, exhibition enhancements, and a marriage of convenience with television. Simultaneously, in 1966, the censorship mechanism that policed the business over the past thirty years dissolved under challenge. New opportunities raised a generation of directors who redefined film's cultural role and transported Hollywood into its experimental age. All things considered, Tusher was correct in marking 1965 as "the death of an era" and 1966 as "the year of revolution and upheaval." From the trade's point of view, this moment set forth "the historic blueprints" for Hollywood's foundational changes. It was the last time the feature film was subject to the censorship codes that had regulated the business for the previous thirty years. New material found eager audiences who did not look back. In Tusher's words, 1966 was hailed as "the year that was in Hollywood."[1]

It was clear in the early 1960s that the film industry either had to change its ways or face serious closures as television rooted itself into American homes even more deeply than studio tycoons were willing to believe. Studios tried to retain their former control by preventing film stars from appearing on television programs or signing on to their own TV specials. Yet, television's capacity for survival forced studio magnates to realize that staying alive meant a conjugal rather than hostile relationship. Thus began the expansion programs during the mid–1960s when adversaries became comrades. Along with tightening cost controls and creating more efficient operations than before, companies transformed half of their production facilities into studios for syndicated television series. Conversely, the television industry realized that a blockbuster in the movie theater meant business for them. "Without theatres — no TV blockbusters," warned Tusher.[2]

To facilitate changes in operations, motion picture and television filmmakers formed the Association of Motion Picture and Television Producers in March 1964.[3] This coalition created a network for successful production alternatives and new economic and artistic relationships between TV and cinema. Film and television consolidation allowed union negotiations and contracts to be conducted in one place by one body. The unification, according to Association C.E.O. Charles S. Boren, addressed problems fragmenting the industry. New alliances defined common ground and brought new opportunities all the way around.[4]

Unification helped pull Hollywood out of deficit years. In the first quarter of 1964, for example, M-G-M brought in $23.6 million worth of television revenues. For the 1964-1965 season the company prepared five television network series. Paramount acquired over eight network projects, and United Artists increased its profits 25 percent by turning to network television. Film and television mergers helped rescue Twentieth-Century–Fox from its *Cleopatra* (1963) disaster, the most costly film in the industry's history. In 1963, the company did not have a single series on television. By the 1964-1965 season, Fox had scheduled five. The expansion program also included the construction of larger office buildings and new sound stages, which meant more jobs.[5] In California, motion picture employment increased 70 percent and, as Tusher put it, created a "rush" of sorts, "resulting in more confusion — and gold fever — than ever." As he claimed, "You need a scorecard to tell the hirelings from the bosses as package deals mushroomed — and paid off— as never before." It appeared that total entertainment "emerged as a new reality."[6]

Ongoing television programming, Saturday night family entertainment, and soap opera-style drama offered the American public something cinema could not. Television's open-ended, unresolved serials created an entertainment market based on episodic intrigue. At the same time, TV easily adopted cinema. Executives understood television and film as natural extensions of each other and the successful integration of the two brought companies a means of automatic recycling and regeneration. Fox's executive vice president, Seymour Poe, saw the undertaking as a sign of the industry's "coming of age."[7] To continue a general revenue turnaround, three major studios sought outside capital for a cure. Paramount merged with Gulf and Western Industries, a "distributing, manufacturing, and mineral-producing company."[8] Columbia offered the Banque de Pares et des Pays Bas 34 percent of its shares and United Artists invited merger talks with Transamerica, a financial conglomerate. As one critic commented, "today's motion picture industry has attracted investors, analysts and acquisition-minded corporations outside the entertainment field to an extent undreamed of a decade ago."[9] As Oscar glittered at the Academies in full golden color, the marriage between theater and television was clear. Yet, new revenue guarantees from television and corporate mergers could not completely rehabilitate a struggling industry, since creating a cinematic product ultimately had to address the problem of the available audience. "Total entertainment" still favored television, with nine out of ten homes in America housing a television set by the end of the 1950s.

Along with film company diversification, studios developed stronger methods of promotion and took a pronounced interest in areas of related commerce such as "recorded music, book publishing, [and] merchandizing" businesses. Expansion through assorted retail markets entailed a new promotional scheme focusing on pre-selling. Marketers cross-promoted with such products as the novel, pins, posters, music, and other merchandise. By the end of the decade, film promotion became a big business in its own right.[10] Marketers intensified mass-advertising practices and circulated film information through commercial ads, TV and radio spots, teaser trailers, and TV featurettes. Ultimately, an Academy nomination or award made a substantial difference in a film's advertising value and became the leading feature in a film ad. Marketing executives tailored ads for particular audiences. Paramount, too, placed ads describing young "film buffs" who displayed their movie buttons of *Romeo & Juliet, Goodbye Columbus,* and *If.* "These young people," the ad claimed, "and thousands like them are doing their movie thing. They are all seeing the three motion pictures that have made their world more meaningful ... like love and the establishment. You should see them, too, if you want to see the great change that is happening."[11]

At the same time that companies diversified and cross-promoted, they were vigilant at pre-selling through noncommercial channels. Marketers led more concentrated campaigns than in earlier periods. Typical publicity for big pictures generated cover stories in major magazines such as *Life* and *Look* and newspapers and local TV news, all of which increased marketing value based on the assumption that entertainment was "real" news.[12] Coverage of a film on the local level as a news item added an element of authority to an object of entertainment and contributed to the "must see" sentiment while developing "the proper frame of mind to receive the picture."[13] Consequently, these persistent methods of promotion further cultivated America's deeply implanted celebrity culture to help charge interest in a film and exploit viewers' acute case of movie-star mania.[14]

Companies by the mid–1960s, however, could no longer bank on the automatic draw of casting greats such as Doris Day, Rock Hudson, Cary Grant, Gregory Peck, and others. As one writer reported, "There has been a notable decline in the number of films that are

written and produced simply as vehicles for superstars whose box office appeal alone suppos-
edly would carry the picture." The earlier era of Gable and Garbo had been turned over to
TV. Producers typically would not touch a package without a "big name," but by mid-decade,
it was not clear whose prowess made money. Certainly there were the most famous — Jack
Lemmon, Kirk Douglas, Elizabeth Taylor, Richard Burton — but studios that waited to match
their script with those names could find themselves without a sizeable project at all. Companies recognized that a "selective moviegoer [would] not automatically parade into the theater." Filmmakers by default attended to new star possibilities when the likes of *Bonnie and
Clyde* registered unexpected box office results.[15] Stanley Kramer, for example, saw a trend
toward unknown talent and believed by this time star power in big names detracted from a
film's dramatic delivery and narrative value. He even wondered if his own films "wouldn't
have been even better ... without the big casts, the Hollywood stars."[16] More to the point, if
casting power was not what it had been, Hollywood faced challenges more critical than just
infrastructure modernization. It now had the burden of cultivating new talent, but that would
have to wait a few years until scripts offered attractive material for rising stars.[17]

While the production end of the industry was busy rejuvenating itself through expansion and diversification programs, new promotional strategies and tie-ins, and a search for
new talent, the exhibition branch entered its own revamping. For most of Hollywood's history, the major studios dominated first-run exhibition, but in August 1944, the United States
government issued a decree requiring the controlling film companies to divest their economic
interest in movie theaters and block bookings.[18] Commonly referred to as the Paramount
injunction, this decree separated the exhibition arm from the body of production. Despite
government intervention, however, changes in exhibition were slow to occur. M-G-M, for
example, did not separate production and distribution from its theater assets until 1959 when
Loews amassed several U.S. and Canadian theaters.[19]

Divestment, at the very least, opened doors to independents who formerly had to compete with studios for outlets. Producers were no longer guaranteed movie distribution because
theater owners were no longer obligated to show a studio film regardless of its quality. Divestment made it easier for exhibitors to cultivate the new interest in the art films. Yet, exhibitors
ultimately faced a greater challenge. It was obvious that the movie-going custom had waned
by the 1950s because of television and the changing patterns of leisure resulting from rapid
suburbanization.[20] During the post-divestment period, many urban movie theaters were
demolished, turned into supermarkets, or converted into art theaters and other venues. It was
not until the early sixties with the automatic draw of suburban shopping centers that exhibition rebounded.

Taking the theater to the shopping center reconfigured distribution from the first-run
theater system to saturation bookings that required more prints and thus circulated more
money. In the New York metropolitan area alone, exhibitors added one hundred theaters to
shopping centers during the 1960s, making convenient movie-going available to such outly-
ing areas as Hicksville on Long Island.[21] The shopping center formula helped theater owners
bounce back from their near-bankrupt businesses and brought new entrepreneurs into the
exhibition market by mid-decade. One such contender was Eugene Victor Klein, chairman
and president of National General Corporation (NGC). Klein brought the company from a
$6.7 million loss to a $3.03 million profit by the early 1960s, making NGC the second largest
U.S. theater chain. "The big thing for the family today," Klein claimed, "is to do everything
in a package — go shopping, have dinner, go to a movie. Nobody wants to schlep all the way

downtown to an old barn anymore."[22] As movies grew into another "consumer lure," an attachment to shopping, what mattered most to many exhibitors was the ability to offer parking and driving convenience in only one stop off the main road.[23]

Regulatory changes and movie-house relocation converged with innovations in exhibition business practices. Vice President Jack A. Chartoff of Automated Theatres of America, Inc., explained that "today, automated equipment and the idea that the picture is more important than the theater is giving birth to a new breed of exhibitor." That new breed came from a variety of fields ranging from the Eastman Kodak equipment sector to the furniture business.[24] Exhibitors also developed investment opportunities by creating and offering franchises in theater chains. Encouraged by Jerry Lewis, who campaigned for exhibitors to join him in "the most successful money-making segment of the entertainment industry," some hopefuls saw opportunity in the franchising business and opened Jerry Lewis Cinema theaters at an initial cost of $15,000 with an equipment package of $40,000. Others such as Trans-Lux/Inflight flooded the market with chains. As Trans-Lux President Eugene Picker asked, "If we find a location that will draw people from a wide area, why not keep the profits all to ourselves?"[25] Theater building rebounded with 40,000 cinemas and 14 million seats filling United States cities and towns.[26]

Mixing movies with suburbs altered the concept of the theater. Unlike monumental movie houses of the Golden Era such as Fox's five-thousand seater in San Francisco (demolished for a parking structure), contemporary configuration introduced functional, economical structures accommodating between 250 and 700 viewers. This translated into a theater design that stripped away ornamental interiors and left only a screen, a large room, no balcony, a mass of seats, and a projection booth. At the same time, an expanded screen, set against "less gingerbread," highlighted the dramatic quality of the picture. This functional interior contrasted with the dense and diverse activity of the movie. Contemporary design placed the screen, not the architecture, at the center of dramatic intrigue.[27] Exhibitors enticed viewers into theaters by offering longer runs, wider screens, an array of food, and a sexy film. The key was to get audiences inside; how they engaged in the setting was up to them. Thus, the dominant architectural theory of function before form fit comfortably with the streamlined, suburban shopping center.

Theater innovation in the suburbs had an obvious impact on movie houses in cities. Urban structures modernized with the glass and marble sleekness of sixties architecture and the twin-theater concept with a side-by-side configuration, a single turnstile entrance, one projection booth, and one manager. The twin-theater trend offered the owner a chance to show the art film alongside the entertainment feature. Don Rugoff, head of an art house chain, explained that "a picture, after running for some weeks in both theatres, might slow down in business, but not enough to justify replacing it. It could then continue on in one of the theatres, while a new program goes into the other." By staggering show times or varying the length of the movie run, an owner could meet the needs of film society viewers, art-house advocates, and general audiences. Moreover, the "concept" theater suggested that exhibitors recognized the diversity in viewer taste and moved beyond the assumption that there was just one audience. Others, such as Walter Reade, emulated the twin concept, adding a 600-seat theater next to his newly renovated 450-seater. Theater buffs never again saw anything like the thousand-seat palaces of the early decades since architectural restructuring went hand in hand with downsizing. With the exception of Radio City Music Hall, built in 1932 with a 6,200-seat capacity, most of the others had vanished or been refashioned. Loews' Capitol in

New York removed 2,000 of its 3,600 seats to make room for the new Cinerama screen and keyed down the décor. In these monotone interiors, screens took up entire walls.[28]

Editor Ernest Callenbach of *Film Quarterly* lamented the passing of grand theaters or at least the appreciation of theaters as places:

> Speaking quite personally, I think it is a bad thing that most of us who are deeply concerned with films have come to regard film theatres largely as necessary evils: ugly, uncomfortable, and noisome on the whole, often managed incompletely, even as to elementary projection quality.[29]

To Callenbach, the streamlined theater suffered from a "fundamental misunderstanding of what such a theater" should provide. Sleek, "stripped-down," and "plastered-over" architecture created a cool ambiance for what Callenbach argued was "a 'hot' medium." The plaster and gilt of old invited the viewer into glamour and mystery and suggested the movie-going experience was not just about the film. In contrast, a streamlined interior, as Callenbach observed, was authoritarian: "It insists that you watch the picture and nothing else." The décor, once integral to the cinematic experience, gave way to the "empty chill" of standard theater design. The object of movie-going now was the picture not the façade; that was just fine with proponents. The streamline contemporary theater forced audiences to focus on film. It was cinema itself that mattered, not gilding, scrolls, or gargoyles.[30]

Theaters, advertising, diversification, and mergers suggest that Hollywood is first and foremost in the business of making money. Yet, economics tell only part of the story of the Hollywood establishment at mid-decade. Expansion programs and intensified marketing reveal industry resourcefulness and restructuring, but they do not describe film's cultural role during this time. Shifts in the Hollywood structure coincided with changes in attitudes, beliefs, and values. These alterations challenged the dominance of the family blockbuster film and opened other avenues of exploration for filmmakers. New content and visuals in smaller budget films revealed changes in film taste and film's function as a cultural barometer and guide. While Hollywood can restructure, cut costs, and seek revenue production outside movie-making, it cannot buy audiences. Perhaps the most important change for the course of the American feature film was the death of controls and review boards that determined appropriate material for mainstream screens. Censorship had been a contentious issue since Hollywood's early days. Filmmakers, the public, and the courts wrestled over proper definitions of film content and acceptable boundaries for visual representation on the screen. Changes in censorship codes at mid-decade put the final touches on the Hollywood blueprints about to reshape American movie-making.

Hollywood producers had traditionally determined their industry's moral responsibility through voluntary self-regulation during the film industry's golden era. To prevent further government intrusion and federal censorship, producers and other trade leaders in 1922 formed the Motion Picture Producers and Distributors of America (shortened to Motion Picture Association of America in 1945).[31] Eight years later, on March 30, 1930, under the directorship of Will H. Hays, the MPAA created the Motion Picture Production Code, a censorship agreement of sorts, to police the industry. The membership entered into "a voluntary agreement," acknowledging its responsibility to the public and making a pledge to raise "the motion picture to a still higher level of wholesome entertainment for all concerned." The challenge for the review board, known as the Production Code Administration (PCA), was to balance successfully the code standards "with the integrity and rigor of the screen as a medium of entertainment." Through that administration, the board enforced restrictions with a $25,000 fine for violations of the 1930 code regulations, which required prudence in references to crime, profanity, violence, obscenity, and the "sanctity of the institution of marriage and the home."[32]

The PCA operated in conjunction with the Catholic Legion of Decency, a social watchdog for the specific guidance of Catholic families.[33] The Catholic Legion, formed in 1934, became an unprecedented pressure group that assumed the authority to prevent the release of questionable films. Catholic priests and bishops pursued motion picture control by negotiating with producers to eliminate offending scenes or words from a script before it could receive PCA approval. Their intent was to make a picture more acceptable to Catholic audiences or even to prevent release at major theaters.[34] Suitable films then received the Code Seal of Approval, indicating that they had the PCA and Legion's consent and were therefore safe for exhibitors to show. The problem for both filmmakers and the industry was not battling the Catholic Church per se but the possibility of 20,000,000 Catholics boycotting a film lacking a Code Seal of Approval.[35] Yet, it was not just the number of Catholics that threatened the success of a film. It was their concentration in major cities like Chicago, Boston, New York, and Detroit, where studio-owned, first-run theaters determined the life of a film. Both exhibitors and filmmakers feared that "negative publicity and Catholic boycott would make it impossible for any Legion-condemned film to make a profit." Films at issue were not pornographic or clearly obscene, but those pictures that had potential for success with an adult audience interested in sophisticated subject matter.[36]

Considering that filmmakers were involved in a number of court cases throughout Hollywood history and even though independent producers tried to skirt the Legion censors by seeking alternative distribution channels, the dominance of censors was not successfully challenged until mid–1960. Two forces coalesced by then to give non–PCA films wider distribution opportunity. First, films without PCA approval began to register their commercial value at local art theaters such as New York's Cinema I and II. Second, by the early 1960s, European films had successfully made their way into the general American movie market. With their mature subject matter and relatively strong commercial draw, both European and non–Code pictures helped demonstrate that social agencies of censorship were losing ground in policing freedom of the screen and engineering audience choice. Non–PCA Seal films had profitable showings at theaters in New York, Baltimore, Los Angeles, Chicago, and Detroit by the mid–1960s and films with Legion condemnation generated revenues totaling in the millions.[37] Both non–Code and European material indicated changing audience and filmmaker tastes in film. Interestingly, the box office was Hollywood's most potent censor and the lack of a Seal of Approval might be a theater's best bait.[38]

Changing tastes cropped up internally as well when the review board could not agree on what constituted obscenity. By 1966, new members with more liberal views of morality and of film's responsibility sat on the industry's review board. The MPAA had also hired Jack Valenti, President Lyndon B. Johnson's aide, who promised to bring some of the "Great Society" vision to Hollywood. Valenti's idea was "to inspire and enlarge the future of the motion picture industry" by making it "part of this new era." He "refused to look back." He would be no dreamer. This Harvard graduate and Texas public relations man intended to shake the status quo both inside and outside Hollywood. Valenti's presidency promised "new ideas, new objectives, new programs."[39]

The watershed came in 1965 and 1966 for both the PCA and the Legion with Mike Nichols' *Who's Afraid of Virginia Woolf?*. Warner Brothers took a risk and invested in the

Jack Valenti gets experience in President Johnson's office just prior to bringing the "Great Society" vision to Hollywood (Photofest).

world's most famous married couple, Richard Burton and Elizabeth Taylor, as Edward Albee's George and Martha, history professor and daughter of the college president. Their love-hate relationship involved a sadistic repartee in front of their guests, a young campus couple played by George Segal and Sandy Dennis, whom Martha invited home for a few nightcaps. Amidst the booze and self-disgust, the Burton and Taylor characters revealed the darker side of American marriage. Completed in the fall of 1965, the same year *The Sound of Music* debuted, *Virginia Woolf* remained in Warner's vault until May 1966 because the script was "unapprovable under Code requirements." The Production Code Administration asked Warner to cut the five "sons of bitches," the twenty "goddamns," the thirteen "christs," the one "hump the hostess," and of course, "screw you."[40] However, Warner was $7.5 million into the film largely because of the principals' salaries and had no intention of changing a script that had received the Tony Award for its Broadway production. When a studio such as Warner defied the PCA's rejection of the project and stuck the script in the vault, the barriers holding back years of contest over the rights to aesthetic freedom, deliberated in court cases and first-amendment demands from filmmakers, buckled.[41]

The Code Review Board ultimately agreed to award *Virginia Woolf* an exemption if Warner would remove the "screw you" and "frigging," which the studio did. After much deliberation, the Catholic Review Board (now known as the National Catholic Office for Motion Pictures — NCOMP) reached a compromise and allowed *Virginia Woolf* an A–IV rating ("morally objectionable for adults, with reservations") and the PCA ceded.[42] The film finally opened in New York on June 11, 1966, with a stipulation on theater contracts "prohibiting anyone under the age of eighteen from seeing the picture unless accompanied by an adult."[43] Review members stressed that "this exemption does not mean that the floodgates are open for language or other material."[44] Yet, exceptions usually lead to new rules. Industry executives, directors, actors, actresses, and *Newsweek* quickly pointed out the hypocrisy in the exemption policy on the one hand and the questionable value of the Code on the other. *Life* magazine highlighted the film's merit, and even the Legion of Decency noted its artistry. The struggle over *Virginia Woolf* made the ineffectiveness of the PCA ever more apparent to the Motion Picture Association of America and, by July 6, Martin Quigley, Jr., son of the coauthor of the original Code, declared the old censorship system dead.[45] By late 1967 *New York Times* critic Vincent Canby confidently wrote, "the major American film companies apparently no longer fear having their films condemned by the National Catholic Office for Motion Pictures" (Legion of Decency). Similarly, exhibitors who previously refused to show a "condemned" film, now received controversial subject matter with enthusiasm.[46]

It was not coincidental that Code restrictions crumbled by 1966. The film industry, the public, and the courts had argued for nearly thirty years over PCA and Legion control of film content. The censorship decision on *Virginia Woolf* in 1965 and the Code's death in mid–1966 were not a coup but a watershed in the history of American culture and film. Confusion within censorship circles, theaters' profits from condemned films, and audiences' demand made it easier for the industry to balance censorship, enterprise, and social expectations. Not only could a braying Martha say "goddamn you" on screen, but she could also bring in profitable returns. The filmmakers whose aesthetic taste competed with typical genre pictures could now find wider public support. Valenti made it clear that "no one had conspired to kill the code, no one was capable of saving it." Warner's pledge to keep the film as written, along with social pressure on the Code administrators, "cohered at one moment in history to change the face of American film censorship."[47] Add to that Valenti's entrance into the industry just as changes in distribution procedures allowed for exhibition opportunity and, beginning in the mid–1960s, filmmaking and watching took on a new appearance. To be sure, as Vincent Canby reported in *The New York Times*, "most of the men who hired [Valenti] are of a younger, more liberal breed than were the first generation potentates who hired Eric Johnson [Valenti's predecessor] in 1945."[48]

The film market now opened wider to independents who wished to use the medium for confronting difficult issues and asking audiences to ponder seriously the complexities of contemporary life. Until November 5, 1968, when the Motion Picture Association of America developed a new ratings system of General, Mature, Restricted, and X, Hollywood could deal with any subject if done "in good taste." The exhibitor and the public, not Hollywood, would "police" the theater. The screen that previously had not been available to explicit scenes of sex and violence changed permanently. Words, images, and bodies "clutched in the sex act became as ordinary as someone passing the toast at breakfast," according to one trade expert.[49] The film industry garnered a measure of poetic license that raised questions about the fine lines between artistic expression and indecent exposure. If images and bodies clutched in the sex act or graphic visualizations of violence — in Technicolor — demonstrated a filmmaker's faith in his intent to reflect reality, to mirror society, then how would one define the role of the artistic component, the filmmaker's vision? Narratives that showed life realistically also advanced frameworks of interpretation and ultimately circulated claims to authority. When mainstream entertainment burst with candidness and passed responsibility for effect on to the viewer, it essentially allowed Hollywood to have its cake and eat it too.

The Code break-up facilitated the move toward independents' film production.[50] Along with the loss of studio mogul dominance, simply put, it was the creative sector's gain. Filmmakers who had been pushing to widen content borders for the mainstream audience welcomed the prospect of legitimizing new subject matter and assigning answerability to parents. When William Tusher claimed in 1967 that American films reached a new level of "respect they had not enjoyed for many years," he meant that industry changes brought filmmakers to the foreground as artists who could turn mainstream films into artistic products, making them "better, more inventive, more searching and frequently more entertaining than ever."[51]

The move toward independents boosted the prospects for the young and ambitious to contribute to Hollywood restructuring. This period saw the transition of the director from subordinate to auteur. In the studio-era integrated system, "the director was usually a hireling along with the writer, the cameraman, the actor, and the wardrobe lady." Directors "apprenticed at the studio, where [they] got ... tutoring in the company way, and ... tunneled as best [they] could through someone else's choice of cast, script, and editor." For the most part, directors were salaried and involved in camera action only, leaving the picture once the action was shot. Arthur Penn recalled of *Left-Handed Gun*, a film he directed in 1958, "I finished shooting, they said 'Goodbye!'" True to form, he saw the film for the first time months later in New York after the editor completed it.[52] There were exceptions — Alfred Hitchcock, John Ford, Billy Wilder, and some others. However, as Joseph Gelmis, president of Film Critics Circle and reviewer for *Newsday*, pointed out, "most of them were hyphenates — producer-director. The rule was that the producer ran the show and the studio put its stamp on each film. Directors were interchangeable. The formulas were sacred."[53]

The most wounded in this change of authority was indeed the producer, the former chief. David O. Selznick, just a year before his death, complained that the producer's artistic control all but vanished. "The movie producer seems to have become an anachronism," he lamented. In the golden era, the producer was the creative force, having "mastered every detail of filmmaking." The producer lost the supreme role as master of supervision, acquisition, and "creative control." Amid the climate of Hollywood restructuring, the producer often functioned as the wheeler-dealer, but his responsibility for the creative project typically ended there. In the words of one observer, "Most young directors and writers prefer to operate on their own without a producer looking over their shoulder."[54] By mid-decade directors had gained enough autonomy and creative agency to be more daring.[55] Individuals such as Sidney Pollack (*This Property is Condemned*) and Elliot Silverstein (*Cat Ballou*) experimented with American film, blending artistic style with narrative invention. Such a synthesis, they hoped, would lead to a "new American cinema" that would deliver directors into a golden age of their own.[56] The challenge filmmakers faced was balancing the artsy element with the financial promise of attracting a large audience.[57] Filmmaker Richard Lester described the concentrated focus on the filmmaker. As he commented, "A director's job ... is to ... produce a personal vision on a subject that he has chosen ... and what the people who pay him are buying is that personal vision." Ultimately, the film "must finally succeed or fail on the success or failure of [that] personal vision."[58]

A changing creative climate was also made possible by revolutionary technology. Tools for the trade added to filmmaking opportunity because the new portable cameras were light, high quality, moderately priced, and available to "anyone seriously motivated to finance and shoot his own film." Lighter equipment allowed filmmakers to go to the streets, and the more mobile and portable technology became, the more location-minded directors grew. Shedding the manacles of the studio setting with "hand-held cameras and airborne mini studios," filmmakers gained "a sense of fleetness and freedom — from shackling below the line costs as well as hobbling geographical limitations — not known before and not noticeably imagined until recently."[59] New technology allowed screenwriters and directors to find their material in daily life on the campuses and in the streets of America.

Directors and their machines constructed a new Hollywood, but it was no simple task. The Zanucks, Warners, and Zukors who had invented the American film industry held tightly to the reigns of power, but before the end of the decade, poststudio filmmakers took their places as American directors. Mike Nichols, Arthur Penn, Robert Altman, Stanley Kubrick, Peter Bogdanovich, Francis Ford Coppola, Warren Beatty, and George Lucas flourished in the industry as auteurs. Martin Scorsese, Paul Schrader, Steven Spielberg, and others followed. By his filmmaking days, Spielberg could claim that "young people were allowed to come rushing in with all of their naiveté and their wisdom and all of the privileges of youth," but they "had to wrest it away from [the older generation]." In Martin Scorsese's words, "You pushed here, and if it gave there, you slipped in. And as all that pushing and shoving was going on, the equipment was changing, getting smaller and easier to use. Then the Europeans emerged. Combine all those elements together, and suddenly by the mid–60s, you had a major explosion."[60] Film pundit Peter Biskind pointed out that the studio heads who still wanted to produce the musical increasingly fell "out of touch with the vast baby boom audience that was coming of age in the '60s."[61]

American film artists took advantage of the relaxed, creative borders and film's potential for intervention and exploration. Those whose films were attracting large audiences — Kubrick, Cassavetes, Nichols, and others — dared to imitate Bergman, Kurosawa, Fellini, and Antonioni with innovative narratives and filming styles. Filmmakers produced likeable nonheroes and experimented with new subject matter and language taboos. Feature films leaned toward a more adversarial view of modern life than the model pictures of *The Sound of Music* and *My Fair Lady*. From 1966, American cinema produced and consumed adversity. The popular film engaged in a more directly political purpose, with fewer features constructing narratives of social harmony and recycled convention, adding to the transformational equation of film's industrial life and cultural role. Undoubtedly, as *Film Daily* editor Vance King concluded, the artist with a new vision never "had it so good." Independents "are getting bookings which they never had before; they are getting terms (if they have merchandise that is sensationally exploitable) better than any of them ever got; and with good campaigns are getting better results than they ever had dreamed of." Indeed, new directors found in film a medium suitable to their aesthetic tastes and entrepreneurial desires and turned the 1960s and 1970s into the "director's decade[s]." As a group, they "enjoyed more power, prestige, and wealth than they ever had before" and more freedom to stylize film because they were unembarrassed ... to assume the mantle of the artist."[62] The day of the "company film" had given over to the companies buying independent stock, making "the entire spectrum, from low-budget films to extravaganzas ... open."[63] Categorically, budget demands still limited the choice of films to make. The high-grossing film, for example, required studio-distributor backing, but for those who had an idea that could attract a large number of viewers and the critics alike, the field had cleared considerably.

From onlooker Peter Biskind's perspective, it appeared that Hollywood changes in the mid–1960s meant that "everything old was bad, everything new was good. Nothing was sacred; everything was up for grabs." He declared, "it was, in fact, a cultural revolution, American style."[64] Censorship renovation and the new emphasis on the director as artist complemented the changing social conditions of the 1960s. While Hollywood searched for new methods of production as well as distribution, the 1960s cultural and social milieu facilitated filmmakers' desires to press for the legitimacy of topics previously forbidden to the mainstream film. The 1967 Academy Awards proved that the industry's values had changed in favor of the filmmaker and the art of cinema with their endorsement of *Virginia Woolf*. Not only did a gritty *Who's Afraid of Virginia Woolf?* receive thirteen nominations — more than any other movie that year — and win five, but a brash Elizabeth Taylor and a dramatic Sandy Dennis also took the best and supporting actress awards. The original singing ladies had competition from a bold Taylor who "enjoyed her finest hour to date as an actress."[65] Hollywood, like it or not, had modernized. One film critic predicted "a technological and aesthetic revolution in movies which [would] inevitably restructure human consciousness and understanding."[66] Maybe film failed to become that powerful, but the popularity of such upcoming pictures as *The Graduate*, *Easy Rider*, and *Alice's Restaurant* suggests something had at least been re-imagined.

Yet, the New Hollywood could not have emerged without a critical mass. A brash generation was on its way to influence the direction of the film industry. As consumers and producers, they acted in, directed and watched films; wrote screenplays; and studied movies on college campuses. Movies for the 1960s youth were what books were to their parents. Hollywood offspring Maurice Rapf grasped the association. "It's their medium," he remarked, "and they love it."[67] Convention and generic formulas gave way to experimentation. Industry restructuring created new prospects for independent filmmakers. Exhibitors who wanted quality films on the order of the European or art film had to compete with studios for distribution. Updated visuals and hard social issues stimulated artistic experimentation in American mainstream film and gave film a new agency. To be sure, American auteurs never had it so good. If ever they could count on an admiring audience, it was then.

CHAPTER II

A New Audience for the Now Movie

Film Societies, the College Campus, the American Film Institute and Making Film Art

Great film-makers need great audiences.
— Bernard R. Kantor, "Film Study in Colleges"

The third dimension of a film is a thousand people, a thousand pairs of ears and eyes looking at it, not one pair.
— John Cassavetes, "Dialogue on Film"

What's new is the audience itself.
— Maurice Rapf, "Can Education Kill the Movies?"

While internal improvements preoccupied industry shapers, selective audiences who wished to raise the artistic bar for American film voiced their opinions at such box office surprises as *A Room at the Top* (1959) and *Zorba the Greek* (1964). Yet, this vibrant art film audience did not push Hollywood through its studio doors like another sector of viewers did. A generation of boomers, as if without warning, had grown up and, with impassioned enthusiasm for the artistic potential of American film, helped prod the moving picture toward new content and style.[1] For those filmmakers (mostly in their thirties or early forties) who aspired to deeper cinematic acclaim, the timing was right. The most experienced and educated American spectators of film to date emerged and widened the borders of Hollywood production formulas. Young people sought screen education on campuses and turned to something other than the time-honored big budget or latest blockbuster. Sophisticates interested in higher quality pictures organized or expanded film societies. At the same time, universities and colleges created academic film programs and helped advance film as an art. Moreover, these advocates contributed to the development of the American Film Institute, the first nationally funded center of its kind in the United States. Societies, campuses, and institutes — shaped by viewers with artistic eyes — gave directors a better chance to make art, money, and entertainment, all at the same time.

Despite attempts to take film into highbrow culture during the movie palace days, American cinema functioned largely as a commercial, popular form of entertainment. At the same time, an interested few professed film's artistic merit and formed societies or joined local clubs. By the 1960s, film society members met for screenings at libraries, schools, museums, churches, synagogues, homes, or even rented local theaters on off nights to acquaint the largest number of viewers with the "best" available films. The more aware of cinematic aesthetics audiences were, members argued, the better the chance for filmmakers to produce films of high intellectual value. Consequently, increased followings by mid-decade made it obvious that viewers found new resources for tailor-making their motion picture enjoyment.[2]

Early societies assembled to safeguard footage from the past, but the primary motivation for members remained the wish to challenge the Production Code that limited public choice, distribution, and production of motion pictures. Societies could access films unavailable through commercial distribution by forming film exchange co-ops and holding film festivals, or by merely meeting regularly to screen a picture and host a knowledgeable lecturer.[3] To further their goals, organizations such as the Film Society Caucus, the Film Council of America, and the Roosevelt College Film Society created the American Federation of Film Societies (AFFS) and drafted a constitution in 1955.[4] The AFFS proposed to devote its total activities to assist in the development of a discriminating general film audience and to increase public consciousness of the film as a mature medium, by initiating and promoting, in cooperation with other commercial and non-commercial organizations, projects for the expansion of opportunities for the exhibition and intelligent presentation of significant films throughout the USA.[5]

Film society members described themselves as devoted to cinema conscientiously conveying an aesthetic experience. They were not just friends and fans of old films, or "FOOFS," as the acronym had it, but solemn aesthetes dedicated to studying, discussing, and advancing film as art.[6] Society members argued that though film had not yet warranted the level of sophistication awarded the great American novel, it could at least distinguish itself from the "tastelessness" of television. Devoted members gathered and distributed program and lecture notes to encourage the education of viewers and the AFFS published society material in the *Film Society Primer*, an annual publication of film information and related material.

Society enthusiasm coincided with increased interest in the art film by the early 1960s, but it did not necessarily mean that Hollywood listened to film societies. To the contrary, as *Variety* reported, Hollywood "unfortunately tends to be suspicious of film societies rather than enthusiastic about their progress and the general upgrading of tastes they engender."[7] As one AFFS director scolded, Hollywood refused to acknowledge audience sophistication in film societies. At the very least, he admonished, producers and filmmakers should have recognized members' love for film as art.[8] Despite the obvious need for "a counter force," as critic Hollis Alpert put it, "the commercial spirit has far too long dominated the American film."[9] Ignoring film societies' insistence on diversity in film signaled Hollywood's commonplace disregard for changes in film taste.

Nonetheless, through alliances, caucuses, and published program notes, the Federation centralized efforts to place film on "the high, dry shores of art."[10] Unfortunately, those high shores left societies a bit too dry and distanced them from their original function of making available more significant films or fine tuning the artistic eye of public audiences. To film expert

Anthony Hodgkinson of Boston University, societies by the mid–1960s seemed overly traditional and self-absorbed. "Film," as he remarked, "has always been and still is a social art, a popular art." Hodgkinson further claimed "to take the viewpoint that 'high culture' is a temple threatened by the invading barbarian hordes of Hollywood-corrupted 'masses,' and calling for desperate defence [sic] by the enlightened, is as unreal an attitude as to fall into the value-less morass of the pop-cultists, who find witless response to any and every untutored screen-scribble of the 'underground,' wherever it may locate itself."[11] The trend toward elitism suggested that with the Code break-up, film societies had served their original function and needed to change or dissolve.[12]

Film society problems ranged from internal disagreement on club goals to organizational challenges to lack of interest. Still, societies contributed to the dialogue concerning the place of film in American culture—what it is for and what the relationship among the audience, film, and the industry should be. They were an important cultural indicator of the changing tastes in audiences and part of the dynamic between the art and mainstream film while codes were in flux. Yet, societies' clearest contribution in developing critical opinion, audience sophistication, and film consciousness was by virtue of their involvement in the institutions of education. The AFFS's newly elected officers, by mid-decade, came primarily from college campuses. A select group of professors contributed to the AFFS's monthly publication, *Film Society Review*, to "keep the reading and the talking going."[13] These film activists helped advance film education on campuses across the country while successfully organizing film conferences, safeguarding society program notes in libraries, and otherwise campaigning for the artistic merit of film.

Film advocacy from societies met with profound enthusiasm from students. One student organization, the United States National Student Association (USNSA), served approximately 1,200,000 students and offered the AFFS a way to create a nationwide film society program on campuses. Together the student group and AFFS contributed labor and information for creating college film societies. *Film Society Review*'s editor, John Thomas, noted the addition of a student film advisory board. It "reflects USNSA's recent and growing interest in the field of film," Thomas remarked, "both as communication and art form."[14] Campus leadership typically consisted of graduate students, undergraduates, and professors from across the disciplines. At Dartmouth, for example, approximately one-fifth of the student body was involved in film society activity by 1967.[15] Other groups, such as the Department of Fine Arts Productions at the University of California at Los Angeles and Delta Kappa at the University of Southern California, drew on the AFFS for the typical film series tailored to university schedules.[16] By decade's end, approximately 90 percent of all film societies were campus affiliated.[17] Members underscored their role in making audiences—"nurtured by film societies"—the "master keys to the progress of the art—to a fuller understanding and richer enjoyment today, to future films of even greater beauty, significance, and diversity than those we now cherish."[18]

General interest in film had long been fostered through regular film series provided by distributors to campuses. Students and faculty at Ohio State University enjoyed film series on campuses from the mid-thirties when Edgar Dal and F. W. Davis instituted The University Film Series and introduced audiences to foreign film. By the 1960s, campus screenings were part of most college offerings. A University of Utah student newspaper, for example, advertised enthusiastically: "variety, quality, and the ability of the film maker to involve his audience will characterize Union Movies this quarter, beginning this weekend with 'The

Golden Coach' directed by Jean Renoir."[19] Another film series organizer advocated the addition of alternative cinema to the regular film sequence. Saturday nights were set aside for new releases and mainstream cinema while Wednesday nights were reserved for the art film. Campuses thus channeled cinematic art for those interested.[20]

Soon, common allure mushroomed into pressure groups made up of students, professors, and society organizers who called for the sanction of film as an academic subject, like literature, to be taught, analyzed, and produced. To be sure, select universities already had film schools. USC's film production program dated to 1929 and its degree program in film was the first in the country. During the 1940s and 1950s, other campuses developed courses for the industrial function of film to train students as audio-visual directors for business, industry, and the medical field. Whether producing a project for the university or the outside community, students created countless feet of film every year for a third less than in the commercial field. Educators saw little value in training students for the entertainment industry, yet the foundational fact remained that film functioned above all as a popular medium, a form of entertainment. Robert Gessner of New York University understood the need for change in the technical emphasis in film programs and pointed out as early as the 1940s that film curriculum should gear itself to mass audiences. He introduced students to a new screen education, training them as "directors, prop men, film cutters, and camera crews" and encouraged them to produce "every thing from Westerns to variations of 'Gone with the Wind.'"[21] New approaches to film education were even suggested in *Saturday Review*, whose editor recognized "that film affects our thoughts, our attitudes, our activities."[22] Generally, though, except for Gessner's pioneering efforts, the dozen-plus colleges offering film programs in the 1940s took a vocational approach. Not for another twenty years would film education become a likely academic subject in the college curriculum.

Key to that change was the arrival on campuses in the mid–1960s of the baby boom generation, born in the aftermath of World War II. Film as a social tool was simply "forced by student insistence and demand."[23] By 1965, the college population had soared to 5 million students; by 1973, 10 million. This compares to the 3 million who attended state universities in 1960 and the 2-½ million in 1950. One-half of eighteen- to twenty-year-olds entered college by 1969 and three-quarters of all college students attended state campuses. Before World War II no university was larger than 15,000, but in 1970 over fifty institutions enrolled 30,000 or more students.[24] Clearly, as administrators reported, "no longer regarded as a 'luxury,' post-high-school education has become a standard part of life in America."[25]

The campus has always been an arena for debating social and political issues and a meeting place for experimental ideas, but from 1965 it became a new space for action and dissent.[26] Campuses functioned as a central location for consciousness raising, but with the growth of the university system, students lobbied administrations for changes in dorm rules, lifting bans on speech restrictions, and allowing students more decision-making in campus life. Through manifestoes, flyers, political organizations, underground presses, marches, sit-ins, and speeches, students expressed their dissatisfaction with the system. Students, professors, and administrators debated the definition of a university. The college campus proved a legitimate site for germinating radicalism and a place to promote and protest an adversarial view of America.[27] It would be difficult not to notice, as one observer commented, that "by the late 1960s ... a massive shift in attitudes and orientations toward traditional American values and support for traditional institutions had taken place on many American campuses, even if most young people did not perceive themselves as revolutionaries or even radicals."[28] Universities approached film education in this climate of social unrest and demands for radical revision of the college curriculum.

Incorporating film arts in the university system challenged the dominance of the traditional arts. Consequently, many campuses resisted the curricular needs of those who saw the importance of studying motion pictures as an art. One professor argued that university administrators "never thought much of film as a bona fide area of study. There were a few exceptions ... but in the main, film, much less film-making, had no substance, no discipline, no ... respectability."[29] Yet, the boomers were the one generation that had grown up with movies more than books as a primary form of entertainment. Thus, for professors who had argued film's artistic function, the college audience provided experience and enthusiasm. Professor and AFFS Chair Jack C. Ellis was one of those who spoke about the possibility of developing serious screen programs on campuses. "We share a belief in the major role the Federation will play," he argued, "in the unprecedented stirrings now affecting the field of film study and appreciation — the increase in teaching of film at the higher and secondary levels."[30] Filmmaker Arthur Mayer, who was already involved with screen education, argued that failing to implement cinema studies made no sense since film has played a "critical role ... in the development of ... students." To ignore the importance of creating film departments with "critical standards" as for "all of the arts" was simply shortsighted.[31]

A significant step toward sanctioning film as an academic pursuit occurred in the fall of 1964 at Lincoln Center in New York City. The national conference on film studies convened to review the American Council on Education's (ACE) six-month survey of screen education in secondary and higher education institutions. ACE, a conservative, nonprofit agency based in Washington, D.C., with 1300 college and university members, was the principal coordinating agency for higher education in the United States. To meet its goal of integrating film courses into campus curricula, the Council brought leading film scholars together. Their ultimate goal was "to have a film study course in every college or university in the country, and as soon thereafter as possible, in every high school in the country."[32] By 1965, the government agreed to fund a film-study seminar at Fordham University with a follow-up conference at Dartmouth in Hanover.

Dartmouth students had a firm investment in film as an academic pursuit since the campus served as a distributing point for AFFS program material.[33] Supported in part by a grant from the MPAA in cooperation with ACE, this three-day conference brought together approximately one hundred academics, film society members, government officials, and reviewers from the commercial market to organize the academic pursuit of film on campuses.[34] The conference at Dartmouth signaled the beginning of film studies' permanent presence in colleges and universities. Participants confirmed that "the question of *whether* to teach motion pictures has been resolved affirmatively." The next step would be to decide "*how*." As Columbia professor George C. Stoney pointed out, "most of our education is concerned with words ... [but] who trains us to look?"[35] New York University's Director for the Institute of Film and Television, Robert Saudek, predicted that his program would help reduce mediocrity in media. He firmly believed that film and television "will be changed only by well trained leaders who have both a respect for quality and a great deal of substantive knowledge." Considerable enthusiasm coming from students brought film studies programs to campuses "with unprecedented speed."[36] Head of the Fordham Center for Communication, Father John Culkin believed that film was such an important art form that "students ought to be learning the fundamentals in grade school ... so that when they finally get to college, they have an opportunity to blossom out, without worrying about the mechanics."[37] Developing film audiences may never have reached that depth, but in the midst of program exuberance, it appeared that it might.

Film arts as a part of the university structure was fostered through another channel, the University Film Producers Association. The organization's journal facilitated dialogues on film studies and advanced methodology.[38] A 1965 brochure listed as one of its goals, "To improve the art of motion picture through the training of tomorrow's filmmakers and film-teachers." Believing that the university would provide a wellspring of capable filmmakers, teachers, and viewers, film academics discussed technical aspects of film production along with how film is seen and understood. Shirley Clarke, educator and founder of a film distributors' cooperative, advocated that the university should be a place to change Americans' attitudes toward film artists and help solve the problem of public perception of filmmakers merely as technicians. A competent program in her estimation would educate an audience "to support, and most important of all, to enjoy ... films that attempt to expand the medium," even experimental films. Film is "not merely escapism," she reminded. "Film is an art just as literature and music are arts: serious, deep, and searching." Developing a "broader basis for enjoyment" meant treating film and filmmaker as art and artist. Clarke recognized the value of the university to do so. As she contended, "University people occupy an important position as opinion makers in this country, so let's use it."[39]

Administrators and teachers, with the support of students, initiated fully-fledged curriculum change and department organization to professionalize film study. More important for the industry, film art took the viewer into the classroom where students were audiences "learn[ing] to experience film as a contemporary art, not as a classical one."[40] As one educator claimed after the Dartmouth conference, "Perhaps no studies in American education are growing with such exuberance as film studies."[41] Besides the well-equipped and developed film schools at USC, UCLA, and New York University, over a hundred other campuses offered courses and degrees in film by 1967. More than 35,000 students took over one thousand courses on campuses ranging from Alabama and Massachusetts to Texas and Utah.[42] In time, university programs extended beyond aesthetics. To address the art form's impact on viewer experience, curricula included courses in the sociological and psychological study of the medium.

Professors trained graduate students who helped create film studies classes and production centers. Graduating teachers took film education to the secondary schools and in turn brought students to the college campuses as experienced undergraduate viewers. By 1969, approximately one hundred campuses added film courses, increasing campus programs by 84 percent.[43] The Director of Educational Programs of the National Endowment for the Arts determined that enthusiasm for film on campuses had "never been more intense." Fervor came from those "articulate and intelligent students on the academic scene [who] not only know where the action is, they *are* [director's emphasis] the action."[44] This new breed was not to be dismissed as rebels. They not only had a cause but were clearly on a mission.[45]

College-aged audiences soon expected entertainment films that had something to say. The "key word" for one university newspaper selection was *involvement*. "Any film which cannot emotionally involve the viewer and make a lasting impression on him can be considered a failure," the writer declared. Prospective audiences were "people who have newly discovered film, who care about it, and want to make it over; they are actively interacting with the flickering shadows at a new level of awareness and intensity." As associate editor for *Time*, Henry

Bradford Darrach, Jr., described them: "The new generation of moviegoers believes that an educated man must be cinematic as well as literate."[46] Series organizers tailored the "long range goals ... to help develop a more discriminating audience for all feature films."[47]

To professors and film society members alike, the sophisticated college student offered a prospective, ideal viewer. Whether a film-course dilettante or a cinema major, as University of Southern California professor David Stewart commented, a film student will "become a more informed film viewer, a better audience." Northwestern professor and AFFS Chairman of the Board Jack C. Ellis pointed to the growing sophistication in film taste on campus by the later 1960s. Students "follow film-makers," he remarked, "rather than stars, and are working out hagiographies of what are to me very minor saints and new canons of taste that challenge the rigidities of my own middle-aged aesthetic." Like other academics, Ellis saw himself as "increasingly in the business of educating future film audiences, critics, scholars and teachers." Instructors saw new film sophistication in young viewers.[48] Thus, academics by the late sixties could not only assume student interest in film but also expect cinematic knowledge. To USC film professor Bernard R. Kantor, "Our colleges and universities are working hard trying to develop these audiences through their film study courses."[49]

While screen education required a classroom, a projector, and passionate followers, incorporating production training was a bit more complicated. For those campuses that were able to provide the space, funding, and equipment, filmmaking labs expanded and programs multiplied. With lighter technology, students literally went out into the world to film. Unlike a previous generation that created the world in a studio with machines nailed to the floor, young filmmakers and teachers saw the camera as the most valuable source of spontaneity. Visual verisimilitude — telling it like it is — connected filmmaking to contemporary beliefs about the value of artistic communication. Film functioned as a path to action for young filmmakers and viewers by virtue of its accessibility and its entrance into classrooms as a legitimate academic study and creative form of expression. Film professor Alvin Fiering of Boston University, for example, explained that "what distinguishes the [B.U.] film program ... is the emphasis placed upon personal expression." Personal filmmaking, professors hoped, would lead to diversity in film content.[50] Similarly, at New York University, as Martin Scorsese remembered of his college experience, production "had to do with more personal filmmaking, with themes and subject matter that you felt more confident dealing with — about yourself, about the world you came from."[51] Student filmmakers' enthusiasm to represent the world by taking their art to the streets did not go unnoticed by one policeman rushing to help a Northwestern student whose shirt was covered with blood. Stopping in "horror and anger," he soon discovered a student filmmaker had set up the entire scene. "Everybody's making a movie," he sighed and went on his way. Students at Northwestern filming for their film class could have been anywhere in America since programs turned to the moving picture as "artistic self-expression" mixed with social activism.[52] Such passionate enchantment mesmerized filmmaker Stanley Kramer as he worked with college students. "All the young people who used to want to be novelists," he remarked, "now want to be filmmakers."[53]

The 1960s provided the social environment of activism that enhanced the development of film studies. Making/watching film gave the under-twenty-fives "a piece of the action, whether in running a university, the country, or the world."[54] One free-standing film department, for example, developed out of the 1960s climate of advocacy. Students and professors "founded [the San Francisco State Cinema Department] amid the political activism and artistic experimentation of the 1960's."[55] Others combined film studies with English and history departments. By and large, what had changed in campus film programs during that time was a shift in values and beliefs about the university. One Stanford professor pointed out that "students come here with the knowledge that this is not a prep school for the industry salt mine." Making room for artist experimentation instead of the purely industrial technician shifted emphasis in screen education. An Ohio State professor explained, "Our theory is that people have to have something to say before we can help them become film-makers. The technical aspect is not the real problem."[56]

The primary advantage of developing film as an academic pursuit during the studio break-up period and 1960s activism was that the university supplied the young filmmaker with an ever-expanding, politically conscious audience and a relatively safe way to experiment with consciousness raising. Universities held film festivals and arranged film conferences to showcase student-artists. This pioneering effort resulted in the first National Student Film Festival at UCLA in September 1965. Festivals increased spectator numbers at UCLA from a few hundred once a year to seven thousand twice a year.[57] The Fordham University in February 1967 drew 1200 participants, both college age and younger from twenty-seven states. Student film festivals helped generate the possibility for film to offer a viable profession, whether as future professor or filmmaker. The university-sponsored festivals also provided a new service to the community, one a bit different from the 1940s' view of film for industry. Students working on projects exposed the university to "the community audience" as a place where film could be art and "endure as powerful experience." Students freely experimented and continually made "films that suggest the untapped potential of the medium."[58]

Yet, not all were encouraged by what they saw. University training to some was hardly more than "amateurs teaching amateurs to be amateurs."[59] UCLA studio director Warren Hamilton claimed he had "never seen production more sordid, sour and sick than some of today's offerings."[60] The posturing of youth as sophisticated filmmakers trained at the university "laboratory" did not guarantee a job as a professional anymore than a class in creative writing led directly to a publishing house. Just where their projects led was a question waiting to be answered. One student on the UCLA campus vowed to hide his degree when seeking a film career.[61] It was all too evident that the university-degreed still had to earn their elders' respect. To industry traditionalists, making a film was not a matter of going to college when they could point to the unschooled Stanley Kubricks of the trade.[62] At mid-decade, turning out sophisticated students "merely meant more well qualified students rejected by unions or studios or both."[63] The truth of the matter was that studio doors were closed "for the great majority of such students."[64] Still, as noted at the New York University's Summer Film Workshop in 1967, "the film industry, the unions, the trade and vocational centers, in giving up long ago the training of young blood for film-making have created a vacuum which has been filled by colleges and universities."[65]

UCLA professor Colin Young saw the value in university training. In his opinion, the sixties crop of students were "more promising than ever before ... [with] greater skill in dealing with their own minority audience then [sic] their predecessor ... both in subject and style."[66] Others, such as *Los Angeles Times* film critic Charles Champlain, "foresaw a good future for students' films because audiences demand not only technical excellence but films that have something to say."[67] Critics failed to note that one could find the likes of several professionals from the industry such as Stanley Kramer, Haskell Wexler, and Jean Renoir working closely with students on campuses or making guest appearances in classrooms.[68] Between facilitating experimentation and conveying film wisdom, film studies and production at least offered alternatives, possibilities for education, and options for the future.[69] Not only did film curricula help develop the discriminating eye earlier advocated by film sophisticates, the university also became a place for an unprecedented place of cultural production. Campus study focused on changing attitudes, teaching respect for film, and understanding film as a craft, an art, and a social tool.[70] Moreover, legitimizing film academically meant arguing its importance along aesthetic lines in a place that could far better institutionalize it as a serious art form and artistic study than the federated film societies or campus series. As one student remarked, feature-length films "thought of five years ago *only* as an entertainment ... are now *in* and regarded as a legitimate pursuit in America. Film education programs encouraged cinema to grow as an art form."[71]

Changing perceptions of what an aesthetic product could provide, be, and do came most distinctly from the campus classrooms that conferred on film a new cultural role. One enthusiast observed, "Students realize that films are an important cultural force, and more and more of them feel that American films do not reflect an accurate view of present values. They want this changed.... The best way to do this is to learn the business."[72] *Saturday Review* critic Hollis Alpert applauded young film goers' progressive sensitivity. "The most important development (and it took the rise of a whole new generation before it became apparent)," he remarked, "was the visual training and orientation the young viewers received."[73]

Campus production centers and college curricula had clearly cultivated the first of the film studies' generations, the industry's future model spectators. As makers and viewers, many young adults used film and the college campus for a site of negotiation and a place to stage their own authority. Young people who grew out of the habit of family movie-going helped create an audience gap of sorts for the industry and found colleges viable vehicles to move in a new cinematic direction. Hopes loomed for film's potential. It was the one art form in high demand. Simply put, the timing was right for young artists who had an eye for contemporary life to break into an industry steeped in tradition. Young audiences provided the reason and force for the shift.

Yet it is not entirely clear just how audience sophistication or production at the university could change the marketplace. Does a literate viewer and filmmaker guarantee film variety and value? Do film "literates" warrant more say than do "illiterates"? On what level does knowledge of a movie's production history or aesthetics influence film's marketability?[74] Likewise, the protective campus environment and the "pre-existing" audience shielded student filmmakers from the daunting task of having to entice distributors, exhibitors, and general public interest. Unquestionably, the university would not be the model for the marketplace, but it did provide an arena where attitudes and tastes developed, and values and hopes were debated. Student film competitions brought student organizations together to create new spaces for developing film consciousness among young viewers. Moreover, campus competitions exposed potential artists. New York University graduate Martin Scorsese won the first prize at a 1965 festival and was filming in London by 1968. The National Student Film Festival, sponsored by the National Student Association, Motion Picture Association of America, and Manhattan's Lincoln Center for the Performing Arts, in January 1968 sported *THX 1138*, a sci-fi picture shot in Los Angeles by George Lucas (UCLA). Of thirty-seven entries, Lucas won in the category of drama and received a contract with Warner's to expand *THX 1138* under the guidance of Francis Ford Coppola. Even though Scorsese's and Lucas' instant success contrasted to the more typical fate of film graduates, their popular appeal proved that the university-trained was well on its way into traditional Hollywood.

If a sizeable share of the movie-watching audience was college educated, then that voice would be heard at production centers and box offices. Exhibitors since the fifties have easily exploited the teenage film, but with a new emphasis on the filmmaker as artist, eager cinematic aesthetes encouraged the production of critical perspectives. College audiences demonstrated that there was room for subtlety and discriminating taste in the feature narrative and gave movie directors a chance to dabble in a variety of film styles. The low budget had a special appeal by the end of the sixties. Audience exuberance allowed filmmakers to develop their vision by cultivating a critical distance from both their narratives and their viewers, and still make money.[75] What began as an art-house product had unquestionably spread into the mainstream film industry with such notice that film critics tagged the new development the "Now Movie."[76] In *Harpers'* estimation, "What these new movies will do to — and, potentially, for — the art and entertainment business, economically, will be of no small consequence." The former "fiscal upheavals" would pale in comparison to Hollywood's dislocation "by talented young people who are no longer clamoring at movieland's golden West Coast gates."[77]

The industry had transformed itself, and perhaps the best visible sign that film production registered audiences' tastes, complaints, and demands for more artistic products was the creation of a national organization that legitimized the intellectual value of feature films. Film enthusiasts saw their quest for artistic merit partially satisfied with the formation of the American Film Institute (AFI), a nationally supported film establishment under the Johnson Administration and the National Foundation of the Arts and the Humanities Act of 1965. The institute was the result of years of discussion, reflection, analysis, and countless proposals. Among these involved entities were the universities, the motion picture industry, the federal government, film museums, archives, and other screen education groups, not the least of which was AFFS. Members of the academic community had submitted a detailed proposal for the American Film Institute by mid-decade. At the Dartmouth conference participants held an AFI session where they pledged not to let the momentum for creating a strong institute dissipate. The critical first step, as the AFFS managing editor remarked, was to establish "how ... each agency [could] best serve the development of an enlightened film public through the relevant channels of the American Film Institute."[78]

The official governing body was formed June 5, 1967, after a great deal of controversy and fear that it would be just another Hollywood since the board was filled with industry celebrities. Gregory Peck was acting chairman of the Board of Trustees during the planning stage and Francis Ford Coppola, Jack Valenti, Fred Zinnemann, Sidney Poitier, and other Hollywood affiliates served as board members.[79] With a substantial contribution from the National Endowment for the Arts, the American Film Institute was well in place by the end of the decade. In 1968, the Institute opened the Center for Advanced Film Studies, serving "as a bridge between film study and film-making as a profession." The Center drew university graduates interested in a tutorial with accomplished directors.[80] Leading filmmakers such as Elia Kazan, Lawrence Turman, and Arthur Penn participated in selecting students who would learn every aspect of the industry. AFI's tutorial program offered filmmaker and student alike an alternative to the studio system and made a career in film after university training not only possible but likely. Arthur Penn chose Jeff Young, a typical AFI Fellow and budding filmmaker, to be a trainee for *Alice's Restaurant*. As Young quipped, "I got my Phi Beta Kappa for my mother, my law degree for my father, and I'm in films for myself."[81]

In addition to centralized training, the Institute also funded the formation of film studies programs across the country. For the first time in America, filmmaking emulated

European models of aesthetic development supported by national institutions, fashioned by university film departments, and filled with promising university graduates. The education arm of the Institute created film libraries for teachers, conducted teacher training seminars, and funded model curricula sessions.[82] As AFI director George Stevens, Jr., remarked, the Institute meant "to transform the essential film experience from making out in the last row of the loges to breaking out of a 70-year straight jacket about the seriousness of *literature* and the frivolity of *film*."[83] The Institute also set in place the foundational purpose of the AFFS's original call for more substantial films.[84]

The AFI brought together filmmaker, filmmaking, film society enthusiast, film education for the ideal viewer, film preservation, and accessibility to advance cinema as an art and address its many industrial changes and cultural influences. Fundamentally, film sophistication became a site of debate about whose experience and ideas of truth commercial film should represent. The wider inclusion of a nontraditional art-form in college curricula, occurring at the same time an uncensored film industry endeavored to clarify its professional stance, converged with growing national support for independent filmmaking. These components made it possible to justify experimentation in film, satisfy audience taste, and affect production in mainstream cinema.[85]

American audiences would soon enjoy the cinematic goods of the young "auteur" coming from film schools and institutes. Until then, filmmakers a few years older caught the attention of mainstream audiences with the artistic "now movie." Critic Arthur Knight confirmed that "what had started out in the art houses had suddenly swept into the mainstream of filmmaking, and with such force, such impact, as to demolish any picture made in the more traditional or conventional modes."[86] Despite the exaggeration, by the end of the 1960s, viewers who grew up mesmerized by a world of ubiquitous images provided the necessary vision for the new energy. What began during the mid–1960s helped set the foundation for the growth of film studies as an academic subject while academics formulated more cohesive film standards, campus departments, and training programs.

A new constituent in American culture who wished to talk about art in mainstream movies would be pleasantly surprised by the currency of films released on American screens in 1967. Directors updated their assumptions about who their viewers were and what they wanted. One filmmaker aptly picked up his camera to shape a narrative about changes taking place on college campuses, in the home, and on the streets. Mike Nichols, the director of *Virginia Woolf*, found the tropes and subject matter to chance cinematic experimentation in the feature film and help viewers understand current social changes. Nichols brought his vision of American film as art in line with broad stirrings about the widening, bothersome generation gap, the counterculture, and campus strife. A key 1960s film, *The Graduate*, fulfilled new audience desire and responded to the call for making film art. Extensively praised for embodying the concerns of a sixties generation, Mike Nichols' *The Graduate* became the purveyor of generational dissent, not because the picture inspired revolution, but because it articulated a belief and a vision about film's revolutionary nature. In essence, *The Graduate* held a mirror up to a generation that saw itself at its most confident and commanding moment.

GENERATION

CHAPTER III

The Graduate

Representing a Generation

This is Benjamin. He's a little worried about his future.
— Tagline from *The Graduate*

It is unlikely that the gap between the young and us vegetables has ever been wider in some respects than it is now.
— Russell Lynes, "Cool Cheer or Middle Age"

But nothing has any meaning until it's released, and the audience decides.
—Mike Nichols, *Playboy* Interview

Why Benjamin Braddock (Dustin Hoffman) of *The Graduate* (1967) should be worried about his future is not entirely clear. He graduated from a prestigious eastern college as valedictorian of his class, has a red convertible waiting for him at his parents' Beverly Hills home, and is surrounded by a crowd of caring friends offering congratulations and innovative business prospects. Mr. McGuire (Walter Brooke), a colleague of Ben's father (William Daniels), lets him in on a secret for a promising life: "The future is in plastics." Despite audiences' resounding laughs, it clearly was. Yet director Mike Nichols had something else in mind for his graduate. His Benjamin would not be satisfied with the older generation's formula for success. Instead, Nichols made it clear that the time had come to discover a new sense of the young, and that meant adjusting the lens to frame Ben's point of view.

No film better exemplifies the convergence of industry and audience changes and no film more successfully exploited the generation gap than *The Graduate*. Nichols integrated unfamiliar actors, nonformula narrative, daring sexuality, and generational discourse into a synthetic whole. His award winner telescoped multiple changes of attitudes, beliefs, and values into the image of an alienated college graduate. This film not only ensured Dustin Hoffman's fame, but it transformed the image of star icons. The open-ended conclusion and uneven storyline added to film's experimental appeal. Most notably, the film discarded an older generation's notion of success and cheered on an "inarticulate Benjamin" who found doing nothing a potent form of resistance.[1] Middle-class youth wishing to distinguish themselves from their parents and challenge an older generation's set of truths now had a co-conspirator.

41

Promotional poster of Mike Nichols' 1967 film *The Graduate* (Photofest).

The Graduate became one of the most popular films following its release in December 1967 and one of the most written about. It grossed over $104 million in its initial offering and over $30 million in its rentals and thirty-year anniversary edition. One film critic called it the "epicenter of Hollywood's 1960s' 'youthquake' movement" and maybe even "the definitive film of its era."[2] Martin Quigley, Jr., pronounced *The Graduate* "one of the phenomenal Hollywood pictures of the 1960s." Those who "disliked it and predicted a commercial failure," Quigley wrote, "seldom ... proved so wrong in advance about any picture."[3] The film had no bankable stars, yet it accomplished what Nichols set out to do — to explore "a subject that has been badly exploited and mangled in Hollywood — the 'youth scene.'"[4] The film caught on and, considering that European films and other American fare had critically approached the youth topic before, it raised questions of why now.

Mike Nichols' mature content for mature audiences took the boomers from the Jan and Dean Surf "epics" into the young-adult SMA category.[5] The film's irreverent, rebel-graduate sat somewhere in between the Beach Party set and the art film anti-hero. As *Hollywood Citizen-News* reported, "The Graduate is bawdy, naughty and a bit rowdy — and is recommended for adults only — but the humorous way."[6] This film validated Hollywood's talk about the directorial touch of Mike Nichols and also underscored the industry's "new climate of creative freedom and adventure" — as William Tusher described it. The success of producer Lawrence Turman and Mike Nichols, both in their early thirties, granted a certain assurance to directors with an interest in the experimental twist in feature films. With backing from Joseph E. Levine at Embassy Pictures, Nichols and Turman turned Charles Webb's perceptive novel into a "Now Movie."[7]

The Nichols team helped crystallize the "under thirty" assumption that materialism was a nasty habit of the older generation. The film became a virtual mirror of resonating symbols — plastic sunglasses, hot cars, California swimming pools, *Better Homes and Gardens* houses — and a vibrant Simon and Garfunkel musical score. Yet, if the film took viewers on a tour of the post–World War II accomplishment of material security, it also advanced contemporary social attitudes: old is bad; new is good. By conferring onto the younger generation the role of delivering society, *The Graduate* justified young people's challenge to the authority of their parent generation. This film combined contemporary concerns over guilty pleasures with deeply-rooted American anxieties about what the effects of materialism meant. *The Graduate* ironically endorsed changing tastes for something new, inventive, and youthful while it circulated images of desire for a de facto lifestyle the younger generation took for granted. As *Cue* reported, the film "is a clarion call to youth."[8] Moreover, this film indicated that Hollywood's "looked-for" audience now existed and did make a mark on the film industry. As *Film Society Reviewer* critic Paul Seydor commented two years after the film's release, "Had it not been so successful, such films as ROMEO AND JULIET, GOODBYE COLUMBUS, MIDNIGHT COWBOY, EASY RIDER, CHE!, LAST SUMMER, ROSEMARY'S BABY, THREE IN THE ATTIC, THE STERILE CUCKOO, JOHN AND MARY, and ALICE'S RESTAURANT would probably never have been made."[9]

The film affected and reflected what circulated in the popular press over generational authority. While *The Graduate* was in production, for example, *Life* reported that the younger generation would resolve the perils of modernization. This popular magazine touted the younger generation as the new conduit of hope by emphasizing their attributes of honesty and authenticity. In such articles as "The Search for Purpose: Among the Youth of America, A Fresh New Sense of Commitment," *Life* clearly separated young from old. The older generation was smug in their financial security, and their world of "technocratic totalitarianism" had created meaningless lives. The young, however, were "fully-alive" and refused to be the automatons of old whose robotic dedication to work, duty, and consumerism threatened to deplete their humanity.[10]

Nichols established the same discourse in the film with opening shots of a newly automated world sucking the spirit out of people. The film opens, for example, with Benjamin having just addressed his graduating class and leaving for his Los Angeles home. He rides the airport escalator while the film's theme song, "Sounds of Silence," plays. Viewers see a close-up of Ben gliding along the LAX walkway while credits roll and Simon and Garfunkel sing about people who hear but don't speak or listen. "Sounds of Silence" defines Ben's alienation and determines his separation from, if not superiority to, those immersed in contemporary society. Ben eyes the figurative 10,000-plus people and establishes the value in his astute observation that he is not one of them. The early sequences determine the validity of the generation gap and echo the same divide as in *Life*'s "Search for Purpose."

Generation-gap arguments also surfaced in the academic setting in the fall of 1967, just before *The Graduate* appeared. Student body presidents and editors from colleges and high schools and executive officers from young people's political groups organized a forum at a "Students and Society" conference on the West Coast. The focus was on ways to proceed in a "severely troubled national and international order they are soon to inherit." Their foundational premise rested on the assumption that "the gap between the generations today is deep and unbridgeable." Evidence for such an indictment included Vietnam, urban racial strife, American imperialism in third-world countries, and the belief that "never has adult leadership appeared so faint and so unrelated to the basic issues." Conference spokesman W. H. Ferry confidently wrote, "This is why, these young people say, they will not, on passing the magical age of 30, subside into the comfortable slots in the Establishment open to them because of their native intelligence and [mostly] middle-class backgrounds."[11]

New York University's Frederick Richman declared at the gathering that "a bona fide generation gap exists today — beyond mere difficulties in transition — and it is qualitatively different from those that have occurred before." As he argued, those under thirty are "raising the possibility that society ought to (or will have to) accommodate itself to youth, instead of youth to society." Yet the problem, he contended, was that "students today tend to dismiss all people over 30, including the older radicals from the 1930s. The rascals ... are neither Democrats or Republicans, but simply adults." Generational accommodation defined the pressure point coming from those who demanded more "involvement of students in society" and political liberation of youth.[12] Age determined separate identity and altered the way political attitudes and stances were grouped and assumptions understood. One student threatened "a full-scale rebellion," with "youth pitted against their elders."[13] *The Graduate* helped confirm the growing sentiment that age was a sign of defiance.

By *The Graduate*'s release in December 1967, the popular magazine *Ladies Home Journal* (LHJ) reported agitation between anxiety-ridden parents and American youth. LHJ released the results of a poll and the findings of psychologists, medical doctors, and politicians concerning generational issues. On the first page of the article, LHJ featured a "Man of the Year"–looking youth, hands in pockets, facing off with his parents — a suit-and-tie-clad father and well-groomed mother. "Talking to my parents is a drag.... The last thing I want to be in 20 years is like [my father]," the son complained. "Our kids have everything given to them. My generation had to work for what it got," retorted the father.[14]

The dialogue in both the *Ladies Home Journal* and the "Students and Society" conference framed the conflict as psychologist George R. Bach and others relayed it to the American public a month after *The Graduate*'s release. "We Can Close the Generation Gap," Bach promised in one of nine articles centered on young people in *Life*. Such notables as Robert F. Kennedy offered advice in "What Our Young People Are Really Saying." All in all, social critics, parents, psychologists, politicians, and writers acknowledged the problems of generational discontent and, in a similar fashion as the Students and Society Conference, agreed that America was a "psychologically divided nation." Both parent and child had chosen to deal with generational conflict by becoming "emotional dropouts." American youth rejected the morality and values of their parents and reacted by turning to social promiscuity and new drug indulgence. Parents, on the other hand, disengaged "within their own dismay and disappointment." Those parents who were baffled about "hippie flower children" met head on with these children who saw the adult world as one filled with "drunks and divorcees, who managed to invent nuclear bombs."[15] Psychologists and doctors attempted to bridge these poignant divisions by creating "new climates of receptivity" through institutes and group therapy sessions. Recognizing that youth culture had far-reaching implications, Dr. Bach argued that "bridging the gap will lead us to a new and better path."[16]

Similarly, Robert Kennedy gained trust as a popular spokesman for the younger generation. He concurred, "The bridge across the generations is essential to the nation ... it is the bridge to our own future." He promised "that our young people ... will be heard." Above all, "They must feel that there is a sense of possibility."[17] The bridge was vital to shift what mattered from age to beliefs. Kennedy optimism found opportunity on many college campuses where students across the political spectrum commonly accused time-honored institutions of being discriminatory, bureaucratic, exploitative, and corrupt. Senators, professors, commentators, child psychologists, and others who wished to reform American society or create marketable goods engaged in the reality of the generation dilemma.

Many distrusted youthful discontent, however. *Look* writer Russell Lynes suspected, "The generation gap [had] never been more publicized ... or ... enjoyed for purposes of self ... on both sides. Everybody seems to ... wallow in being misunderstood — the young by the middle-aged, the middle-aged by the young." The usual baits with which the young seemed to shock the older generation did not particularly dismay Lynes. Mini-skirts, long hair, rock music, and other superficial extravagances were only youthful indulgences. The rub for Lynes went deeper, since lifestyle and manners always change. The insult lay in the permanence of the young's disapproval of anyone over thirty and the sacrilege that disapproval seemed to imply. Lynes wanted at least recognition of the contradiction in calling for personalized status within one institution while demeaning those over thirty.[18]

Nonetheless, youth oppression, though a bit perplexing in reality, became a vital means of transforming age into a discourse that confused it with the condition of alienation and disenfranchisement.[19] Using thirty as the separating mark enabled the most affluent generation to date to adopt a sense of powerlessness. Thinking of a younger generation as "unique" meant claiming psychological oppression and correlating it to the effects of materialism. This discourse allowed young adults to understand themselves as revolutionaries whose role was to re-fashion society. Demanding accommodation from adults by creating new ideals and making new promises out of the "under thirty" dividing line also re-defined how one understood American values and beliefs. The under-thirties discourse masked generational diversity and created new lifestyle possibilities for both youth and adult. Film aided in the process and marked its role as an agent in that change.

Benjamin Braddock came along at a time when many of the young, as Hollis Alpert put it, were "suspicious of all this bourgeois opulence."[20] In this milieu, to one young viewer who was "more than a little worried about [her] future," Benjamin presented the truth, "with all its crudeness, shock and beauty."[21] Representing the young as the potential truth-bearers functioned as a popularized form of indictment against American politics and the older generation. As critic Pauline Kael sharply complained, "The graduate stood for truth. The older people stood for sham and corrupt sexuality."[22]

Yet, to popular commentator David Brinkley, the film's unforgivable transgression was its dishonesty. "One night at our house," he wrote in his feature column "David Brinkley's Journal" for *Ladies Home Journal*, "my son and several of his college-age friends found themselves in heated agreement. They thought *The Graduate* was absolutely the best movie they ever saw." Brinkley countered by declaring *The Graduate*, "except for a few minutes at the beginning ... pretty bad." Most distasteful in his opinion was the film's representation of the parent generation as "self-centered and materialistic ... licentious and deeply hypocritical ... walking advertisements for ... affluence." What seemed to be "the enduring conflicts between parent and child have now, suddenly, been phrasemongered into something called The Generation Gap." In Brinkley's eye, "All that is new about The Generation Gap is the phrase itself."[23] Like Lynes, a little justice was all Brinkley wanted. Others agreed. One viewer walked out on what she saw as "a protracted, dull dirty joke, concerning a namby-pamby, self-pitying mama's boy, an idle, stone-laced drunk, and her apparently easily manipulated daughter, none of whom possessed an ounce of self-respect, wit, or talent."[24]

The simplistic division between the "ludicrous, corrupt" parents and the "honest, idealistic, pure, loveable" young people made *The Graduate* "a piece of calculated pseudo-innocence" from filmmakers "with a shrewd eye on the box office," critic John Simon suspected. He had no patience with a world reduced to an aged and outdated Holden Caulfield who was nothing more than "an idealistic, sensitive, confused innocent."[25] Like Brinkley and Simon, Pauline Kael accused Nichols of pandering and explained the picture's appeal as clever publicity that brainwashed viewers through new distribution tactics and market research on demographics. Kael discounted the film's relevance and meaning by arguing that when the "worst inflated pompous trash ... is the most talked about ... we want to see the movies because so many people fall for whatever is talked about that they make the advertisers' lies true." Kael charged the filmmakers with "demagoguery in the arts."[26]

Distributors certainly promoted *The Graduate* based on generational conflict. Reaching the public through newspapers, radio and television ads, magazine features and panel discussions of considerable interest, marketers exploited the film as a news event. Even the political sector saw potential. Senator Jacob Javits argued that "honesty and integrity are what the young are demanding from their Senators and teachers," and when young people see *The Graduate*, "they bring ... a desire to believe" in "broadening ... values ... of honesty and understanding others' view points." The senator believed that Mike Nichols "inspired the young to believe they care," and he encouraged adults "in public and private life ... to emulate them."[27]

Media hype and critical review created a "must-see" aura around the film. After all, critics and advertisers have long delighted in their authority as movie messengers and taste managers, but good marketing cannot carry a bad movie. As Joseph E. Levine pointed out, "You can only do so much with advertising. After a while, they don't believe all the lies we tell them. You have to have a film to back it up."[28] *The Graduate* did just that. What appeared as trivial trash to some critics transformed youth into something that mattered. A college student recalled at the time that Hoffman's character tapped into "my world so well. I remember thinking my problems were also his."[29] A Stony Brook New York University student claimed that "if any of the films of the past year was truly a young people's film, it was 'The Graduate.' 'Bonnie and Clyde,' too, but especially 'The Graduate.'" Ben's gentle nature contrasted to the more "callous and violent" portrayal of the Barrows and offered many young viewers a reasonable point of connection. Certainly, as the writer continued, "You don't have to be young to dig it, but it helps.... I identified with Ben.... I thought of him as a spiritual brother. He was confused about his future and about his place in the world, as I am.... It's a film one digs, rather than understands intellectually."[30]

In some of the coldest weather in Manhattan that winter, viewers waited in lines blocks long. This was not the *Sound of Music* family bunch but the teens and young adults who did not seem to mind the eight-degree temperature. As Hollis Alpert noticed, "They stomped their feet, they made cheerful chatter" because "they ... knew they were going to see something good, something made for *them*." Conversely, "no one waited outside in the cold" at other nearby theaters. A Dallas fan bragged in a letter to Joseph Levine "that he had seen *The Graduate* more than any of his friends, no less than fifteen times." A Columbia University graduate student remarked to Hollis Alpert that no one should assess the film until having seen it "at *least* three times." She argued, "You see, it has meaning and nuances you don't get on just one viewing." The "multiple attendance" by young audiences transformed the film from a success into a phenomenon.[31] With such obvious interest, marketing strategy changed from a simple sketch of a graduate in cap and gown standing under an outline of a woman's leg to a picture of Dustin Hoffman entering a doorway with the tagline, "Now you can see 'The Graduate' again or for the first time."[32]

Where most top films opened to large grosses and then thinned out, the reverse was true with this picture. The first week it brought in $21,000, and by the ninth it totaled $90,000. Moreover, the film topped the charts without mentioning Vietnam. Rather than a specific event, it was the effects of conventional society that most stirred the hearts and minds of viewers. *The Graduate* became the film to see because it was the first effective cinematic manifestation of young adults' open resistance to middle-class ideals, embedded in the famed generation gap debates of the 1960s. By placing the advent of dysfunction in the previous generation's need to build a world of material security, *The Graduate* sparked debate, generated commentary, and incited enthusiasm for film as a means of action. *The Graduate*'s screen version of generational discourse made alienation a condition of age and generational solidarity an instrument of change. Together these components helped it earn some $104,000,000.

The film created an identifying process that personalized the screen and offered a new way of being in tune with changing attitudes and taste. It did this by reconstructing the meaning of *The Graduate* in its immediate context and in relation to the specific ways of understanding and feeling the predominant generational questions in the mid-to late sixties, which begins with the personal appeal of Ben's characterization and Hoffman's persona. Ben's growing awareness that something in his life is not quite right is sidetracked when he discovers the possibility of sex with Mrs. Robinson (Anne Bancroft), the attractive wife of his father's business partner. At first startled by her sexual aggression, Benjamin later invites her to a local hotel where they engage in one of American cinema's most memorable affairs. In the meantime, Ben falls in love with Elaine Robinson (Katharine Ross), his mistress's daughter, who came home from college for the summer. When she discovers his sordid behavior, Elaine hastens back to Berkeley to her boyfriend Carl (Brian Avery), known as the "makeout king," and Ben pursues her. The film ends with Ben proving his sincere love for Elaine; the two of them escape on a bus, departing from their parents' material world.

The camera follows Ben from the airport to his bedroom and zooms to Ben's face through a fish tank. Images of entrapment, repeated throughout the film, invite viewers into Ben's alienation. Later in the film, a much loved shot comically shows the older generation's outdated notion of what makes young people content. Benjamin's parents have thrown a birthday party for him with their adult friends who applaud when he steps outside the house and jumps into the pool in his birthday present, a new frogman suit. Ben peers out of the goggles and sees an older generation as outdated and immaterial as the diving gear.

The real appeal of this birthday scene, however, cannot be explained without contextualizing Dustin Hoffman. Nichols and Turman delayed production for months looking for just the right young man to portray the main character and key to the film's success was that decision. It was well known that Nichols held out for a new look, but most assumed that meant a handsome young face from television.[33] Instead, the picture debuted a short, dark-haired, large-nosed Dustin Hoffman who, in the words of reviewer Joseph Morgenstern, "wears the world like a new pair of shoes."[34] When Hoffman walked into Mike Nichols' office on a rainy day, he did not turn heads. Embassy's chief mistook him for the plumber.[35] Likewise, Katharine Ross, who played Elaine, was surprised when she first saw Hoffman on the set. She remarked, "He looks about three feet tall, so dead serious, so humorless, so unkempt." Dismayed, she worried that the screen test was "going to be a disaster."[36] This "homely non-hero," as *Life*'s David Zeitlin described the 5-foot-6 Hoffman, "with a schnoz that looks like a directional signal, skittish black-beady eyes and a raggedy hair-cap ... slouches like a puppet dangling from a string."[37]

An unpretentious Hoffman even frightened Embassy's publicity personnel who asked what "that ugly guy [was] doing as lead of the picture." The company's advertisers doubted the possibility for recovery of the highly leveraged $3,100,000 and wondered if Embassy's chief had "lost his touch" with this one. Needless to say, many remained skeptical following the casting of Hoffman and believed they were helping to prepare for a big flop.[38] Yet, to Mike Nichols' discriminating eye, Hoffman added a touch of the offbeat and brought a psychological tension to the story.

Benjamin Braddock was originally cast for a California surfboard-type — tall, blond, blue-eyed, and athletic. The western blond in the book and screenplay had not only gone to an eastern college but had come away with scholarships to Harvard and Columbia graduate schools. Mike Nichols initially took that route. He had Robert Redford and Candice Bergen in mind. To complete the California family, he offered the role of Mrs. Robinson to Doris Day who turned it down because it offended her sense of values. As for Redford, at that point in his film career, he just "could not ... play a loser like Benjamin, 'cause nobody would ever buy it," Nichols recalled.[39] Instead of an idol merely reproducing just "another portrait by the well-loved so-and-so," this inarticulate manner would allow room for improvisation.[40] "It's the hardest thing I ever tried to cast," noted Nichols. "These people are so far removed from stock characters."[41] Even Hoffman fought Nichols' reinterpretation. "Benjamin Braddock is just not Jewish," he complained.[42] Yet Nichols sought what Hoffman's look offered on screen — a young man "simply living his life without pretending."[43] Nichols' guess proved brilliant. Hoffman began the film as an off–Broadway actor and ended as a star.

The Graduate turned Hoffman into a symbol of the here and now. New Hollywood changed its face from the pre-war generation look of "vanilla features" to an ethnicity that engendered a new kind of realism.[44] The timing was right. As Stanley Kaufman pointed out in 1967, "It would be hard to imagine [Hoffman] in leading roles a decade ago."[45] His offhanded and unassuming acting manner, as head of Embassy's publicity remarked, was "absolutely new to the screen." From a young person's point of view, Hoffman's demeanor of "insecurity" simultaneously exuded an "inner core" of strength. Embassy's representative described it as "the way that you and your friends act but that you've never seen on screen before."[46] Alongside the western surfer now sat the eastern, European, dark-haired youth. Hoffman himself observed that "suddenly, our tastes have become so anti–American image — anti–Saturday Evening Post [*sic*] Norman Rockwell."[47] When the slouchy Hoffman dons the frogman suit, he takes viewers with him and projects the popular sentiment against parents. Floating and drifting mock the value of work, so vital for the parent generation, and symbolize the disillusionment of the rebellious younger generation whose worry was not economic security.

Charles Webb's 1963 novel touches on common elements of the classic father/son debate that would pique both generations' attention. Ben challenges patriarchal authority by trading his home for the road. He values people, "simple people," he tells his dad. "I want simple honest people that can't even read or write their own name. I want to spend the rest of my life with these people ... farmers ... truck drivers. Ordinary people who don't have big houses. Who don't have swimming pools." Yet, his father is not a simpleton. "Ben," he accuses, "you have a romantic idea of this," and the classic conflict of father and son continues.[48]

Four years later, the son's discontent shifts in emphasis. Nichols downplays the parent's role as teacher and supports the younger generation's romantic notions about human nature and American ideals. "It's very comfortable — just to drift here," Ben explains to his father. "Have you thought about graduate school?" asks Mr. Braddock, to which Ben replies, "No." When his father asks him to explain the point of those "four years of college" and "all that hard work," Ben impudently replies, "You got me."[49] Ben's plastic swimming pool raft helps remedy his summer melancholy.

The Ben/Hoffman combination, therefore, personifies what Stanley Kauffman speculated was a new "being ... not otherwise" possible in an earlier time.[50] It was not a rite of passage that the film highlighted nor an on-the-road rebellion but a specific generational identity transmitted through familiar icons of rejection. Hoffman exuded the tweed-sports-coat ambiance throughout the film. His "eastern" formality and ethnic appearance competed with the "all–American," seductive, masculine composite, commonly known as the "walking surfboards," born in California and popularized during the Beach Boys era and surfer films.[51]

The fresh impact of Hoffman mixed well with the witty script and brilliant musical score.[52] Whether Benjamin Braddock drives the red convertible sports car on the freeway while listening to Art Garfunkel and Paul Simon's "Scarborough Fair" or floats on a plastic raft in the swimming pool to "Hello, Darkness, My Old Friend," the combination is striking. Lyrics that tell about Ben talking to his friend Darkness help distinguish his torment as both typical and universal by identifying Ben's privacy as a safe environment in contrast to public spaces. These beloved songs were not just a backdrop for the rhythm of the film but an assertion of Ben's identity and a validation of the irreducible core of Ben's good soul. He broods but is not neurotic. He is disappointed, not despondent.

The music adds pertinence to the film and vice versa by bringing the realm of the psychological into the context of the younger generation's self-proclaimed disenchantment with its parent society. Rock music's increasingly political function as a mode of dissent for a younger generation coming of age during the late 1960s offered filmmakers songs with political voices. Since just "Mrs. Robinson" was written specifically for the film, movie-goers identified instantly with the soundtrack. The power of music helped make *The Graduate* more than just a classic story about a college graduate's difficulties, adjustments, or psychological struggle with his father.

Music also distinguishes Ben intragenerationally by identifying what he is not. The film establishes Ben's place in the generation gap by separating him from the hippie culture and ensures that he is not a campus agitator. A key moment comes when Ben is at a Santa Monica hamburger drive-in. Noisy youth listening to "The Big Green Pleasure Machine" surround his red convertible. Ben orders them to turn the music down and when they do not, he pulls up the top to his convertible, annoyed with their presence. This symbolic gesture contrasts Ben to the raucous celebrants of Sunset Boulevard who were attracting attention at the time and thereby distinguishes him from the coming counterculture and its youthful radicalism.[53]

Just as he separates himself from the Sunset Boulevard hippies, he also differentiates himself from political radicals. Halfway through the film on the Berkeley campus, he defends himself from being mistaken as a long-haired Berkeley disrupter. In the book, Ben's new landlord near the Berkeley campus, Mr. Berry, becomes wary of Ben's behavior and inquires, "Are you booking me or something?" To the contrary, in the film, his landlord, Mr. McCleery (Norman Fell), concludes Ben is trouble.

"Are you a student?"

"Not exactly — no," Ben answers.

"You're not one of those agitators ... one of those outside agitators?"

"Oh, no sir," Ben assures him.

Ben establishes his lines of identification and clarifies Mr. McCleery's confusion between the Braddock type of youthful rebellion and those marginalized as "outside agitators." The film maintains the element in Ben's character that Lawrence Thurman saw as the work's relevance — "wildness, yet an underlying decency."[54] Ben stands as a twenty-one-year-old ideal rebel who helped define the proper form of rebellion against middle-class values, but Nichols would have been remiss to ignore his own generation.

The Graduate garnered iconic status because of its new star and music but the film's most egregious act, the affair between Ben and Mrs. Robinson, gave it its most prominent feature. In her daughter's bedroom shortly after Ben's graduation party, Mrs. Robinson drops her clothes and reveals her willful intent to allure the young graduate. Specific shots of Mrs. Robinson, through Ben's eyes, reveal her suntanned shoulders, white breasts, and her bikini underwear. Attempting to discard the empty formality of being a married woman, Mrs. Robinson forces Benjamin, still in his sport coat and tie, to look at her. Fearful of the consequences of her aggression, Ben escapes her home, but the thought of sex with her lingers, and he soon makes a phone call.

Mrs. Robinson, nearly twenty years his senior, accepts Ben's invitation to meet him at the Taft Hotel bar. After he telephones Mrs. Robinson, he leaves the phone booth and "moves about uncomfortably for a few moments." He "removes his jacket" and "crosses to the doors that lead to the main lobby," as the script explains.[55] Just before he settles in, he holds the doors open for a group of elderly men and women dressed in traditional tuxedoes and formal wear and then a group of high schoolers going to a prom. Though each group confuses him as a guest for its respective parties, he escapes to the bar and shows he is independent of these personalities. The hotel is where Ben's sexual identity defines his generational revolt and confirms that Ben is neither teenybopper nor social conservative (despite his sport coat and tie).

The hotel room is a meeting place for the generations. The scenes portray both a predator and a middle-aged beauty shown through Anne Bancroft's strong demeanor and evocative shots of her body in lacy, leopard-pattern underwear. The visuals consist of bare shoulders, of the two lying side by side, Hoffman in his boxers, and Mrs. Robinson suggestively taking off and putting on her nylon stockings. Her outstanding beauty and California tan lines bring to the screen a stylish appeal that also allows her character to transcend sordidness by being provocative — victimized and victimizer at the same time. She is Nichols' answer to what happened to the prototypical, martini-drinking, 1950s woman. Anne Bancroft's screen appeal seeps through the character's alleged corruption. Her glamour adds another aspect to generational sensibility, placing her outside the caricatured parents and their frogman gifts. If one could not trust Mrs. Robinson, it was and was not because she was over thirty. Her attractiveness and association with the possibility of fantasy seen through the eyes of Ben further publicized West Coast affluence upon which the film's stance on sexuality depended. Sex with Mrs. Robinson made the film memorable, current, and critically acceptable.

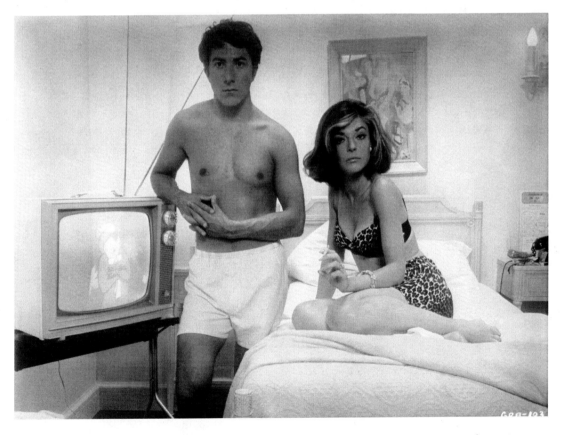

The two generations meet in the Taft Hotel in *The Graduate* (1967); Anne Bancroft as Mrs. Robinson, a sexual outlaw in leopard underwear, is not exactly the Doris Day prototype (Photofest).

Once in the hotel room, Mrs. Robinson cleverly cajoles Ben out of his anguish. "For God's sake, can you imagine my parents?" Ben frets. "If they were right here in this room right now, what they would say ... they brought me up. I think they deserve a little better than this—than jumping into bed."[56] Though Mrs. Robinson's strength as temptress is powerful, Ben is fully capable of refusing her seduction, but stays in the room after Mrs. Robinson derides him:

> Benjamin, is this your first time...? It is, isn't it? It is your first time.
> That's a laugh, Mrs. Robinson. That's really a laugh.
> You can admit that, can't you?
> Are you kidding?
> It's nothing to be ashamed of ... of being inadequate....
> Inadequate!?

The attraction between the older woman and the college graduate is not anything new, but its treatment of sexual transgression in the "safe" mainstream is. Ben of the novel, for example, hitchhikes, sleeps with prostitutes, and lives with the homeless. His healthy sex life parallels his curiosity for life on the road. The film, on the other hand, discounts the novel's emphasis on the fabled journey as a rite of passage. Instead, Nichols connects the generation-gap debates with hotel sex. This film extends the boundaries of where the progressive picture could go regarding sexual territory.

Mrs. Robinson is the sexual outlaw and seducer of Ben but is comfortable with sex without love.[57] By contrast, Benjamin's engagement in hotel sex appears necessary for his rescue. The affair attracts him for its liberating potential. Sexuality will be his generation's last emancipator.

Hoffman's nakedness is memorable enough but not because he is a sex object. Rather, he made new sense of the star phenomenon through his small body and being casual about his activity with Mrs. Robinson. A bit nerdy, common, and unconventional, Ben failed one viewer's assumptions of pin-up poster material. In a letter to the editor, the viewer complained that "it is next to impossible to believe the older woman ... could be attracted to a boy who is physically and socially far from the American Dream."[58] The controlled sex scenes make Hoffman's character seem real and vital and add a touch of "telling it like it is" to the fantasy of sex because he is not the poster boy.

Hollis Alpert was convinced that Benjamin's affair with Mrs. Robinson was "probably the funniest and maybe the saddest affair yet shown on the overexperienced screen."[59] Another critic described the affair as "wildly funny, revealing and free."[60] Andrew Sarris of the well-known *Village Voice* argued that it was "easier to be interesting with an unconventional sexual relationship than with a conventional love pairing."[61] Sexuality on screen asserted the film's contemporary attitudes toward common taboos. Whether one described the affair as wildly funny or critiqued it as timid, it still leads to the same point. Both perspectives confirm the film's "truth" about sex because the issue centers on taste and levels of sophistication rather than moral legitimacy. Against traditional authority that once claimed sexuality as a religious and private matter, this film helped the younger generation advance its adversarial position.

The relative endorsement of the film's portrayal of sexuality in view of the picture's widespread popularity suggests that the feature film entered a new safe zone, despite bending borders of acceptability through sex with Mrs. Robinson. Her matter-of-fact involvement with Benjamin helped transcend earlier Doris Day prototypes. In addition, Bancroft contrasted to other stars such as Marilyn Monroe or Ann Margret by drawing attention to female effective-ness and away from overt sensuality. The mature siren and her $175,000 worth of jewels and furs displayed willful strength. Ben's straightforward engagement helps reinforce his role as truth seeker and takes the narrative to its provocative resolution. Her seduction of Ben exposes the real American tragedy—an empty marriage. As Ben later tells Mr. Robinson, "We got into bed with each other. But it was nothing. It was nothing at all. We—we might just as well have been shaking hands."

Since the film encouraged audiences to identify with Benjamin's relative naiveté as Mrs. Robinson's prey, *The Graduate* also suggested that sex without passion was destructive, thus balancing rebellion with Mrs. Robinson's cool beauty and casual sex, but still exploiting the changing social environment and sexual attitudes. Ben is torn by equally powerful feelings of loyalty in contrast to the pathos of Mrs. Robinson, produced obliquely by her life of mate-rial affluence and leisure. This contrast is necessary for the film's generational statement about those over thirty. Ben ultimately succeeds in his critique of modern American society when he rejects Mrs. Robinson and chooses her daughter, Elaine. She is the proper contrast to his moral dilemma and to his revolt against objectification—both material and sexual. She becomes his way out of adult confinement and the film's tool for building its final critique of the parent generation. Passion for Elaine begins the de-objectification process and leads to Ben's personal investment in his future. Mrs. Robinson represents the prospect of fantasy and a bit of wildness for the young man, but Elaine grounds the story in its theme of "underly-ing decency."

Ben's first date with Elaine begins at a striptease bar. First, Ben forces Elaine to watch the stripper and then runs after her when Elaine hurries out of the club, humiliated in front of the stripper. Ben later apologizes by telling her the story of his adulterous affair without revealing his mistress' identity. For the first time in the film, he has a genuine conversation (though not completely truthful), revealing sincere feeling. Once his attention shifts from disingenuous behavior with Mrs. Robinson to true love, the narrative ceases its satiric innu-endo. Reinforcing the shift, the setting moves from places of adult authority (hotels and sub-urban homes) to the red convertible and the symbolic college campus, the University of California at Berkeley. The switch from critique to love establishes Ben's truthfulness, sincer-ity, and authenticity, thereby, reinforcing generational duality and confirming the value in escape from material objectification and alienation. Mrs. Robinson's sexuality in the public space of the Taft Hotel threatens Ben's emotional security; his red car and campus apartment restore it. Sexual liberation both establishes and contrasts to authentic true love outside of the space of parental authority. What was at stake in this example of private/public, adult/youth was the affirmation of generational identity. The hotel sex scenes with Hoffman's image as authentic and honest empower the younger generation and offer it a chance to imagine itself as those who have discovered the hollowness of the older generation's lifestyle.[62]

The strongest indictment of Mrs. Robinson's character, despite her sexual vitality and inordinate beauty, occurs when Elaine discovers her duplicity. Mrs. Robinson is rain soaked with black, stringy, dripping hair. Her drenched black dress contrasts to the white wall where she stands outside Elaine's bedroom as her daughter discovers the truth.

The sympathetic shift to Elaine frees Ben from objectification by her mother as a con-ventional sex object and by his parents as an intellectual showpiece. The move allows him to recover his humanity, despite his former affair. Through his pursuit of Elaine, Ben challenges the conventional image of antimaterialism. He is not a victim but an agent for generational reformation. He is quite the opposite of what Kael and Simon accused him of trying to be, the Tolstoyean peasant, the dripping innocent.[63]

Considering Hollywood's newfound freedom amid changing social expectations, *The Graduate* places Ben squarely inside the society that produced him. At the same time, instead of perpetuating the image of the mythic victim, Ben negotiates new boundaries for mainstreamers and represents the younger generation's "truth task."[64] Ben, both truth seeker and transgressor, invites viewers to cross social borders "politely" and provokingly.

The picture drew interest because of Mrs. Robinson but ultimately returned to its theme of transgression with the concluding sequence. Until then, it appeared that the film would return Elaine to her boyfriend Carl. Shortly after Ben locates Elaine on the Berkeley campus, he manages to catch up with her walking with Carl at the local zoo. As if in a showdown with the pre-med student, Ben sandwiches Elaine between them — tall, blond Carl, Elaine, and short Ben. Later, Ben seeks information on Elaine's whereabouts at Carl's fraternity house. He searches for leads in the locker room amid the "walking surfboards." Hoffman's smallboy image contrasts to the southern California fraternity brothers who chide and joke about Carl, the "makeout king."[65]

Ben's quest of honor is to convince Elaine of his worth, but that ends when Elaine has already married the blond-blue-eyed Carl. Ben proves his commitment to Elaine through a speedy chase down California freeways in his red convertible to the Santa Barbara Protestant church where Carl and Elaine have just been pronounced man and wife. Carl kisses Elaine and is about to leave with her when Ben pounds on the church's glass partition, shocking the congregation and shouting for Elaine. "It's too late," Mrs. Robinson screams at Ben. "It's not too late for me," her daughter yells back. Elaine runs for ethnic Ben, who swings a wooden crucifix before an angry congregation. He rescues Elaine from them by jamming the church doors shut with the cross and the two escape. The film's one last transgression occurs, most clearly, through the sacred image of the wooden cross. Swinging that image gives the film one final inflammatory but fashionable means to rebellion. As one *Graduate* fan remembered, "I was shocked that he swung the cross. I didn't know you could do that."[66]

Ben in his casual shirt and Elaine in her designer wedding dress flee from the angry crowd and jump onto a city bus. The camera pans the faces of working-class people who stare dumbfounded at the frivolous runaways rushing past the filled seats on the city transit. The couple sits at the back of the bus and stares enigmatically straight ahead. Not embraced in a love grip, nor engrossed in their fondness for the triumph over those left behind, they remain disconnected from the public peering back and the film ends. The successful challenge makes a critical comment on what would become a passionless marriage if Elaine stayed with Carl. Ben rescues Elaine from the hurtful future as wife of the "makeout king" by using the most immediate resource — his own two feet. He has also produced an authentic and genuine reality of rebellion by breaking through the glass barrier and redefining a most sacrosanct symbol, the wedding vows. Elaine's desire and Ben's resourcefulness rescue young people from parental and religious authority inside traditional institutions.

The ending dismembers the sacred institution of marriage and conventional sexual rules by representing rituals as optional. This sequence targets the sizeable religious population that grappled with the effects of the liberalization of tradition during the 1960s. As Andrew Sarris remarked, the film "not only shatters ... monogamous mythology; it does so in the name of a truer love." Sarris admits he "was with *The Graduate* all the way because [he] responded fully to its romantic feelings." The film was "moving precisely because its hero passes from a premature maturity to an innocence regained, an idealism reconfirmed." Sarris pointed out that "even the overdone caricatures that surround the three principals cannot diminish the cruel beauty of this love story."[67] In the words of filmmaker Stanley Kaufmann, the film conveys "a new kind of love: a love based on recognition of identical loneliness on their side of the generational gap, a gap which — never mind how sillily it is often exploited in politics and pop culture — irrefutably exists."[68] True love outweighs hotel sex and formal vows. Thus, Elaine's compliance exposes her mother's limitations and engenders possibility for a rebellious younger generation.

Subverting the narrative by taking a disheveled Ben into sacred territory — which causes Elaine to discard her new husband, the families, and relatives in favor of boarding a bus to nowhere — brought a film era to an end. With Mrs. Robinson, the Production Code's "Doris Day" and "twin bed" formula receded into the archives. This film endorsed Hollywood's function of portraying sexual love more in tune with social changes in attitude and also challenged the industry's invented regulations with its sexless marriages (with one foot on the floor). This film critiques that past as a sham and a superficial control by the industry, not for the good of society.[69]

Nichols' ending shifts the tragedy from Ben and his moral development to the older generation and its moral failing that denied the likes of Mrs. Robinson a choice.

Anne Bancroft's performance never convincingly leaves Mrs. Robinson destroyed. The film allows a complexity for her character that is missing in her husband and Ben's parents and therefore encourages empathy. When Benjamin and Elaine opt for an honest love relationship, they implicate Mr. Robinson as much as his wife. Ultimately, his success remains both the cause of his wife's loneliness and the means of her exploits. She has stepped outside the marriage parameters in the most immediate way possible. Her agency and relative effectiveness deliver her from the burden of having only two choices — to be happily married or to be a sensual commodity. All in all, the film portrays Mrs. Robinson's tragedy and her sadness as the older generation's limitations, now corrected by both Ben and Elaine. What is "too late" for her mother will be salvaged by Elaine, who makes sure viewers understand her words, "not for me."

Charles Webb argued that the ending did not vindicate anything. Rather, "as such, there is little difference between [Ben's] relationship to Mrs. Robinson and his relationship to Elaine, both of them being essentially immoral." The book's traditional ending has Ben interrupt the marriage ceremony *before* the couple has said their vows. In a letter to *The New Republic*, the author complained about the film's changed ending. He questioned whether the story had retained any moral stance at all. Webb argued that Benjamin, in his book, "does not disrespect the institution of marriage" but focuses on his moral development. "Reach[ing] the girl before she becomes the wife of somebody else" characterizes his "moral attitudes." The ending was Charles Webb's way of giving the story and character moral depth. Nichols reverses the emphasis and creates an ending that makes moral attitudes irrelevant. "If it were not for the ending," Hollis Alpert remarked, "I doubt that 'The Graduate' would have aroused as much enthusiastic favor as it has among the somewhat inchoately rebellious young."[70]

Nichols' ending determines the film's success and marks a moment not of moral bankruptcy, when Hollywood had forsaken public need for moral lessons, but a new sense of goodness. In Hollis Alpert's words, "Mike Nichols ... has lined up old Hollywood with avantgarde Hollywood." The "positive" ending favors "honesty" as that which refuses sex without love and delivers one from "ancient taboos" that paraded as moral safeguards but operated as "hollow formality." An attraction to the ideals of the earlier sixties — to change society and make it more honest — continued in this film and merged with the trend in the later 1960s toward "dropping out." Though 1968 would bring forms of protest and demonstrations with more serious acts of rebellion than climbing on board a bus, Nichols saw his film's connection. As he told one Columbia University audience, those expressions of defiance were about a younger generation's "nerve" and "necessity, to break the rules."[71]

Not all were convinced that "making the bus" raised any questions at all about generational honesty. Nor did the final image make the least attempt to clarify the meaning of Ben's liberation and purpose. Paul Seydor complained about the couple's fleeing to never-neverland. It did not solve any of the pressing social issues of the time.[72] Even Mike Nichols joked that the couple would "end up just like their parents in five or ten years," not changing much of anything at all.[73] The ending's ambiguity — do they stay on the bus or become like their parents? — is the picture's strength and most telling moment. Ben and Elaine indeed carve out a road, a path to action for more than just the two of them. Climbing on board the bus is a defiant act, a symbolic act, and a representation of the younger generation's agency. It is a reassuring conclusion to Ben's pursuit of a life of difference. As one fan wrote, "He was chasing an ideal in spite of all the obstacles that society put in his path in the attempt to co-opt or eliminate him."[74] Elaine and Benjamin's jump on the bus signifies the final challenge to authority and tradition. Ben dumps his fancy red car, the graduation present, for his own two feet and redefines himself as a representative of the younger generation, not as a victim of an older one.

Moreover, the script in many ways seems to belong to the pre-antiwar demonstration period in the 1960s, when generational conflict rested largely on parent-child differences. The young publicity team at Embassy, for example, questioned the relevance of a script that did not even mention the word Vietnam, let alone a film with 103 minutes of running time that portrayed the younger generation without campus or street protest. Young staff members wondered, "What ... *The Graduate* ha[d] to do with them?"[75]

Edgar Z. Friedenberg of *The New York Review of Books* called the film a "pseudo-documentary." "The social commentary," he pointed out, "is expressed as it would be in a nightclub sketch, almost entirely through exaggerated characterization." Friedenberg scorned what was absent — "nobody in the picture mentions the draft or the war; dissent in Berkeley is symbolized only by a hippie-looking couple leaving a jewelry store and by the landlord's hostility." *The Graduate* may have been an "'in' movie," Friedenberg continued, "but the realism doesn't extend to burning draft cards or smoldering police." With the absences of these daily occurrences, Friedenberg saw "no issues, only scenes" and certainly none of the "wilder, angrier, more uncertain," mood of California. Friedenberg was impatient with the everyman portrayal of Benjamin, whom he called a "muttering inarticulate."[76]

Reviewers noted that the shift from a critique of society to a love story was a betrayal of "its own expertise."[77] Some denounced the anti-hero Ben as a fake and indicted the Nichols team for "gang banging" Mrs. Robinson by ignoring her victimization, thus making Ben's rescue of Elaine from her mother's fate a fraud. "She's their real masterwork, a character to rank right up there with the best of Lillian Hellman. Stewing in her own misery, symbolic of a parasitic society anxious to suck the vital red blood of youth," claimed Paul Seydor.[78] Others found the romantic hero suspect, completely unlike "the present-day graduate [who] is much more complicated, sophisticated and involved."[79]

On paper, in the political climate of 1967, it may have seemed out of touch with the radical behavior of thousands of young people, but on screen the film's success suggests it both transcended its context and was immersed in it. Lawrence Thurman explained the story as completely "pertinen[t] to the present scene." Director Mike Nichols agreed that Benjamin provided a way to inquire about the behavior of the prosperous young. Similar to other baby boomers at that time, "Benjamin has been surfeited with objects," finds them confining, and seeks "something to arouse his passion." The element of affluence lent the story an attractive "pungency."[80] The script highlighted the dilemmas and points of rebellion in middle- and upper-middle-class kids who also wondered about the point of all that education.

The Graduate let go of the earlier California beach movies that had already popularized swimming pools, rambler houses, casual clothing, spider convertibles, sunglasses, and free-ways as icons, for as the sons and daughters of the "lounge culture," the "plastic fantastics,"[81] the "barbeque-pit society."[82] At the same time, the film certainly circulates the same desire for the products argued on the surface as the older generation's materialism. Ben throughout the film floats on the plastic raft, wears stylish plastic sunglasses, listens to plastic records, and eats at hamburger stands that uses plastic-ware. "The plastic," Friedenburg chided, "is a lot tougher than the movie admits; but there is real blood under it."[83] In that respect, the film self-consciously derides affluence as an older generation's affliction while unselfconsciously rein-forcing a culture of "cool," favoring sunglasses not frogmen suits.

The lounge-culture teens would have to give way to new identities on screen, however, that were claiming American individualism by tuning in, turning on, and dropping out. *The Graduate*'s satirical representation of southern California engaged a New York intellectual crowd that could fully accept western affluence as intellectually vacuous and see Benjamin as a yokel. "Benjamin, as an individual, is a pathetic figure who would be tragic if he had any *hubris* at all," Friedenburg of the *New York Review of Books* disparaged. "Benjamin's lack of pride and selfhood on which to mount his feelings is just the point; middle-class life in Amer-ica—and Southern California is America, is it not?—makes us all like those loveless people and their pathetic victims, surely," the reviewer continued.[84]

Friedenberg's argument that *The Graduate* seemed "basically a copout," despite its power to capture "the look and sound of much of the contemporary California scene so skillfully," also reveals the developing forms of rebellion of the time.[85] *The Graduate* was released just before widespread antiwar strife, before the Chicago Convention of 1968, Woodstock, and the height of campus bombings, but after the widely publicized Summer of Love. With its December release, it makes sense that the film's currency would be measured against social challenges coming out of counterculture behavior and more radical activity than rebelling against American materialism. Yet, if the film lacked historical and political insight by not asking what was really happening in the streets and by condescending to the hippie counter-culture, it was by no means backpedaling. The film engaged in the conversation about social changes and cultural values already alive and well in the public arenas.[86]

Ben and Elaine ultimately challenged attitudes about the older generation's upper-mid-dle-class lifestyle and conventional social relationships. At the same time, the two runaways, as film critic Simon sneered, did not exactly set up a paradise or offer "perceptible [*sic*] resources or qualifications" for a new society. No doubt, Simon argued, "it is an exigous Eden they can look forward to."[87] Thus, are the red sports car, Ben's sunglasses, and the sounds of Simon and Garfunkel ultimately what define the characters' appeal or does the film resonate as a honest critique of traditional society? To drift in the swimming pool of the parent gen-eration, albeit on plastics, symbolized the ironic result of material satisfaction. Through

Hoffman's persona and Ben's appeal as passively resisting his parents' objective for him while floating in the symbol of success, the film establishes its critical perspective and derisive tone.

Hoffman's inarticulate manner should have seemed idiotic to those who made up the largest population of college students in the country's history. Seydor doubted that if Benjamin were indeed a star graduate from a prestigious college, "he would be smart and brash and cynical; he would be astonishingly well-oriented and incredibly well-informed" and instead of muttering his way through the film, "he would be very articulate."[88] Ben also challenges the role of the enlightened adult teaching the young college student. The film's focus on Ben's "decent" rebellion helped articulate an acquired sense of generation, not defined solely as a coming of age but as a preoccupation, a sensibility, a style, and a rhetoric.

The Graduate favors the couple's successful defiance of the older generation and leaves it at that. In this sense, the film measures the limitation of the affluent middle-class rebels. Certainly, like Ben and Elaine, revolutionaries could board the bus but they would not stay there. Nor would they engender social change for those whose faces stared blankly back at them, for to do so would be to take them to the place the young people had just fled. Rejection of materialism as a means of generational legitimacy was thus contingent on literally being able to afford to rebel. Their revolt occurs after the fact, after Beverly Hills affluence and university education have given them the choice to do so. Establishment values of success and conventional beliefs in work as productive adversely affected Benjamin because they were incompatible with his wish to be different, not because of his physical discomfort or literal disenfranchisement. The desire for a different future became an honorable cause only because of its legitimate association with the rejection of materialism and the belief in the liberating powers of youth. Between the publicity, the response from the younger generation, Pauline Kael's charge that *The Graduate* was highly inflated trash as it utterly pandered to youth, and David Brinkley's objection to the adult put-down, social authority was argued. Kael, Brinkley, Simon, and others' discontent over this film likely exposed the growing impatience with the rising adversity toward American affluence, not because consumerism did not deserve critique but because the criticism released the privileged young from full responsibility and exposed the rebellion's contradictions.

The ending answered the question raised at the beginning of the film when Ben delivered the graduation-day speech: "And today it is right that we should ask ourselves the most important question: What is the purpose for all this demanding work.... The purpose my fellow graduates — the purpose is —... there is a reason, my friends, and the reason is —." Searching for the final page of his speech, he flounders at the podium when the pages blow away in a whirlwind and prevent him from answering the question. The camera then cuts to Ben for the opening sequence at the Los Angeles airport. In the house full of guests at his parents' graduation party for him, Ben listens to an older generation define who he is. "Hey — there's our award winning scholar." Yet, Ben does not engage. He has left the purpose, education, and future behind, in the East, where he could not even find the link between the diploma and a good job. To the contrary, Ben's triumph in rescuing Elaine from a fated marriage defines his purpose as a graduate. Love and rescue liberate him from boredom, objectification, and the pressures of a fake future.

It would be tempting to discount the plastic fantastics in favor of the intellectual authority of reviewers and college honors students. Yet, it was not difficult for thousands of fans to identify with the film's vision through Benjamin's eyes with Hoffman's convincing performance, not as a star or a celebrity, but as an ordinary and confused college graduate, stumbling around in a useless frogman suit. As one fan admitted at the time, "'The Graduate' affected me more deeply than any other movie I've ever seen.... Most of the young people I've talked to who've seen it have also responded deeply to it, though maybe not in exactly the way I did."[89] *The Graduate* gained its social authority from Hoffman's inarticulate character—a romantic but irreverent upper-middle-class rebel who definitively established the dividing lines among teenager, young adult, and the establishment. As music also took on a more clearly antiestablishment stance and as serious campus activism among college-aged students became ever more associated with unruly appearance in the larger society, what Ben came mean in generational appeal measured the kind of change that mattered to young people in rebellion.[90]

The youthful eye of Benjamin Braddock from the beginning devalued an older generation's established systems. They were simply expendable. He qualitatively defined the meaning of the generation gap in terms different from demonstrators and counterculturalists. How viewers who identified with the narrative and character in the midst of rising social strife into 1968 explains the film's significance. Most telling is the film's visualization of the break between generations. The two young people, whose lives shone with the same sort of middle- to upper-middle-class home culture as was featured in popular periodicals, sorted out their own identities and places within a changing culture by defying conventional expectations not in bizarre dress and behavior but with "an underlying decency." If the picture short-circuited the critique of the consumerist society by not making victims out of the characters, it also gave the narrative a logical connecting point between young and old. If *The Graduate* failed to highlight the political setting many critics expected of a popular and artistic feature film, it also resonated more clearly on a level that enhanced the human drama in social relationships.

The Graduate received industry kudos with five Golden Globes for Best Picture, Best Director, and Best Actress in a musical or comedy and, for both Ross and Hoffman, most promising male and female newcomer. The Hollywood Foreign Press Association awarded Nichols' showpiece with two more citations than the 1967 Academy Award winner, *In the Heat of the Night*. *The Graduate* was nominated for seven awards and received Best Director for Nichols' innate sense and shrewd eye for "visual comment."[91] Hoffman did not gain Academy patronage, but did become a phenomenon. On the street, he was the man of the moment, suddenly known as the graduate. People "thought I was an innocent," he recalled, "who walked around with 'The Sounds of Silence' always playing in the background wherever I went."[92] In Joseph E. Levine's eyes, *The Graduate* was "the most successful film I ever made." No one could have predicted the success of the film since the novel already "had been to every film company in Hollywood." Indeed, author and director were lucky they found each other in the midst of a generation's rebellion with a cause.[93]

The film, as a sixties emblem, made Dustin Hoffman a star and carried "formative influence" on the generation that was to leave their mark on American society by the end of the decade.[94] "I remember exactly where I was sitting in the movie theater, and with whom, all three times," recalled *L.A. Weekly* reviewer Ella Taylor. Nichols' film was the "movie that my generation clasped to its bosom as the prophecy of our coming revolution," she continued.[95] Susan Lydon of *Rolling Stone* recognized Mike Nichols' "unerring comic sense, light touch, cleverness, and perception." All of these added up to "an excellent, highly entertaining, and hilarious movie."[96] *The Graduate*'s social and intertextual life has far out-run the film's aesthetic value. References to the film have popped up as late as the 1990s in *The Player* and *Used*

People. The Lemmonheads revived Simon & Garfunkel's "Mrs. Robinson" for MTV and there has been talk of *The Graduate: Part II.*

Clearly endorsing the "under thirty" discourse, *The Graduate,* despite Hoffman's real age of thirty-one, made a charming argument for the entrance of the "now movie," to which *Saturday Review* devoted an entire issue by the end of the year. The Nichols' team proved to exhibitors that good filmmakers did not have to start with the bankable star. The release of *The Graduate* indelibly marked "newness" as a blending of youthful discontent with antimaterialist posturing, sexual frankness, and a director's phenomenal style.[97] Mrs. Robinson had a lasting impact on representations of sexuality in the bedroom. "For," as Hollis Alpert noted, *The Graduate* "has taken aim, satirically, at the very establishment that produces most of our movies, mocked the morals and values it has long lived by. It is a final irony that it has thereby gained the large young audience it has been seeking and has been rewarded by a shower of gold."[98]

The most contemporary of arts, the seventh art, by the end of 1968, found a new expression outside of the adult narrative, the "safe" teenage rebellion story, and the wholesome family entertainment picture. The protest was not an intentional overthrow of convention, just an alteration in thinking. "Rebellion ending in conformity," Gary Dauphin called it in his *Village Voice* review thirty years later.[99] Whatever its revolutionary strength, the film made available to filmmakers "hard-hitting cultural themes that were more risqué"—and ultimately more adversarial than in previous decades.[100]

Whether one objected to or praised the film, *The Graduate* opened the range of social and political discussion by projecting a sixties generation as college-aged, antiestablishment, and materially secure enough to risk rejecting tradition. Audiences responding to Nichols' *Graduate* helped speed up a renaissance of sorts for Hollywood. As the *New York Times* reported halfway through the film's first year, "Mike Nichols and Jean-Luc Godard have become the heroes of many college campuses. The American Director [*sic*] and the French moviemaker are the pied pipers of a movement" for the 60,000-plus students enrolled in college film courses across campuses.[101]

Before nascent social and political rebellion became more militant in the larger society, *The Graduate* seemed radical in its endorsement of attitudes and identity. A film that Doris Day refused to sign onto looked tame, however, in comparison to films coming to movie theaters by 1969. Benjamin's tweed-jacket-and-tie image were replaced in the feature film by a new, popular counterculture look of men and women who donned robes and sandals, sat cross legged in Golden Gate Park, and openly recited mantras. Mixing the exotic with the primitive and bringing them both in line with the politics of dropping out, these rebels challenged middle-class dominion in ways that not only separated young from old but also young from young. By the last year of the decade, deep splits within the sixties generation surfaced and bestowed the younger generation with its most famous icons. Political insurgency melded with a counterculture sensibility and created a mode of rebellion through lifestyle.

One filmmaker responded to the rhetoric and actuality of the culture politics and added a guitar player and an eating establishment to American mythology. Arthur Penn's *Alice's Restaurant* defined the camaraderie in young people eager for revolutionary distinction. The docu-drama/comedy starred a folk-singing hippie, Arlo Guthrie, who identified even sharper lines of generational distinction than did Benjamin. *Alice's Restaurant* helped legitimize the folk music and counterculture movements. Penn contributed a narrative voice to the radical perspective generated through appearance. Hippies and postgraduates ventured boldly onto the screen, asking the American public once more to adjust its lenses and accept a new vision.

CHAPTER IV

Alice's Restaurant

Constructing Hippie Folk and Legitimizing Revolutionary Distinction

Every Generation Has A Story To Tell.
— Tagline from *Alice's Restaurant*

At the Newport Folk Music Festival in 1967, when Arlo Guthrie debuted his song "Alice's Restaurant Masacree," little did he know that two years later he would be on location in Stockbridge, Massachusetts, shooting a film with Arthur Penn. "Alice's Masacree" may have indeed died a natural death had Arlo's friend not taken the album to Penn's house one night. A Stockbridge resident, Penn saw the cinematic potential in the twenty-minute song about a littering incident in a neighboring town.[1] Although countless movies have been inspired by single hits, Penn was the first to "film" an entire album.[2] The result was *Alice's Restaurant* in August 1969.

If audiences were not interested in another epic by the end of the decade, it was because the world had changed. Arthur Penn took on the challenge of making film more relevant to what young people wanted from their world and, unlike *The Graduate*, his picture not only directly addressed the commotion in the streets, including stirrings about Vietnam, but also highlighted the social divisions over lifestyle and fashionable "dropping out" associated with the hippie counterculture. Penn sensed that the counterculture movement was more than a fad and he resolved to make a statement about it. He offered new ways to negotiate boundaries of acceptable counterculture distinctiveness at the height of contentious activity and general struggle between mainstream America and "the many hippies," as one trade magazine identified them.[3] *Alice's Restaurant* asked viewers to accommodate the counterculture and identify with its perspective. This film fabricated a power of desire for a counterculture ethos by circulating its icons — the van, long hair, bizarre clothing, and a noncommittal social position of detachment. In particular, the film identified hippies, long hair, and communal living as central to American freedom of expression and part of a long tradition of American bohemianism. To be sure, those who refused to see the counterculture as an enhancement of American society would now have to respond to a veteran director.

At the same time it legitimized counterculture distinction, *Alice's Restaurant* was not so kind to the traditionalist. This longstanding symbol of America was shown as a leftover of a bygone era. In attitude and appearance, these everyday citizens, the plain folk, represented bigotry and oppression. Restaurant owners, truck drivers, law enforcement personnel, Montana educators, and Westerners in general appeared suspect. Old Left activists who championed the "people" similarly drew criticism. The picture instead presented the true progenitors of a better America — a hippie couple, Arlo and his girlfriend Mari (Tina Chen). Together they carried counterculture vision away from the commune and into the larger culture.

Yet, even as this film humanized the counterculture and derided convention, it did not ignore the reality of dropping out in 1969. Penn's critical eye caught the irreconcilability between joining communal life on the one hand and scorning middle America on the other while denying that dropping out was a choice, contingent and dependent on having the means to do so.[4] In its exuberance for shedding material identity by dropping out and forming free societies of togetherness, the hippie counterculture absorbed chances for further social agency. Based on a belief that reorganizing America could occur through lifestyle, cultural politics came to serve a revolutionary agenda bound by its own obstacles. *Alice's Restaurant* reflects the same discursive mirror and therefore remains a testimony to what was possible in the new society's most compassionate bid for freedom, love, and peace.

The American movie business reacted to the new artistic taste in young-adult audiences most strongly in 1969. Paramount released *Goodbye Columbus* and the docu-drama *Medium Cool*. United Artists backed *Alice's Restaurant* and *Midnight Cowboy*. Columbia picked up *Easy Rider* and *Bob & Carol & Ted & Alice* and Fox signed *Butch Cassidy and the Sundance Kid*. These films were proof that the generational message had reached studio heads. As Axel Madsen of *Sight and Sound* observed, "youth is openly displaying its strength, appeal and power. Having lost the 'other' half — at least in affluent society — movies must now forcefully reflect the hungers, hurts and needs of this junior half of the population."[5] The success of these films demonstrated the potential of Hollywood to adjust to a generation's newly-found cultural voice, despite the still favored *Paint Your Wagon*, *MacKenna's Gold*, and *Hello Dolly* big-budget types.

Movies such as *The Graduate* brought the new Hollywood into view by 1967, but the low-budgets in 1969 took the industry into its era of revolution and experimentation. As film reviewer Stephen Farber contended, these were films "no studio would have dreamed of making even last year — for *Alice's Restaurant*, a crazy quilt of autobiography, farce blackout sketches, melancholy romantic ballad, melodrama; or for *Medium Cool*, an angry, passionate indictment of the forces of repression in Contemporary America."[6] Films such as *Getting Straight*, *The Strawberry Statement*, *Move!*, *Joe*, *Little Fauss and Big Halsey*, and *Cisco Pike* made experimental efforts — once a reserve for the art house, college film festivals, and film societies — into a mainstream commodity. As *Film Quarterly* editor Ernest Callenbach observed, "The appeal of *Midnight Cowboy*, *Easy Rider*, *Medium Cool*, and *Alice's Restaurant*" nearly caused the "art-house films [to be] deserted by their customary young audiences."[7]

Experimentation did not enter the American mainstream screen without criticism. Non-linear technique and inventive story lines had not earned complete respectability in American feature film the way it had in European cinema by *Alice's* release in August. To some, cinema as a site of dissension seemed like pandering. Hotshot filmmakers were accused of using the medium as an "instrument of rebellion" for "the lunacy fringe of the modern hippie generation of today." It was "insidious propaganda against law, religion, military and patriotism" disguised as "comedy and hilarity."[8] But others argued that experimental film made sense. It was part of a new and likely artistic evolution. On "the box-office front," Ernest Callenbach maintained, "these new films constitute some kind of break-through," especially for the filmmaking rebels.[9] If film were to become an agent in social change as many hoped, then these objections proved that pictures like *Alice's Restaurant* accomplished their goal.

Penn built on the experimentation market for general release. Where he touched on the artistic in *Bonnie and Clyde* (1967), he distinctly emphasized innovation in *Alice's Restaurant*. The former film offered young audiences a chance to identify with angry populists of the 1930s. Faye Dunaway as Bonnie Parker and Warren Beatty as Clyde Barrow sold a mesmerizing glamour in a film that, for the most part, followed a conventional story line, ending in idolizing two renegades. Two years later, artistic innovation fell into place for Penn with the "Masacree" song, since it was already a popular anti-establishment symbol, recalling Arlo's actual run-in with local police when he was arrested for throwing Thanksgiving Day refuse over the side of the road. In *Alice's Restaurant*, Penn saw an opportunity to experiment with nonlinear technique by not tightening the narrative around a central, epic character. Instead, he fashioned anti-heroic individuals and opted for improvisation. Officer Obie, for example, who actually arrested Guthrie in 1965, played himself as the Chief of Police of Stockbridge. Judge James Hannon, a blind judge symbolizing the American justice system, also played himself. The actual commune parent Alice played Suzy, a commune member. Arlo's former girlfriend Carol and many college students responded to United Artists' advertisements and accepted roles as extras. Geoff Outlaw, Arlo's real-life friend, played an assortment of characters. Arlo played himself, as did Pete Seeger in the hospital scene with Arlo's father, Woody, played by Joseph Boley.[10]

An improvisational cast mirrored the hippie aura of spontaneity on the screen, authenticating the film's social plea for tolerance and approval of the counterculture endeavor. A meandering story line and relative formlessness as if a jazz number, the portrayal of nonheroic characters, the blurring of fact and fiction, and the use of ambiguous endings captured the context of a 1960s perspective. The sum total of these effects added up to a transformational endorsement of popular antiestablishment, anti-authority, and antiwar sensibility.

To set the story's tone and Arlo's subjugation by the institutional side of America or, in the words of co-screenwriter Venable Herndon, the "increasingly militarized, demagogue-craving and authority-addicted society," the picture opens to a black screen with credits rolling and sounds of young men swapping war lore as they await registration at the Selective Service Center.[11] In voice-over, Arlo begins the theme song, the darkness fades, and the camera focuses on a brash, African-American female administrator sporting a gray flannel suit and wearing her hair tightly back in a bun. Peering through horn-rimmed glasses, she scolds Arlo for putting "Scorpio" instead of his birth date on the Selective Service application. "I want the specific date," she demands. Arlo complies, puts on his floppy brown hat, walks toward the door, wishes the induction worker peace, and the sequence ends.

In later draft-board scenes, *Alice's Restaurant* brings the counterculture into its larger social role and legitimizes the problem with hierarchical America. At the Whitehall Street Selective Service Center in New York City, Arlo lines up with other young men to get "inspections, injections, infections, neglections, and all kinds of stuff." Inside the white and blue cinder-block building, potential draftees drop off urine samples, receive complete physicals, and parade before the camera in only their jockey shorts. These are not the seasoned, tough marines of old war films but the weak, unsightly, flabby, and skinny young men in everyday life. Arlo attracts the attention of military officials and medical personnel when he goes on a tirade, jumping up and down screaming, "I wanna kill, I mean kill!" When induction personnel ask, "Kid, have you ever been in court?" they direct him to the "W" bench, a holding room for "mother rapers, father stabbers, father rapers," and other criminal stock.

The scene exaggerates Arlo's relatively diminutive body to help raise questions about the power in traditional images of male physical strength. The American man in this film is witty, intelligent, and gentle. Arlo honors the autonomy of this man through his detached stance from traditional society and in his many satirical swipes at the draft board by delivering the film's obvious indictment of the Vietnam War. The World War II model fails if it depends on the traditional authority of the brawny American soldier. This sequence gives voice to pacifists who admonished the American public to make love, not war, and takes satiric swipes at a country that questions young men's worthiness to serve while it engages in acts of war.

It would be difficult to argue against the film's antiwar stance without acknowledging the simple truth of the induction sequence. The impersonal experience of the military centers and the assembly-line process of selection connected viewers to the antiwar perspective by showing that Arlo, like the other dutiful Americans at the center, are simply eighteen-year-old boys, scared, anxious, and fragile. With antiwar activists taking on the appearance of counterculture resistance in the late sixties, anti–Vietnam sentiment, dodging the draft, hippies, patriotism, oppression, and arguments of dropping out became parts of the same trajectory. War protest was not political in this film but ethical. Objecting to the war was the right thing to do and the proper position to hold.

Portraying America as "authority-addicted" appealed to young viewers who found themselves, like Arlo, indifferent to school and the military or passionately spiteful toward authority. Penn described that audience as the "intelligent, confused, middle-class kids — the same kids who troop[ed] to the Woodstock Music Festival by the hundreds of thousands" simultaneously with the film's release.[12] As producer Joe Manduke pointed out, the film spoke for those "'subculture kids' who have rejected the system and created a fragment of reality that they can escape to."[13] Critic Roland Gelatt identified them as "the under-twenty-fives who wear long hair, groove to rock, and burn draft cards."[14] In Arlo's words, they were the ones who had little patience for the "plastic education and plastic consumption [that] allow a system like the draft to exist at all."[15]

It was not mere teenage rebellion that Penn saw as the most valuable characteristic of this part of the sixties generation. It may have been confused but it was not lost. As he described these genuine revolutionaries, one of the things these kids were trying to do was to go back to a first premise. They had been saturated with the well-being of the affluent society and found it very unpleasant. They wanted to get out of the rat race — credentials, grades, upward mobility — the whole thing. They were getting back to the first principles of using their hands. These kids were fighting up from the mat.[16]

Discarding the tailored, preppy style of Benjamin Braddock, hippies reorganized their lifestyle and fashioned a new look with folk-like peasant blouses, loosely fitting gowns, leather sandals, and the most enduring symbol of a pre-modern time: long hair. Added to that was an interest in mysticism and prairie primitivism. Folkish attire and free-flowing hair gave counterculture hippies a sense of return and a hope for appropriating American authenticity imagined as a simple life. Thus, young people advanced their sincere enthusiasm for redefining American society.[17]

Rhetorically, counterculture attitudes fit well with the folk traditions of plainness and

Arlo brings a bit of the counterculture to the Whiteall Street Selective Service Center in *Alice's Restaurant* **(1969); he and the other unseasoned young draftees defy the image of the conventional heroes of Hollywood war films (Photofest).**

anti-elitism. Shaking off the appearance of affluence gave young Americans a way to identify with American distrust of wealth, but appropriating the rhetoric and not the history and place of common folk left the counterculture with little connection to the reality of "the people" or small-town America. Rather than time-honored principles such as work, production, individualism, and a sense of duty grounding everyday life, the counterculture advocated the ideology of peace, love, freedom, and other "first premise" indicators. Counterculturalists did not concern themselves with social dislocation or with protecting traditional institutions from whatever alien force threatened their security. Nor were they vigilant about preserving the bourgeois version of the American dream.

Typical folk sensibility from popular iconography recalls rural Oklahomans of the Joad family in John Steinbeck's and John Ford's *The Grapes of Wrath* and the Westerner as Will Kane from *High Noon* or the urban populist Terry Malloy in *On the Waterfront.* The villains in this mythology were the social, political, and cultural elites whose greed brought the destruction of the traditional community held together by family, responsibility, and work. Of utmost importance to these American "folk" was the promise of "a fairer, more egalitarian America." Their role was to preserve the American dream. The intent was "not to destroy the institutions but to unmask the power of elites" and make their institutions "serve the people." Such images went hand in hand with the vow "to uphold Americanism as the promise of individual mobility and the antithesis of plutocracy and greed." This "noble assemblage" of American folk, the everyday and ordinary, reflected not rhetorical distinctiveness but a hard-earned legacy.[18]

Thus, the folk that viewers saw in August 1969 on Penn's screen was not the "little" guy so long distinguished in popular culture, literature, and film as the protector of patriotism. Self-reliance and heartland individualism were flattened and the sanctity of work caricatured. Instead, marketers positioned a folk music hero with a counterculture sensibility. Early advertising, for example, showed Arlo in long hair in the center of a United States postage stamp and Liberty coin with the words "e pluribus Arlo."[19] Here, the controversial aura of long hair both signified revolutionary identity and functioned as a site for claiming individual rights and freedom of expression.

Legitimizing the counterculture by devaluing traditional society comes early in the film when Arlo drifts around the country until he heads for college. As he explains, "With the draft breathing in my face, I'd figured I'd get some education." He enrolls at a Montana school because he "liked the country there" but once in Big Sky territory realizes he is too different to fit in with the local community. His music teacher scolds him for improvising instead of playing Brahms. The young Guthrie irritates his gray-haired landlady with noisy guitar playing, and the Montana police sneer at him because he smokes marijuana. Most egregious, however, is that he dares look like a girl in Marlboro land. Arlo waits to order at a town restaurant when three locals (two sporting cowboy hats, jeans, and denim jackets, the other dungarees) chide him about his hair and ridicule his feminine demeanor. "Doesn't she look pretty," one of them remarks. Arlo defends himself by rubbing a slice of pizza in the joker's face. Subsequently, the men throw him through the restaurant's plate glass window, and he lands alone on the street. Arlo is cited for the cost of the window and put on conduct probation. He then concludes that the academic world of Montana does not permit "freedom of thought" and, as in real life, he leaves after three weeks for the East, disappointed in the educational system and Montana's prison-like atmosphere.[20] In his own words, "Montana was weird.... Everybody seemed uptight about long hair and me."[21] The film garners sympathy for Arlo by caricaturing Montanans as bigots, tyrants, and otherwise contemptuous Americans. Even the college professor is an antiquated, rural fool.

Upon leaving town, Arlo next encounters hostility from blue-collar America. He hitches a ride east with a truck driver whose good-humored manner turns to loathing and anger when Arlo removes his brown leather hat and lets the hidden locks fall to his shoulders. The hefty trucker indignantly lights up a stogey, turns the radio station to a football game, and all but growls at this imposter, clearly drawing lines between his guest and him. The trucker completes the film's exposé on the American working-class ideal. Bigotry in the everyday worker contrasts to the open-mindedness of the victimized hippie.

The construction of Arlo as the new folk is clearly demonstrated in a New York hospital where he visits his father, who is dying of Huntington's disease. During the third visit, Arlo joins Pete Seeger and his father in an old Woody song, suggesting a generational tie. This hospital encounter appears to parallel Woody's social activism and his generation's use of folk music for political voice, but although both Guthries turn to music for protest, Arlo has shed the burden of Woody's politics. Arlo simply does not share the pragmatics of the "old movement's" people. Instead, he chooses to turn on, drop out from, and detach from "the system" altogether. Where optimism fed his father's movement, derision nourishes Arlo's. Accordingly, the young Guthrie ignores a system Woody sought to change. Woody's objective was to strengthen unions. Arlo's is about raising consciousness. As Penn recognized, "Kids especially — aren't interested in [Woody's] kinds of politics."[22]

The conditions generating folk songs in Woody's day were the Depression, poor working conditions, and poverty in general. His line of folk singing championed the worker — the people — and the active pursuit of a "worldly utopia."[23] Woody's books and songs "reflect[ed] the restless yearnings of Americans during the thirties and forties — 'Pastures of Plenty,' This Land is Your Land,' 'So Long, It's Been Good to Know Ya,' 'Geugen James,' 'Roll On, Columbia.'" He wrote and sang about "people threatened by fascism, war, and Depression."[24] Woody's subject, as *Sight and Sound* reviewer Philip French noted, was "the unrealised promise of American life" and "the decency of the exploited poor."[25]

By *Alice*'s release, Woody had been canonized as a "new folk hero of America's alienated young." The dedication occurred at the Newport Festival where Arlo delivered his "Masacree" ballad and ironically reflected Woody's connection as a historical fact.[26] If anything, Arlo's generation sang the Woody ballads were sung for posterity. "Many, like the Dust Bowl Ballads," Arlo explained to one critic, "don't have much meaning for a general audience, and you hear 'This Land Is My Land' mostly on the radio."[27] In the film, Arlo makes Woody's songs seem like nostalgic mementos, reminding viewers to put the past to rest. "Seems like Woody's road might 'a passed through here sometime," Arlo muses in the film upon seeing a gospel revival meeting where the southern folk proclaimed they had found their lost souls.

The hospital scene serves as metaphor for Arlo's generational sensibility and measures how much had changed in the radical hopes of the Old Left compared to the activists in the 1960s. His father's death confirms the dissolved ties and intimates that Arlo is delivered from Woody's shadow. The film, as the junior Guthrie explained, was the "piece that gave me a separate identity from my father." By and large, Arlo's distancing from his father shows the son's refusal to be the mediator between generations, whether on screen or in person. With the film and folk music's focal point, Arlo made it clear that Woody's "today had passed."[28]

Arlo was part of the folk music trend during the early part of the decade that encouraged folk artists to advise men and women about the evil of violence, the greed inherent in capitalism, the illusory nature of progress, and the importance of resisting the "plastic" society. Folk musicians such as Judy Collins; Joan Baez; the early Bob Dylan; and Peter, Paul, and Mary became American bards, echoing the voice of the new "people." Musicians pined for a purer, simpler time. Peter, Paul, and Mary, for instance, debuted an album with the cover title, "Honesty is Back." The music of folk authenticity encouraged a "solidarity" that would lead believers toward something better.[29] Singers such as Phil Ochs and Bob Dylan, who dropped out of prestigious colleges, took guitars to free speech protests, civil rights demonstrations, and antiwar marches on campuses, in Washington, D.C., and many major cities across the country. By the late 1960s, folk singers were more than just entertainers. They became icons of a special kind of protest.

Baby boomer affluence had helped turn rock music into a thriving industry of big business with concerts, albums, and other promotional enticements. The folk singer, on the other hand, managed to keep an image of purity in contrast to the highly commercialized venues of rock music. When popular folk singer Bob Dylan walked on stage at a folk concert with an electric guitar and was booed off, he symbolized the break between the authenticity of folk music and the commercialization of rock. This incident indicated the contrasting authority of these two types of music, despite similar degrees of venue profitability.[30]

With middle-class kids dropping out of society by the film's release in August 1969, the sanctity of the folk no longer held together but the idea of "the people" did. The trucker, policeman, judge, and government administrator bowed out to the new "people," the "beautiful people" building the simple life of a commune community. As one reviewer noticed, the film "implicitly contrasts two conflicting responses to the hugeness and complexity of America — the committed, popularist, political approach that seeks to change the system which Woody symbolises [sic]; and the urge to opt out and found an autonomous community."[31] *Alice's Restaurant* exploited this discourse and sold the film as "a Folk Movie — superb, fantastic, touching, wise, wildly funny!"[32] Arlo's fame as a folk singer by the movie's release made him the 1960s version of the autonomous individualist, the folk-singing, pot-smoking, freedom-seeking counterculture missionary.[33] Guthrie, therefore, brought to the screen a collective separation for a younger generation, whose politics centered on showing themselves as the deserving innocents — progressive, tolerant, and free thinking — despite their unique liberation's clash with worker experiences and ideals of progress.

In the film, Arlo opts for autonomy, leaves Woody's legacy at the hospital, and heads to a place that Ray (James Broderick) and Alice (Pat Quinn) Brock built. The Alice of real life was the librarian of the Stockbridge boarding school that Arlo attended and Ray was a New York architect. Both were part of the artists' and literary scene, but dropped out of the professional, urban society to found the commune. At the time of the Thanksgiving Day incident, Ray and Alice lived in the bell tower of an old church where Arlo stayed during his boarding school days. The Brocks opened a restaurant and housed several young travelers.[34]

In the film, the two middle-aged hippies represent a serious attempt to implant hippie philosophy in the Northeast through the commune. First, they accept the keys from the pastor of the church, who had just completed a de-consecration ritual. This building is now "secular and unconsecrated and no longer under our canonical jurisdiction," he proclaims. Next, Ray and Alice rush inside and, as if in a Charlotte Brontë novel, they twirl around in admiration of the new glass, old wood, and the attractive interior. It is "all ours," Ray declares as he steps to the lectern. With open arms, he confirms that it is "a place to be the way we wanna be." Their band of drop-ins proceeds to remodel the interior, placing signs of communal life inside the body of the church. The commune members rip out pews, rearrange the floor plan to include bedrooms, a bath, and a kitchen, and the commune comes together. There they reorganize traditional society and create a new, benevolent family setting. Like the others, Arlo is both member and guest.

The church renovation recalls similar attempts at the time in the famous hippie enclave, Haight Ashbury, where participants converted the old Victorians into utopian households. Based on assumptions that nonfreedom was "an attitude," one such group, known as the Sutter Street Commune, formed a "free community" in San Francisco. Part of an intercommunal organization called Friends of Perfection, members circulated weekly flyers declaring their revolutionary agenda. One such circular explained that the commune offered, "BOTH AN ALTERNATIVE TO THE VALUES OF decadence/greed, AND A MEANS FOR DESTROYING THE PRESENT SYSTEM OF mind/body slavery."[35] In this revolutionary agenda, the goal was "to get out of the economic stereotyped treadmill of capitalism."[36] Hippie members reclassified themselves as citizens "of the Good Earth" and turned the San Francisco streets into a contemporary American frontier.[37]

Proponents of hippie philosophy redefined the relations of power by hoping "to end repressive laws regarding personal behavior." They petitioned for, "open public buildings for development by the PEOPLE of the city." This brand of populism reconstructed America not as "a nation of 'plain folk' pitted against a small but powerful bank of elitists," but members in a global — if not universal — society connected in attitude and spirit.[38] Of course part of that spiritual connection included dropping out through experimental drugs. Drugs promised heightened perceptions of self and the sensual world. One experimentalist explained that "there is no life for those who try to identify with their job, society or anything outside themselves ... you've got to go inside to find it [identity]."[39] A new word, *psychedelic*, described the essence of revolutionary experience and helped turn a subculture into a cultural phenomenon. To one degree or another, attempts to create a communal lifestyle surfaced across America, from the streets of San Francisco to the parks of Chicago to fields of upstate New York.

More than any other act, dropping out by traveling to one of the many hippie enclaves classified one's legitimacy as a counterculture member. A Haight-Ashbury publication, a *Communication Company* flyer for associated communes, for example, distributed advice for dropping out. "DON'T DROP HALF OUT," one flyer taught. "Drop out. All the way." That meant one had to "reject the whole system" or "what's making you unfree," for "if you have to be cool, you're not free.... Be free."[40] Arlo's friend Roger said early in the film, when Arlo considered taking a teaching job for Indian children, "Man, you's only be helping them to go where you're already leaving." Rejection of convention through changing appearance and attitudes or fleeing to the free streets of counterculture communities, especially the Haight epicenter, marked the intention to "confront the machinery of power." One flyer announced, "It's great to live in a city with a free street" and offered "hope [that] your street is free soon if it isn't already."[41] The film highlighted these attempts as "first premise" reality and circulated visually what was being negotiated in the national culture.

At Alice and Ray's commune in the film, Arlo enjoys a blissful setting. Throughout the picture, Alice and Ray welcome wayward travelers hoping to replenish familial stability. Ray, for example, suggests to Alice that "if we had a place like this before," Roger (one of the kids) "might not have drifted off." The commune brings the film to a critical moment in the judgment of traditional America. Juxtaposed with the embracing family is Officer Obenhien (Obie) who keeps an eye on the commune kids. He is friendly with Alice and stops by her place for coffee, dressed in traditional police uniform, blue shirt, tie, badge, and hat. When he and his police officers turn the Thanksgiving garbage into a crime scene, they are described as bumbling fools. As Arlo narrates, they "took twenty-seven 8×10 colored glossy pictures," an aerial photograph, and marked the evidence with circles and Xs. The police chief, his officers, and the blind judge fine the perpetrators and become the enemies. Alice calls Obie a "meathead" and "stupid bastard," and mocks his "play-acting" as cop of the day. Considering the kind of social strife across the country by 1969, especially after the Chicago Democratic National Convention in August 1968 and the clash between hippies, political activists, and police, representing law enforcement officers as simpletons made sense to numerous young viewers.

To offset insinuations of hippie un–Americanness, Penn spends several minutes on the famous Thanksgiving dinner and paints the commune in American tradition. The picture spotlights several churches in the autumnal Massachusetts countryside filled with congregations singing "Amazing Grace" in preparation for the feast day. The sequence ends by bringing the Brock church/commune into full view and the camera takes us inside where the communal family finishes the last few lines of the song, "I once was lost but now am found / Was blind but now I see." Within the converted church and its display of plenty, Ray dons his pilgrim hat and blows the dinner trumpet. "Gather," he says; "praise be to us for coming here to dig it [the dinner] because we're beautiful." The camera pans the long wooden table set with pumpkins, autumn leaves, and a bountiful spread. The commune members have come from far and near by motor bikes, trains, trucks, cars, horses, or "anything that moved," Arlo explains. These wanderers indulge in the dinner and frivolity, the pinnacle of counterculture beauty. The most ritualistic of American commemorations brings the most contemporary family its own share of early folklore and legitimizes its claim to an American past of survivors who met a hazardous and violent world with unique determination.[42] These new "pilgrims" manifested the counterculture's essential argument of "Americanness," even as they "did their own thing."

As rightful inheritors of American tradition, this new voice of the folk critiqued the older generation harshly when it came to materialism and the Vietnam War. Counterculture pilgrim and patriot posturing as the liberator of bigotry, discrimination, and other everyday absurdities that challenged American ideology of equality fit well enough within the changing social attitudes, but the most visible component, the lifestyle changes, remained too subversive and unstructured for many to accept as a new, free society of reconstituted humanity. The film tries to comment on the failure of the commune and the problem with the younger generation's entitlement to frivolity through a sequence that ultimately shows the movement's undercurrents. The commune parents sit inside a dark restaurant, exhausted and in self-reflection, after Shelly (Michael McClanathan), a rehabilitated drug addict and adopted son, feels betrayed by Ray and Alice and interrupts the commune's idyllic setting by committing suicide. "I guess our beauty wasn't coming through," Alice infers. "Maybe we haven't been so beautiful lately," Ray returns.

To stave of further destruction, Ray coordinates a wedding, "a real weddin'," "real church weddin'," he says, and the Aquarian parents marry again at a more festive gathering than their drive-in special at the Justice of the Peace. Alice and Ray walk down the isle in their church home. Complete with flowers in her hair, Alice takes Ray for her "lawful lovin' man" and the party begins. Costumed guests engage in chaotic revelry with electric and folk guitars, banjoes, balloons, and festive dancing, but the excessive merriment drains the emotional vitality of the crowd and the commune members depart. Ray begs Mari and Arlo to stay, but they opt for a life on the road, leave the madness behind, and the story shifts back to the commune parents. Ray walks inside the church where he sees disorder. In a point-of-view shot, the camera pans the litter and remaining mess from the merrymaking and shows, sadly, that Ray's dream has reached its logical conclusion. Ray, the commune-maker, hoped for a better society as he imagined the countryside's regenerative strength and insists that if only the kids would stay, "we'd all be some kinda family." Ray and Alice represent the honest but weak who have donned the hip folkishness of the 1960s to offer a solution to the medley of youth congregating around their lifestyle. As Penn remarked, "It was a benign family Alice and Ray and the kids created, a therapeutic family, based on their judgment of what a family should be. Those kids were going back, redoing life from the beginning, working out parent-child relationships that had never been resolved." Alice and Ray offered "different forms of family — a coming together to find love and security."[43]

A filmmaker as astute as Arthur Penn would have been remiss not to recognize the underbelly of the counterculture and commune phenomenon by the late 1960s when the free communities faced serious problems of sustainability and disenchantment. The darker side of communal journeys seemed to be more than perception when communes became sites of "depression and emptiness" instead of hippie Edens. One New York observer noted, "the East

Village, despite its new Bohemian name, is still the Lower East Side. It is not a garden of flowers. A teeming, turbulent neighborhood, it is not quite a slum, but it has slumlike aspects." Those who saw hippieness as a social problem described enclaves as places where one "pedels [*sic*] the exotica of hippiedom — underground newspapers, incense, bells, cigarette papers for rolling marijuana 'joints.'" Instead of men in golden robes, "one finds joyless youngsters prowling its incense-heavy strobe lighted interior, aimless and disinterested." One observer recalled the sight of one young boy "stretched out asleep on the floor," sleeping on a "pile of rags."[44] As one worker for the sanitation department in San Francisco pointed out, "They just dump their garbage in the street.... I've asked for a transfer," he told one reporter.[45] In addition, it was getting more difficult to argue free love when "four girls ha[d] been raped ... in the past few days" as one flier reported.[46] Drug experimentation also led some to reconsider the notion of mind expansion as the ultimate form of freedom. One cynic proclaimed in a San Francisco handbill, "EXPANDED CONSCIOUSNESS IS A SELFISH HIPPY [*sic*] KISSING THE SYSTEM'S ASS FOR THE GREATER GLORY OF THE LONELY DROPOUT, ISN'T THAT RIGHT, UNCLE TIM!"[47] Counterculture legitimacy now appeared to be a delusion.

Whether in utopian moments or the practice of everyday life, the failure of the commune to prevent its descent further shows up in the narrative's resolution. The pastoral setting of the church commune disappears when the wedding guests leave a once-liberated Alice vulnerable and alone. With a slightly bitter face, she stands outside the church/commune as if in a portrait framed against a discolored background and milieu. The camera pans from right to left in a slow, long shot, revealing glimpses of the free society's matron through autumn tree branches. The scrutinizing lens moves around a knotty tree trunk and closes in on an anxious Alice, who clasps her hands and stands in a tattered peasant-style wedding dress against faded, weather-beaten, gray wood. Her veil blows in the wind, and the camera freezes the somber Alice in a bleak still-life. The mythic sixties hope, the first premise of building a better world complete with free love, fades out. The final scene lets go of the enthusiasm for the communal project and leaves viewers with a haunting image of Alice's isolation.

One of the marks of cinematic newness at the time was the merciless use of ambiguous resolution. Those "now" movies such as *The Graduate* and *Alice's Restaurant* ended with vague conclusions as a way to solve narrative tension. On the one hand, ambiguity enticed debate and serious thought about meaning, but the unresolved, open endings on the other hand avoided addressing outcomes. In this film, ambiguity glibly paints Alice as the tragic figure. She single-handedly carries the film's burden of failure and faces a life rife with profound loneliness. Certainly, the over-spirited Ray fails to create the extended family when his "kids" drift away, but he walks inside the commune as if proceeding to the next event. He disappears and leaves Alice with the burden of unreconciled relationships and lost dreams.[48]

The weight of reconciliation rests on Alice's shoulders and, through her, the film ultimately exposes the counterculture impasse. The polemic of free love advanced the notion that passion would be freely given and gotten. "IF THE WAY IS OPENED THROUGH LOVE," one circular argued, "THEN LOVE OPENS TO US."[49] Free love posed the contingency of counterculture liberation with new standards of mainstreaming female bodies. In the film, free love is a method of staging visual liberation. Concurrent with new standards for film, *Alice's Restaurant* shows women's bodies in new ways and the story's rendition of a new sexuality reveals the counterculture's hardest truth. Early in the narrative, Arlo sings at a Greenwich Village coffeehouse where a fourteen-year-old groupie takes him to a psychedelic hippie crash pad following his gig. "Got a handkerchief?" she asks and proceeds nonchalantly to unbutton her oversized denim shirt (a souvenir from a rock star). As she exposes her young, fourteen-year-old body, she justifies her exploit. "I wanna make it with you 'cause you'll probably get to be an album." Her long hair drapes over her shoulders and in only her bikini underwear, she recaps the list of rock stars and other celebrities with whom she has slept. Arlo is neither shocked nor aroused as he stares at her aggressive demonstration of emancipation. Instead, he hands her his neck scarf and coolly tells her to keep it as a souvenir. "Same as if we made it," he explains and leaves.

The groupie scene offers the possibility of seeing teenage sex as normal by making the girl the aggressor, not vulnerable but available. Arlo's refusal defines the film's stance on underage sex and makes sex between singers and groupies suspicious. The refusal, however, occurs after the camera makes her unclothed body available to the viewer. Engaging in teen sex may have pushed the film over the line of acceptability, but representing a young girl's body on screen also gave the film a certain social authority in the post–Code days. The scene obliquely displaces prudish notions of age barriers in sex by presenting the option but at the same time objectifies a teen body through Arlo's (and thus the audience's) voyeurism. This scene contradicts its critique of the establishment by producing teenage fantasy (sex with music stars) as an object of desire through Arlo's authority as final judge. By contrast, later in the film, a commune woman (older but closer in age) seduces Arlo. "Are you going to make your move or not?" she asks and, upon his approval, they engage in their moments of free love.

In *Alice's Restaurant*, a fourteen-year-old's advances and a commune member's subscription to free love signify the counterculture's power to subvert convention. *Saturday Review* critic Roland Gelatt applauded the film's "casual, no-hangups attitude toward sex that is currently fashionable." He admired the way "girls here get down to business without so much as a tentative paw from the young man who catches their fancy."[50] Both scenes promote free love as a female desire and represent that as a sign of female empowerment. Ultimately, however, the film's women discover it is neither as free nor as legitimate as these scenes and reviewers claim.

Arlo's booking agent and father's peer, Ruth, offers herself to Arlo, but he refuses. "Girdles feel funny," he tells her and severs both his personal and business relationship with her. Arlo's next cross-generational sexual affiliation involves Alice, the earth mother of the contemporary culture. In her quest for the 1960s liberated experience and its promise of a free society, Alice performs as the sexually liberated woman who breaks taboos against adultery, incest, and age. The counterculture sensibility of free love offers her a way to come to terms with a less than satisfying marriage to Ray. She and Ray snuggle and make love in the barn and the loft and show affection in front of their family, but crossing conventional lines is more flattering than her stale relationship. Alice engages in sexual exploits with Shelly and travels to New York City where she finds Arlo and wants to share his bed. Alice's infidelity in a world of free love must be allowed, but she also must face the ultimate truth of communal sensibility — how to reconcile personal authority and sexual liberation with lasting social relationships. She breaks down halfway through the story when Ray bursts into her restaurant to take her swimming during the restaurant's busy lunch hour. "Ah, hell! Let them all go in the kitchen and help themselves," Ray tells her. "Hey, you're lettin' this place eat you up, baby," he scolds and takes a car-load of kids swimming, leaving her behind to run the business. Later, Alice throws a tantrum when Ray horses around in her kitchen. She screams, "I've had it," and leaves.

The real Alice explained to *Newsweek* that that scene opened a dialogue about her role in the commune and the problems of Ray's youthful fantasy. Because of the film, "We found ourselves talking about things we should have talked about three years ago," she explained. "They shot that scene" and "during that time, I was working seventeen hours a day in the restaurant and making sandwiches for them while they were singing and going to the beach. Following the take, some of the kids said, 'Gee, Alice, was it really that hard for you? Were you that unhappy?'" As in the film, Alice found the weight of work unevenly distributed in the communal arrangements of freedom. "And, man, during that time," she recalled, "I was dying. But nobody really related to one another. We thought we were on just one big happy trip."[51]

The film invites the viewer to identify with Alice's sadness but is unresolved about what it means. At the same time, the story releases the hippie couple Arlo and Mari-Chan from implication when they climb aboard their Volkswagen bus. Their departure obliquely suggests that the hippie culture works best when participants are free to wander and those at the helm stay behind. The tragedy therefore rests with Alice and not with the 1960s myth of dropping out, despite Penn's allowance for critique and choice of ambiguity as a narrative resolution. *Alice* mirrors the popular image of the counterculture but does not account for reality beyond the van. The film's sadness is not Arlo's.

Alice's collapse into ambiguity avoids solving the same problem the counterculture left as its legacy. As a film of its time, it best captures the spirit of the communal hope to establish new models for family living. Ray's church, as Stephen Farber suggested in 1970, "revitalizes the frontier dream of freedom and makes it relevant for" its youthful audience.[52] The film, for all of its critical leanings, leaves whole Arlo's identity as countercultural representative. But Penn's rendering of the pastoral life for the Vietnam generation solves neither the problem of detachment and commitment nor the importance of ties that bind and sustain. The criticism boils down to a problem of failed relationships, not failed ideas. Redirecting the conclusion as a personal situation rather than a larger social issue merely continues the good hippies/bad establishment dichotomy and shifts the politics of Woody's generation from a revolutionary argument of class equity to a focus on new cultural codes of behavior and appearance.

Hippie folk spoke for the critical view of American involvement in war and did not need a class argument to make the critique work. In this film, the personal is not political. Ray, for example, is a member of the older generation but is portrayed as a good-hearted hippie whose sympathy the film encourages. Urban professionals such as Ray and middle-class kids such as Arlo can still negotiate a counterculture identity and therefore escape the film's critique and hippiedom's irreconcilability. The film validates commune identity and counterculture idealism from a male point of view while the narrative shows the nature of free societies in relation to the female. At the same time, the film leaves intact a critical judgment of the working class and its established authority. If Alice at least provided the practical means to make the communal idea work but could not sustain the family nor meet the impossible demands of free love, then the question of who is the victim remains.

It was not a one-way process. Changed affirmations had their limits, as Alice's tragedy demonstrated. Communes were fated from the beginning. By 1969, the contradictions of the movement were too visible to ignore. Where "dropping out" seemed noble and productive to those who indulged, hippie lifestyle ultimately contained its own demise. Censuring everyday America for its relative affluence seemed disingenuous to many when, as one tax consultant commented, "A lot of these people get money from trust funds. Or parents send them regular checks." The irony in this common practice was lost on those who demanded their subsidy. "One young fellow came in here," the accountant mused, "very angry that he had to fill out a tax form. He was getting money both from his mother in Miami and his father in Manhattan."[53]

Walking off the treadmill was certainly contingent on other inequities. As one observer asked, "How can a Negro drop out?" To be sure, "He's there, at bedrock all the time."[54] If hippie freedom was racially and class encoded, the politics of hippie lifestyle emerged yet again. One observer noticed that "they can stand there and smoke pot [marijuana] and no one says a word. But a black cat [man] standing on a corner not only gets busted, but gets the full penalty."[55] Hippie rejection of establishment lifestyle also provoked resentment from those who had invested a great deal in endowing their young with promises of success. As one argument went, the counterculture is made up of children whose parents "make all kinds of money by climbing over other people until they get to the top."[56] Unlike Penn's rendition of the Barrows in *Bonnie and Clyde*, valorized for their heroic efforts to break the banks, Arlo can speak only for the counterculture whose discontent was less a problem of class than identity and attitude. Arlo's character invited the viewer to question the face-value prestige of American institutions, but bashing the heart and soul of America had its own consequences. As one angry viewer asked, what justified the film's "mockery of sacred and respected precepts of society?"[57]

It was easy to see the irony in the claim to oppression when the safety net of home lay close by. For many who came from upper-middle-class, professional lifestyles to join the counterculture, theirs was a dominant class position. The younger generation molded hippieness as a return to a first premise, but as *Newsweek* showed, "Arlo and his friends are the children of the McLuhan age" who may prefer "a wood fire to central heating" but whose "exuberance for simplicity did not expunge a television set on the list of things to buy."[58] The 1960s counterculture likely manifested the class privilege it tried to rebel against. Often, as one observer noticed, "Law school followed a quick shave and haircut for many former hippies."[59] The alleged role as deliverers of peace, love, and freedom alienated those who identified with a traditional past, a conventional lifestyle steeped in day-to-day work and ideas of American liberty. Dropping out through "hippie clothes and ... swinging locks of hair" would not garner the same results. As one pundit put it, "When [Arlo] says no, he has other options. He has the money to take himself off to his institution of higher learning, and he leaves it again in the full knowledge of what will happen next. He comes not from a ghetto full of rats but from a middling-well-off family with its own private troubles."[60] In the words of one reviewer, most young viewers will not have "the more than $100,000 pouring in from the album alone of 'Alice's Restaurant.'" Of course, "Arlo will be able to realize his pastoral dream of independence in a green place, an American dream rooted in Thoreau, Emerson, and Whitman."[61]

The two commune parents, Alice and Ray, the thirty-something, ex-professional dropouts from New York City, substantiated the underlying truth of counterculture philosophy — that constructing oneself as counterculture proves one's resistance to middle-class values. Liberation of attitude and belief, however, re-confirmed rather than deconstructed the freedom of choice and therefore exaggerated rather than reduced the problem of social standing. Ray and Alice represent urban desires for the country, imagined as the life of ordinary folk. By 1969, for example, the real Alice lived on five hundred acres outside of Stockbridge.

Salvation in wide, open spaces popularized during the 1960s by urbanites gone rural seemed a proper stay against material-driven America, but the draw of the country allowed the urban professional to remain relatively safe from critique, escaping any derision aimed at others, such as the truck driver. Finally, Alice channels her energy into the commune project, only to be dismissed at the end, left alone to deal with her own tragic situation. By contrast, Ray sees no reason why the experiment cannot continue and, in some ways, he was right. It did.

This film crossed almost all levels of cultural, social, and economic borders and in one way or another was obliged to pay attention to the discursive impact and fantasy fulfillment of the counterculture phenomenon.[62] The hippie form of "folkism" gave American cinema a way to speak to changes in attitudes regarding American society at the end of the decade. Viewers could engage vicariously in the natural, simple, and authentic, helping to dislocate representations of the traditional "folk" and hero of the parent generation's era. Arlo Guthrie's travels west and east accomplished the construction of counterculture folk heroics undergird with simplicity through a new kind of people — young, whimsical, good-hearted hippie folk. The film underscored the counterculture sensibility and helped answer the question about what "role ... the 1960s play[ed] in the ongoing public discourse regarding American values and policies." *Alice's Restaurant* showed how the counterculture phenomenon was a site of struggle for meaning and power in the 1960s. It showed that the counterculture was neither an "annoying interruption" nor the essential, golden moment of hope,[63] but what one pundit labeled "the leading social phenomenon of [that] time."[64] Like intellectuals in Woody's era, counterculturalists spoke for and became the voice of the people. Underneath that claim lay their break by virtue of economic contentment and therefore their burden.[65] *Alice's Restaurant* remains a testimony to the revolutionary role of the counterculture in the generation known for its Woodstock distinctiveness, even in its contingency.

If experimental film indeed broke ground in American culture, one of the effects of *Alice's Restaurant* was popularizing counterculture ethos. In its positive rendition, the film helped define the meaning and value of the hippie phenomenon. Certainly, counterculture kitsch blended well with popular consumerism. Bangles, bold colors, rock music and tie-dyed clothing became fashionable along with beards and beads. By the end of the 1960s, these simple accessories carried substantial messages of intervention into everyday life. The material for the narrative was supplied and self-proclaimed in the message of free love and in the Haight itself, but the synthesis for generating cultural meaning was constructed by the film. Penn had heard the counterculture's voice and forwarded its message. To him, "The most important function of movies, their very essence, is the number of bells of recognition they ring in their audiences' conscience."[66] *Alice's Restaurant* became a visual intercession, for the counterculture ethos came clearly into view. A new reality remained. American society had, indeed, changed "through lifestyle rather than politics," in attitudes, values, and beliefs. Thus did the counterculture's pleasure policies indisputably subvert "straight" society.[67] Penn's praise was no simplistic exposition. He put these kids squarely in America and indicted those resisting their message.

While the narrative stabs at exposing counterculture contingency, Arlo, garbage, and the draft produced a popular ethos, fostering a long-lasting commodification of dropping out. True to consumer formula, commodities in one form or another served as a means of communication, a language of sorts for the film's message, and thus helped place counterculture discourse into the practice of everyday life, preserved yet consumed.[68] Marketing executives negotiated opening several restaurant franchises across the country during the release of the film. A deal to publish a cookbook containing a record and spices and authored by Alice followed. Next, the plan was to develop a line of frozen foods with *Alice's Restaurant* as the label. These opportunities made possible the strong identification with the counterculture perspective and completed the recipe for the successful integration of its perspective in the world of popular culture.[69] To spread it even further, Arlo engaged in marketing T-shirts, records, incense, candies, books, and videos.[70]

While the critical merits of films measure their historical worth and ticket sales gauge the value of production, in many ways the weight of these experimental films rests on the health of their cultural longevity. Like *The Graduate*, the film has enjoyed a hearty afterlife. It was screened at the Royal in Los Angeles for the Common Cause 1981 Summer Film Festival weekend series of classics. Film critic Jack Slater explained that the "movie about a youth in search of commitment and identity in the late 1960s, apparently still has the power to evoke strong reactions." Quite possibly, he added, *Alice's Restaurant* "reminded many in the audience of their own youthful search for commitment and identity."[71] In January 1994, the Sundance Film Festival advertised the film as central to Penn's work. The Festival catalog offered it as a "definitive portrait of the tumultuous and frenetic sixties" and a "consummate expression" of "the longing for family and a sense of stability." The ad described Arlo as "a kind of Everyman of the sixties."[72] To be sure, *Alice's Restaurant* enjoys the status as "one of the best of the films examining the 'hippie' subculture of the late 60's, that phenomenon which ended up touching, either directly or indirectly, the life of almost every American."[73]

For many in the cast and crew, the process of filmmaking turned fiction into reality, changed perceptions permanently, and became an endearing emotional experience. As Alice recalled, "During the shooting we all learned that we're all just human beings — vain, silly, confused — whether you wear a badge or long hair." She further commented, "that, because of the filming, 'Obie and us got to look past uniforms and really dig each other. He saw past our weird costumes and long hair, that we weren't just dirty hippies to arrest. I dig Obie now. He's a pretty good actor too, sort of a John Wayne type.'"[74] The real Alice remembers that "when Obie picked up Arlo for littering he was a real Fascist. He would handcuff anybody ... two or three years ago," she reminisced "I walked into a bar with a long-haired friend of mine, a kid named Billy Russell, and Obie asked me, 'Who's that girl you're with?' And started giving Billy the business about his long hair." Yet, during film production on location, the three of them "went into the same bar and some of the tough guys there started taunting Billy. Obie grabbed one of them by the collar and said: 'Take it easy, this kid's a friend of mine. He works hard and if his hair bothers you it's because you're bald and jealous.'"[75]

In Obie's words, "Before the film, I didn't like these kids very much. They had long hair. They dressed weird."[76] When the song came out, Officer Obie was furious. "Kids kept passing through Stockbridge to ask him to sign album covers or pictures of the local garbage dump, and Obie muttered a lot to himself about that punk kid who was making millions on his [Obie's] story." Obie contended, "If I knew I was goin' to cause all this fuss, I would've picked up that garbage myself."[77] Later, when Penn decided to make the film, Officer Obanhein accepted the job of playing himself because, as he maintained, "In the end if someone was going to make a fool out of me, it had better be me." From there, attitudes changed. Obie "learned making the movie that ... these kids ... were really thoughtful and polite and damn nice. They work as hard, some of them, as any ten people in Stockbridge. As long as they make $90 a week, they're OK with me."[78] When Officer Obanhein's obituary appeared in *People Magazine* in September 1994, Guthrie reminisced, "He was a wonderful guy.... Even when he arrested me I didn't hate him. He was nice even then. We ended up becoming friends and stayed friends all these years."[79] Even the church that inspired much of "Alice's Restaurant" took on a life of its own. The Old Trinity Church of *Alice's Restaurant* became the Guthrie Center. There, Arlo provided a variety of services for everyone from preschoolers to interfaith spiritualists. Residents generally liked the idea of Arlo buying Alice and Ray's church until he moved in and began working. Annoyed neighbors pointed out that Arlo's philanthropy encouraged "unwanted outsiders."[80] The struggle for ownership of the community surfaced at one point when locals objected to a big bash there and the prospect of setting up a "meditation center for AIDS patients." Neighbor Winona Harding complained, "It wasn't supposed to be some guru running in and out with beads. We're tweed people."[81]

The film's success lay in helping set the standards of the "now movie" and showing that its audience was out there, opening the possibilities of what *Sight and Sound* critic Paul Warshow predicted: that the 1970s would be a decade offering filmmakers "no other limitations than themselves." Filmmaking in the 1960s had displayed a "subtle shift in sensibilities, perception and awareness." The hope, to Warshow, was for American cinema to "continue to explore its own subterranean wealth and find out 'how' to reach out." The result would be a "true renaissance."[82]

Two young filmmakers in the same year reached far and wide to redesign cinematic narratives in a counterculture mode. Peter Fonda and Dennis Hopper brought *Easy Rider* to America that December and decided for viewers the right way to look back at the last few years of the decade. In a film that would revisit the Western, *Easy Rider* introduced Captain America and Billy to show viewers how to convert subversion into hipness. These two young rebels revisited the frontier to redesign cinematic narratives and give them a more popular language for the younger generation. The experimental film exploited the stunning manliness of Hopper and Fonda by rerouting the Western from the West to the Southeast and bringing film, hippies, and men in line with generational debates and conventional westernness by the end of 1969. *Easy Rider* both reinvented and restored the rebellious, rugged-individualist cowboy on the road. Where Arlo's character departed from virile masculinity as a component of his identity, *Easy Rider* flaunted it. Rounding out the year with their Cannes Film Festival winner, these two sharpshooters rode into town in a new, revved-up Western and discovered not only how to win the West again but also how to sustain that discovery.

CHAPTER V

Back in the Saddle Again

Men, Westerns, Hippies, and *Easy Rider*

Taos, man, Taos, New Mexico. There's freedom there. They don't mind long hair. The herds mingle.

— Dennis Hopper, *Easy Rider* Original Screenplay

Peter Fonda and Dennis Hopper had a hunch about the importance of two men with long hair riding Harleys cross-country during the late 1960s. Fonda's passion for biking and Hopper's penchant for defiance turned into an experimental project that led to *Easy Rider*, released in America in December 1969. This film updated rugged individualism by reimagining contemporary men in open spaces and made a statement about an eroding patriarchal authority. Fonda and Hopper produced, directed, and acted in what would become a cultural icon and one of the most memorable road trips in American film history.

Fonda's "modern Western" was conceived at the Toronto Film Festival following the release of his biker movie, *The Wild Angels* (1966).[1] "It all started with an image" for Fonda. He wanted to make a film of "ultimate freedom" where two men would have "no schedule, no timetable, just the desire to 'dig' the country along the way." It would be "both odyssey and ballad" but most of all a search for the truth about America.[2] Hopper and Fonda transformed cowboys into hippies, horses into bikes, and guns into joints.

Rather than dusty desert trails, his characters glide along open highways, but in the spirit of the Western, they do get chased, thrown in jail, and run out of town. The film draws on the authority of the Western to test the concept of freedom and the older generation's America. At the same time, Peter Fonda as Wyatt (a.k.a. Captain America) and Dennis Hopper as Billy subverted convention by legitimating a counterculture sensibility. Not only did the characters question the meaning of the American dream, but they also answered it. "We blew it," Captain America lamented.

Two newcomers took a chance with western mythology to produce an innovative image of men with legendary potential, but *Easy Rider* does not just place modern-day men in the genre again. Rather, the picture remythologizes a male persona that incorporates old with new and legitimizes a new man. Reinventing the rugged individualist by placing the cowboy/outlaw on a bike, *Easy Rider* integrates the counterculture sensibility into the old

Western formula. Drawing on the authority of the Western to test the concept of freedom and American manhood, Fonda's "hippie manifesto," as *Hollywood Reporter* called it, reinstates male authority in the process.[3]

The essential American genre, the one narrative most strongly embedded in American mythology, facilitated the film's perspectives and recorded the latter sixties. *Easy Rider* touched a generational nerve by gathering together essential realities of the 1960s and ensured it would be widely revered in popular culture. With its classic reference to the buddy ride on the Harleys and its famous soundtrack, how it brought Western mythology into a counterculture discourse and became a cultural icon defines its importance as an American cinematic emblem.

Revisiting the Western in the late 1960s meant making sense of a dying genre for boomers who grew up on thousands of its images. This most nationalist narrative imprinted its American heroes on the minds of audiences with countless popular serials such as *Gunsmoke*, *Rawhide*, *Have Gun Will Travel*, and others.[4] These television staples paralleled numerous movie reruns on TV and provided a constant link to the American past and its particular landscapes.[5] Filmmakers grappled with the loss of interest in the Western by 1969 but refused to let it die. *True Grit*, *The Wild Bunch*, and *Butch Cassidy and the Sundance Kid*, in one way or another, updated the conventional narrative. Clint Eastwood safeguarded the genre with post–1969 renditions in *High Plains Drifter* (1973) and *Pale Rider* (1985), but his pictures lamented the loss of the genre itself. The 1990s saw a resurgence of the classical formula with *Dances with Wolves*, *Unforgiven*, *Tombstone*, and others. While these films expanded the Western's stock collection, making sure the traditional Western did not disappear, after 1969 its popular dominance did. *Easy Rider*'s December 1969 release marked the waning of the old Western's function as a central national narrative.

For over a century, Westerns have appropriated the West as a proving ground for national character and male identity. American filmmakers such as John Ford and Howard Hawks drew on the open territory of the West to draw connections among westward expansion, American exceptionalism, and masculinity. Classic Westerns promoted American ideals and values of Manifest Destiny while also serving as an allegory for social and political realities. *High Noon* (1952), for example, critiqued the Cold War and *Cheyenne Autumn* (1954) addressed America's blemished settlement history. By 1969 these competing discourses evolved into a question about what had been accomplished in the West and what settlement ultimately meant. Whether promoting or censuring America, classic Westerns typically depended on a central white male persona whose heroic identity was inextricably tied to the frontier. In this model of American progress, the training of men was critical. Except for a few revisionist pieces, the genre has remained about men and their task of cleaning up the West.[6]

Billy and Wyatt reverse (with an attitude) the standard role assigned men in the Western. Two hip counterculture outlaws appropriate the rugged individualist ideal, give it a new look, and challenge their elders' world. Instead of following the ethos of the professional world embodied in Hollywood veteran ideals such as John Wayne and celebrated through a myriad of cinematic Western classics, they quit their jobs as circus performers, where they were "headliners," and commit a crime. With no witnesses to alert authorities and no posses to chase them, they make a drug deal and there begin the pursuit of personal fulfillment and their emblematic cross-country ride.[7] Shedding any burdens of ambitions and goals, save their own desire to make it to Florida their way, Hopper and Fonda's characters show the John Wayne-trained how to cast aside patriarchal responsibility and authority.

Like youth in the larger culture, these rebels exemplified the younger generation's new guide, a "premise of self." As sociologist Charles A. Reich wrote, "real needs," satisfaction, and a "change of goals" enticed many. Rather than being men "dominated by technique ... and training" and instead of "deriv[ing] meaning from the function [they perform] for society," it was personal fulfillment that mattered. Reich astutely noted that the younger generation preferred to replace "achievement by character" and a "meritocracy of ability and accomplishment" that required "dedication to ... training, work, and goals" with a search for self. Their decision to enjoy, relax, and dig the country along the way left no room for the task-oriented professional. Those who ignored personal search were targets of ridicule.[8] Wyatt and Billy validated that critique. After all, they would die for the right to decide the length of their hair, thus converting a symbol of rebellion into the ultimate sacrifice for freedom.

Marketers explained that the picture would show its viewers "the truth about America," and the bearers were none other than two young "hippies," as the production notes officially labeled them. The promotional poster explained, "A man went looking for America and couldn't find it anywhere," and showed a Ray-Ban-clad Fonda standing like an explorer on a rock gazing into western terrain and claiming his role as captain of the "search for the real America of today."[9] Wyatt and Billy represent the rugged, handsome, prototype "heroes" of the counterculture discourse of antiestablishment and dropping out. They are, as the Steppenwolf song title says, "Born to Be Wild."

The film was marketed in the context of a hippie-generated consumer market defined by collage, bright colors, and new artistic expressions of liberation. The visuals of radicalness suggested that one could denounce America's claim to freedom (in view of its myriad inequities and incongruities) by dropping out of society and donning a new appearance. The commercial potential of counterculture rebellion confirmed the power of hippieness to resonate and take on a life of its own. More than just criticizing middle-class excess, participants reproduced an alternative lifestyle, blending hippie counterculture with the already popular concept of the generation gap and formed a hippie frontier of sorts. The city streets and country communes provided places for proclaiming freedom from the production-directed, goal-oriented society of modern America. There, they could replace the values of straight society.

The hippie counterculture also blended with political activism and antiwar protest on campuses and in the streets during the latter sixties and helped heighten an environment of antiestablishment. Through appearance, attitude, and lifestyles, the lines between political and cultural rebels blurred. The famous San Francisco Be-ins blended signifiers, resulting in a shared generational identity based metaphorically on the belief in the "anyone-under-thirty-credo." Hippieness was fluid and elusive and generally built on the belief that it was as much a sense of being as it was a practice.[10] Beads and flowers came to signify that state of mind. Like Billy and Wyatt's drug deal, counterculture revolution involved a level of affluence that allowed young people to opt for a freer lifestyle.

Hippies and film had a two-fold significance in American culture. Film's productive direction, following mid-decade industrial changes, depended in part on the hippie narrative as authentic America. Appropriating a counterculture experience of dropping out provided filmmakers with subject matter that could claim a truth for the popular rebels, based on the American fondness for the popular over the elite. As Fredric Jameson has argued, popular culture gained its place as a valued preference because it was believed to "clearly speak

Fonda as Captain America drops out of society, dons his stars and stripes, and brings his search for truth to the screen in *Easy Rider* (1969)(Photofest).

a cultural language meaningful to far wider strata of the population than what is socially represented by intellectuals."[11] The popular argument of antiestablishment suited film's standing as a medium for the masses.

It especially made sense for independent filmmakers to draw on the counterculture experience to connect with the general feeling that film should be art. Fonda and Hopper experimented with both and helped force filmmakers to pay attention to the heart and soul of the young's rebellion. An antidote of sorts, the power of pleasure was the motivation for Billy and Wyatt to "head out on the highway" in the first place. The importance of the counterculture was its tie to the consumer culture and to the politics of upsetting middle-class America. As one historian claimed, it was a "genuine subversion of the status quo through pleasure rather than power."[12] Rejecting the parent generation's middle-class civility convincingly challenged bourgeois authority. Thus, Wyatt and Billy become counterculture prototypes, defined by their degree of hippieness and their resonance as classic Western individualists. In this way, Billy and Wyatt reinstate the masculinity of the Western by finding the experimental screen. They represent the 1960s version of the "under thirties" men on the road and transform a nearly exhausted narrative into a mode of resistance.

Easy Rider claimed its radical perspective by converting sacrosanct American icons into fashionable and sympathetic counterculture symbols. Fonda as Wyatt transposed the American flag into a popular fashion statement by placing the stars and stripes on his jacket, helmet, and bike. The flag was thereby deconstructed, reinvented, and reborn with a new patriotic function. Hopper's character, Billy, maneuvered Hollywood westernness by wearing a Codyesque suede, buckskin-fringed jacket; cowboy boots; an Indian-style necklace; tattered cowboy hat; and a "hippie-style" headband. He insisted that familiar frontier symbols become forms of resistance. Sporting unruly hair, Hopper updated Western signifiers and changed the iconography for the eternal cowboy.

The Western hippies begin their journey once they seal the drug deal with a gum-chewing, dark-haired man (Phil Spector) sitting in a Rolls Royce at the Los Angeles airport runway. Fonda's character stashes the cash in a plastic tube fitted into his chopper's gasoline tank and the film begins its search for truth. Between California and Louisiana, where they end up, they stop at a ranch, a motel, a commune, a local town parade, and a café. The script describes these riding sequences as a "traveling montage," a simulation of "the Chrisler [*sic*] commercial approach to Traveling Visuals, establishing the feeling of adventurous freedom that is experienced in riding a bike full-out — a romantic treatment of motorcycle riding, such as is used about SKIING AND SURFING." The camera "impart[s] to the audience the ultimate sensation of the abstract, ballet-like experience of the BIKE-RIDE." Images of "telephone poles whipping by, white lines, double white lines, road-signs, signals, etc., flash[ing] past" allow "the bikes [to] erupt from the center, crisscross, change directions, make circles, and come into FRAME from opposite sides."[13]

Key to these sequences is the panorama of the land.[14] A virtual reality tour of open space, the land seems to be, as *Sight and Sound* critic Tom Milne put it, a "vast, mysterious continent, forgotten and ignored by its tribes of city-dwellers." It is "America, naked and unashamed, as Columbus might have seen it."[15] Romantic and real, the open territory, as seen from the view from a bike, harkens to classic Westerns' use of the land where male identity was defined through action. These satisfying images reinforce the importance of the road experience and give the film its most significant moments of fantasy and desire. The untrammeled land regenerates the two men. Although the setting is contemporary in *Easy Rider* and the obvious narrative is absent, the film's dependence on the Western's centering of men and landscape remains unquestioned.

Billy and Wyatt reclaim the value of openness as American ideals within the Western's tradition. Riding in the brilliance of desert sunlight, they celebrate land as freedom. Billy trick-rides his Harley as if performing in a circus and Fonda contemplates the cleansing effect of the open space. They pull into an Arizona ranch where Wyatt fixes a flat tire. Wyatt pines for the life of a yeoman farmer. "You do your own thing in your own time. You should be proud," he tells the man in jeans and cowboy hat (Warren Finnerty). This scene advances the narrative's search and confirms the urban fantasy of country life as real America, the icon of pure independence.

The open land as a wholesome space is repeated later when the bikers stop at the "naked and unashamed" landscape of the site John Ford made timeless, Monument Valley. Wyatt and Billy tour the site at sunset. The camera shows their silhouettes as they climb to the highest points of the land formations. Against the setting sun, backs to the audience and gazing into the distance, they pause in a moment of silence, as if to pay respects at a holy shrine. This land site connects the two trekkers to popular landscape aesthetics and the counterculture to American heritage.

At the same time, their visit changes the meaning of this space of Hollywood cowboys from historical significance to a sacred memorial of a time before westward expansion. Their new companion, a hippie hitchhiker (Luke Askew), tells Billy, "The people — this place belongs to the ones buried right under you." Thus, what traditionally functioned as a stage for westward expansion now becomes a memorial to Monument Valley's hidden history, dedicated to Native American ancestry rather than remembered as backdrop for stagecoaches. The "under-thirties" West updates Monument Valley's reference point through the film's visuals. Once again, the counterculture bears truth about America. Less national, the monument is now more personal.

By advertising the journey as a search for truth, circulated through a younger generation's view of America, the narrative convincingly draws on the counterculture sentiment to presume its own innocence and begin its story of tragedy. The Monument Valley sequences legitimize the new male image, the contemporary man's rugged individualism, and sets up the narrative's turn to its most obvious indictment against America as a bigoted place. Open spaces turn into nightmare lairs when the riders face their adversaries. To this point in the narrative, the riders have convinced audiences of their trek as a freedom of expression. That they are really criminals never surfaces.

The next episode in their search takes their hitchhiker friend Luke to his commune. This southwest commune recalls others that popped up during the latter 1960s to give youth meaning and provide "food for the stomach and rest for weary feet" or "food for the soul and joy for the mind."[16] The camera pans what one critic described the "Christ-like faces" of those who pray together, eat together, plants seeds together, and sing folk songs. As one member tells Billy and Wyatt, "This could be the right place. You know your time's running out." Billy scoffs at the communalists' silliness and ineptness when he sees the members' impractical choice of farming on the desert. "This is nothing but sand," Billy jokes. "Man, they ain't gonna make it. They ain't gonna grow anything here," he scoffs. The sequence documents "the pathetic, hopeless optimism of a marijuana dream" for the white middle-class radical who connects to the sanctity of the land and advocates the rejection of bourgeois material security.[17] Billy and Wyatt finally reject the commune despite the invitation to join.

Clearly, the commune is not for the individualist. It is claustrophobic and demanding. Through Billy's perspective, the film recognizes the commune as a manifestation of a new kind of delusion. The commune members have taken hippie sensibility to its literal conclusion. As a practice of rebellion and even liberation, the hippie hope of generating a new society has little foundation and chance for sustenance. They are pipe dreamers (no pun intended). The search for the real America must continue and the two buddies cast aside the desert for the open road. The commune is important as a point of reference for the protagonists' solidarity with counterculture sensibility. Yet, rugged and handsome compared to the hippie communalist, they show how to appropriate counterculture discourse without indulging in the lifestyle.

Underpinning the film's main argument is that there exists a deeper malice than deluded communalists. For that reality, the narrative proceeds to the South, the one last pocket of prejudice in American society. It is impossible for the younger generation's hope for an ideal America to survive if such hostile territory is allowed to exist. At this point, the story draws on the authority of the Western's connection to openness to legitimize the bikers' place in American narratives. The bikers' entrance into Louisiana begins when Billy and Wyatt ride into a local parade, interrupting the flow of marching bands. Entering as counterculture and biker outsiders, the two get arrested for "parading without a permit" and are thrown in jail. When Billy asks for a cigarette, he and Wyatt are derided as "animals [who] ain't smart enough to play with fire." Billy concludes that the sheriff and deputy are "weirdo hicks, man; a bunch a weirdo hicks here." The camera makes much use of Western mythology with pans of dark, shadowy jail interiors and close-ups through iron bars. Inside the cell sits George (Jack Nicholson), the southern American Civil Liberties Union attorney, a local rich kid and an alcoholic. He is dressed in a stereotypically Southern white summer suit. He befriends the two and finagles the bail. George scrounges around for his high school football helmet and joins Billy and Wyatt on the ride to freedom. Together, the three of them leave town.

In football helmet, George sits on the back of Fonda's bike. He is the everyman who educates his fellow travelers in the ways of the South. "You're lucky I'm here, see 'at you don't get into anything," George explains. "They got this here ... scissors-happy-beautify-America thing going around here. They're tryin' ta make everybody look like Yul Bryner," he jests. George describes what happened to "the last two longhairs they brought here and I wasn't here to protect 'em." Nicholson's character is necessary to implicate the South and validate Billy and Wyatt's point of view and innocence. His charm deflates his vices and legitimates his insight. His fraternizing and antiestablishment stance provide a point of identification for the younger generation and differentiate him from those people Billy called a "bunch of weirdo hicks." George symbolizes hope for a new society if attitudes change. "This used to be a hell of a good country," George observed earlier. Like the bikers, he "can't understand what's going on." He has now become a "hippie's natural blood brother," as the *New Yorker* put it.[18]

Following their break from the local jail, Billy, Wyatt, and George pull up on their Harleys to a Southern café, a typical place to test the American ideal of equality. With Billy's long hair flowing and the American flag pasted on Wyatt's jacket, they enter, sit down, and proceed to order a meal. A slow pan of the café ends on a close-up of the sheriff. "What the hell is this?" he asks. "Troublemakers," he concludes. A farmer in a CAT cap joins in, "I think she's cute." A local businessman remarks, "Look like a bunch of refugees from a gorilla love-in." The everyday, Southern worker is the paranoid conspirator plotting against interlopers. As critic Paul Warshow explains, the film intends to argue "that the rednecks hate, fear, and

Jack Nicholson as George in *Easy Rider* (1969) joins Dennis Hopper as Billy and Peter Fonda as Wyatt on the back of the legendary Harley Davidsons for their ride to freedom (Photofest).

will even murder the hippies for what they 'represent'; and what they represent is 'freedom.'"[19] By contrast, the Arizona rancher/cowboy remains the American archetype of independence.

The café scene foreshadows the fate of men who choose to make hair length a heroic act and confirms the journey's imminent danger. As in the Montana cafeteria in *Alice's Restaurant*, the café in *Easy Rider* is a place where the male patrons display the contemptuous assumptions about long hair. The trouble with the South is that these men are not only bigoted, but homophobic. A young (under-thirty) local generalizes about long hair. "I saw two of 'em one time," he chides, "they was just kissin' away. Two males." "Some Yankee queers," the farmer joins in.

Outside the restaurant, Wyatt and Billy start up their bikes in front of six giggling teenage girls who beg flirtatiously for a ride. Well aware of the consequences, the bikers enjoy the moment but leave without them. The girls establish the bikers' sexual attractiveness. "Tight pants revving up a pack of giggly teenaged girls," with white Southern men watching, as *Playboy* described it, fuses together long hair, bikes, and virility.[20] Filmed at a Louisiana restaurant for regional authenticity, this sequence provides the freedom riders with a point of connection to the reality of humiliation and prejudice in the larger society. The girls validate the bikers' masculinity even if they are denied their request and substantiate representations of the "small towners" as hickish men — obsessed and threatened by Billy and Wyatt's form of freedom. As George shared earlier with his hosts, "Don't ever tell anybody they ain't free, 'cause they're gonna get real busy killin' and maimin' to prove they're free." The frightening

Fonda and Hopper on the film set for the café scene in *Easy Rider* (1969)(Photofest).

nature of establishment America is located within the legitimate claims of café oppression. It is a regional problem.

The riders become the progeny and progenitors of the self-reliant, self-righteous fabled men in frontier mythology, born to be wild in the counterculture sensibility.[21] Like prototypical cowboys on thoroughbred horses in archetypal Westerns, the rebels on their Harleys represent the moral point of the narrative. Billy and Wyatt rolled into Louisiana, having already established the "bond" among masculinity, hippieness, and the wide, open spaces of American landscape. Recalling the rugged individualist portrayed through heroes from John Wayne to Clint Eastwood to Robert Redford, the film establishes the value of counterculture protest. White marginalization, based on the choice to appear different, is now just.

The film's principal argument about the search for truth also recalls the culture wars over long hair. One young resident of New York City, Paul E. Martin, complained about the power and problem of hair in a letter to the editor of the *New York Times*. "May I add a final chapter to the subject of long hair?" he asked. Addressing a former statement, he explained, "Tom Andrew's letter about his experience after he saw 'Alice's Restaurant' and 'Easy Rider' was no surprise to me." Martin's appearance gave him a chance "to set myself apart from the rest of the world" and to be instantly recognized "in the Village ... and on public transportation but mainly on the street." Long hair on men seemed like a liberating mechanism. "I am happier now than I was, with my crew cut, which I had up until the age of 20." Martin used hair as a "symbol of independence and ... freethinking. We do not expect to be accepted all over," he conceded, "and we have to deal with the objections and the retaliations (like the boys in 'Easy Rider') in an intelligent manner." Hair politics became a way to contest the elders' value of conformity but also to claim discrimination. It meant tolerating "the feminine name-calling, the giant shears ploy, the two bucks for a haircut, and the ever-popular, 'you look terrible!'"[22] Martin's references to *Easy Rider* in his letter personalized the movie's fight and further defined long hair as symbolizing both oppression and a lack of bigotry.

The film recognizes the ambiguity in the counterculture argument of dropping out of society but not the irony in claiming hippie appearance as liberating. The common denominator — hair as freedom — depends on the discourse of contention representing men as innocent rebels. Wyatt and Billy look the part. Billy has long hair and a mustache and Wyatt has appropriated American symbols in ways that some Americans would find insulting. Long hair reinforces the film's ideological viewpoint of the South as bigoted but also circulates a view of the younger generation's struggle and opens a potential avenue of solidarity for middle-class whites with racial and class oppression. The contentious sign of long hair during the decade could have it both ways. Appearance and difference became at once controversial and matter-of-fact. Long hair on men was controversial enough to carry the film's argument of freedom but matter-of-fact enough to put to rest any justifiable resistance to it as a legitimate mode of expression and taste. *Easy Rider*'s popularity depended on neutralizing hair but keeping it shocking, too.[23]

The story is a saleable fantasy and produces and validates popular thought about staking a claim to social change in America and resolving generational issues. The two bikers' tragic odyssey is consistent with counterculture sentiment that insists on the evidence of their own oppression. To be current, however, the film has one more task to fulfill. Its historical status as a generational emblem rests on successful naturalization of the 1960s counterculture, clearly legitimizing middle-class youths' claims of oppression and struggles with their inherited establishment. American autonomy via 1960s symbols resonated through the one component that confirmed cutting-edge counterculture: marijuana. During the latter 1960s, marijuana was advertised widely. Posters and t-shirts marketed the craze at a time when law enforcement was not prepared to crack down on white middle-class rebels.[24] Similar to popular use, joints smoked throughout the film signified liberated minds.

In a visual tutorial, George learns the world of marijuana. At the campsite following their release from jail, alcoholic George appears provincial in comparison to Billy and Wyatt's revolutionary practice. "What's that? Marijuana?" George asks innocently. Wyatt offers a joint to George who refuses. "Oh, ah couldn't do *that*. Ah've got enough problems with the booze and all; ah mean ah can't afford to get hooked." But Wyatt reassures him that he "won't get hooked" and George eventually partakes. "You say it's all right, well ... all right, then, how do ah do it?" George's collaboration suggests an aspiration for the younger generation. If attitude separates him from the bigoted Southerner blamed for America's fall from grace, then it is neither George's money nor his social status that defines him as a good American. To the contrary, it is but raised consciousness and new attitude.

This colorful treatise about the benefits of marijuana compared to the effects of alcohol produces a convincing marketing strategy for the drug and unites counterculture politics with open spaces under the open night sky. The Captain of America releases the Southerner from his past addiction and places him in open-mind territory. A freer and lighter George, still

dressed in white Southern respectability, transcends the local community of hard condition-
ing and is emancipated by comparison. Yet, having George smoke a joint does not carry the
same political message that it does for Wyatt and Billy. George may have been liberated in
mind by Wyatt's drug culture, but not in body, since local predators beat him to death while
he sleeps in his own backcountry.

The film produces a provocative but not risky demonstration of marijuana's positive
value. Portraying sympathetic characters smoking joints was relatively safe in 1969 if the *now*
audience was the college-aged who understood LSD and marijuana as a sign of generational
identity and independence. *Easy Rider* is the quintessential counterculture movie signified by
drug use on and off screen. Completely comfortable with his own habit, Hopper volunteered,
"this is my 17th grass-smoking year. Sure, print it, why not? You can also say that that was
real pot we smoked in Easy Rider. I've already been busted once for possession, in L.A., but
that's another story."[25]

Both narrative and cinema interlinked attitudes with social practices and constructed an
idealized America, declaring marijuana a new form of independence and alcohol an old form
of addiction. Making Billy and Wyatt the counterculture "authentics" imparts counterculture
sophistication and knowledge and affirms the general authority of the younger generation's
advocacy for lifestyle changes. Counterculture discourse fit with Hollywood's Code break-
up, the move of a younger generation into the experimental mode of filmmaking, and the
popularity of university film courses. The nuts and bolts of the young's structure of independence were solidly in place and added one more layer to America cinematic tradition.

Easy Rider updates American autonomy by bringing together timely elements of counterculture vision, antiestablishment attitude, masculine desires of travel, and the mythic
grandeur of the American landscape. Hence, the film's burden successfully foils fear of and
opposition to counterculture identity. Yet promoting the counterculture as authentic America depended on connecting hippieness to something more substantial than drug use. That
critical connection between counterculture and oppression comes in the film with a lyrical
bike ride past the shanties of the South.[26] Watching the riders zoom through town, a couple
of black bystanders wave. The film implies a gesture of solidarity. The scene recalls freedom
marches and civil rights protests played out in previous years. Audiences could connect Dennis Hopper's personal participation in the actual freedom marches and his role as advocate in
the film. Hopper once commented on the friction between marchers and locals at the Selma
march. "There was this guy," Hopper remembered, "at the side of the road who was urinat-
ing on us as we passed and yelling 'White trash,' and I thought, 'Wow! Can't he see ... we
only look different, we're all part of the same herd.'" Hopper continued, "he kept shouting
at me, 'Hippie, Commie, long-hair!' Wow, I mean, *I* don't care it *he* has *short* hair!"[27]

The shanty scene unselfconsciously draws viewers into the connection between hair and
oppression, yet the film's dependence on counterculture oppression also depends on solidarity with blacks to convince a sixties audiences that appearance is legitimately an expression
of liberation.[28] In view of black farmers and their historically limited social liberties, this passing gesture ironically points at blacks' location socially and the South's place regionally. The
psychology of the film and the psychological investment it confers gloss over the contingency
of individualism and autonomy that emphatically rests on being white, not black, in America. Freedom, as one reviewer explained about the film, was simply the "concomitant health,
leisure, and affluence (their Harley-Davidsons, their luxuriant dress)" accessible to whites.[29]

Billy and Wyatt, meaning to separate themselves from the racial attitudes symbolized by the "redneck" South, become an affront to those whose struggle has not included the choice of movement. The standing, waving black Southerners contrast to the roaming riders who leave behind those unable to share in real solutions to racial and class struggle, if what freedom takes is a bike, a helmet, and money in the tank. As critic Paul Warshow recognized at the time, the sixties generation finds "the aims of the industrial society ... no longer satisfying" and in turn "reject[s] materialism because it takes abundance for granted." The "oppressiveness of industrial society is psychological and that salvation lies in the inner sanctuary of the senses, where the young can be in touch with themselves and aware."[30] Psychological marginalization versus economic and racial displacement in the context of 1969 appears naïve. Signifying brotherhood, this micro-scene invites viewers to imagine the counterculturalist as facing the same struggle as the racially oppressed. Indirectly, the wave reinforces the hippie as black, as part of the oppressed on a mission to create a more equal America.[31]

Billy and Wyatt arrive at the heart of the Mardi Gras celebration and they track down the "best little whorehouse" according to buddy George's recommendation. The film indulges in psychedelic visuals and engages in its most experimental features. Billy and Wyatt drop acid but the trip goes bad. The surreal sequence superimposes images of crucifixes and Virgin Marys. New Orleans becomes the American monster, a dream skewed, and guarantees that the narrative of pure landscapes way out West remains real America. As one reviewer remarked, the "wacked-out motor-psycho nightmare collid[es] with the breathtaking landscape of the western."[32] Instead of being saved by the grace of the Western, the story ends with the individualists' annihilation. At the last campfire, Billy gloats. "We've done it, we've done; we're rich, Wyatt ... we're retired in Florida now, man." In a reflective moment, Wyatt replies, "You know, Billy, we blew it." Underneath the veneer of weed, open skies, and counterculture discourse lies the one fact of freedom — that it costs.

Bob Dylan's "It's Alright, Ma, I'm Only Bleedin'," portends the final tragedy. The lyrics warn about "darkness" in daylight that "shatters" fortune. The isolated, two-lane Southern highway appears lush initially but, at high noon, Billy and Wyatt inadvertently face a showdown. A white pick-up truck pulls to the side of the bikers and one of the occupants points a shotgun at Billy. Meant as a joke to "scare the hell outta them," the passenger jests, "Why don't you get a haircut?"[33] They are intruders in an America that does not recognize "their kind," but Los Angeles-bred Billy flips the driver off and the farmer fires. Billy lies dying and Wyatt heads back on the two-lane road for help. Deciding to finish the practical joke, the southerners also turn back. In four quick moments, the camera alternates point of view shots between the pickup and Wyatt on his Harley, each speeding head-on toward each other. The last image shows in slow motion Wyatt's bike blown to pieces. The camera pulls back and leaves viewers seeing a ball of fire burning in a jungle-like setting of the South.

The final scene denies Wyatt's words, "we blew it," their full impact. Instead of the words, it is the image that determines the film's worthy message. *Easy Rider* validates a 1960s era of social activism amidst racial oppression because the real meaning of America is senseless murder. The white pick-up truck becomes the fiend for a 1960s generation of social activists. By killing off the innocents instead of restoring order, as in classic Westerns, this film denies the possibility of a renewed society. The deaths prove George's earlier statement about "maimin' to prove freedom." Those men who defy convention and risk their lives for the freedom to ride and sport long hair reflect generational authenticity. The two bikers retain their masculine appeal for a younger generation that sees appearance as a form of selfhood and defiance as an entitlement. "They die gratuitously," one critic remarked, "for the way they look. We identify their innocence with our own, and in pitying them, we pity ourselves."[34]

At the same time, if the film illustrates the desire for freedom from material trappings, it also holds up for audiences the most important contradiction of a 1960s rejection of materialism as Wyatt's remark intended. Long hair and shabby appearance determine the bikers' outlaw status, but not without ambiguity. If hair and appearance opened for middle-class whites a potential avenue of solidarity with the oppressed at the time, that bond also depended on appearance's ideological features — injustice alongside individualism and autonomy. Reconciling collective oppression as a matter of injustice places the counterculture outside the problem of racial and class oppression and especially outside the system that fostered inequities. Billy and Wyatt have no investment in that momentary wave to black farmers, for example, other than to show a lack of bigotry. The bikers are really just passing through. This "passing gesture," more than anything else, signals divisions.[35] Shared discrimination is impossible simply because of choice. It is as obvious as the money in Wyatt's tank. While Wyatt's comment advances the rebellion against materialism, the ending avoids reconciling the mistake in claims of oppression.

With the help of cycles, the film shows that untrammeled spaces mean freedom and ultimately the salvation of society in general and men in particular.[36] If the reductive West signifies the real America, then its objectification is the imperative that validates the two men's own authenticity and empowerment. Similarly, to justify the riders' ideological impact, to represent bigotry as commonly Southern and responses to those criticisms as backlash, the film perpetuates the South as metaphor for everything racist, wicked, and predatory. The shrinking of place is the film's larger truth.

Easy Rider connected counterculture truth to ideas about oppression and assumptions of privilege. The time-honored western autonomy was mythologized once again. Like the view from the horse, the view from the bike confirmed the men's identity. This particular vision of what counterculture, oppression, and Westerns have in common suggests the discursive role of Fonda and Hopper's film. The bikers accomplish untrammeled manhood discursively, since they retain a measure of heroics as representative rebels against a corrupt society. Locals (as themselves) stand for the "telling it like it is" mantra and the film convincingly conveys the notion that freedom exists only in the lyricism of wide, open spaces. The result is reification or materialization of freedom as a place. The movie's utopian desire for valuing where the bikers had been versus where they end up answers its question about bigotry obliquely because places of freedom contrast to places of oppression.[37] Counterculture discourse mixes with western icons, set against southern racism. The film subverts conventional ideals of the Western's ethical stance, and solves the problem of real America, the truth about it. Like the assumption about hair's connection to political consciousness as expressed in Martin's letter to the editor, *Easy Rider*'s argument of counterculture oppression sidesteps personal implication.

This "now movie" had some critics refuse it a standard of experimental excellence belonging to other films of the time. Certainly, "*Easy Rider*'s content *is* contemporary," Stephen Farber admitted, "but only on the lowest level — the level of mass fantasy." Farber quipped, "Artists are always distinct from the herd, ahead of it, challenging it to catch up; but the people who made Easy Rider still *belong* to the herd." Farber was bored with "men born wild and living free" and tired of their Western victimizing. "Even in frontier folklore," he contended, "the celebration of individual freedom often slipped indistinguishably into a glamorization of brutal self-reliance and self-righteousness."[38] Stanley Kaufmann pointed out how the film's imaginative "sense of journey" gets trite and "tedious" with the "pseudo sagacity and rue" found in the story's ending.[39]

Village Voice reviewer Andrew Sarris called it a "dope opera" and argued that the film pandered to the generation gap sensibility just like soaps did to bored housewives. Just like "adulterous wives [who] were always neglected, mistreated, or misunderstood by their husbands," he mocked, "so now are the young people neglected, mistreated, or misunderstood by their elders." Sarris detested the simplistic collapse in the film of "all young people" into the generic group of having "exactly the same problems and the same values despite differences in class, income, race, sect, or even sex." Moreover, as he remarked, "The pot-smoking hippies, like the adulterous wives before them, come predominantly from the ranks of the bored bourgeoisie." Sarris refused to accept Fonda's character as an embodiment of "an entire culture — its heroes and myths" or to see Billy and Wyatt as "sacred cows beyond criticism, judgment, or disbelief." Captain America, a faddish anti-hero, also seemed "spoiled, jaded, corrupt."[40]

Yet the film, not the critics, prevailed. The widespread acclaim of the story of two counterculture characters cannot be ignored. In the spring of 1969, *Easy Rider* received two awards, with Dennis Hopper taking Best Film for a First Director at the Cannes Film Festival. That same month, the Protestant International Interchurch Film Centre (IIFC) granted the film the International Film Prize.[41] The organization based its decision on their observation that "this film expresses with authentic emotion, through the bewilderment and wildness of today's youth, the search for a sense of life and the search for God in a world without pity."[42] In December, the New York Museum of Modern Art enshrined it "as a landmark film of the 60s" and one of three American examples chosen to represent the country's artistic merit in the eleven-day run of the "Decade's End" program. *Easy Rider* enjoyed being "the only [American] film chosen since 1966."[43]

It was a film of the time, for the generation that made up half the audiences. Said Roland Gelatt of *Saturday Review*, "Fonda and Hopper evidently intend the gentle hippies they portray to stand for that entire sector of contemporary youth who want only to love and to live their own lies — and who are constantly being thwarted by an abrasive, corrupt, and intolerant society." This older-generation critic admitted he felt "hopelessly out of tune" with this "under-thirties" viewer who "seemed persuaded of the movie's truthfulness."[44] Similarly, as even Farber admitted, it "is so phenomenally popular because it is so completely in tune with its college and teenage audience — the movie-makers and the movie-goers share identical fantasies and anxieties."[45]

Columbia exploited generational discord by mandating the press to "go after the 'Easy Rider' Generation." Publicists sold it as a film that "dramatically shows the many faces of America, from Los Angeles to the East Coast." Touting it as "the official U.S. entry at the Cannes Film Festival," marketing specialists appealed to art audiences, film students, and local independents. Some selling strategies included "arrang[ing] for school publication reviews of the film, as well as ample advance publicity — school paper, bulletin boards, college radio stations, etc." The publicity guide recommended that local venues "involve students, parents, and educators in panel discussions, forums, etc. on the so-called 'generation gap' and the manner in which the meaning of 'the American way of life' is so differently translated today." Parents and other adults could get in touch and "see the America their children see." The idea was to have students and parents meet with film personnel in person to set up roundtable discussions. Marketers encouraged church groups to show their youth that "there is much that is beautiful in 'Easy Rider'" and a great deal of material for sermons about truth and beauty. Strategies for getting the film out there reminded church leaders the film had IIFC endorsement. Peter Fonda became the "actor who probably is closer to the younger generation than anyone since the late James Dean!" The "Hollywood Profiles" program aired interviews with Fonda and Hopper over 850 radio stations while Columbia's profits soared.[46]

Ultimately, the search for America passed the most crucial test of all. It became Columbia's biggest box office draw at that time and made the production company one of the few reporting a profit by the end of the 1960s. By September the film had vanquished Columbia's box office slump by earning $256,694 during its four-week run in Westwood, California, at the Village Theater.[47]

Underneath its updated look, the film reinforced the myth of masculinity and open space as the source of renewal, but it was not restricted to the screen. Waging war through the lens of film could not have successfully carried a generational voice without the power of one more component, the flawless musical score. The beat of masculine rock completed the film's governing argument and the generational endorsement of it on its own term. Like *The Graduate* and *Alice's Restaurant*, *Easy Rider*'s musical score became its own legend. Biking became synonymous to the sounds of The Byrds, Steppenwolf, Jimi Hendrix, the Electric Flag, Roger McGuinn, and others from the soundtrack. Those who passed judgment on the narrative and style praised the soundtrack. Through rock music, as one enthusiast reported, the film "treats the youth-dropout thing successfully. You can't have one without the other."[48] Fonda's musical tour made advertising simple. "'Hear the Music — See 'Easy Rider'!" ads read. "Arrange for credit cards on all juke-boxes in town," instructed Columbia's publicity notes. "Offer guest tickets to record collectors who bring all 12 of the discs listed below (and keep discs for return after your 'Easy Rider' engagement has been concluded)!" The musical score cemented identity to activism and brought the 1960s revolutionary onto the screen in a lasting way. The legendary odyssey highlighted nostalgic desires for untrammeled freedom, landscapes of grandeur, and rock music as the liberating truth.

Along with *The Graduate* and *Alice's Restaurant*, the success of this film helped open studio doors to low budgets and identify the reality of the new national audience. Faddish rider-heroes or not, they satisfied and spoke for those who saw generation as advocacy itself. To think young meant confronting fears as Hopper suggested: "What I want to say with Easy Rider is 'Don't be scared, go and try to change America, but if you're gonna wear a badge, whether it's long hair or black skin, learn to protect yourselves.'" Protest was a means to enlightenment and a necessary step toward self-fulfillment. "They can't tromp you down," Hopper explained, "maybe they'll start accepting you. Accepting *all* the herds." As he told one interviewer, "I took a chance, man, but I believe in the picture, and it's going to give me my freedom — to make more like it, and to get out of cities."[49]

If the film used rock well and did what one reviewer called "justice to its spirit," their production odyssey encouraged filmmaking to tell it like it is.[50] The band of stars and technicians loaded up semi-trucks and produced the film on the road. As the press book noted, "Fonda and Hopper simply went out looking for Americans — to play themselves." When they found a regional location, they "set up cameras and recording equipment and then scout[ed] around for interesting onlookers, many of whom usually ended up in the film itself."[51] New-found actors would react to a situation and show life "out there." Digging the country was tried, true, and tested.[52]

In keeping with 1960s form of social life, the film did not conclude with its final scene. On September 17, 1999, at 7:00 P.M. at the Samuel Goldwyn Theater in Beverly Hills, the Academy of Motion Pictures Arts and Sciences commemorated thirty years of *Easy Rider* prominence. At the same time, Fonda raced through New Orleans on his star-spangled chopper to commemorate thirty years of "the counter culture film," as *Entertainment Today* called it. Fonda shared his last lines of the film, "You know what Billy? We blew it," he remarked. "Hell's Angels has more family values than most U.S. families." Fonda warned, "We better wake up or my prophetic words at the end of Easy Rider will come true."[53]

The filmmakers reinstated *Easy Rider*'s panoramic road journey, the search for the real America, in their own lives. Today "I travel with a tent and sleeping bag," Fonda says. "On the road there are no fences and an extraordinary sense of freedom," he explained to the *New York Times*. It could have been this way 150 or 100 years ago," he explains, "the Old West, with the sense of endless possibilities.... I ride as many summits as I can. I never ride freeways longer than necessary.... So free."[54] Moreover, as Fonda related to *The Los Angeles Times* in 2000, "I've become an icon, wherever [sic] I go in the world, I'm introduced as 'Captain America' or 'Easy Rider.' And that's 25 years of it. And it'll never be different. But that's OK."[55] Fonda enjoys a gracious and subdued life in Montana and proves that attitudes toward that place seem to be a bit different now than they were in Arlo's time. Big Sky country has become a repository for the Hollywood sect, those who grew up on the Western, and hippies gone Bobos, as writer David Brooks calls them.[56]

While the stars-and-stripes-Harley and Fonda are inseparable, the film's attitudes about counterculture rebellion followed Dennis Hopper through thirty-some years of cultural status. Broadwing, an Internet company, chose him for its marketing strategy. "When Americans think Dennis Hopper," the company proclaimed, "they'll think cutting-edge services and products." Broadwing explained they chose Hopper because "he exemplifies the image the reborn company is seeking"—edgy and not afraid to attack the marketplace. He brought the magical element of futuristic credibility to the product as he ranted about dinosaurs in network providers; "When you say jump, they fly."[57]

The spirit of rebellion in *Easy Rider* provided the marketing world a timeless image of America. In the business magazine *Forbes*, a Diner's Club advertisement promotes travel with the classic photo of Fonda and Hopper riding side by side on their Harleys. The tagline tells consumers to "travel in good company."[58] In a Pepsi-Cola commercial on television in 2006, a white-collared professional (an organization man) takes a break from work. Middle-aged white collar men can be wild in their suits and ties with a little help from the Fonda-style Harley and the sound of "Born to Be Wild." On a break from the office, the businessman imagines he is one of the men on a Harley speeding along in the open space of the outdoors instead of confined to the inside of a car. Pepsi, Steppenwolf, and a balding office worker escape, if for just as long as it takes a stop light to turn green.

The biker image was changed forever as it melded with the rising status of the customized Harley Davidson. An experimental project from beginning to end launched both of the filmmakers' careers as celebrities, cost less than $400,000 to make, and has amassed some $58 million. Somehow this outcome gives Wyatt's words at the end of the film new meaning. The video re-release and the advertising market's appropriation of *Easy Rider* icons speak as much for the value of the film.

The film has entered the world of websites and chat rooms. There, fans share stories about heading out on the highway with their adventure groups. Like tourists, they seek to relive the landscape's promise and participate in momentary fantasies of their own. One adventurer wrote, "We didn't own Harley's but we had the coolest Suzukis to be found in Idaho, Wyoming and parts of Utah." The explorer and his side-kick "had the forks extended, changed the handlebars, attached highway pegs and added the much needed 'sissy bars'" and "roamed the highways ... looking for ... adventure."[59] Rumblings about a sequel keep surfacing. In the 1980s Hopper had planned a "Biker Heaven," a fantasy about a "post-apocalypse America in 2068. More recently Miracle Entertainment fabricated "Easy Rider AD." The story has Wyatt in jail for the murder of George and brings George's son on the scene to prove Wyatt's innocence.[60]

Hollywood had spent nearly a century constructing and refining the American male riding, shooting, and cleaning up the frontier. In the last quarter of that century, *Easy Rider* took the Western back to the future, recycling, reinventing, and redefining the genre. The film's long cultural prominence suggests it was more than a dressed up Western or lyrical biking ballet since moving through open spaces on chrome and metallic technology naturalized the Harley as an ideal of independence. Taking two hippies into hostile territory to show what's wrong with America in 1969 and romanticizing the land with a Harley Davidson, a contemporary form of independence, turned a two-wheeler into an American icon and bike-riding into a favored sport, like skiing. At the same time, the bike defined the divisions between old and young, open and closed, pure and impure America. Untrammeled space was celebrated as freedom and ultimately as the salvation of masculinity, if not society in general.[61]

With the help of the bikes, the film showed again what the West has won. The two men's counterculture authenticity and empowerment depended on the vibrant West as the sign of real America. In 1969, as in earlier decades, the truth about America was romanticized once again — this time with a view from a motorbike instead of a sleek, black stallion. The mere longing for western rather than southern landscapes places these regions on both sides of the same coin, engraved and fixed. Like Hopper, who located freedom on New Mexican territory where "the herds mingle," the riders customized Harleys to prove where freedom can exist. The bikes, in turn, brought back an America lost and managed to promise a younger generation its own form of reconstruction.

Giving meaning to America through Wyatt and Billy as 1960s representatives, however, also meant bringing hippie identity in line with conventional masculinity. Hippies and cowboys side by side retained masculinity's dependence on open space at a historical moment when familiar signifiers of convention were breaking down. The film exchanged images of Gary Copper, John Wayne, and Fonda's father Henry for long hair, popular drugs, and mechanical bikes. It also defined itself against the grimier image Clint Eastwood promoted in the Spaghetti Westerns and his tiparillo fixation, yet not at the expense of the mythic Western man. This 1960s treatise on the ideal of freedom melded rugged individualism with the counterculture outlaw and provided new ways to consume and imagine old ideals of freedom.

Underneath its updated look, the dichotomy of rebellion in America can be seen. *Easy Rider* found America in the narratives of old as much as it did in the activism of the new counterculture debates. Fonda's bet about the "modern Western" reinvented men for a 1969 audience in the midst of generational debates and hippie discourse and a younger generation that would carry "the Sixties" with it into the next decade. Not surprisingly, the story continues its life today in the consumer marketplace.

At the same time the counterculturalists were going back to the commune, a Texan meets a Forty-Second Street New York hustler and together they ask audiences hard questions about men in buckskin jackets. Cowboys of a different type made their debut the same year as *Easy*

Rider in John Schlesinger's *Midnight Cowboy*. Schlesinger paid attention to issues arising out of people's experiences with American pop culture and ignored the stirring issues of hippieness and generational rebellion. *Midnight Cowboy* validates other experiences as the filmmaker asks new questions about a difficult subject to resolve — the gender debates.

GENDER

CHAPTER VI

Under the Influence

Representing Masculinity
in *Midnight Cowboy*

> Everybody's talkin' at me.
> —*Midnight Cowboy*

On April 7, 1970, seventeen actors and actresses presided over the forty-second Oscars. With no master of ceremonies, "Friends of the Oscars" ranging from Bob Hope to Elliott Gould read their cue cards and paraded before an ABC-TV audience of millions. Except for the talk about the 1.5 million-dollar Elizabeth Taylor diamond, the night belonged to the men of the Western. Of the many films nominated in 1969, the top Awards went to *Midnight Cowboy*, *True Grit*, and *Butch Cassidy and the Sundance Kid*. Robert Redford and Paul Newman slid easily into new categories of Western individualism with their historical buddy roles as Butch and Sundance. Their hair a little longer than the cowboys of Westerns past, they still fit the mythic mold. The contrast of the night was clearly in *True Grit* and *Midnight Cowboy*. Would it be John Wayne as U.S. Marshall Rooster Cogburn, Jon Voight as Joe Buck, or Dustin Hoffman as Ratso Rizzo representing the West, America, and American men?

Wayne's larger than life image did not go gently into the night. He won Best Actor for his role in *True Grit*, a film hardly remembered and rarely referenced today. In the spirit of *Shane*, *True Grit* did what old Westerns guaranteed audiences they would do—show that a man, like his country, uses all resources to fight injustice and to make the frontier safe for American progress and expansion. Perhaps the quintessential symbol of the "West-ethos," Wayne accepted his Oscar for Best Actor, beating Dustin Hoffman and Jon Voight, but the night belonged to *Midnight Cowboy*. Winning Best Picture, Best Director, and Best Screenplay "based on another medium," the film was clearly acclaimed as the best of the best.

Less than a year earlier on July 11, 1968, as if to foreshadow the Oscar night, *Life Magazine* featured Wayne and Hoffman on the cover of the issue. The title read, "Dusty and the Duke: A Choice of Heroes." In a bright and artsy collage of purple, red, green, blue, and yellow, Wayne the cowboy covered two-thirds of the page. Much like the close-up in his debut film *Stagecoach*, his cowboy image clearly dominated the space. On top of Wayne's cowboy hat stood a black and white profile of Dustin Hoffman, bent in the shape of a question mark. "The two heroes may well face off when the time comes to give out the Academy Awards," the writer predicted.[1]

On both of these stages — Oscar's and *Life*'s — popular culture registered changes in American society. The Duke's certain, decisive persona on the one hand and Dusty's alienated, uncertain, and agitated new man on the other represented the contrast between two cinematic worlds, two generations, and two political sensibilities. Explained *Life* photographer John Dominis, they "are the best examples I know of the way America seems to be polarizing."[2] The representative New Yorker, the thirty-something liberal Dustin Hoffman argued on the streets of Manhattan for consciousness raising and changing social relations. The other, a sixty-two-year-old cowboy of the dusty trails of the West, stood his ground on the deserts of Durango, filming yet another Western.

Larger than his surroundings in the popular imagination, Wayne mirrored his conservative politics and common-sense approach in *True Grit*. The Marshall "feels the same way about life that I do," noted Wayne. "He doesn't believe in pampering wrongdoers, which certainly fits into the category of my thinking," he continued.[3] Having won no previous awards for what he considered his best performances in *She Wore a Yellow Ribbon* (1949) and *The Searchers* (1956), he presented and accepted awards on Oscar night. There, he stood clearly showing the Western as an American icon if not institution. Even if the Western's heyday had faded, he made the identity very much alive. The Oscar moment brought the male ethos, so completely represented by the Western during the 1940s and 1950s, to a point of departure. It was a standoff between two strong, parallel identities played out in one national narrative defining both older and younger generations.

Cinema had indeed played a central part in establishing American cultural roots. What it produced and circulated had even become a source of knowledge about masculinity. Considering the depth of the Western's cultural resonance, it was time, however, to question its effects. It is thus both ironic and fitting that a critical challenge to this deeply embedded American representation came from overseas, from British filmmaker John Schlesinger. In his interpretation of James Leo Herlihy's novel, *Midnight Cowboy*, Schlesinger posed the possibility that there existed a perverse consequence to the rugged individualist formula propagated in the cinematic and popular West. American masculinity may have been coded into the consciousnesses of viewers through the Western, but an irresistible politics of gender arising in the late sixties simultaneously challenged that transparent construction. Schlesinger questioned what the tenacious hold of this myth meant, even in its waning moments.

Midnight Cowboy asked viewers to consider Hollywood's impact on the production of identity, especially in the Western's representation of individualism, masculinity, and Americanness. Schlesinger's picture helped forge new narratives about men's experiences in the wake of antiestablishment sentiment, which asked for more authentic individualism than convention would allow. Contemporary filmmakers addressed changing taste in men's images by updating the old Western in the manner of Sergio Leone's trilogy, Sam Peckinpah's *The Wild Bunch* (1969), George Roy Hill's *Butch Cassidy and the Sundance Kid*, and Clint Eastwood's later films.[4] Schlesinger, on the other hand, offered a space in which to liberate stories about men from the subjugation of masculinity circulated through the genre of the old frontier, its popular rendition of the cowboy, and cinematic updates.

The Western had long offered viewers a grammar and vocabulary for male identity in men's place in American history. Eastern journalists, artists, novelists, and others had portrayed two

John Wayne with Oscar in hand for the role of Rooster Cogburn in *True Grit* (1969), bringing the Western's heyday to an end, with his wife Pilar (Photofest).

centuries of Western myth in writings, paintings, travelogues, and novels. The frontier West was an attractive myth for commodification in popular culture, politics, land, music, tourism, rodeo sport, and fashion because it brought action and strength together in a national identity. The image of the cowboy resonated with young and old who saw the story line performed live in the days of Gene Autry, Tex Ritter, and other touring cowboys riding decked-out horses in Fourth of July parades, at county fairs, and other local venues. On Saturday morning television, boomers learned how to dress like Roy Rogers, Dale Evans, and Autry, with guns, holsters, and chaps, and to perform their own reality shows as summer cowboys and cowgirls. Real cowboy boots were a luxury and a keepsake for many children.[5]

By the 1970s, urbanites such as Ralph Lauren conceived a world-wide consumer market based on the image of the West as territory of the masculine individualist.[6] Western regions saw the fabrication of the "old West" towns such as Jackson Hole, Wyoming, and Sundance, Utah. Likewise, just a few pages away from the Wayne/Hoffman article in the July *Life*, a Marlboro advertisement with a virile man in a cowboy hat, equated cowboyness with smoking. Holding a cigarette in one hand and leather reins in another, he stood in his tack room preparing to ride. Westerns, Marlboro men, and cowboys like John Wayne pieced together alluring ideas about what it meant to be masculine and American. By appropriating frontier history, popular culture, and celebrity personae, marketers and developers appealed once again to the already familiar American interest in expansion and the need for nostalgia.

As a place and idea, the West confirmed the potency of change and action. Advancing the opinion that the West was "won," the Western helped prove the value of pursuit. By consuming the products of the West, whether wearing, smoking, or viewing them, one could identify with the manliness of western lore and imagine possibilities for action. Handsome celebrities compelled imitation. Jimmy Stewart, Gary Cooper, Paul Newman, Robert Redford, Clint Eastwood, Jack Palance, Ronald Reagan, and of course John Wayne, to name a few, helped fuse the look of a western persona with a particular power of desire. These men had become their own story line, winning wars, shootouts, and fistfights and teaching film buffs what it meant to be an American and a man.

With *The Great Bank Robbery* in 1913, the Western's long screen life began its relatively unquestioned reflection of masculinity. Certainly the genre managed relative updates, but its key feature — the ability to link masculinity, open spaces, and Americanness — held strong. The genre forged an American superego and men stood as the dominant historical force in the middle of that space. Like a parent, the genre drilled viewers on the rules and conditions of social interactions. Considering the long life of the narrative, its representation of gender is revealing. As historian Joan Scott explains, it is not just experience alone that produces identity. Rather, "signifying systems" influence the production of "gender." The Western is part of the "processes of signification" that give experience meaning. Not only does the genre itself produce meaningful stories but the genre's long life functions as a part of the construction of Americanness.[7]

What Schlesinger contests in *Midnight Cowboy* begins with John Wayne's ubiquity as the star of Western discourse of individualism and masculine authority. *True Grit*, for example, was a reiteration of those fundamental stories of men with integrity, principle, and moral unambiguity who sacrificed themselves for the greater good. The marshal, as Wayne described him, is "such as the screen has never before seen."[8] As the production notes illustrate, he is "a hard-bitten, whiskey-gulping, mean-tempered rapscallion ... [a] one-eyed U. S. Marshal" who brings the outlaw to justice. Like typical narratives, *True Grit* stresses justice, responsibility, and accountability. The characters "go through plenty together and, each in his own way, exhibits true grit," Wayne explained. Cogburn helps Mattie Ross (Kim Darby), the "perky young girl from a family of good substance," learn the lesson of grit. An Annie Oakley of the South, who has "the best little head on her shoulders of anyone in the state of Arkansas in 1880," she learns how to track down her father's murderer, survive a rattlesnake

Joe Buck (Jon Voight) transports the buckskin and fringe image to New York in *Midnight Cowboy* (1969), only to find his new buddy Ratso Rizzo (Dustin Hoffman) ridiculing it as "cowboy crap" (Photofest).

den, and ride with men.[9] The world is immoral and unjust but in educating Mattie, Wayne shows that moral action conquers pain and suffering. Thus, *True Grit* enables viewers to identify with the men teaching young women about clear moral choices. Masculinity, action, endurance, and strength connect, as if universal and transparent.[10]

The Western of Wayne's era failed to maintain its prominence in movie theaters during the Vietnam era and *Midnight Cowboy* registered that change. Schlesinger's film asks what happens if the genre has consequences beyond moral education. Certainly the test of the Western's endurance was its strength as a pedagogical center, a place where both identity and morality could be passed on to its audiences as one and the same. For Schlesinger to critique that potency was a risk at best since Americans may have lost interest in Westerns at movie theaters but were still mesmerized with *Gunsmoke* on CBS and *Bonanza* on NBC, the second and fourth most popular television shows at the time. Schlesinger gambled on the possibility of reevaluation during this time. Though the image of the cowboy was a persistent one, Schlesinger's success as measured by box office revenues and Academy recognition suggests that American viewers willingly widened the scope for the representation of masculinity.

Schlesinger's first American-produced film opens to the sound of horse hooves, shooting, yelling, and a large white screen. It is an outdoor theater where families once sat in cars to catch the latest release. The camera pulls back and shows the drive-in as a thing of the past. Against the massive, white screen in the middle of the weeds and rusted speakers, a young boy rides a plastic horse, and the story begins. A young Texan, Joe Buck, who had been raised in a fatherless household, is about to seek his fortune as a hustler in New York City. In voice-over, he sings, "Get along little doggie." The camera cuts from the Big Tex Drive-In and focuses on him. Joe prepares to leave Texas and his job as a dishwasher at a local café in search of a dream. He carefully unfolds a fringed buckskin jacket in a motel room and puts on a Kelly-green cowboy shirt as he imagines telling his employer, "You know what you can do with them dishes." Joe lights a cigarette, walks out of the motel, down the local street and past a '50s-style, dilapidated movie theater. On the marquee the letters JN WAYNE THE A AMO dangle as if falling. At his work, he announces to his fellow employees that he is starting a new career. "What the hell you doin' in that get up?" his employer mocks him. "Grab an apron and clean up the crap," but Joe happily boards a bus and heads east for his new urban life as a cowboy, albeit one out of place and time. This first sequence establishes the meaning in the "get-up" and sets up the narrative's critique of Joe's misappropriation of the image.

Amongst a bus full of travelers, Joe listens to his transistor radio and picks up a New York City talk show where women describe their ideal man. Why, "Gary Cooper but he's dead," bemoans a caller. "Tall, definitely tall.... A Texas oil man.... Young," another imagines. Joe believes he is now at the doorway of opportunity. He is sure of its power to attract clientele and imagines his future prospects. At a sleazy New York City hotel, he unpacks his western gear, tapes a poster of Paul Newman to his room wall, and convinces himself of his new life and image.

Joe Buck unselfconsciously strolls about Manhattan in cowboy outfit. He finds his first New York City customer, an upscale call girl (Sylvia Miles), has sex in her swanky apartment, gets swindled out of his money, and is thrown onto the street. He faces repeated rejection when a new teacher appears, "a sickly, undersized Bronx-born grifter." "Terrific shirt," Ratso Rizzo comments. "Just admiring that colossal shirt. That is one hell of a shirt," he continues. "Bet you paid a pretty price for it," he concludes and Joe responds, "I ain't cheap," but little fortune is to be found for naïve youth in Manhattan. As one film critic put it, "Joe Buck ... proved to be not so much notorious as naïve, inept and lonely — touchingly, if just a bit too sentimentally, lonely."[11] Thus, Schlesinger carefully separates Joe from the savvy, alert, and committed hero of the Western.

The production notes describe Joe Buck as "a good-looking, uneducated Texas youth," the "synthetic cowboy" who fills his suitcase with red, green, purple, and blue cowboy shirts. Joe's notion of what makes a man is mediated, as his suitcase shows, until Ratso's cynicism meets his optimism head on. Eventually, they "join forces," the notes explain, "to bilk a hostile world which rebuffs them at every turn." The "unlikely pair of loners" commonly dream about how "to start a new life." For Joe, it is "the answer to the prayers of many lonely, love-starved New York women," and for his friend it is "to be called by his rightful name, Enrico Salvatore Rizzo."[12] In the meantime, Rizzo does his share of conning and sets Joe up with a bizarre and hideous Mr. O'Daniel (John McGiver), who fantasizes about the future with Joe when he sees his cowboy garb. "I ain't a for-real cowboy," he tells McGiver upon suspecting his corrupt intentions, "but I am one helluva stud." Joe is once again conned and learns yet another New York lesson.[13]

Traditionally, Westerns highlighted valor through the cowboys/Indians or sheriffs/outlaws dichotomy, but above all advanced masculine identity through the magnificent physiques and faces of men. Sergio Leone, for example, made a fetish out of Clint Eastwood's strong, linear jaw and penetrating eyes. Jon Voight, however, steps into this role as the antithesis of such pop culture heroes of the West and alters the iconic significance of the Newman/Eastwood looks. Voight's baby face, which defines his character, clearly contrasts to the Eastwood jaw. In addition, Schlesinger films Joe Buck inside the hotel room, imitating the poster-types. Joe flexes his bare torso in front of a mirror flanked by the Newman poster and a female nude fold-out and is happy with what he sees. Rather than riding through the expansive western landscape, Joe wanders the streets of New York.

Hollywood Westerns in Manhattan turn Joe into a contrived type, a statement, and a copy. Ratso complains about his friend's affectations as a Texan stud and tells him that in New York, "nobody buys that cowboy crap any more ... that's faggot stuff." Joe defends the identity. "John Wayne? You goin' to tell me he's a fag? I like the way I look. Makes me feel good," he argues back. Joe is a pathetic creature, entranced by Western potency and its meaning. His disappointing, unappealing persona is unlikely material for typical theater voyeurs. Compared to previous and current idols on screen, Voight makes a pronounced break. Likewise, Dustin Hoffman, fresh in the minds of viewers as the preppy Benjamin Braddock, now appears as a Times Square rat with tobacco-stained teeth, greasy hair, and thrift-store clothes that reeked through the screen. Rizzo is the voice of reason, claiming that Houston in Manhattan appears hideous. Hoffman and Voight muddy the glamour portrait that drew audiences to the likes of Paul Newman, Robert Redford, and Clint Eastwood. Schlesinger subverts the typical screen images, "the human material," as critic Pauline Kael describes, "so much of what we respond to in fictional movies." It is not "the sensuality of the actors and actresses" that draws spectatorship into this film. Instead, it is the actors' performances that "involve us emotionally."[14]

Rizzo's comments to Joe raise the stakes for a John Wayne ethos by calling cowboy paraphernalia "faggot stuff" on the streets of Manhattan. Voight's unsensual cowboy kitsch and Hoffman's ratty, grifter lifestyle complicate the Western's buddy image of masculinity. This film subverts the lure of the typical cowboy gaze by diverting attention from the silent stalwart on the desert to the talkative, conversational Ratso on the streets. These buddies talk while they walk Forty-Second Street. They tell stories, argue, apologize, and dream over the butane "campfire" in Ratso's dilapidated, rat-infested, abandoned building. Joe's array of cowboy costumes juxtaposed with the urban space of his chatty friend highlights Schlesinger's critique of the Western. *Midnight Cowboy*'s American male has little use for the individualist, gallant hero fostered by Hollywood. Instead of Rooster Cogburn parenting the younger generation, Ratso Rizzo raises Joe's consciousness and points out his delusion.

At the heart of the story is the nature of Rizzo's offer to help. Rizzo takes Joe off the streets, and Joe makes money so he can take his friend to Florida, the place of Ratso's American dream. By "assum[ing] responsibility for another," and by "car[ing] about the welfare of someone else," the notes explain, each can be released from his dreary trap.[15] Rather than the Western's model of regeneration through violence, the film shows that compassion — real and intense — connects men. Masculinity becomes more nuanced than the rugged individualism of the John Wayne type, because, in short, *Midnight Cowboy* is a love story that transcends convention and revises what has been constructed and produced in the popular arena through the Western genre.

In the Western's formula, the individualist proved his worth through valor, whether protecting the town or following the outlaw. He was subject, however, to the inevitability of domestication and settlement. Women figured in the narrative as both the threat and the stability in a region prone to modernization. Women were typically the basis for protection, but since the cowboy was usually the loner, women served in prominent roles as the prostitute with a heart of gold. *Midnight Cowboy* reverses the roles of the male loner and questions the place of women in that narrative. As if to mock both the "heart of gold" and the loner, Joe Buck neither protects nor fights for the safety of women and America's future. Instead, they are potential capital and the means to his wealth.

Joe's knowledge of women is rooted in his abnormal childhood. As a young boy, he was dropped off at his grandmother's house and abandoned by his mother. He was raised in the middle of a quasi-prostitution trade. Sex for money was not unfamiliar to Joe since his impression of women was established through this experience early on. At the same time, his self worth is at stake through his performance in bed as an adult male. In the film's most explicit scene between Joe and his wealthy client Shirley (Brenda Vacarro), Joe faces himself as a man. He has stripped himself of his cowboy hat, red shirt, and cowboy boots. In his nakedness with Shirley, he fails to perform sexually and must come to terms with who he is. "Joe could be anyone," Shirley teases him. "I like that: move over, Joe; come here, Joe; kiss me, Joe," she continues. Shirley excites Joe with her word games, and Joe's sexuality kicks in. Joe's accomplishment confirms that he is both stud and man. "I'm not exaggerating," Shirley tells her friend over the telephone. "You should try it. It might be terrific for you," Joe hears her say as she lines up another client for him on Thursday at 8:30.

Joe returns to Ratso as a provider and a success. "She went crazy," he tells Ratso. "Turned into a damn alley cat." He has used the money he earned from Shirley to buy Ratso socks, mentholatum, and soup. "We ain't gonna have to steal no more.... I got eight bucks in my damn pockets and twenty more comin' in Thursday," he eagerly reports to Rizzo. Yet, Joe's dream is dashed when Ratso explains he is scared because he can no longer walk.

The sex scene with Shirley continues the film's critique of celebrity sex in cinema. The camera shows close-ups of buttocks and breasts but does not allow viewers to enjoy typical sensuality in such images. What is revealed instead is that the celebrity culture and its clothing are neither sources of knowledge about manhood nor possibilities for change. Though the draw is powerful, the camera for Schlesinger functions now as a way to identify with Joe differently than with pin-up men such as Newman or Eastwood and father figures such as Wayne.

Donning the hat, boots, shirt, and buckskin coat should help Joe shake his anxiety, but Joe's attachment to the power in the image of the Western male works only if the icons retain their potential power. Joe must learn that what he knows has little to do with reality. If his pursuit for a better life depends on going east with the paraphernalia that empowers him, Joe's heroism — and therefore viewer empathy — will be found in the discovery of the emptiness in the image. As Dotson Radar put it, "The use and application of this heroic, sentimental, wholley false interpretation of actuality ... makes the hustler Romantic and American, and makes him touching." The empathy enables him "to deny the real cause of his estrangement from the straight world, and to dismiss it by laying hands on the John Wayne/Wild Bill/Jesse James America that exists out there west of the Hudson nowhere."[16] Thus, "laying hands" on the Wayne-Billy-James America fails ultimately when Joe faces the reality of Rizzo.

Coming to terms with the power of the Western that once taught young people morality meant separating the genre's story line from its link to masculinity and American exceptionalism. The Western broke down as a model for American identity in the wake of civil rights strife, antiwar demonstrations, and the counterculture's rejection of consumer society.

The frontier thesis — that the West was a place to be conquered — and the popular notion — that it is also a place to test manhood — gave way to more sympathetic notions of American land and identity. The counterculture's "back-to-nature" movement popularized the landscape as sacred, not a place for conquest and development. The civil rights movement, followed by federal legislation, gave voice to minorities, which asked who the real savages were in the expansion of the West. Young men formed antiwar protests and refused to accept the Vietnam War as a proving ground for their manhood. *Midnight Cowboy* questioned America's cultural inheritance in this socially turbulent time by placing western signifiers on Joe Buck and taking him east to the heart of the American success story, New York City.

The film shows that what Americans have drawn on for symbolic meaning through countless references to the Western was contingent on place and experience. By transporting cowboy icons to Forty-Second Street, Joe has appropriated a westernness that correlates to no real experiences and is available only as a fantasy, not a promise. The use of westernness for personal search, ingenuity, and success is nothing new, but in this film the Western reference highlights Joe's discovery that the frontier image of manliness now has little meaning as a resource of power for a working-class young man and a homeless friend. In that context, the cowboy complex holds true to its cinematic renderings only as a distortion of male authority rather than a declaration of it.

If the Academy Award recognition of Wayne's art both validated his Western politics of moral clarity and influence on the one hand, *Midnight Cowboy* opened up the Waynesian narrative to a discussion of the Western's link between masculinity and moral superiority on the other.[17] Joe and Ratso embody a new direction that suggests Waynesian ambition and iconic significance are inconsistent in rationale and outdated in their educational role. *Midnight Cowboy* does not just deconstruct John Wayne patriarchy as portrayed through his Westerns and therefore liberate all the Joes from under its influence. To the contrary, the film shows the point at which discourse fails experience and produces consequences. For the midnight cowboy, the effect has been both too real and too fantastic.

"Gotta get outa here," Rizzo tells Joe. "Miami Beach — that's where you could score," he points out. Ratso imagines himself in a place where rich, blonde women wave from balconies and call him Rico. "You got more ladies in Miami than in any resort area in the country," he explains. The Florida escape takes him out of dark, urban Italian New York and places him in the bright sunlight of Florida's expansive beaches, a place of comfort and no struggle. In much the same way as the West was imagined as a space for renewal, Florida for Ratso regenerates him and makes a new life possible. There, he will engender authority in the middle of the nouveau riche. A place of ultimate pleasure — of sunglasses, bikinis, swimming pools, palm trees, and luscious food — Miami clarifies Ratso's idea of what makes a man. He would be tan, running along the beach or at the pool, calling the bingo game for wealthy women. He would wear white and not be crippled by the paradigm of hard work, progress, and strife. Miami indulgence would free and empower him.

For Joe, Miami is a practical goal. He recognizes their desperation as failed hustlers in the city so seeks $50.00 for a bus ride south. When a conventioneer propositions him to go to his hotel room, Joe turns the moment into an opportunity. After a tirade of sorts, he asks the man for all of his money. When he is refused, Joe beats the patron unconscious with a telephone and steals the cash. Joe has now completed his task as Rizzo's helpmate, and the two of them share a ride to Florida. The telephone scene mimics Westerns and becomes a sinister rendition of the Cogburn code. As John Wayne explained about his characters, the only ones who got it deserved it. Said Wayne. "I've killed men on the screen, but it was always because they didn't follow the code."[18] On the Western's terrain, violence is manly and straight-forward. One critic explained how "even murder is pure for being apolitical, done in the name of no cause, party, or abstraction." Action is immediate and autonomous. "Brawls," cheat-ing, stealing, and murder require retribution and a straight shooter.[19] Wayne himself explained, "In Rooster's world, a kick in the face is clean fighting, particularly when it's a struggle for life."[20]

The West was a place of retribution where the ends oftentimes justified the means. It is easy to see why, then, frontier individualism as the core identity for American strength has historical construction in the Western and the height of its popularity in the 1940s and 1950s during and after World War II heroism. Traditional Westerns, like conventional war films, acted to instruct young men while affirming a masculine ethos, a code of conduct that included violence as the right and justified method of validating maleness. Like the young boy riding the plastic horse at the beginning of Schlesinger's film, Joe has to discover the place where he can discard the fantasy and cast the image away as a youthful artifact.

In *Midnight Cowboy*, violence runs helter skelter with no arguable justification and no code. Violence is predatory and tenacious. Survival for Joe means shoving the telephone down a patron's throat for nothing but money. A sort of Freudian response to the repressive nature of the Western's influence, the exploit turns into an act of rescue. Joe transfers violence from the Hollywood screen to the sleazy hotel room and renders pain visible. His pain is displaced rather than projected. With money in hand, he is now the subject and agent of his own story. He is saved from the ever-present Western that lived for over two hundred years on book-cases and in theaters of American culture. As a practical matter, he now has the means to save his friend.

Along the way to Miami, Joe throws his buckskin jacket, cowboy boots, hat, and shirt in the garbage. He buys new clothes and slips on a seersucker cotton shirt and summer khaki pants. Joe saves the bright palm-tree shirt for Rizzo and discards his New York black. "That was the last one they had," he tells his friend. Now, it is Joe's pragmatics that balance Rizzo's fantasy. His resourcefulness brings opportunity. "Hell, I ain't no hustler," he tells the once rugged and discontent friend. Joe explains that he will get "some sort of outdoor work" when they get there. *Midnight Cowboy* empties the West of its ideological reference with the icons in the garbage can and releases Joe from the silver screen of narratives and emblems. Miami, not the West, is the place of possibilities. Joe — not the "get-up" — is the source of strength.

Midnight Cowboy asks audiences to reconsider the muscular strapping of Westerns and their formula for maleness when Joe Buck at the end of the film throws the cowboy props in the trash. He exorcises both Forty-Second Street appropriation and failed narratives. Free from the costume, Joe has not simply banished the past. Rather, he has acknowledged his mistake. Joe Buck's image, like the suitcase full of cowboy shirts, was pure commodity. Oth-erwise, the theme of Hollywood's impact on identity would have been gratuitous in the con-text of the late sixties. Instead, the film advances a critique of the Western and its role as one of the discourses most available to the post–World War II generations.

The Academy's approval when Wayne accepted his Oscar in 1970 as Voight and Hoff-man looked on made that moment a symbol of what had transpired in context of the sixties. The narrative was still potent by nature of its critical resonance, but the Schlesinger critique complicated the progressive notion of the rugged individualist advancing American society.[21] Joe taking his friend south resolves the story's tension, even if it is too late for Rizzo, who dies on the bus before they arrive. Joe reaches over to close his dead friend's eyes, puts his arm around him, and protects him from the glaring stares of the other passengers. Masculinity now encompasses tenderness and vulnerability.

The scrawny and sickly Ratso, like Hoffman's question-mark physique on the July cover of *Life*, gave "picking oneself up by the bootstraps" a humorous and pitiful sadness when applied to the bus headed to paradise. The film fit with the 1960s idea of moving beyond traditional relationships and offered audiences a chance to re-evaluate the nature of male identity as drawn by the Western and its reliance on a specialized buddy code constructed in American cinema. Joe validates Rizzo's significance by legitimizing his pursuit of happiness and by showing that a man can draw emotional support from another man. In turn, independent Ratso leaves his grifting. Joe finds his aspiration — to attract women through his cowboy studliness — an oppressive ideal because, in the "get-up," Joe existed outside of experience.[22] Miami allows Joe to shed the "cowboy crap" fantasy and find manliness in his resourcefulness. Considering the underlying theme — that Joe was under the influence of imagined identities and universal icons such as Paul Newman and John Wayne — Joe's education, the truth about the consequences of iconic embodiments of American ideals, came from experience. Thus, Joe's presumption about westernness ends when he returns to work, to his task of caretaking rather than living an identity defined by other sources.

Midnight Cowboy was the first successful mainstream film to question the consequences of the historical construction of masculinity through the Western, but the issue transcended the matter of construction. The film asked hard questions about male identity and the use of the Western to contain and control the meaning in male experience. It did so through a new story about the damage done to a young Texas man who identified himself through the potent image of strong actors. Sex failed because it was a business for the experienced, not the mistaken. The film resonated because it was not the exchange of goods nor the hustling enterprise that brought reprieve; it was showing an emotional exchange that lifted two men out of their squalid environment. If anything, it asked viewers to recognize the value in those identities often derided and denigrated, if not typically abused.

By shedding Western garments, Joe Buck refuses "to accept the terms in which the dominant culture has chosen to define [his] reality." Side by side, the nouveau blond from Texas, paired with the dark-haired Italian from the Bronx, share a history of oppression and humiliation. At this point, Joe and Ratso recognize each other's vulnerability as their own. Drawing power through helplessness, these characters echo the popular "He Ain't Heavy, He's My Brother" mantra. Hence, the screen opened wider for those who could transform what was once a cause for guilt into personal and eventually political power as a new tradition of masculinity was available.[23]

The possibility of rethinking concepts of men at the end of the decade was simple enough for most, but others argued that Schlesinger avoided the seriousness of social pressures on men to conform to convention. Schlesinger was booed at the Berlin Film Festival for not taking the film far enough in critical social issues.[24] Detractors accused him of avoiding the subject of Vietnam and reviewers suspected that the exaggerated attention to the friendship's platonic nature was evasive. Male bravado and repression would suggest the issue was latent homosexuality or was it identification with a universal concept and idea of love between men that was neither concealed gayness nor personal denial?[25]

Roger Ebert complained that the film "comes heartbreakingly close to being the movie we want it to be" with the painfully accurate performances of "America's underbelly," but "there has been a failure somewhere in the director's faith in his materials. John Schlesinger has not been brave enough to tell his story" and has dragged these memorable characters into "an offensively trendy, gimmick-ridden, tarted-up, vulgar exercise in fashionable cinema." The result is nothing short of a "soap opera" about the "urban jungle." It was the "sloppy psychology" and failed character development that weakened "a movie that could have been great."[26] Likewise, Joseph Gelmis wrote, "There was more attitudinizing than character development."[27]

Schlesinger has been criticized for perpetuating homophobia by stereotyping gayness and denigrating that identity in *Midnight Cowboy*. The argument is well taken considering Joe's last desperate attempt to save Rizzo by stealing money from the conventioneer. This especially offensive act, critics accused, allowed Joe off the hook at the expense of a gay patron he had just brutalized if not killed. As one British comment went, "Joe may forget about the telephone he has rammed into the mouth of the badly bleeding queer, but surely we are not expected to forget as well."[28] Schlesinger denied that he set out unequivocally to bash gays. He repeatedly explained that the film was not about the characters' latent or obvious gayness. Having just come out of the closet himself, he was more interested in reshaping conventional narratives than collapsing personal experience into yet another commodified identity. He insisted the film was about "how two men can have a meaningful relationship without being homosexual."[29]

Even as late as 2006 he explained: "It was viewed as somewhat antigay, which I'd never intended ... but ... if you look at it with a ... gay sensibility and want everything to be positive about gay life, it could be interpreted as antigay." His real and only intent, as he commented, was to make a film about love between two men and undertake "a theme that had never been really tackled before."[30] As it was, because the relation between Ratso and Joe remained uninhibited, asexual, non-erotic, and un-sensual to many audiences, the film carried well its essential burden of questioning the universal influence of American westernness. Otherwise, Schlesinger risked making this specialized story unambiguously a gay film and the sex scenes exploitative nudity. Some critics, for example, applauded the director's refusal "to patronize his characters" and romanticize their relationship as "pure." By refraining from a good homosexual/bad American society split, Rizzo and Buck became part of "a realized world," thereby "uniting diverse audiences with them."[31] Avoiding the more blatant sexual direction than the book, Schlesinger made room for artistic ambiguity and direct address of the debate about masculine identity.

Thus, it would be a stretch to say *Midnight Cowboy* is an emblem of gay rights or even an attempt to humanize homosexuality. The critical point of arguing the film's impact and meaning did not lay in that discussion. Since the gay rights movement had not yet formally mobilized and, with the Stonewall Riot still a few months away at the time of production and release, sympathy for homosexuals' civil rights was yet to garner strong public attention. In addition, how far American society was from homosexual acceptance can be measured in the unselfconscious use of denigrating language in the film script and in critical comments such as *New York Times'* Vincent Canby when he casually writes, "Joe Buck ... comes to New York to make his fortune as a stud to all the rich ladies who have been deprived of their rights by faggot eastern gentlemen."[32]

Receptive audiences responded to the disparagement of the romantic myth of the cowboy, the effects of the top-down impact of the media, and the exposure of male hustling, but those interests would not explain the litigious nature of the picture that angered film critics such as Roger Ebert. If anything, this film measures the divisions over identity, power, and social relations.[33]

Yet, Joe Buck's restored humanity provides a means of agency, of choice. He becomes a person, not an unenlightened dupe reacting to false aspirations nor a straw man merely responding. The film allows a personal touch to come through Rico Salvatore Rizzo's street cynicism. A reconstituted innocent and a redefined cynic made intimacy possible for men. "I'll just tell 'em — you want me? I don't go nowhere without my buddy here," Joe asserts. Hence, what was threatening about this film was its attempt to define masculinity outside of the standard John Wayne discourse without choosing its opposite. *Midnight Cowboy* added a question mark to traditional representations and the meaning of popular personae. The story connected the most available notions of masculinity to the personal experience of the two characters.[34] The source of strength shifts from the silent man on a horse to the pair of outcasts on the bus heading south. The rugged individualist recedes from view as the bus stops at their destination. Vulnerability and the profound experience of dependence affirmed a new ethos, a code of conduct reserved now for men.

Western icons were potent tropes for debate about identity as proven by *True Grit* and *Midnight Cowboy* running within months of each other. In the Academy's choice of nominations for best actor a year later, the pull of that debate can be further felt. Though the latter is not a Western, its appropriation of the genre's signifiers defines the intersection where the narrative of progress and masculine individualism met the challenges to these dominating patterns. *Midnight Cowboy*, therefore, contested the quest of the rugged Western individualist by asking viewers to consider the consequences of such an ideal when it functions as a form of repression. Its "Now Movie" realism on the streets of New York City drew audiences in; the superb performances of Hoffman and Voight confirmed that one more cinematic boundary could be pushed by sixties agency.

Released a year after the new ratings system (G, M, R, X) in 1968, the film defined the meaning of an X rating while avoiding the category of pornography. Fans saw it as "one of many groundbreaking films made during a period when there really was no 'official' watchdog over the content of American films and ... was acclaimed as the kind of quality 'adult' film the X was supposed to allow." Critics complained that the radical dream ended somehow in 1969 and that Jack Valenti's system was co-opted by 1975 when X-rated films meant pornography. Divesting directors of more possibilities for X-rated films seemed like a "backlash against the 'excesses' of the '60s" and seemed to open the door to pornographers to co-opt the legitimacy of the X rating.[35] As one viewer commented, "Those of us who loved 'Midnight Cowboy' in its first release saw a whole new potential in American movies ... but ... now ... we feel a sadness ... for a brave new world that was promised yet somehow slipped away."[36]

The X or R debate is moot if the film, indeed, broke ground and influenced future filmmaking. *Midnight Cowboy*'s original rating says more about the difficult subject matter of gender than about its emblematic promise to lead film out of dark ages of control. Americans' resistance to unconventional representations of the Vietnam War and popular culture's inability to portray gay identity with dignity provide the allegorical play in *Midnight Cowboy*. They are the shifting grounds of debate about how mainstream cinema approached masculinity beyond the totalizing image of the individualist Westerner. A new persona depended on audience empathy with familiar victimization claims in top-down stories, balanced out by self-reliance. The film refused to identify Ratso and Joe as merely victims of society and chose instead to indict something else. It gave a chance to those who feel "everybody's talkin' at" him or her to be less peculiar. The brilliance lies in bringing together the acting, the candidness, and the vision to make Waynesian eyes watch another option for male relationships at the turn of the decade.

If United Artists felt the film was risky, the film's popularity cannot be explained by its subject matter alone and, if American society were in the midst of instead of at the beginning of debates about masculinity, the box office would have produced different results. Similarly, the place *Midnight Cowboy* has held in cinematic memory shows its cultural worth, for it is neither the filmmakers' decisions nor the intent that provides historical evidence for the film's social agency but the reception and afterlife. In hindsight, original viewers confirm that we still care about these lost souls — the "weaselly, hobbling Ratso is the original American icon of homeless despair." The "preening faux-cowboy stud" and their "peep-show vision of Manhattan lowlife" allows *Midnight Cowboy* to ride again, vivid and disturbing.[37] From the vantage point of the "unsentimental '90s," as *Washington Post* writer Desson Howe remarked, and despite the film's "unrelenting grimness," it was still "somehow ... all wonderful to watch."[38] Reviewers agreed by the film's anniversary that it still stands as a classic.

Just in case American kids listened too intently "to the echoes of" the American dream, a British director was there to caution them, but the film took on a life of its own, through Hoffman's greased-down hair and Voight's cowboy garb. References to the two have appeared in everything from orange juice commercials to Disney's *Hercules*, an SCTV spoof, and as the name of a fingernail polish. If anyone cares to travel to The Monarch in the city of Ooty in Tamil, India, for a Taj holiday, one can find "a discotheque that captures the timeless essence of a typical Western atmosphere and ideal gathering place for friends." Called "The Midnight Cowboy," this bar offers snacks and the finest spirit and wines with the latest music for those mavericks vacationing in India.[39]

Even in political discussions, the film serves as a historical reference point. During a panel debate held on December 20, 2006, about the role of Hollywood in spreading anti–Americanism, law professor and author James Hirsen held John Wayne as the standard for American ideals. "In the past," he pointed out, "Hollywood provided a positive American image to the world — back when John Wayne as a cowboy exemplified ruggedness, independence and fairness, but films such as 1969's *Midnight Cowboy* ... represented a turning point in American cultural representation of the cinema."[40]

In an interview on CNN News in August 2003, Anderson Cooper asked *The New York Times* critic Elvis Mitchell about his article on the disappearance of sex in current film. "No," said Mitchell, "there's this real fear of dealing with adult sexuality in movies. Movies are now teasing about sex. They're sexy without being sexual." Cooper asked him to "go back to 1969" to *Midnight Cowboy*. Mitchell explained it "was a movie about male prostitutes, and it was more the material than the actual picture itself ... this movie that didn't shy away from the fact that sex was messy, complicated. Adults ruin their lives by it." Mitchell further pointed out, "And that was the year of 'True Grit,' a year of ... staid, quiet, boring, all-square Hollywood movies."[41] The discussion circled back to the same questions about American identity and masculinity represented in John Wayne's iconic status, *Midnight Cowboy*'s iconoclasm, and *Life* report of the polarization of America.

The event that brought back the debate more directly, however, was Ang Lee's *Brokeback Mountain* in 2004. "Is Brokeback this year's Midnight Cowboy?" Emanuel Levy asked on his website in his article "Oscar 2005 — Midday Cowboy," and his answer was yes.[42] The echoes between the two are striking. Thirty-six years after Schlesinger's release, Ang Lee takes us back to rewrite a fantasy about what might have happened had *Midnight Cowboy* been a love story about two gay men. *Brokeback*'s characters are portrayed as cowboys, called cowboys, wear cowboy hats, ride horses, and carry ropes, but they do not fight Indians, beat up outlaws, sleep under the stars around a campfire, nor hustle on the streets of Times Square. Instead, they "herd" sheep, "gather" them, and go fishing. They are not pursuing the American dream like Joe Buck and Ratso and they make love in the idyllic setting of lush, pastoral mountains next to clear, crisp river water. As *Village Voice* film critic J. Hoberman jested, the film "is less a movie than a chunk of American landscape."[43] Personalizing open country in a narrative that looks back on the 1960s as a historical reference point, the filmmakers adjusted the lens of history and imagined social processes developing differently.

Brokeback's social agency exists on the boundary-pushing that critics such as Elvis like to see. Boundary breakers hype film's progressive ideal as the last frontier for creativity in the social and political context of making money. If a film like *Brokeback* gets made in the context of the same-sex marriage debates and at the pinnacle of gay rights, it ceases to operate as an allusion but stands as an agent in social change. Thus, when *Brokeback Mountain* appropriated traditional western mythology to challenge male identities and relationships, it proved a safe bet in 2006. John Wayne was dead, Robert Redford had already built his empire from western iconography, and the only Westerns young audiences watched were Clint Eastwood's revisionists or possibly reruns on "Nick at Night." Memories of families watching "Bonanza" in living rooms and playing cowboys on plastic horses faded with boomers aging. To strike a cord with Western analogies and allusions would be esoteric. Besides, if intimating that the Western cowboy struck a nerve, it was because variations of the Western ethos had become a hot commodity in popular culture. Ranging from country music to Madison Avenue's Ralph Lauren $1200 cowboy attire to bull-riding on cable networks and the NRA's professional competitions, Western identity plays out still on another surface, a potent battleground for gender debates and Americanness.

The delicate balance Schlesinger achieved between innuendo and straight storytelling gave the film the power to be successful at the box office and sustain itself in film history. Yet, landmark as it was, *Midnight Cowboy* competed with a more potent attraction by the 1970s. The other male genre, the war story, that was invested as deeply in patriarchal relations and traditional gender roles as the Western, was the next target. Robert Altman debuted a transitional film just months after *Midnight Cowboy* earned its viewer and critical admiration. While audiences were getting a taste of the hustling life in Manhattan, others were waiting to see two United States medics in Korea shake off sacred cows in *M*A*S*H*. Donald Sutherland and Elliott Gould sealed the deal for the new war look on the silver screen and had a heyday reconciling counterculture ideas with the shifting meaning of masculinity and social roles in America. These medics were not the Ben Caseys or Dr. Kildares that boomers grew up watching on television. Rather, they were the military's nightmare — independent, rebellious, but experts in their practice. Through their antiestablishment extremism, the gender debates took yet another turn.

CHAPTER VII

_____

No Icon Left Unturned

*M*A*S*H* and the Project
of Antiestablishment

Fox didn't release 'MASH.' It escaped.

— Robert Altman after the Cannes Film Festival

The film is so thoroughly American that one fears it may not be justly evaluated abroad.
— Thomas Quinn Curtiss in a review for *M*A*S*H*.

Following the Academy Awards in 1971, Twentieth-Century–Fox publicized Frank J. Schaffner's *Patton* and Robert Altman's *M*A*S*H* in one advertisement, side by side. "Winner! 8 Academy Awards including Best Picture, Best Director, Best Screen Play, Best Actor, Best Film Editing, Best Sound, Best Art Direction, Best Set Decoration; both proudly presented by 20th Century–Fox," the ad read.[1] Oscar stood stately in the middle of the advertisement with George C. Scott as General George S. Patton on the one side and an image of a woman's two naked legs topped with a man's hand giving the piece sign on the other.

Like *Life Magazine*'s front cover of John Wayne and Dustin Hoffman two years before, this ad brought together more than just two movies. Not only did Fox reinstate the importance of the World War II narrative through the image of General Patton saluting while standing in front of the American flag, but it defined a new sensibility with the *M*A*S*H* logo — a peace sign and naked legs in high heels. With Oscar in the middle, the seamless joining of discourses created a quirky juxtaposition of complex social issues wrapped in war and military symbolism. While Franklin J. Schaffner won Best Director over Robert Altman, Altman's treatise turned audience endorsement of a look into an icon of protest. If Schaffner's portrayal of Patton adjusted itself to an antiestablishment sentiment by portraying the general as a cold-blooded killer, Altman's surgical unit better suited the taste for iconoclasm. *M*A*S*H* clearly produced and advanced a sympathetic image of the "sixties" man — part counterculture, part locker-room jock, and part escapist. Where *Patton*'s playing field consisted of reinterpreting the meaning of a renowned general's legacy, Altman's film determined how audiences should resist familiar World War II persona and embrace another one built of its alter ego — anti-patriarchal, anti-authoritarian, and anti-protocol.

114

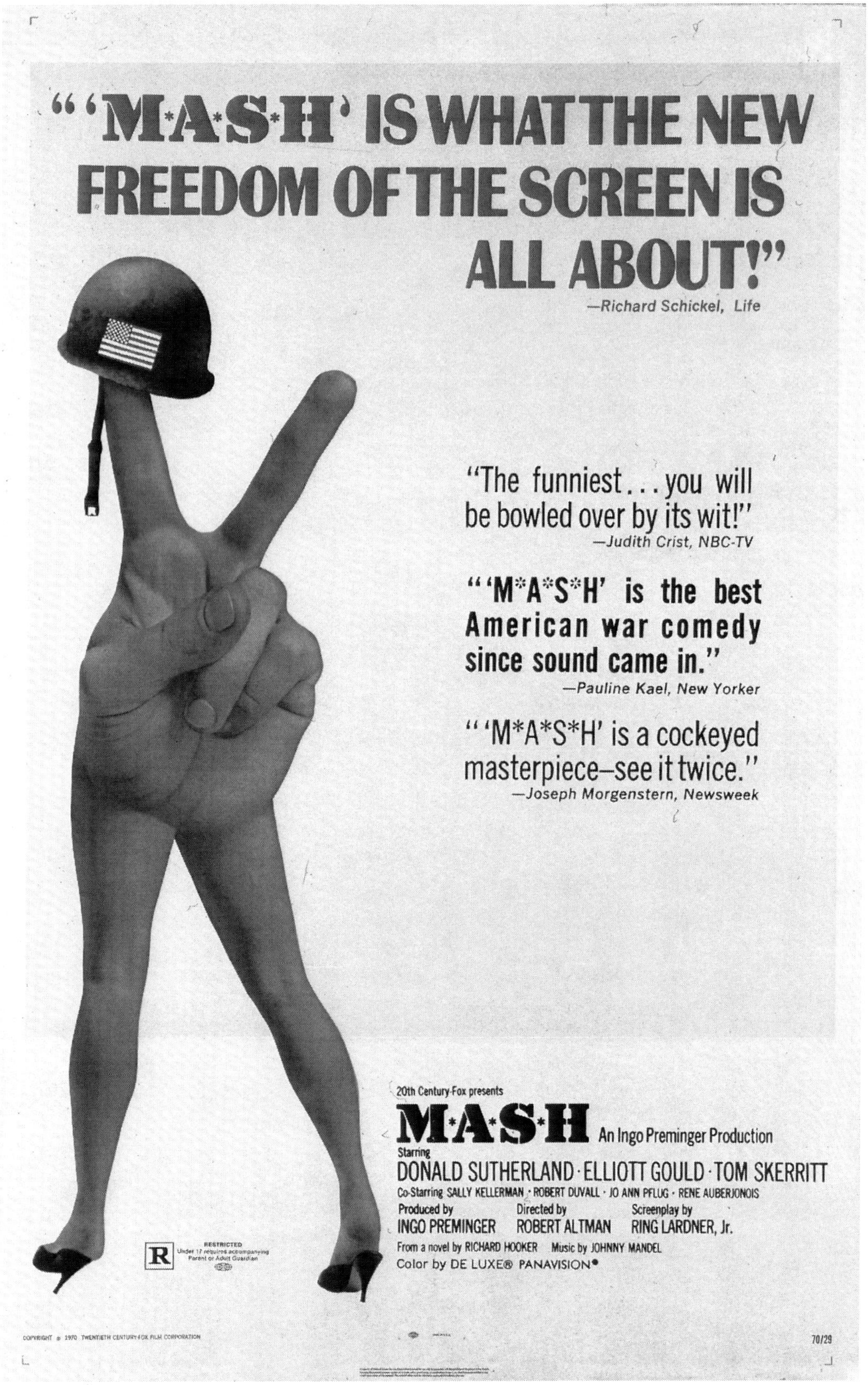

Promotional poster of *M*A*S*H* (1970)(Photofest).

In 1970, in the pre–Watergate Nixon milieu, three war films appeared — *Catch-22*, *Patton*, and *M*A*S*H*. Though temporally set in the middle of the Vietnam debates, not one was specifically about Vietnam. The only mainstream feature to be intended as a Vietnam film was John Wayne's *The Green Berets*, released on July 4, 1968, after the Tet Offensive, the My Lai massacre, and President Johnson's March announcement not to seek reelection. In the film, Wayne is clear about Vietnam, its link to communism, and the importance of America's involvement in Southeast Asia, where the United States Special Forces were clear about their mission. By 1970 a popular image of the disillusioned, disoriented, young draftees entering a war they never understood replaced the earlier Green Beret figure. Now clichéd, those images framed a new cinematic discourse about Vietnam, war, and manhood.

The closest a film came to engaging the anti-military sentiment toward the Vietnam War at the time was *M*A*S*H*. Robert Altman put it aptly about his picture, "I think we've tricked everybody in the United States into seeing the film ... even if they don't lay down their guns and pick up banners." In an interview overseas, following *M*A*S*H*'s award in France, Altman unleashed on Americans. "The vote for Nixon," he argued, "was ... an endorsement of the Kennedy assassinations." He continued, "I'd do anything to help my son, or anyone, escape being drafted [including going] to prison over that."[2] Altman found in the screenplay "the opportunity to do something [he] had been working on for about five years, which was a World War II farce."[3]

The war hero had been transformed into a medical professional who could have his cake and eat it, too, but that sort of regeneration carried its own contradictions. Altman's cinema unselfconsciously stylized the look of male authority but failed to redesign new relations of power between men and women. Sixties masculine imagery in this film was therefore contingent on degrading images of women, suggesting the same problems in the larger culture, considering the film's popularity. *M*A*S*H*'s fame measured the inability of popular culture to extend the progressive project of social change to women. Substituting conventional masculinity with clear versions of updated men but not of females reveals the limiting level of insurgency in Altman's antiwar call. For as far as filmmakers saw themselves liberating Hollywood from old models of male representation, sexual identity for women remained constant.

Patton and *M*A*S*H* framed the debates over war and men at the beginning of the decade. The former personalized the war for soldiers on the battlefields and placed them in the discourse of epic history. "Duty is the essence of manhood," the general says in his speech to the audience, and "battles decide who is coward and who is magnificent." In *M*A*S*H*, soldiers are silent, brought in on stretchers and laid to rest on surgical tables. Surgeons trying to piece bodies back together ask audiences if the ends indeed justify the means. Cameras zoom in on close-ups of wounds, surgeries, and the gruesome side of battle. Blood is everywhere in *M*A*S*H*. *Patton* depersonalizes "the bursting of flesh" and "the shedding of blood" that *M*A*S*H* exposes almost boastfully. In *Patton* soldiers are restored to valor by the paternal leader. Their efforts are honored by their courage. *M*A*S*H*, on the other hand, removes the correlation between liberty and war, duty and action.[4]

For General Patton freedom is not rhetorical but always a battle as the general tells his audience in the opening sequence of the film where he stands for two long minutes in front of the American flag covering the entire screen. As the camera zooms into a close-up of General Patton addressing the unseen audience, the viewers, his troops, he orates about what it means to overcome weakness. In *M*A*S*H* duty is pragmatic, not gallant. Discipline is mocked. *Patton* returns to the classic qualities upon which American myths were built — what

"THE EPIC AMERICAN WAR MOVIE
THAT HOLLYWOOD HAS ALWAYS
WANTED TO MAKE BUT NEVER HAD
THE GUTS TO DO BEFORE."
—Vincent Canby, New York Times

"YOU MAY NEVER HAVE ANOTHER
EXPERIENCE LIKE IT! EVIDENTLY
SOMEONE BELIEVED THAT THE PUBLIC
HAD COME OF AGE ENOUGH TO
TAKE A MATURE FILM ABOUT A
REAL WAR WITH A HERO-VILLAIN
IN ALL HIS GLORIOUS AND
VAINGLORIOUS HUMANITY."
—Liz Smith, Cosmopolitan Magazine

PATTON

The posters of *Patton* (1970) and *M*A*S*H* (1970) on page 115 symbolize the debates over men and war; one personalized heroism and the other personalized fun (Photofest).

Scott himself called the "immortality of individuality" or the measure of a man on traditional, heroic terms.[5] *M*A*S*H* replaces the value of individual honor with men and women responding to circumstances.

With the draft in full force but Vietnam's outcome yet a few years away, popular debate centered on America's role in the world. Was it a heroic nation or an imperialist one, an intruder or a savior, progressive or barbaric, liberating or subjugating? Americans could not reconstruct ideal manhood easily, since America's moral call to enlighten the rest of the world now seemed like another example of "westward" expansion. Thus, the popularity of these two films showed competing arguments about deciding the meaning of the present.

Ten days after the release of *M*A*S*H*, the same New York audiences flocked to Schaffner's *Patton*. The films ran neck and neck in gross sales. *M*A*S*H* edged *Patton* by approximately $12 million, with *Patton* bringing in $61-plus million and *M*A*S*H* over $73. A year later, however, on April 17, 1971, at the Dorothy Chandler Pavilion, *Patton* swept the Academy Awards. It took seven of its ten nominations, winning Best Picture (Frank McCarthy, producer), Best Screenplay (Francis Ford Coppola and Edmund H. North) about a historical figure, Best Director (Frank J. Schaffner of *Planet of the Apes* fame), Sound (Douglas Williams and Don Bassman), Art and Set Direction, Film Editing (Douglas Williams and Don Bassman), and Best Actor, which was scandalized by Scott refusing to attend the Oscar ceremony. *M*A*S*H* received five nominations and won one Oscar for Screenplay Adaptation (Ring Lardner, Jr.), but its most prominent claim to fame would be measured by the eleven-year run of the namesake's famous television series for a generation that did not know about the film at all.

The film's ultimate role in deestablishing the establishment began with the conversion of the book into film. The general aim of the book, as author Richard Hooker (alias for Dr. H. Richard Hornberger) wrote to Lardner, was to "know doctor is human," a bit screwy in behavior but "dedicated, too." Lardner said of the characters, "I've tried to follow not having the Swampmen do anything gratuitously defiant but only things in keeping with their general aim of asserting their independence in order to get their work done and live their lives without bureaucratic interference."[6] Author Hornberger quibbled with Lardner over the use and characterization of the medics. In referring to the team's dentist, Captain Waldowski, Hornberger prodded, "Is slob the right word?... For some reason ... slob has no special meaning for me." Hornberger suggested to Ring that he should "avoid confrontation of goofing off, drunken surgeons and dying patients." Himself a medical doctor, Hornberger worried about the script misrepresenting the medical profession and helped Ring with medical language ("ask technical advisers what gauze is ... another classical non-word" and "change 'vital indications' to 'vital signs'").[7]

Hornberger felt uncomfortable with overly gratuitous close-ups of bloody hands inside mangled bodies. Showing so much "exposure to wounded ... [may] just leave bad taste in everyone's mouth," the author cautioned. He also objected to Lardner's focus on the gruesome side of life. "How many movies," Hornberger wrote, "that I was thoroughly enjoying have I left with bad taste in mouth because a tragedy was thrown into relative happiness? Hell, us grunts don't demand that much reality. We want to escape it." The quibble was over the script's treatment of an "adopted" Vietnamese youngster, Ho Jon, whose death Lardner added in the second draft because "of imbalance favoring comedy over grimness," he explained. "We felt it advisable," continued Lardner, "the audience should realize death was a constant factor on the scene."

The author and scriptwriter bantered about including a description of Colonel Merrill in an unfavorable light. "I plead guilty," confessed Lardner, "to inserting a bit of propaganda reflecting my own view that the Korean War was part of a mistaken policy that has culminated in Vietnam ... but I don't defend it and certainly don't assume any right to imbue your characters with attitudes you find distasteful."[8]

Generally a traditional narrative about the value of medics in war, Hornberger's novel placed the experience of Korea in print. It was a testimony to the value of service in the Korean War. While the focus was on the medic not the soldier, the novel's conviction to portray men as human, a bit screwy, but "dedicated, too" kept masculine representation within conventional identity of power and authority. Yet, to convert this story into a sixties sentiment meant fetishizing the "screwy" behavior as a sign of liberation for the American man from the authoritarian hold of the past. The Lardner screenplay was marked "FINAL" by February 26, 1969, six months after he signed a contract with Aspen Productions, Inc. Adapted from the novel, the script tried to remain faithful to Hooker's intent and, after several meetings and correspondences, the author thanked him for honoring his request.

The film opens to the theme song, "Suicide is Painless," and shows MASH-unit helicopters flying wounded soldiers on stretchers attached to the runner. The song finishes as choppers take off for other wounded soldiers and the camera focuses on surgeon Hawkeye Pierce (Donald Sutherland) as the phrase, "And then there was Korea," rolls by, followed by statements from General MacArthur and President Eisenhower. Other than those specific references, the film was anywhere Asia and the medics similar to the popular press's pictures of American soldiers in Vietnam.

The Korean War is typically written as a stalemate, largely ignored in cultural representations but remembered by Korean War veterans as a victory. It was sandwiched between the endless representations of exceptionalism through World War II heroics and the public's larger denial of meaning for Vietnam vets. This "forgotten" war provided Altman with open ideological terrain. Not established as a sacred icon, there was no mass-culture narrative to be suppressed or built upon, little to be resisted or reinstated. Simply put, Korea was a safe bet. Creating a new war story of Korea directed toward Vietnam meant bringing a new consumable, a new means of regenerating the male image in the military without turning audiences away. Certainly humor was a viable narrative tool, but a comedy about the Korean War carried little cultural transgression. To override that liability, Altman combined the fact of Korea with the look of contemporary subversion. The fusion was a veritable success.

"Fade In ext. landing area outside 4077th; see large letters 'M-A-S-H,' Mobile Army Surgical Hospital," page one of the script reads. The "sex-starved men on the post" run the unit with nurse "Lieutenant Dish, twenty-four, blond and clearly, even in her winter fatigues, the sexiest looking nurse in military history" (JoAnn Pflug). Captains, majors, lieutenants, men and women, attend to the wounded and assist the two central characters, the top-gun surgeons, Hawkeye Pierce played by Donald Sutherland and Trapper John played by Elliott Gould. Major Margaret Houlihan, "who will soon be known" as "Hot Lips," "tallish, willowish, blondish, fortyish, prettyish" arrives at MASH by helicopter and introduces Sally Kellerman to the viewing public.[9]

The 1960s presented a challenge in representing vets, soldiers, and the military. To begin with, Vietnam was the first war to receive extensive television coverage. Media coverage quickly dashed ideas about heroism in war, pride in battle, and honorable return. To American viewers, it was clear wars were not movies. The value of war could no longer be assumed, nor could the value of the soldier as the persona of what Scott called the "immortality of indi-viduality." Despite *Variety*'s claim of *Patton* being "100% American, in every way," America, in definition, vision, and image, was anything but clear. *M*A*S*H* could fill the Korean War's empty representation history and use it as an allegory for Vietnam at the same time. The film and the later turn in television to *M*A*S*H* reconstructed the image of the military but did not spark a national preoccupation with the Korean War. Thus, the issue for a viewing Amer-ican population was clearly Vietnam.

After settling on Robert Altman, Fox's fifteenth choice for director, the company was ready to produce what would be a defining film for the beginning of the new decade. Con-verting the script into a film Altman-style meant creating the texture of a community instead of building a story around individuals. The actors Donald Sutherland and Elliott Gould were essential to the film's overall effect of antiestablishment. Sutherland had a healthy TV and movie career before *M*A*S*H*. He appeared with the stellar cast in *The Dirty Dozen* (1967) and later starred in Paul Mazursky's *Alex in Wonderland* (1970). Elliott Gould had convinced an American public of his quirky talent in *Bob and Carol and Ted and Alice* (1969). Gould charmed viewers as the liberated, dark-haired husband who finds "swinging" a satisfying addi-tion to conventional marriage in Mazursky's hit. In *M*A*S*H* the Gould persona signifies the professional class that negotiated new terms for the organization man. With his buddy Hawk-eye, Trapper defines the ethical center of Altman's film. Creativity, flexibility, and autonomy are more heroic and necessary than hierarchy, loyalty, and lofty military ideals.

By April 1969, the film was well into production with Robert Altman at the helm. A common Altman strategy — texture over plotline — operated in this picture to advance his argument that society and its institutions destroy men.[10] Hornberger would have agreed that the screenplay stayed with the book's thematic integrity, but Altman has never been known merely to adapt a written work. Matching his impromptu style to the subject of sanity against insanity, Altman transformed a straightforward script into a timely signature piece. As one reviewer put it, "*M*A*S*H* crashed through all defense lines, obliterating any trace of respect for such cherished conceptions as army discipline, precedence of rank, male virility, wom-anly virtue: nothing is sacred in the climate of an absurd war." These two "anarchic actors" look and dress the part.[11] They easily take on the discourse of appearance as a sign of rebel-lion.

Altman laid the groundwork for the forgotten Korean soldier and the un-representable Vietnam vet by arguing that masculinity is measured by performance not adherence. When Trapper John, for example, enters the MASH unit, he is unrecognizable as an officer. He sits covered in a makinaw, complete with fur-trimmed hood when the camera slowly focuses on him. In Altmanesque darkness, Trapper is finally revealed but not who he is. Unshaven and unkempt, he has just been transferred to this unit and arrives fully out of uniform. Through-out the film, he redefines the identity of the medical establishment by making a fetish of appearance. Except for his surgical scrubs, he is in Hawaiian floral print much of the time. This laid-back identity and over-attention to appearance undercuts the glamour of handsome men in power and shows that scruffy can be attractive, but this guise of anti-authority has nothing to do with dismantling established male power.

By January 1970 the film was well on its way to box office success, but this time Ring Lardner confessed his ambivalence about what Altman had done. At the first screening, Lard-ner remarked to Altman that he had "ruined the script." He wrote to Hornberger, "My main objections, for the record, are to a bad beginning and a weak ending, a stupid routine with

Onward Christian Soldiers [*sic*] and the use of a song called *Suicide is Painless* [*sic*]. I also dislike the asterisks in the title and the loathsome picture in the ads."[12] Yet by the summer of
1970, the film's popularity made it hard to deny its importance. As Hornberger was convinced,
"There is no question in my mind that this is one of the best movies I've seen" and was already
writing his sequel to the film, enjoying his "screaming public."[13]

What had transpired from book to script to film was the conversion of a relatively conventional portrayal of medics in the service to an updated, socially relevant treatise on the
Vietnam War masked as a 1950s historical event, but its stylized use of the historical past
allowed the film its most egregious discursive transgression. Reviewers applauded the film's
"irreverent ... blasphemous, and destructive" diversions from traditional military movies. It
is notable because it is "dirty, disrespectful and crammed with carcasses—and, of course in
its fast-cutting modern style," said Dilys Powell of *The London Times*.[14] *Film Quarterly* critic
William Johnson applauded its "hilarious antimilitary satire" and its lack of piety.[15] Yet, what
some lauded as "anti-war, anti-establishment and ... anti–American," others saw as reestab-
lishment.[16] Johnson, for example, questioned its value as anti-military since the hierarchy's
characterization was largely one-dimensional. "The higher authorities are clearly willing to
turn a blind eye on Mash [*sic*] so long as it [did] its surgical duty," he pointed out. The realism of surgery "work[ed] hard and well," but asking an audience to dislike commanding officers simply because they were bores or idiotic evaded a clear central strength of the film's
potential.[17]

Altman explained his motive. He never intended his films to make political statements.
Rather, he filmed like an artist painted. He was more "interested in the look and feel of a
film," in the audience's emotional work as active viewers of his stylistics.[18]

Certainly Altman's talent as a boundary breaker goes unquestioned in terms of "Now
Movie" qualities, but the new realism in film standing in as progressive social agency is less
clear.

"Telling it like it is" is not a transparent transmission of experience but a re-presenta-
tion, an interpretation, a meaning-making action, too. In one scene, Hawkeye and Trapper
John, for example, have been summoned to Japan to perform surgery on an American congressman's wounded son because "Trapper is the best there is." They travel in golf attire to
Japan, taking their clubs and expecting to play golf. As the military jeep approaches the course,
Trapper and Hawkeye engage in a conversation in what is supposed to be Japanese. Meant
for comic effect, the scene pokes fun at the sound of the language, much in the style of an
old Jerry Lewis movie. Certainly this moment also works to expose the ethnocentricity in
people who behave like the two renowned surgeons. On the other hand, viewers have already
identified with Hawkeye and Trapper as the best there is, the representative men of the new
antiestablishment. Thus, the scene's antics betray mere realistic comedy.

Five months after release in America, at the twenty-third International Cannes Film Festival on May 16, 1970, by a vote of six to three, Cannes Film Festival judges gave *M*A*S*H*
the Golden Palm for best motion picture of four hundred entries.[19] Over ten thousand
viewers and eight hundred journalists participated in the two-week event. At the end of the
week, Robert Altman stood on stage in the Festival Palace with producer Ingo Preminger
and actresses Sally Kellerman and Jo Ann Pflug (Lt. Dish) to receive the grand prix at the
awards ceremony.[20] By the end of May, the film was showing continuously at the Rialto in
London. As was advertised, "following the Cannes Award and the unprecedented popularity
of the film in the United States, special arrangements were made by the Rialto with the G.L.C.

Authority to allow the film to be shown round-the-clock from the opening."[21] *M*A*S*H* was the first film from overseas to get that kind of approval for a twenty-four-hour straight run at the Rialto Theatre in London. It was liked because it was fashionable in the sixties style of rowdiness: long hair on men, obvious antiwar stance, and anti-authoritarian in attitudes. Londoners continued to praise its "fast-cutting modern style" and its "actors, writers, directors and of course the producer who had the nerve to make the film."[22]

Alongside the approbation, several renounced the film's true mission. "I hope nobody will tell me," Dilys Powell wrote in *The London Times*, "that M*A*S*H is anti-war."[23] In Europe, Altman and producer Ingo Preminger were booed when they went on stage to receive the Cannes Festival awards. The jury president, Miguel Ángel Asturias, boycotted the award ceremony in protest against the decision to award Altman and Preminger the grand prize, but the award stood.[24]

What some saw as iconoclasm, others saw as anesthesia. Graduate students at New York University, for example, questioned the film's social commitment in view of its commercial tie. A flyer from "the Graduate Cinema Strike Committee of N.Y.U." implored students to ask, "What is the price of your entertainment?" The committee argued that the film industry "is frantically diluting, commercializing, and exploiting the political and cultural revolution taking place in this country." More pointedly, "Directors who claim to have a social concern make films which distort and exploit the socio-political ideals of youth in a greedy attempt to capture the 'youth market.'" And following that statement, advocates asked, "why is *M*A*S*H* about Korea instead of Vietnam?"[25]

The N.Y.U. flyer argued from an anti-capitalist perspective declaring, "Ironically, the exploitation films produced by these powers are largely supported by those whom they exploit; the young, the blacks, the women, while at the same time perpetuating the lack of comprehension common to the misinformed 'middle American.'" If only enlightened, America would be governed by a new morality of nonexploitation, ultimately redeeming and empowering the socially abused. Objecting to popular film's duplicity, this flyer highlighted the flawed agency in *M*A*S*H* and its exploitative, capitalist character and circulated a directive: that viewers resist and reject Hollywood projects.[26]

Not everyone was willing to resist the likes of Hawkeye and Trapper John when a cultural revolution meant shaking off the authority-driven past. How that was understood at the time was up for grabs; venues from Hollywood to NYU graduate students mediated its meaning. If, as Altman told reporters, his goal was "emotional" rather than "literal accuracy" and if he was correct in assuming that "no company would have financed a film about Vietnam," then the internal structure of the film doggedly did subversive work.[27] On the other hand, if Altman's iconoclasm merely exploited changing attitudes, then a harder question of its anti-establishment achievement remains to be asked. The process of reconstructing America to fit changing attitudes and social pressures meant deconstructing American manhood. Like the Western, iconic narratives such as the war story no longer stood as the unequivocal perspective of American history. *M*A*S*H* entered into theaters as that kind of cinematic rebel, product and producer of the displacement of convention. Yet its ideological break is not so clear and in some ways the film remains guilty of the perpetuation of convention, typical and predictable. Somewhere in between a rejection of all popular films and a filmmaker pleading innocence through art stood the reason for *M*A*S*H*'s success and failure.

The larger power of this film, its discursive function as an agent in social change, can be appraised properly when considering the role and function of its female characters.

Improving the social status of women was obviously not the film's purpose, but the question of its pigeonholing of women while liberating men raises the issue of what representations in film were possible. Men's major roles outnumbered women's twelve to one at the time, but that should be of no surprise since the Producers' Guild claimed over twenty-three hundred male members and only twenty-three women. Of course, the popular assumption was that "women's pictures" just didn't sell, especially if they did not star Barbra Streisand at the time.[28] It made sense to assume things had changed for women when viewers saw liberated women such as Jane Fonda in *Klute* (1971), gaining power through liberalized images of sexuality on screen. The breakthrough visuals seemed at the time a measure of success, but for the most part women's roles remained exploitative.

Feminist Betty Friedan responded to the clever way American society answered to her call for unleashing the "feminine mystique." Hollywood had helped take women out of the kitchen and put them onto the streets with lively flair. Friedan asked "that we rate the movies W + or W- or even W---, depending on the image of women in a given movie." Why can't filmmakers come up with a respectful liberation giving women a "new identity as people?" she asked. A mystique of the masculine kind seemed to have sprouted in the years since Friedan denounced the subjugation of women. Friedan called for a more complex discussion of the changes in relationships between men and women and in the effects of those changes in conventional families. Now, in the form of "latter-day Hardy Boys," with "that convenient poignant bullet through the long hair," the new age man was quickly founding his new establishment.[29]

By mid-decade, Hollywood's distorted treatment of women was so annoying to some that during the New York Film Festival the National Organization for Women and the Screen Actors Guild organized a conference entitled "Filmmaking U.S.A.: A World Without Women" to discuss the matter. Three hundred people packed into a library to hear a panel discuss the situation for women. The contradiction was clear as *New York Times* journalist Judy Klemesrud reported: "At a time when feminism seems to be in full flower, there is a dearth of good roles for women in American film." Then, she argued, "when women do get parts at all, they are usually cast as prostitutes, empty-headed blondes, sex kittens or neurotic housewives." At least in the Katharine Hepburn and Bette Davis days, audiences saw strong women on screen assert some authority.[30]

Women's power in Hollywood seemed to be compromised with the studio break-up because producers no longer had to honor women's contracts. Says movie critic Molly Haskell, "When you had actresses under contract you had to find parts for them." In addition, "There were also a lot of women screenwriters in the thirties and they wrote good repartee between men and women." What she called the "mammary gland" fixation, inflated with actresses such as Marilyn Monroe, translated into the sixties version of women as victims and subjects of men's violence.[31]

Friedan and other feminists forced the discussion of representation out of their closet and into the mainstream. In the wake of buddy films, "this whole slew of 'boys together' movies, in which I also include 'M*A*S*H,'" Friedan contended, "women are not seen except as shadowy waitresses, or virtually faceless bodies, call-girls, paid or unpaid — non-persons." With gratuitous sexuality, films "seem to feed death wishes, in sexual disguise," Friedan concluded. As she remarked, "The more explicit the sex, somehow the more anti-human, anti-life the movie." Friedan's comments raised the question of whether the extremely popular "Hardy-boy" format of that time was engendering social agency or offering "cheap escapes" from harder issues of gender.[32]

The magic in reconstructing establishment thinking during Hollywood's most historically liberalized moment lies in the inscrutable way a film such as *M*A*S*H* manages women's
liberation. The degrading treatment of women was often buried under the guise of shaking
off Puritanism. Puritanism and prudishness were discredited as old-fashioned and limiting
for women, while sex outside conventional marriage meant liberating the body from yet
another authoritarian figure and therefore regenerating. Reviewers, for example, wrote of Sally
Kellerman's character as the "prudish nurse whose Puritanism thaws in the heat of battle."[33]
Sally Kellerman's "Hot Lips" was a justifiable target of ridicule because she was, as *Newsweek*
described, "the Calvinistic but libidinous WAC."[34]

To test that Calvinism, the medics played pranks. Houlihan's wondrous thaw began when
she was the butt of two humiliating, practical jokes. Corporal Radar O'Reilly (Kim Atwood)
wired the inside of Officer Frank Burn's (Robert Duvall) tent and transmitted over the loud-
speaker Burn and Houlihan having sex. The medical unit became privy to her sexual raven-
ousness and hence made her conversion a public goal. To get her to melt even more, the
jokesters rigged a cable on the shower tent that lifted the cover to expose a naked and mor-
tified officer Hot Lips. As if at a movie, rows of medics, male and female, applauded as she
groveled naked on the ground.

Not everyone ignored the effects of "Hot Lip" representations. One New Yorker protested
in a letter to the editor. She objected to *New York Times* reviewer Vincent Canby including
Altman's film in his "Ten Best List" of 1970. As she remarked the "inclusion ... is further dis-
heartening evidence that movie critics see nothing wrong with dehumanizing women in the
name of humor." Like the film's logo, "Women ... are regarded not as people but as sexual
parts to be patronized and humiliated for laughs." That this misogynistic pattern went largely
ignored by public and critics alike speaks to the discursive power of the anti-military and
antiestablishment image to take on a male persona at the time. The letter pointed out that
the obscenity in such films lies in the endorsement of the film's "blatant misogyny" and its
"bland" acceptance. The film's humor further legitimated the wish fulfillment of those game-
players whose debasing antics toward women get buried in what Canby called "unequivocally
funny" pranks.[35]

Similarly, the book's author objected to another scene when the medic team tricked Captain Walter "Painless Pole" Waldowski (John Schuck) into a "cure" for impotence. Lt. Dish
agrees to sexual intercourse while the captain is asleep, preparing to die, but when he finds
himself awake after Dish's performance, he finds himself restored to health and manliness.
Lt. Dish's sudden change from a virtuous nurse to unpaid prostitute made no sense to Hornberger. As he remarked, "in the finale to Painless Waldowski and Lt. Dish ... [I] think her
decision to cooperate based, as implied, only on how Painless is hung — after her virtuous
buildup — may be a little too much. Would it be any less effective if she was, fairly obviously,
wavering for humanitarian reasons, before the private showing finally moved her?"[36] This savior of impotent men — the available nurse — played into male myths and served to reinstate
men's sexual identity.

In both Lt. Dish's humanitarian gesture and Hot Lips' mortification, Altman's wish of
the Hugh Hefner kind — the forbidden fruit, the virgin and the whore — overshadowed singular protests as the film resonated with the millions of viewers as an American icon over the
next few decades, but, practical jokes aside, the last sequences of the film bring the egregious
nature of the film's discourse to the fore. Major Houlihan's transformation and liberation
from a rigid disciplinarian to a member of the humane community is complete once she joins

the surgeons and alienates herself from the quintessential military authority, Major Burns. This membership was confirmed when she became head cheerleader, a non-person, instead of Major Houlihan, a professional nurse in the U.S. Army.

As the publicity folder suggested, those who have the most humanity staged the most games, but humanity in this film turns into saving the impotent dentist from suicide and gets subsumed in bullying tactics. One reviewer, "a minority report," as he called his perspective, saw the style of these "heroes" as ruthless and imposing. "Any admiration their coolness may inspire," he commented, "is torpedoed by the ruthlessness they show in imposing their style on the recalcitrant uncool."[37] Their antiestablishment is thus qualified for only those whose "jugular" is exposed when bugging the tent of Major Burns and Major Houlihan. In short, those who can make and take jokes win.

Major Burns fails the test but Houlihan survives the humiliating prank where she is exposed while showering and passes with flying colors when she sleeps with one of the heroes and joins the game as the cheerleader of men. Sally Kellerman commented on how enthralled she was with the character since Houlihan was the only one to change. Yet, that change meant going from a military officer and competent professional to a subordinate and "acquiescent bedmate," as one reviewer called her. Critics who soured on *M*A*S*H* repudiated the ending as the return of the "Sigma Nu Frat Party," sixties style.[38]

M*A*S*H dishonored war games but not game playing. The medics challenged the general to a football game and after a few pranks such as stabbing the opposition with hypodermic needles filled with drugs, *M*A*S*H* medics win the game and take thousands of dollars in bets back to camp. The football game wraps up the film's American identity and etches the gender lines clearly on the screen. The medics establish male intimacy in their coming together as men to win the hierarchical battle. Women dutifully play their role as cheerleaders, thereby confirming that they are not as deserving of the kind of intimacy as are men. This is the sequence that made Hot Lips feel good enough about herself that her anger subsided. The elimination of women from the narrative's action and their placement on the sidelines of the football game is a sinister reflection of women's place in American society in antiestablishment disguise.

The press book sent to advertise the movie included posters of the picture of the woman's legs and man's fingers with Sutherland and Gould flanked on both sides. Another option for theaters had a shirtless Gould holding a cigar in his mouth and Sutherland with a scotch in hand and, "where newspaper censorship exists," fingers were covered with a glove. Press marketing described the characters as "the best surgeons in the Far East and they are hell-raising lunatics who make a shambles of army bureaucracy" but "never [lose] sight of the purpose and dedication of the three human doctors and the wounded they try to mend and save." They learn to "survive the tragic waste of war ... by cling[ing] to their sanity and humanity" and, for the women, "Major Hot Lips ... whose exposure to the rigors of life in the raw brings about a wondrous transformation" and Lt. Dish is the "sexiest in military history."[39]

In between representation and the everyman medic, the film refuels the truth and contradictions of a higher authority. They were surgeons not 42nd Street hustlers but in a sense still hustling. In the words of reviewer Richard Corliss for the *National Review*, "*M*A*S*H*'s heroes are experts at beating the system, not smashing the system."[40] Hot Lips was a literary tool to shape the unit up, but as in the former logo and a *New York Times* article, it was all about the legs. The film clip of the actress getting out of the helicopter with her skirt above her thighs, revealing nylons and garter, became a widely circulated photograph for reviewers' articles because that was the film's point. Power to women meant shaking off prudishness and for that they could become the leading man's girl or the next "woman singing the blues," as one feminist complained.[41]

Robert Altman had once explained to an interviewer for *Action* that his decision to dispense with much of the script was based on his style and nothing else. "I'm interested in the behavior pattern of the characters," he claimed, "not in what they say [and] if I had done his script the picture would have been a disaster."[42] Lardner was not sold on all the "adlibbing" but thankfully received his Oscar in 1971. Renowned filmmaker François Truffaut applauded Lardner for his "excellent script" but ridiculed Altman for his "disastrous direction."[43] Somewhere between Lardner's objection and Truffaut's insult lies the film's value as a "new breed of movie," distinctly stamping it Altman-made for a Hollywood scrambling to redefine itself.[44] Altman's boundary-breaking men reflected his attitude toward the subject of war and film's common treatment of heroes, but in his language of seeming verisimilitude, he reestablished an unforgivable social reality, unambiguously degrading for women. In doing so, he helped his film define the establishment in antiestablishment that protected the power of men's authority.

M*A*S*H subverts the overdetermined war image to keep free the social status of men as the agents of action. If Altman was adventurous in his direction of this film, he was less so in his motives. When pressed to explain why directors have not widened the roles for women beyond "mammary fixation, " losers, or victims, Altman once replied, "well, isn't that the way most women really are?"[45] *Knight Ridder* reporter Judy Gerstel agreed. "From 'M.A.S.H' to 'The Player,'" she said about Altman, "he's been criticized for the way women are presented in his movies ... women are naked, vulnerable or abused... [but] far from being a misogynist, Altman is a feminist."[46] Yes, if only through the slightest of imagination. Perhaps more accurately, *The Observer Review* reported it best about Altman's iconoclastic truth-telling, "It is perhaps the supreme example of an anti-establishment movie making a box-office *coup* for the establishment."[47]

The surface appearance of insurgent authenticity in *M*A*S*H* is exactly what gave the initial story its afterlife. The *M*A*S*H* television series began on CBS on September 17, 1972, and ran for eleven seasons and two hundred fifty-one episodes. Its finale in February 1983 drew over three-fourths of the viewing audiences. Major Houlihan's actress, Loretta Swit, was occasionally invited to speak at nursing graduations. Altman was honored with a lifetime achievement award at the seventy-eighth Oscars and appeared on the honorary tribute screen for the deceased a year later at the seventy-ninth ceremony. Hornberger lived his life feeling comfortable with the initial results of the film, but he snubbed the television series' rendition of Hawkeye Pierce. Alan Alda as Pierce guaranteed the life of the original film, but Hornberger, who died at seventy-three on November 24, 1997, "disliked the TV series because of the liberal bent that Alda brought to Hawkeye, the character Hornberger modeled on himself, a political conservative." Said Hornberger, "I intended no messages in the book. I am a conservative Republican. I don't hold with this anti-war nonsense."[48]

At a dedication ceremony in 1997, the U.S. military closed the MASH unit thirty-five miles from Seoul. "Today you are joining us in making history," unit commander Colonel Ronald A. Maul remarked as onlookers said good bye to "America's MASH."[49] The American Film Institute hosted a *M*A*S*H* reunion in November 1995 at the Cecchi Gori Fine Arts Theater in Beverly Hills to celebrate both film and television history. What Altman began, the television series etched permanently in American consciousness. Most notably,

Korean War vets refer to the story as a personal reference and validation for their sacrifices. A group of fifteen vets staged a "serious" production of *M*A*S*H* to tell their stories. Among the actors were "Purple Hearts, Bronze Stars, combat pins and other medals" recipients, said director Gary Baumgartner. "We wanted the tenor of the show," he said, "to reflect that this was a real war.... These guys are true heroes." With advice from the chairman of the Iowa chapter of the Korean War Veterans, the production provided "an all-encompassing experience" as it combined the movie with live theater. Patrons were able to see artifacts and photographs from the war, forgotten in the aftermath of World War II and used as a narrative tool to engage in the debate about Vietnam.[50]

The seminal *M*A*S*H* (1970), a story about a compassionate surgical unit serving in Korea, made Altman "the 'new' Hollywood's prodigal son."[51] Taking popular movies into the next decade meant deconstructing formulas that had defined Americans for decades. With *M*A*S*H*, Altman reconstructed the idea of heroism in war and found his subject matter not on the front lines but in the surgical room where men were still in charge. Altman saw to it that the war film would be forever changed, but in a general antiwar social environment, it captured rather than radicalized conventional notions of the other half of the population.

Altman caricatured the military system in a way that resonated with 1970s counterculture attitudes through Hawkeye and Trapper. They were the younger generation's "authentic" and "honest" men who redirected their ideals from obsession with masculine strength to softened professionalism.[52] These "easy riding elitists," as film historian Diane Jacobs has described them, brought the new "scruffy, non-verbal heroes of Woodstock" to the screen and updated the image of men in the cinematic war zone. These characters were the men of the seventies, the "peace marchers" who, in Jacobs words, claimed: "If we ran the world, not only would it be a lot more amusing, but a good deal more efficient as well."[53]

Cheers from audiences immortalized the film's correlation between cool as sanity and anything square as ineptness.[54] *M*A*S*H*'s sarcastic medics confronted the gallant warrior image.[55] At the same time, Franklin J. Schaffner's "anti-war and anti–Patton" picture inadvertently reaffirmed conventional male identity with George C. Scott's portrayal in *Patton* and gave "Americans a new hero." Schaffner's project meant to question war by portraying a maniacal commander as an "impulsive ... hungry militarist." Instead, viewers identified the eccentric and merciless General Patton as a dedicated leader, the warrior as the essential man.[56] In *M*A*S*H*, using Korea as a stand-in for Vietnam provided a space in which not only to question combat but also to reject Pattonesque essences. Men's protest was not centered on questions of equal rights but on the freedom to determine their roles and identity. The resounding box office success of both films and the long-running career of the television series clearly revealed two sides of the same coin. Both venues sat on the battleground of manhood. Protest was both specific to Vietnam and to the other war within American culture.

If Altman closed the power-door to women in *M*A*S*H*, he attempted to open it in his next film, released in 1971: *McCabe and Mrs. Miller*, starring a resourceful, independent woman entering a man's landscape with authority and determination. Julie Christie as Mrs. Miller took on Warren Beatty and the elegant, panoramic Western. A successful businesswoman in a turn-of-the-century northwestern mining town, Mrs. Miller asks a gender-conscious society to permit new representations of women in the West. Her stunning performance takes up where Major Houlihan feared to tread and suggests there might be more to the image than just telling it like it is.

CHAPTER VIII

Out of the Saddle, into the Seventies

Gender in *McCabe and Mrs. Miller*

> I tell ya, Ida, you start payin' special attention to one man and you just end up with a lot of misery.
>
> — Constance Miller, *McCabe and Mrs. Miller*

In November 1970, *Look* magazine underscored the importance of American film. "The movies, America's favorite and most enduring entertainment," the editors wrote, "take over this entire issue." Feature writers collaborated with members of the industry to assess the poststudio environment. "Movies today are more alive, more filled with surprises, more talked about than ever," they said. United Artists president David V. Picker declared "this is a great day for creators, for those with new ideas, for people whose first love is making good movies." Martin Baum of ABC Pictures proclaimed the new decade "a golden age, the best of times for creative people because, with far lower budgets, we can gamble with new ideas and new talent."[1]

What the seventies offered American cinema was certainly a determination to experiment with new material ranging from American lifestyle changes to newly spirited movements. American cinema recorded and redesigned its society; whatever appeared real was meaningful and whatever seemed "emotionally unstrung" was real.[2] Considering the passionate plea from the "under thirties" audiences to make film art, any audacious trumping of convention would appeal, but iconoclasm in Hollywood fit one director's style perfectly. Robert Altman, who had twenty-some years of experience in both television and film, found his antiestablishment viewers and began what would be his most memorable movies. The changes in the industry offered him a chance to develop his taste for the European-style art film and spark his interest in revising sacred American myths. From 1970 to 1975, he cut nearly ten films. The trade touted him as "the new *enfant terrible* of the cinema," the "boy wonder" of moving pictures.[3] In the eyes of the industry, he and a handful of others ensured film's future and guaranteed its place as "the greatest entertainment medium ever."[4] Altman, with his anti-genre projects, held very little back.

Disrupting Hollywood formula meant adding a new dimension to stories that revolved around men. Tackling a most masculine and ingrained narrative to find a strategy for speaking about social change in America was gutsy in *M*A*S*H*, the war genre, but necessary in the Western since women's liberation emerged as a national priority. To address the quest for women's equality honestly, Altman turned to the Western.

The Western could work as a treatise on social issues of gender if the hero were an incompetent but likeable businessman/gambler instead of a cowboy protector. Add a strong, independent businesswoman who knew the way to financial success better than anyone in town and the conversation about women's liberation could begin. In his 1971 experiment, *McCabe and Mrs. Miller*, Constance Miller (Julie Christie) meets John Quincy McCabe (Warren Beatty) and begins to deromanticize the magical West. As a strong feminist movement converged with antiwar protest, changes in gender roles became obvious, but the meaning Altman made of these shifts did not. Altman's work sheds light on the uncertainty men and women faced as they came to terms with the myriad controversies of their time. The result was a veritable treatise on men's and women's relations. *McCabe and Mrs. Miller* represents the pressures, accomplishments, and limitations in the gender debates at the beginning of the new decade.

While many men newly rejected conventional assumptions about manhood in the early 1970s, women turned to larger contests over authority and legitimacy. The women's movement emerged as a demand for equal rights with provisional alliances in the early stages, growing out of radical politics on and off campuses during the 1960s. Educated women rebelled against New Left organizations that restricted their participation in radical organizations. Women in Students for a Democratic Society and the Student Nonviolent Coordinating Committee, for example, suffered sexual stereotyping and discrimination and argued against the limited world of men's ideas about participatory democracy. While Americans protested the military and called for a more honest government, women in particular pointed to their own subjugation in radical advocates' organizations.[5] This gender gap represented the degree to which traditional hierarchies operated even in the most liberal spaces and, by comparison, provided the perfect symbol of larger, more difficult tasks ahead than war protest.

By the time *McCabe* was in production, radical advocacy for women's equal opportunity had made significant progress in mainstream arenas. As one study reported, where women's liberation during the 1960s "ha[d] virtually no impact on youth values and attitudes," just a few years later, a "wide and deep penetration of Women's Liberation precepts [was] underway."[6] Popular magazines such as *The Ladies' Home Journal* yielded to pressure and inserted feminist writings. In 1972 *New York Magazine* published forty pages of feminist articles, leading to *Ms. Magazine*, the first widely circulated popular feminist periodical. That year, Congress passed the Equal Rights Amendment and Title IX of the Education Act, opening new avenues for the equal rights discussion.[7] When *McCabe* hit theaters across the country following its release in 1971, the feminist movement to date developed its widest exposure and most dynamic influence.

Once unsettled by politics of the generation gap and campus radicalism, American society now found deeper tremors when women's liberation mutated into a debate about reproduction and the control of women's bodies. With a new political Right responding to Left politics, the issue of abortion and the Equal Rights Amendment dominated the women's movement. At the same time, the sexual revolution became a nationwide struggle. The birth control pill by the seventies was accessible and widely considered the contraception of choice, enabling defiance of dogmatic religious institutions. For young people the pill became "a tool of revolution." As historian Beth Bailey argues, youth "attempted to use sex as a weapon against 'straight' society." Youth, as the logic went, "celebrated sex as a 'natural' act that symbolized an alternative to materialism, capitalism, or the military-industrial complex." Young adults pressured college administrations to establish co-ed dorms where men and women could enjoy "relationships (including sexual) based on a common humanity."[8] On the popular front, Americans read *The Sensuous Woman, Everything You Always Wanted to Know About Sex but Were Afraid to Ask, The Joy of Sex*, and countless sex-advice articles in magazines such as *Cosmopolitan, Mademoiselle*, and *Redbook*.

Both feminism and the sexual revolution overlapped with the counterculture that had already professed free love in the late sixties and therefore deluged popular culture anew with sexual attitude and its connection to women's liberation. In Bailey's words, the sexual revolution defined an "emerging national culture."[9] Traditional morality was challenged in permanent ways.

The most private room, the bedroom, now symbolized the public state of men's and women's relations. Making the personal political brought the bed into the center of the pursuit for liberation. Women's issues became a multivoiced site for social change. Ideas about liberation flowed into and out of an everyday consumer culture that sold the image of uninhibited females and sexual suggestion as normal. Turning sex, the women's movement, and bedroom roles into a viable commodity gave one publication its cultural voice. The fashionable *Cosmopolitan* advocated that the sexes forever bid "farewell to prudishness and unreasonable taboos." Its popular editor, Helen Gurley Brown, determined sexual enlightenment, not sexual modesty, to be the sign of liberation for the 1970s. As one expert declared in a 1970 issue, "In a world where contraception, abortion, and divorce are legally accepted means of preventing or correcting errors, yesterday's sexual inhibitions seem inappropriate."[10] Brown, whom some called a female Hugh Hefner, turned her publication into a showcase on sexuality. She invited readers to "step into my parlor" and ask questions about "promiscuity," find answers about the "(hard won) sexual emancipation," and make comments about personal experiences. Readers found answers from sex therapists, from advice columnists, and in everyday stories.[11] The publication, largely geared to single, working women, turned gender strife into an education workshop on fashion, general sex appeal, and bedroom strategies.

If *Cosmo* and such recorded the different ways women and men addressed issues of sex, sensuality, and gender roles, film offered a unique opportunity to decide the shape and tone of women's liberation. In a post–Code environment, film turned the sexual revolution into the dominant story of change in the relations between men and women. Yet, in some ways, the challenge for film would be more difficult than the call for equal rights and sexual freedom. Film's visual discourse depended on images of men and women deeply embedded in American thinking. Men on screen were repeatedly defined by their tasks, work, abilities, and action. American movies typically defined women in terms of their relationship to those men in public roles. It made sense in film to declare women's independence by awarding action roles to females.

If women could unleash their resourcefulness, then maybe they could shed the shackles of Hollywood, too. Altman adjusted the lens for the Western to allow his film a chance to test a most challenging assertion. Adjusting a genre that was almost synonymous with America meant letting go of heroes revered for decades and detaching the West itself from a most masculine image. In other words, how might equality look on a woman in a Western without merely flipping the coin and putting a woman in a conventionally male role? While the genre was updated over time, the central concern was men's role in the West. Women figured in the Western as both the threat and the stability in the frontier process. Consequently, the Western offered few central roles for women. No woman has won an Oscar for a role in a Western. Julie Christie was at least nominated for her role in a genre that had extraordinary ability to be uniquely American, universal, and specifically male.

Similar to the women's movement at the time, the film's critical perspective recognized "that the notion of 'power' for a man is different from 'power' for a woman: it is acquired and manifested in different ways."[12] In the first sequences, to reverse this kind of typical dependency, *McCabe and Mrs. Miller* reinvents masculinity's tie to the frontier and sets the stage for an Altmanesque emancipation of Mrs. Miller. *McCabe* opens to the Warner Brothers logo and the sound of a high gale wind blowing across the Northwestern landscape of green foliage, pine trees, and rain. The film's signature ballad filters through the sound of blustery weather as the folk guitar of Leonard Cohen, a Canadian balladeer, introduces the film's perspective. The miners "were dealers," Cohen sings, kind of homeless creatures who sought "shelter" in the West for their deals.

As Cohen finishes the song about the wandering "Josephs," the camera brings Warren Beatty's character, John McCabe, into view. He wears a full-length muskrat fur coat, white dress shirt, and vintage suit and tie. A short distance from town, he prepares his entrance by sprucing up his clothes and putting on a black derby. As the ballad continues, McCabe rides on his horse in "Wall Street" attire, down muddy streets, across a suspended wooden bridge, and into the town of Presbyterian Church — the Northwestern destination named for "the tallest structure in town," as the production notes say.[13] He makes his entrance as the patriarchal dealer/Joseph who will become the small-town big shot in a thriving gambling enterprise.

The opening frames set the ironic tone of the film. Altman interrogates the frontier myth and, rather than building on a Fordianesque mystique of the West as a place of American progress, Altman highlights the flux in the turn-of-the-century West. The community of Presbyterian Church is not the steadfast, consummate settlement but part of "a thoroughly ambiguous process." The script explains, "The town ... was born in the early 1890s. It was never conceived, it just happened." As executive producer David Foster explained, the film would more closely mirror "the way [towns] grew" from "a tent under a tree for protection" to a mining camp to settlement.[14]

Once imagined as a place in which to perform the ethical act — the regeneration of America — the West in *McCabe and Mrs. Miller* is a chaotic frontier, a space where deception and cunning pay. Instead of the resourceful man of solitude in the context of a progressive American past that allowed men to settle wide, open spaces, making the way safe for democracy, the center of this Western's screen is an incompetent opportunist whose sole aim is making money. Reshaping the classic role of men in Westerns meant instigating their role as protectors of the town. In typical John Ford Westerns, for example, if men do their duty, the town survives the terror and the violence of the frontier. By performing acts of heroism and bravery, the central character confirms the noble role of the rugged individualist in the process of westward expansion. Altman casts this formula aside and suggests towns often could not sustain themselves and were not symbols of order. As the script explained, five years after McCabe arrived, the town died.[15] It never developed a main street, and buildings are half constructed. By the end of the film, the one constant in typical Westerns, the church, burns down. Instead of the rule of law, church, and family, money is the tie that binds. Zinc, whiskey, and prostitution hold each character to this place and, according to Altman authenticity, that's the way it probably was.

Easily enough, the film destabilizes the most enduring element in the genre, the West itself. Dank exteriors and dark interiors replace dusty, sunny deserts. A rainy, cold Northwest brings the realism of "smelly shacks and stinking mudholes of the mining town," as the production notes described the setting. The sepia-toned visuals portray an unfinished frontier with less than glamorous characters. Altman-style dialogue offers the "here and nowness" and confirms that things had changed for America. Actors donned rough-hewn wardrobes with dirty flannel shirts and well-worn suspenders. Muddy boots and calloused hands deromanticized the characters. If the film was to be real and meaningful, it had to show "cold air coming out of the characters' mouths," the miners' unkempt long johns, and the girls' patched petticoats.[16]

Shooting on location in the Northwest near the Washington State–Canada border and insisting that cast and crew live like the story, Altman drove home that the West was also about the cold and uninviting surroundings experienced by many but generally absent from iconic imagery in American popular culture. As the production notes explained, everyone, including "the carpenters, plumbers, brick-masons, road-builders ... lived in places they built themselves." Not only would the entire crew understand the story, it would feel the frontier "way of life long before the picture started." Altman's three-dimensional style direction made the actor/citizen "completely at ease among the mudholes, donkeys, pigs, goats, chickens and zinc mines."[17] Lest the promotion for this film suffer, however, marketers had to exploit frontier iconography to sell "anti–Western" revisionism. Who would want to see dirty miners when *Butch Cassidy and the Sundance Kid* was quickly becoming a legend? Promoters had people dress in "western" costume while handing ticket holders mock shares of a mining stock promising the bearer a fortune. The handbills for Pacific Pantage Theater in Hollywood read, "100 dollars in zinc ore." These certificates showed the path to opportunity with Warren Beatty and Julie Christie on Warner Brothers' publicity poster selling the turn-of-the-century Northwest. It was a place where one could get "plenty of good hootch" and find "honest gambling tables, a steaming twenty-five cent bath and a turned-on sporting house." Warner's offered viewers a walk into "way back when," to show that "things were simpler then." This "campy nostalgia" playfully eased viewers into a critique of westward expansion.[18]

The story begs for a heroic individual to lift the town from hardship and misery. For a few sequences, it looks like that man might be John McCabe, but in the spirit of revisionism, Altman next re-casts the image of masculinity. Altman's *M*A*S*H*, which played during the production of *McCabe*, had already introduced two Hollywood newcomers, Elliott Gould as Trapper John and Donald Sutherland as Hawkeye Pierce, capturing the younger generation's interest in a persona analogous to an "urban Everyman," or as one writer put it, "today's ... she-he man" not the burly "he-man."[19] Trapper and Hawkeye's enduring personae gave credence to the anti-genre and prepared the screen for *McCabe*. Altman's *M*A*S*H* grounded his authority to buck the system and question whether the rugged individualist with the seductive leathery face is the proper symbol of American masculinity.

John McCabe, the man who needs money, is hardly visible. He wears a scruffy beard and is cast in shadows until he promenades past the unkempt miners who watch excitedly as they try to discern his identity. He carries "an impressive handgun"—"it was huge," one of the townsmen exclaims. The sexual innuendo allows viewers to laugh at the Western's fetishization of guns as an icon of masculinity and begins the film's task of reinventing the American male.

In keeping with the frontier town's image as the place where "lusty workers ... stomped into town on Saturday night looking to tie one on," John McCabe's first stop is the saloon.[20] Once inside the town saloon, John collects a crowd for a poker game. The "suckers," as the script describes the townsmen, fight for the chance to sit next to McCabe, and he begins his hustle. Men engage in side conversations and mythologize his identity. "Man's got a big rep, boys," Patrick Sheehan, the saloon owner, interjects. "Gentlemen," he continues, "the dealer is none other than John McCabe ... the man who shot Bill Roundtree."[21] Sheehan approaches McCabe to confirm the story, "You Pudgy McCabe? The gunfighter?" Sheehan asks. "Business man — business man," McCabe answers. "The one who killed Bill Roundtree?" Sheehan prods. McCabe mumbles, "The very same." Presbyterian Church now claims authority with the gambler with a rep, even if most of the men had never heard of Bill Roundtree. If Sheehan says so, the "legend" must be valid. With their new man of renown in town, men spin the gunfighter's story. "*I* knew him," one boasted. The patrons are among the privileged and when John McCabe raises the poker stakes, he easily dominates the games.

With his winnings, he travels to nearby Bear Paw, a more settled town, to purchase prostitutes for his new business in Presbyterian Church.[22] He barters for the women, like livestock. "Eighty dollars a chippie? I can get a goddamn horse for fifty dollars," he tells the trader. He works out a deal and buys three ladies, one who is toothless, another who is obese, and a third who is a psychotic teenager. Back in Presbyterian Church, these "sisters of mercy," as the film's song intimates, perform their transactions in a row of tents since McCabe has opened his business before building a bordello.

To this point Presbyterian Church is a man's town. Opening the genre to women begins by reversing the typical entrance into town. Instead of the decorative stage-coach, Mrs. Constance Miller crosses the threshold in the front seat of Webster's Sawmill steam-engine: "flippin' contraption," as she calls it. After a six-hour trip, she steps into Presbyterian mud in Western style and takes center stage. At a cursory glance, Constance Miller appears to be typical — a genteel lady forced into the harsh living conditions of the Northwest. She wears a velvety Victorian cape, feathered hat, and gloves. Men help her down from the wagon. The camera follows her as if promising a glimpse of her beauty but purposely avoids the beauty and zooms in on the muddy pathways she will have to negotiate by herself.

Independently, she seeks out John McCabe, the town businessman. "You John McCabe?" she approaches him. "Mrs. Miller," she reaches out to shake his hand and informs him, "come from Bear Paw to see you." Startled by her forceful demeanor, he stares at her, chews on his cigar, and watches her walk to his unfinished bordello. "This your place?" she asks. "Yes, ma'am," he answers, still puzzled by her abruptness. At the construction site, she gazes through the wood frames to tent-city and watches one of McCabe's girls carry laundry water to a campfire. Her simple glance at oppressive and offensive working and living conditions indicts McCabe as a victimizer of women and pushes the film into its treatise on women's issues. Calculating her next move, Mrs. Miller turns to McCabe and tells him, "I'm bloody starving."

The two walk to Sheehan's saloon. She sits across from McCabe, lights a cigarette, and orders "four eggs fried, some stew and ... some strong tea." McCabe expects a bit of flirting but is stunned when Mrs. Miller insults him, "Hey, you know if you want ta' make out you're such a fancy dude, you ought to wear something besides that cheap Jockey Club cologne." He is taken aback, perplexed, hurt, and humored. The camera frames Mrs. Miller

John McCabe (Warren Beatty), local gambler and businessman, greets Mrs. Constance Miller (Julie Christie) on the muddy streets of Presbyterian Church and is about to learn of women's rights on the frontier in *McCabe and Mrs. Miller* (1971)(Photofest).

in close-ups, alternating between her hands stuffing her mouth, dipping her bread in runny egg yolks and her cheeks bulging with food. The camera slowly zooms in and shows McCabe staring at Mrs. Miller's mouth and hands as she overindulges in her meal. She leans across the table, looks him straight in the eyes, and unequivocally announces, "Listen, Mr. McCabe, I'm a whore and I know if you had a house up here you stand to make yourself a lot of money." Her manly language stuns McCabe. He is now her captive audience.

Warren Beatty as John McCabe expects to flirt with Julie Christie as Mrs. Miller but finds something different when she lights up and destroys his illusion of what women should be in *McCabe and Mrs. Miller* (1971)(Photofest).

Feminist consciousness raising of the 1970s challenged the notion of women's dependence on men for survival and especially questioned women's subjection to the value of "dress[ing] decoratively, look[ing] attractive, be[ing] compliant." If they were to enjoy any power, feminists argued, women had to ask serious questions about the "overattention to appearance." Some believed women's stress on "overcorrectness and overgentility of speech and etiquette" were both "merely the result of being forced to exist only as a reflection in the eyes of others." The walk to Sheehan's saloon and the eating scene establish the film's ideological stance by attempting to define Mrs. Miller against the conventional habit of assessing women's worth by "the impression she makes upon others."[23] If women's validity depended on appearance alone, then Mrs. Miller denies others the right to decide who she is by challenging conventional expectations of lady-ness and the meaning of velvet clothes.

Just as feminists alleged that sexual liberation contained its own objectification, Mrs. Miller challenges Hollywood at its center. The restaurant scene establishes her authority to reject "appearance" dependency. She controls and owns her subjectivity by demanding that McCabe first recognize her power to speak intelligently and assertively, making it clear from the beginning that she is different from the women portrayed in typical Westerns.

Mr. McCabe has no answer for her everything-you-always-wanted-to-know-about-running-a-whorehouse-but-were-afraid-to-ask list. "What do you do when one fancies another?" Miller asks. "How do you know when a girl really has a monthly or when she's just takin' a few days off? What about when they don't get their monthlies, 'cause they don't? What do you do then ... what about when business is slow? You gonna let the girls sit around on their bums?" In this West, she speaks. John listens. Still he takes a stand. "What makes you think I ain't thought of that already? Them tents, that's just temporary," he defends himself. But Mrs. Miller is the expert and McCabe the novice. She presses, "Do we have a deal or don't we?"

She cleverly wagers a fifty/fifty partnership and begins the clean-up. Under her rules, the "filthy and unshaven" men must install a bathhouse because the bath is mandatory before anyone visits the bordello. The "sportin' whorehouse" completes the town's center and Mrs. Miller reigns as madam of Presbyterian Church.[24] McCabe's fantasies about his future success have been refined, defined, and redirected. Mrs. Miller's business sense reveals McCabe's foolish notions about women's capabilities. He becomes defensive and arrogant as he later spars with the men about who is in charge. The more successful Julie Christie's character becomes, the more exaggeratedly male Beatty's appears. Just after the partnership agreement, for example, John McCabe is alone and sorts out what Mrs. Miller's proposal means. He complains about the imposition of Mrs. Miller's list of demands for a successful business. "Shit, I ain't takin' no goddamn bath; I don't give a shit if I...." McCabe belches, grunts, drinks a shot, and belches again.

The men construct the bathhouse and grumble about the new policy—"I can't imagine nobody paying no 25 cents for a goddamn bath." McCabe inspects the site. In a kind of "locker-room" moment, a buddy jests, "Hey, McCabe, why don't you go ask Mrs. Miller when the new whores are comin' into town?" McCabe refuses to defer, "You think I'm gonna listen to some goddamn chippie come up here and tell me how to run a gooseberry ranch? You got the goddamn saddle on the wrong horse. Them girls will come up here when I goddamn tell them to." With these new demands, the narrative shifts from McCabe, the man with a "rep," to McCabe the fool or, as his one-liner goes, the frog who "bump[s] his ass so much." By now, all the men, including McCabe, accept that Mrs. Miller, the businesswoman, is legitimate.

Juxtaposed with the "locker room" scene, McCabe courts Mrs. Miller. Standing outside Mrs. Miller's door in the damp night, he entreats her to let him enter. Instead, she makes him stay outside in the cold and speak through the door. Man has a right to know when the girls are arriving, he says. "Paid for them, the transportation; you think I'm nothing but a bank," he whines. Aloof, Mrs. Miller lets him ramble, ignores his plea, and enjoys the comfort of a warm, incandescent bedroom.

This film, like feminist speeches and treatises, argues for equality and change of social roles by adding a woman's voice to historical narratives. Imagining a woman in stories traditionally dominated by male characters, it was hoped, would change the status of women by showing what female authority would be like. Constance Miller smoking a cigarette at

Sheehan's saloon, placed within a frontier setting, brings her inside the Western formula and defines her agency, but how successful Altman's smart madam could be was limited if McCabe, like the larger society, denied what placing women on equal footing really meant.

The feminist standing of *McCabe* rests on accomplishing what Joan Scott argued history should do, that is, impart "not just new information but new knowledge—another way of seeing and understanding what counted as history." Including women's capabilities and strengths to encourage positive portrayals, as Scott explained, simply "to establish ... women's presences" was not enough. Advocacy must show "their active participation in the events that were seen to constitute history." Women's "emancipation," Scott continued, "might be advanced by making them visible in narratives of social struggle and political achievement."[25] If Altman's movie can be considered a treatise on women's social struggle and if American cinema at the time provided a place for advocacy, then it is worth asking how Constance's presence in this narrative advanced women's call for equality. Inviting the viewer to imagine liberation meant de-gendering Hollywood and reversing a century-long history of cinematic representation of conventionally perceived women. If feminism's aim was to expand options open to women and if Altman's story could show the same, how exactly does Mrs. Miller expand that scenario?

The first sequences redirect the understanding of women by demythologizing the spectacle in female representation while not forsaking the power in a sexual, feminine appeal. The early scenes establish the reality of attraction. Close-ups of her beautiful face, lovely hair, and piercing eyes alternate with shots of her cheeks bulging with eggs. These combined images show she is both real and conventionally attractive. The camera frames Mrs. Miller in radiant light against a dark saloon to bring attractiveness in line with her power to speak intelligently and convincingly. She conveys experience and redefines rather than diffuses the power in beauty. By centralizing a woman's perspective in the narrative and defining work within female experience, she determines her subjectivity; she speaks for herself. She is attractive, capable, and focused.

Striking a deal with John McCabe allows her autonomy. She does not just work at the bordello but transforms the work environment. She recruits more sophisticated prostitutes from Seattle than those women McCabe bought earlier at Bear Paw. Together these women improve their workplace and exude dignity as employees. Mrs. Miller teaches women in this frontier to enjoy playful romances, dance to the sounds of the gramophone, and even celebrate birthdays. Accordingly, Mrs. Miller gentrifies prostitution by creating beautiful interiors and outfitting her women in attractive clothing. Velvet draperies glow in soft, golden lighting. A homey oasis compared to McCabe's tent row, Miller's house provides the town with warmth and a protection against the ravaging, cold winter. Yet lest they appear too "wifely," these women also swear with men, actively enjoy sex, and otherwise are neither innocent nor remorseful. They are attractive but not overly glamorous. Here, sex is a lucrative business, a form of female authority, and a means of negotiating social power. Altmanesque realism is not forsaken.

Altman positions Mrs. Miller with the voices of those who questioned the taken-for-grantedness of sexual roles in conventional marriage. In the script, for example, McCabe touches the wedding band on her finger and asks, "What about your old man?" She answers, "I don't have one. I just wear this to be respectable."[26] The film does not include this short scene. There are no heart-to-heart conversations between John and Constance about her "old man." The filmmaker lets the viewers fill in the missing pieces in her history, but within the ironic tone of the narrative, her demand to be addressed as *Mrs.* mocks the significance of marriage as a sign of respectability. Another moment advancing the idea of women's self-determination, for example, comes poignantly into view when a newly married couple in the film is split by the husband's untimely death. Bart Coyle (Bert Remsen), a miner who married mail-order bride Ida (Shelley Duvall), dies in a brawl. At Bart's funeral, miners, prostitutes, and entrepreneurs join in typical fellowship, singing "Asleep in Jesus." There, Mrs. Miller and Ida make eye contact.

Later, in a job orientation of sorts, Ida discovers her potential as a single woman. Mrs. Miller trains her prospective employee and outfits her with proper clothes. They share a moment of tenderness. "Well, it just hurts so much," Ida tells Mrs. Miller. Constance advises, however, "You just got to take your mind off it. Think of something else. Look at the wall, count the roses in the wallpaper.... See, the thing is it don't mean nothing.... I mean, you managed it with Bart, didn't ya?" Ida replies, "I had to. It was my duty." Constance responds, "It wasn't your duty, Ida. You did it to pay for your bed and board. You do this to pay for your bed and board, too." With Mrs. Miller's matter-of-fact style of independence, the film allows the narrative to support the feminist agenda of sexual freedom. The confident madam not only questions the assumptions underlying the institution of marriage but also subverts its prominence in women's lives.

Discursively, Mrs. Miller represents the popular argument at the time that intercourse outside of marriage is an important part of women's liberation. A *Cosmopolitan* type of assertion, sexual freedom was a way for women to challenge patriarchy's dependence on the conventional marriage model. Mrs. Miller, like Helen Gurley Brown, offers to reshape women's social identity. They both walk into virgin territory and begin the process of reconstruction. A half-built town allows Mrs. Miller a fair chance to create an additional business that will help determine the town's social structure. Rather than the sheriff's office as the central location of action in *McCabe*, it will be the saloon and bordello. Sexuality with dignity establishes the "house's" "civic" importance.

With new freedoms of sexuality in popular culture, however, a more complex issue concerned feminists. How discrimination based on sexual difference explained women's oppression was clear enough. Yet, as advocates argued, sexual promiscuity as the liberating feature of women's lives seemed to be another way to recycle the "dominant-submissive relationship." Sex outside of marriage looked surprisingly like the "sex class system" which kept women as receivers and men as actors. Assumptions about women's sexuality were still stuck in the belief that women had an obligation to satisfy men rather than the freedom to find sex "an expression of her general humanity."[27]

Mrs. Miller's job-training session raises Ida's consciousness to these false assumptions. Obligatory sex in or outside marriage was just legalized prostitution. At least Constance made it possible for women to be paid for their labor. Thus, visualizing prostitution with a new frankness allowed the narrative to comment on the politics of the bedroom to a certain point. As countless manifestoes claimed by the time of the film's release, opening the bedroom for public debate took women's liberation beyond equal opportunity of the 1960s and exposed points of incongruity in the feminist movement and a *Cosmopolitan*-style liberation in general. Both popular and intellectual culture needed to address an incongruity. As one manifesto argued, if "love and sex" were the "emotional cement" for "dominant-submissive relationships," then the bedroom also functioned as a space of "control" rather than for "the growth of another."[28] With the sexual revolution looking like a step toward women's equality, the inhibiting features of sex as a forum for liberation surfaced. Where some women found newly-claimed rights to sexual pleasure a revolutionizing proof of independence, others pointed to its exploitative aspects. Between the joy and rage over what constituted liberation, feminists insisted that women beware of a new subjugation.

In the context of feminist caution, the question of commodification arises in *McCabe and Mrs. Miller*'s use of prostitution as the film's way to imagine female freedom from convention. The complex issues of power had to be addressed. Like the early stages of women's liberation, Altman's film gives women access to men's language and signals a common assumption about female emancipation — that the standard of freedom is masculinity. Altman offers Mrs. Miller a way in by relaxing the taboos against women's speech. The argument claims that a gap between men's and women's speech directly related to women's lack of power in the public sphere. Expecting proper forms of speaking from women and allowing strong expression to men pointed to a form of "linguistic sexism" that "submerge[d] a woman's personal identity" while predetermining her social value and limiting her choices. To address this "lexical disparity," popular culture portrayed women speaking men's language. If speaking the language of the dominant group changed deeply embedded values that prevented women from political and entrepreneurial success and could equalize vanity as the same mark of distinction for women as men, then why not start with cursing?[29]

Mrs. Miller negotiates new terms of condition with John McCabe by intruding into the men's saloon. She symbolizes the moment in history when the implications of men's public control and dominance surfaced as gender discrimination. In the larger society, it became increasingly clear that neither inserting women's voices into history nor making demands of sexual freedom would automatically lead to social equality or personal empowerment.

McCabe and Mrs. Miller questions traditional and gendered spheres by awarding Mrs. Miller a pragmatic resourcefulness typically reserved for men. The film creates a capable woman for its central character in a genre about men and in her construction as a woman. This film's negotiation of that narrative space reveals the challenge for women. Constance's leadership gives her the chance to speak confidently for equal treatment. She is an agent in this narrative. It is her business to protect and manage women. Ultimately, however, while being their advocate on the one hand, Mrs. Miller is their captor on the other.

For all of Constance Miller's independence, prostitution as a form of women's (especially Ida's) security and therefore the means to liberation ironically reinforces typical male/female division. A means to independence, prostitution is at the same time a form of dependence. The narrative mirrors the early stage of the feminist movement, just as feminists realized the connection between sexual liberation and the reproduction of sex-centered representations of gender. Had women really gotten very far cinematically when they still appeared in very limited roles, some were asking?[30]

The film accomplished its task of deconstructing the paradigm of marriage in similar ways as *The Graduate* and *Alice's Restaurant* by representing the church, once a sacred stronghold, as inoperable. Typically, many Westerns respected the place of the church in the frontier town. In *McCabe*, the town minister, Mr. Elliott (Corey Fischer), literally has no voice throughout the story. The scene with Ida and the half-built church shows a building without people or pulpit and a preacher who roams without direction and purpose, in and out of the saloon and along the muddy streets. The townspeople, not the reverend, conducted funeral ceremonies at the gravesite for Ida's husband.

Taking up the task of feminism would be limited in this film to Constance Miller's portrayal as a smart businesswoman. From there, the narrative turns to a traditional love story. In the logic of romance, an independent woman and a mediocre businessman find their magnetic pull when financiers from Harrison-Shaugnessy offer to buy the town businesses. Pulling their resources together, they come up with their own wagers, but McCabe holds out for more money. Eager to share the story with Constance, he surprises her with a bouquet of flowers. Proud of his courage to up the ante and assuming the role of typical hero, McCabe struts in front of Constance, but she quickly trumps his glory. "Well, you just better hope they come back; [they'd] as soon put a bullet in your back as look at you," she warns him, but she is high on opium and so smiles seductively at McCabe. They engage in the most romantic moment of the film. "You're a funny little thing," he smiles at her. "I'm tellin' ya you're just as sweet ..." but lest he gets too secure, she smiles mischievously and playfully reminds him he has to pay before he gets into bed. He counts out the money and they make love. This scene confirms that he will stay with Constance at his expense.

In Mrs. Miller's space, he defers to her in exchange for intimacy and romance. As one critic put it, "McCabe needs Mrs. Miller to do more than balance his books, for he comes to love her deeply."[31] McCabe's terms of endearment, however, redirect Mrs. Miller's purpose, and from this point on change her from an independent entrepreneur to a fretting lover, overprotective of McCabe. Following their night of intimacy, she storms into the saloon, interrupts McCabe's poker game, and reprimands him. "Now I'm your partner and you gotta listen to me. What're ya plannin' to do about them boys up there?" she questions. McCabe is curt with her and offhandedly remarks, "I'm gonna make a deal with them.... If they won't make a deal ... I'll just have a drink," he condescends. Casting aside her concerns, McCabe continues, "I appreciate your worrying about me; I appreciate that protection; but there's nothin' to be scared of." He then turns on his charm and proudly explains, "Tell you the truth ... I feel sorry for 'em. They old guffers been workin' the company twenty years ... hell, when they come up side a mule like me, I feel sorry for 'em ... tell you the truth I do ... I know what I'm doing." Irritated with his naiveté, Constance recognizes her loss and is heartbroken. She looks pleadingly toward McCabe, hoping to convince him of his gamble. "They get paid for killin,' nothing else," she adamantly warns him about the Harrison-Shaugnessy bounty hunters. McCabe departs and the camera zooms to an extreme close-up of Mrs. Miller's cheerless desperation.

In the privacy of his quarters, McCabe stands in front of a mirror, straightens his top hat, pours a drink, and adjusts his image. He engages in a monologue proclaiming his love for Constance: "God, I hate when the bastards put their hands on ya. Sometimes when I take a look at you; I just keep a lookin' and a lookin'; see your little body up against me so bad I think I'm a gonna bust." Complaining about her insensitivity, he says, "I keep tryin' ta tell ya in a lot of different ways just one time you could be sweet without no money around." He is the romantic one. "Well, I tell ya something," he proclaims, "I got poetry in me. I do. I got poetry in me but I ain't gonna put it down on paper." He prefers his rational, pragmatic, and intelligent side to the poetic, despite the fact that he "ain't no educated man." Her determination is his infirmity. "I got sense in me.... If there's just one time, let me run the show I — you're just freezin' my soul, that's what you're doin,' freezin my soul." Regaining his poise, he admonishes, "Well, shit, enjoy yourself girl; just go ahead and have a time; what the hell." McCabe's romantic declaration of love ends by depersonalizing Constance. "It's just my luck — the only woman that's ever been one to me ain't nothin' but a whore, but what the hell; I never was a percentage man. I suppose a whore is the only kind of woman I know." McCabe rationalizes his ineptness and projects it onto the woman who freezes souls and "ain't nothin' but a whore."

Determined to declare if not restore his masculinity, McCabe visits Mrs. Miller and lets her in on his wisdom, "Comes a time in every man's life when he just got to stick his hand in the fire and see what he's made of." Annoyed with this romantic notion of himself, Constance berates him, "What're you talkin' about?" True to McCabean idealism, he reminds her of his heroic wager and informs her, "I'm talkin' about bustin' up these trusts of monopoly, that's what I'm talkin about. Somebody's got to protect the small businessman from these big companies and I'm gonna be the man.... I know it don't mean nothin' to ya' but I got a reputation in this town." She cries back, "They'll get you, McCabe. They'll get you and they'll do something to you" and sobs quietly in front of him. He is touched by her emotional flare-up and runs to her side. "Now, now little lady, ain't nothing gonna happen to me," but Constance is not a fool nor does she accept the bait of McCabe's self-image as a tough operative. She enjoys the spar. "Don't you give me any of that little lady shit. I don't care about you. Just give me my $1500.... If you're not gonna make a deal with them, then I'll make a deal with 'em."

Yet, her assertion is an act of desperation more than conviction. The two exchange words in Mrs. Miller's kitchen while she is cooking for and serving McCabe. "Eat your meal," she tells him and sets the food down. He partakes of his final dinner. This scene reverses the original saloon sequence where she downs the eggs, makes McCabe the offer, and walks away as an equal in a potentially lucrative business. This scene thwarts her competence and function as a partner for profit. She no longer has a voice in the partnership.

The film encourages viewer identification with an intelligent and independent female until the narrative makes her McCabe's helpmate and returns to a critique of the Western through the bounty hunters. Three assassins infiltrate the town to murder McCabe. The powerful mining company sends Dog Butler (Hugh Millais), a six-foot-six-inch Englishman; Breed (Alexander Diakun), a Russian-Canadian; and seventeen-year-old Kid (Manfred Shultz) to take over the bordello and saloon.[32] Dog and Breed are classic figures of the Western — handsome, tall, strong, quiet, steely-eyed, and professionals at their job. They serve to comment on the logical conclusion of conventional violence portrayed in countless Westerns. Through them, the film challenges the accepted association of firearms with masculinity.

Altman critiques both the ideal and the irony in social form of masculine violence via the film's most macabre scene. The seventeen-year-old Kid eagerly practices quick-draw heroism by staging a shootout. He challenges an endearing visitor, Shorty (Keith Carradine), who stops by the town for a night of fun. After having become one of the women's favorites, Shorty leaves the bordello and the women bid him come back soon. "Goodbye, cowboy," they wave, and Shorty steps onto the bridge where Kid fires several shots at a whiskey jug. "Hold up on your target practice a minute," Shorty yells in a friendly manner. The blond Kid, eager to test his competence as a novice gunman, walks toward Shorty in standoff style. After several words, Shorty realizes the danger and retreats, but Kid is hell-bent on continuing this game: "What're you wearin' that gun for?" His "Colt," Shorty explains, is for show because he "just can't shoot good."

The all–American Kid bullies him into pulling the gun out of the holster and, as Shorty reaches to show it off, Kid shoots him in cold blood. Shorty dies, falls into the icy river below, and Kid walks away, proud of his skill as a straight shooter. Kid has contrived a standoff with an innocent traveler and serves as the narrative's critique of the source of violence in American society. The gruesome act critiques Hollywood's complicity in the dis-cursive circulation of shootouts and assumptions about a man's privilege to display his prowess as a gunfighter. The film stays consistent with its task of deflating icons of the Western, for Kid's action astounds even the professional assassins.

In its deconstruction of the Western's brand of violence, the narrative now switches to the charming lover, McCabe. The film argues that the real violence in American society is still the destructive forces of international corporations. "I'm talking about bustin' up these trusts and monopolies," McCabe promises Constance and so begins a shootout of his own. "Man is fool enough to go into business with a woman," he complains, "she ain't gonna think much of him." He chastises himself and validates gun power over verbal negotiation. Turn-ing to the real business ahead, he confronts the three Harrison-Shaugnessy hit men. McCabe kills Kid first; then Breed. Dog, the toughest and most cunning assassin — the out-of-date icon of violence — chases and shoots McCabe in the back. Tracking his victim to make sure he is dead, Dog gets it in the head when McCabe musters his last bit of strength and shoots him dead center.

Pudgy McCabe is convincingly portrayed as an attractive, charming lover and now a skilled and calculating straight shot in this classic standoff. McCabe kills all three assassins and dies in this fight, but he leaves a legacy of skill after he proclaims his love for Mrs. Miller. As one critic aptly recognized, "What he defends, at bottom, is the purity of his own image ... to state what he is." McCabe, therefore, is "a genuine candidate for the role of traditional hero."[33] John McCabe shoulders no burden as protector of the town like Sheriff Wills in Zin-nemann's *High Noon*, but he does defend his personal investment. All three bad guys are dead. The gunfight gains audience sympathy because of the romantic connection to his role as pro-tector of the little guy, even if McCabe lies outside, frozen like a marble statue in several feet of snow. His image fades against the sound of the same howling winds as brought him into the picture in the first place.

Mrs. Miller refuses to watch her lover die. Consequently, she accepts his fate and seeks the Chinese opium den for shelter. McCabe leaves the Western icon-less and suggests that women best carry on the narrative and the tradition. The ending seems to empower women since it refuses to move a traditionally masculine genre forward. The camera zooms into an extreme close-up of her face where she lies inside the opium den. In controlled zoom toward her eye, the camera forces itself inside and ends on magnified, jittery blood vessels and finally shows only the white of her eye, used as a background for the rolling, black lettered credits. Her behavior betrays her words that all she wanted was to protect her profits. She is left painfully alone at the end of the film, having lost her security and authority. The film has moved through her into a blank silence, the point of mirage. She is voiceless and isolated from both lover and community of women. She is confined to the interior space of her emo-tions and divested of agency.

The film's revisionist intent slips by the end into ambiguity except that the film actually confirms the moral center of frontier order, the central part of classic Western formula.[34] The insistent hostility toward progress and mining conglomerates coupled with the townspeople as victims substantiates old-type Westerns.[35] This stylized genre picture, sold as a Western, became its own burden. If men were to make sense of and even embrace feminism, address-ing the Hollywood stronghold was a place to begin, but Altman's film relinquished its posi-tion as a voice for female oppression because power and authority were still defined through men in battle.

McCabe softened the burden of the individualist hero cowboy as a representative of America and quashed the use of the West as the ethical space in American narratives. Through its "counter-aesthetics" of landscape and real people, the narrative parodies the over-used image of masculinity in classic Westerns. This strategy worked as what Laura Mulvey calls "a motor force," a boost to push a more serious issue forward.[36] If this film is about the power of the female and her skill as a resourceful businesswoman, it is as much about coming to terms with the changing images of masculinity. The "little-guy" standoff displaces Mrs. Miller and brings McCabe into the center. The ending reinforces the tie between men and physical power. He saves and is saved.[37]

The ending erases McCabe's earlier image as victimizer of women but also presents the film's ambiguity. If he is a genuine helper of the victim despite his tent row, then Mrs. Miller's plea to him to accept the mining company's bargain redefines her as his opposite. Certainly, his winter shootout saves Mrs. Miller from the henchmen but not the town from Harrison-Shaugnessy. The Western as a site for questioning gender relations ends in paradox. It was easy enough to stylize the setting and let women curse on screen, but opening the space wider for gender disputes once again proved more challenging, even to the iconoclast Altman. Placing men and women together, in partnership in a man's genre, only to lay the latter quietly aside, denies subversion its full power.

At the same time, released in the early seventies, it makes sense that the film would grapple with the same contradictions present in the women's movement. Claiming and legitimizing female subjectivity and calling for gender equality had to begin with imagining women as central characters in traditional male narratives. Adjusting the boundaries was a first step toward declaring women's experience legitimate; women as history-makers was part of the logic in feminism. It assumed that adding positive roles for women in society would lead to the social construction of more even social relations. Certainly this period of "utopian optimism," as Laura Mulvey characterized the early 1970s, sparked the imagination and widened the possibilities for women's agency. Robert Altman contributed to the call for women's liberation through the portrayal of an astute businesswoman who challenged the certainty of the male gaze. Ultimately, however, fitting the formula with a new face ignores the discursive processes — the narrative dependence on men as active and women as passive — by which the genre is constructed in the first place.[38]

McCabe and Mrs. Miller is one "engraving" in the cinematic history of "Now Movie" experimentation. Altman's film, some thought, proved that America had answered the Europeans' art-cinema with a director of its own. If others had not filled the shoes of the "Bergmans and Fellinis," *The New Yorker* claimed, Altman did with this film. "Here is an American artist who has made a beautiful film," the writer declared. Altman's product corroborated claims of film art for mainstream audiences, but even the pundits wondered, "Will enough people buy tickets?"[39] Julie Christie's Academy Award nomination for her role as the entrepreneurial madam, two years after John Wayne walked away with his Oscar for best actor in *True Grit*, seemed to mark a turning point for women, but Mrs. Miller lost the contest to Jane Fonda (another prostitute) in *Klute*. A traditional story that was released a day after *McCabe*, *Klute* brings a brash Fonda in line with a glamorous sexuality and shows female bodies parading across the cinematic screen in red lipstick, black leather, and high spikey boots.

McCabe's relative failure at the box offices confirmed the public's disinterestedness in Altman's most compassionate attempt to reconstruct the cinematic past. *McCabe and Mrs. Miller* stands as a record of what was possible for women in film of the 1970s. The picture gave power and authority to Mrs. Miller but risked commodifying her jovial prostitutes. As feminists sought changes in social norms that exercised control over women's behavior and choices, filmmakers continued their quest of consciousness raising, but for the most part, directors speaking for and representing women were still men. As feminist film critic Teresa de Lauretis argued, women have rarely represented themselves as subjects, nor have "images and subjectivities — until very recently, if at all —... been ours to shape, to portray, or to create."[40]

This aesthetic integration of changes in attitudes and lifestyle abetted the cultural revolution of the seventies to the point that it was possible. Film helped define the shift in cultural authority from an earlier time when local communities, churches, families and other traditional institutions played a more significant role in determining sexuality and gender roles than popular culture of the 1970s. Movies provided an omnipresent source of reaffirming or adjusting perceptions in a broad way.[41] It took another decade for feminism itself to recognize its own limitations and for filmmakers to find new strategies in the struggle for liberation on screen.

Vibrant writing, advocacy, and public organizing undoubtedly forced filmmakers to rethink female roles. Altman's picture commented on the space women might occupy in that story. Just as academics talked about the politics of the image and the role of cinema as an apparatus, a social technology, filmmakers experimented with their art for the mainstream screen and attempted to redefine convention in contemporary terms. These cultural stirrings brought to film a new political dimension. Defining gender roles during this time offered exceptional possibility for the film industry's growth, as Mike Nichols discovered with the controversial and gutsy film *Carnal Knowledge*. A bit more seasoned since *The Graduate*, Nichols collaborated with cartoonist Jules Feiffer to experiment with a gender-conscious society, bringing harsh language and portrayals to the screen forcefully and energetically. If experimentation in a conventional industry were to mean anything, Nichols' film would be the test.

CHAPTER IX

What's Sex Got to Do with It?

Carnal Knowledge and the Delusion
of Telling It Like It Is

And I found myself nostalgic for a period in my life that I absolutely hated. But I wasn't nostalgic for my real past. I was nostalgic for my MGM past, the past that, on Saturday afternoons back in the forties, I saw as my future, which took me out of the East Bronx and into these incredible movie mansions, the real life duplicate of which I have seen only once — at Hugh Heffner's house in Chicago. Because he saw the same movies I did and had it built according to specifications.
— Jules Feiffer's Speech at YMHA

Lights, camera, action. A beautiful co-ed walks into a college party. Tommy Dorsey's "I'm Getting Sentimental Over You" plays in the background, and screenwriter Jules Feiffer tears up and yearns for the Andy Hardy days of fantasy, illusion, and dreamy Saturday afternoon visions of women. Then, cut. It is September 1970. Feiffer is watching his screenplay transformed into what will become a controversial film — loved, hated, banned, and placed on the top-ten best films list. Amidst the sexual revolution, the generation gap, and political upheaval, the New York cartoonist and Old Left socialist finds himself immersed in the then and now on the *Carnal Knowledge* set with director Mike Nichols and crew.

The East Bronx native sent his script intended for the stage to Nichols in the late sixties, but when the director read the play, he saw a film. After a year of negotiations, Feiffer's original "True Confessions" became Mike Nichols' *Carnal Knowledge*. The project began and ended with substantial paring down but few major changes in theme. Feiffer's screenplay did not betray his two basic premises: that the truth of men's and women's relationships is that "men really don't like women" and that the likes of MGM had gotten it wrong for decades. With those two perspectives untouched, as Nichols explained, the script was "essentially the same work with the same spine and soul."[1]

Carnal Knowledge is a meeting of the generations — the middle-aged director and writer — and the newcomers, boomers more than ten years younger. Certainly the two groups joined in mocking the romantic tradition of movie telling. Yet Feiffer was no advocate of the sexual revolution, boomer style. Instead, he cynically pointed to the failure in the sixties' sexual revolution and the seventies' discourse on gender and feminism to bring men and women any closer to healthy relationships. His narrative was harsh in its honesty, with realistic language and mean-spirited banter. Its abrasiveness delivered audiences from the romantic past, all in a seemingly lusty fashion.

Key to the relevance of *Carnal Knowledge* in the early 1970s was the separation of the sexual from the amorous in a legitimate way. The film discards the classic structure of love stories by refusing to portray heroic individuals discovering their one true love. Instead, the main character, Jonathan Fuerst (Jack Nicholson), ties several loose episodes of love and lust together. He faces the camera in head-on close-ups of clinical-style confessions, pleading his case as viewers learn of his buddy Sandy (Art Garfunkel) and the women in their lives. Jonathan controls the information and leads viewers to his concluding remarks about his sexual interests. With a black and white slideshow of the women that mattered, he brings the film to its finale.

Nichols and Feiffer made sense of changing cinematic standards by filming provocative nude scenes alongside daring dialogue. The film was "honest" and gutsy, even in what one critic called "these ultra-liberated cinematic times."[2] Yet, getting sex and love right on screen actually promoted old stereotypes more than it enlightened viewers. The new visuality of both men and women along with frank, unprecedented language invited a voyeurism that perpetuates exactly what irritated Feiffer about American film in the first place — that it peddled fantasy. The Nichols/Feiffer project produced a new myth — that telling it like it is could dispel the enchantment of film. In its attempt to shape the meaning of debates about social relationships and show the absurdity in thinking that the sexual revolution had changed things between men and women, *Carnal Knowledge* stands as a critical gauge for measuring what was possible in dismantling old notions of romance and replacing them with the way it really was.

According to what audiences see in the movies, "sex in America," Feiffer once wrote, "is a foreign object" with which Americans merely "coexist." Sex "is what happens before and what happens after. What happens during ... is basically irrelevant."[3] We have been fed a "gag," he wrote, and that is the fifties' "Dagwood and Blondie" fantasy. He pointed out how mass circulation magazines, from *McCall's* to the *Ladies' Home Journal* to *The New Yorker*, peddled the family stereotype. In their representations of American life, movies, like the popular publications, "studiously" evade "one fine point," which is "the attraction that brought father and mother together in the first place. Sex." Rather than complexity, the media peddled "a false dream." Feiffer's art meant to disrupt rather than reinforce the myths of America. As he noted, "art offends"; it "wants 2 violate" the community, "subvert it, and outrage it."[4] *Carnal Knowledge* had to be just that cruel.

The packaged image of romance and marriage delivered a promise of stability and affection in family life. These conventions defined the moral framework of American society until, as Feiffer put it, "God died in the early sixties, then the two Kennedys and King, then America died, and finally hope." While his generation let America die, the younger generation let hope die. "So at last," he wrote, the generations have met. "We're given something solid with which to bridge the generation gap: our mutual failures."[5] The solution was the problem to Feiffer. He suspected that the sexual revolution was one more subterfuge. Sexual liberation led men and women to another false "reality" of love yet did not get them closer to intimacy.[6] *Carnal Knowledge* presented it another way — with raw honesty. As Bosley Crowther remarked, the film "is merciless toward both its men and its women in order to reach some kind of understanding of them, of their capacities for self-delusion, and for the casual infliction of pain."[7]

If the young and old met in failure, the movies had something to do with it; at least, that is how Feiffer told his love story.

The characters in *Carnal Knowledge* are typical postwar college kids at the beginning of the film who were of the "bobby sox" and "saddle shoes" generation. They used words like "conceited" and "stuck-up" and wore their hair short. They danced "the fox trot" and "the lindy" and made out in the back rows of movie theaters.[8] Moreover, they held the notions of romance — the moonlit nights, dreamy fantasies of star-crossed love and the tragedy of love lost — that most American youth who went to movies absorbed. The story takes this generation through the 1960s to the film's present time, covering twenty-some years of episodes in the quests and conquests of Jonathan and Sandy. The episodic treatment of a love story allows the film to avoid the conventional scenario and skirt the details of romance in favor of the knowledge this film will pass on.

The film opens to two men's voices heard over a black screen. It is October 1946 at Smith and Amherst colleges. Red-lettered credits appear and Jonathan and Sandy discuss women at a fraternity party. "If you had a choice, would you rather love a girl or have her love you?" Jonathan asks. Sandy just wants a nice girl who "doesn't have to be beautiful," someone who would be a companion. Jonathan counters, "I want mine sexy lookin ... tall, very tall ... big tits ... ahead of me" in sexual experience. The back half of a red car then appears and a slow pan recalls the symbolic back seat. Out of the dark, Susan (Candice Bergen) comes into full Technicolor view. The camera follows her into the Smith/Amherst mixer where couples dance "cheek to cheek," sorority women sit on the sidelines, and fraternity men in suit and tie smoke, drink, and prepare to make their moves.

Jonathan and Sandy debate the reality of romance and sustainable, loving relationships when Susan passes by. Sandy is mesmerized by Susan's beauty — a classic strong chin, blonde hair, black sweater, and beautiful, shiny skin. Jonathan begins his game. "You like that? ... I give her to ya." When Sandy accepts his offer, Jonathan tutors him in ways to advance and "talk to girls." Sandy cautiously walks over but immediately returns to Jonathan: "I fucked up," he says and his friend claims, "It's my turn ... you struck out" to which Sandy bargains, "I get two more times at bat." Still shy about his quest, Sandy approaches once more, but Susan is the one who breaks the ice. "This is the first time I've ever been to a college mixer," she acknowledges to Sandy. "It's such a phony way of meeting people," Susan continues. She has engaged Sandy in conversation and initiates the dramatic love triangle, the tension, and the tone set for the rest of the film. Sandy is prodded by Jonathan's brash, confident bravado to "score." Jonathan, however, is attracted to Susan and takes full advantage of Sandy's naiveté. Not until the end of the film during a slideshow does Sandy learn that Jonathan seduced Susan. Sandy and Susan marry and later divorce. She disappears from the story when the three are still in college and is later replaced by the film's central beauty, Bobbie (Ann-Margret).

The "male talk" at the mixer defines reality from the men's perspective, since Susan does not hear them speaking. Their brash language appears to liberate the mainstream screen from the MGM past and invites viewers into a new possibility of truth. The film begins its cinematic transgression with "street" talk and then progresses to provocative nudity of Ann-Margret's and Nicholson's characters through engaging images of sexual intercourse, bare bodies, and other myth-shattering visuals.

Ann-Margret proved a perfect choice to advance the film's critical comment on the problem with men and women. Nichols had considered Jane Fonda, Dyan Cannon, and Raquel Welch, but when he settled on Ann-Margret for the role of Bobbie, he brought a very specific persona to the screen.[9] By 1971 she was a box-office star, teen idol, and television favorite. Her most famous screen roles were opposite Elvis Presley in *Bye Bye, Birdie* (1963) and *Viva Las Vegas* (1964). These films helped begin her career and marked her as the American sex-kitten. Critics applauded her acting in *Carnal Knowledge* where she made "a shattering impact in her portrayal as ... an aging sex kitten who longs for marriage" as Avco-Embassy's publicity department put it.[10] The sex-kitten plays the sex-kitten and fulfills Jonathan's fantasy of sex on demand. She is the most important female of the film and the only one in the cast of *Carnal Knowledge* to be nominated for an Oscar.

The camera brings Bobbie into view out of a pure white image on screen. She is glamorous and graceful as an ice skater at Central Park. Viewers hear Jonathan and Sandy talk about the "cans" on Bobbie. Jonathan then speculates, "I'd get marred in a minute if I could find the right girl." But children with their mother walk by. Jonathan points to her and remarks, "She's a real ball buster ... her kind.... Think a girl goes for you and you find out she's after your money or your balls or your money and our balls," he informs Sandy. Just a few scenes later, glamorous Bobbie, in a plunging black scoop-neck, seduces Jonathan. They have sex to the song "Dream, Dream, Dream" while the screen fills with Ann-Margret's sensuality. She lies on Jonathan's bed as if a "Playboy" bunny. The camera then follows her complete nude profile as she walks to the shower.

The torrid sexual encounters between Jonathan and Bobbie begin in little time and eventually lead to Bobbie's question, "Do you think it would be a fatal mistake in our lives if we shacked up?" The request stops Jonathan dead in his tracks. He sits unclothed in an easy chair with only a small towel draped loosely across his lap and replies that shacking up might just be "very good ... with open eyes." Bobbie vows, "I'm not asking for your hand in marriage" and Jonathan accepts her offer. She leaves her job as a fashion model and in due course finds bedroom fun turning into formidable bickering. As if in a business deal, Jonathan effectively controls the union until Bobbie realizes her interest really is marriage. In little time, Bobbie, the siren, becomes "the girl who craves marriage and babies," as the *Daily Mirror* put it. She is no longer an available body who sacrifices her successful modeling career for Jonathan.[11] Bobbie is, instead, a victimizer and Jonathan's expendable "other." She rails against him, "I'm a maneater or ballbuster and castrator." He yells back, "You spend more time in bed." Jonathan accuses, "You're trying to kill me.... Get a job" to which she replies, "I don't want a job; I want you." And Jonathan's famous line, "I'm taken by me," ends the sequence.

With no commitment from him, Bobbie simply displaces herself and falls into depression, pills, and booze. Jonathan makes it clear, lest audiences should empathize with Bobbie's victimization, that the trouble is with her. The "shacking up with Bobbie" sequence advances Feiffer's treatise on the MGM past and the sexual revolution present. What happens to Bobbie and Jonathan is the real conclusion to romantic love stories and the new sixties fantasy about sex as liberation. Was it love or lust, deception or honest desire that defined this relationship in all of its progression? Bobbie exemplifies women's capacity to break men. As one critic complained to Feiffer, Bobbie is the film's sacrifice, a submission to "the theory of women as manipulative (Bobbie using emotional blackmail to get Jonathan to marry her)."[12]

The sexual promiscuity that was to save Jonathan from sexual impotence brings him back full circle to feelings of powerlessness, but just as he tires of Bobbie, he meets Cindy (Cynthia O'Neal), the feminist and Sandy's girlfriend. Cindy intrigues Jonathan. "Man, she's really something," he tells Sandy at the tennis club. "Know her problem? She wants balls," and

Mike Nichols' *Carnal Knowledge* (1971) tells it like it is between men and women. Ann-Margret's allure became the film's primary marketing tool. She is shown here with Jack Nicholson (Photofest).

Jonathan covets the challenge. Feminist Cindy, however, is not stuck in the lost era of Bobbie. Cindy is athletic and aggressive. Her independence, for a moment, frees Jonathan from Bobbie's dependency and offers Jonathan a chance for sex without love. She entertains Jonathan's seduction and then rejects his idea that he and Sandy swap partners. Cindy, who is willing to have sex with Jonathan but not be humiliated by Sandy's one-night stand with Bobbie, subverts male fantasy about women. She tantalizes Jonathan's desire to seduce her but has transcended the sexpot image of Ann-Margret's excessive character because she sets the rules.

Carnal Knowledge diverts its attention from the beauty of Bobbie to the trouble with her dependence once Cindy enters the screen. Rather than Cindy's feminism, it is Bobbie's weakness that is a threat to male power, since Jonathan accepts his fate after Bobbie's two attempted suicides, marries her, has a child, and divorces. From a feminist point of view, which Cindy represents, women's social status stems from their neediness. The narrative proves that the logical conclusion to the problem with women's inclination to mix lust with love leads to disaster. The trouble, as Feiffer would have it, is with women's desire and men's obligation. Divorce frees Jonathan physically from the burden of Bobbie, but the effects are lifelong.

Though Cindy's screen presence lasts a few minutes, the impact of her image goes unquestioned. Her prototype was clearly visible off screen in the personality of *Cosmopolitan*, the magazine that legitimized women with drive, ambition, and promiscuous entitlement. They were the females who could deliver the Jonathans. Voice, drive, and an upper hand were cer-

tainly not bestowed on Bobbie. Bobbie's last image as "a tub of lard" keeps her inert and unconscious. Cindy, on the other hand, reconfigures women's image and reconciles the Cosmo Girl
with the new focus on feminism. She sadistically destroys the illusion of Bobbie and allows
Jonathan the possibility of a new fantasy and life. Both Cindy and Jonathan prey on the sex-
kitten's fear that her future is limited if sexuality cannot be reconciled with the conventional
value of marriage. Indeed, Bobbie must now ask what's sex got to do with it, since shacking
up resolved nothing for her.

Cindy does not break or destroy Jonathan but clarifies his situation and obligation. She
establishes her authority but is by no means a sympathetic character and is attractive only as
an authority figure. She walks out of Jonathan's and Bobbie's apartment, out of Jonathan's
life, on her conditions. She is the flip side of Bobbie, with the two representing both ends of
the spectrum defining the trouble with women. The Bobbie/Cindy sequences have proven
the film's argument about the myth of romance. Both assumptions lead to the same point —
that not only does love have nothing to do with meaningful relationships but neither does
sex.

The fourth female prototype enters the film in its most sinister part. Sandy brings a
younger generation love child, Jennifer (Carol Kane), into the story. Sandy is now the intellectual hippie, the prototype of what irritated Feiffer about the sixties response to social strife.
Sandy wears bell bottoms and has long hair and a hippie mustache. He is now attached to
Jennifer, who brings both the carnal and the knowledge to Sandy. She "knows more at eighteen than Susan knows to this day," Sandy boasts to Jonathan. "She's my love teacher," Sandy
explains and offers to help Jonathan in the future of love. "You don't need any of those games,"
Sandy clarifies. "Games don't impress Jennifer, just life, just love," Sandy instructs. Art Gar-
funkel's character shifts lanes and walks through reality into Jennifer's "free" love and life.
She takes this forty-year-old out of male crisis and transforms him into a new-age man.

Jonathan, however, will have none of the love generation. He pulls the mask off romance,
whether it be from the MGM past or the hippie present, to reconstruct male and female identity in his slideshow, "The Jonathan Fuerst Ball Busters on Parade." "In those days we had
illusions," he begins. Sandy and Jennifer obediently watch as Jonathan shows his bizarre black
and white slides, in which Bobbie earned a starring role. Once "the fastest tits in the West,"
Jonathan says about her, she is now "king of the ball busters." His narration of the sexual
encounters he had from the time he was five years old to the present day consists of harsh,
sexist, and racist language. "This was my Jap in the sack," he laughs. With each click of the
projector, he dehumanizes those objects of desire and reduces them to crude labels.

As feminists explored the production of women's identity in the age of sex on screen,
they questioned how telling it like it is in film could be seen as more truthful. Reality is no
less guilty of stereotyping than the MGM past. Even deconstructing the romance to liberate
women's image as passive receptors seemed to turn the camera in a new direction toward a
new use of women's sexuality. By bringing women to the screen as "ball busters," the film
constructs a collective male anxiety and diverts the film's project from romance to fear of
women in general. This split is constructed through Jonathan, who is the self-determined
male on the one hand and the victim on the other. Through him, in the interest of subverting the romance, Nichols cast a spell of another kind on women.

Through the slideshow, the film advances a fantasy for men about women's dependence
that further stereotypes women as burdens who merely "demand things, manipulate, take you
out of your self, ask for contact, want to be loved, want to be talked to, want to be thought

about, are a hindrance once they've been screwed," as Feiffer once chided. When the film removes love from the equation, women like Bobbie, Jonathan knows, are simply not relevant to the world outside of the bedroom. If it weren't for sex, Feiffer continued, "women would have been wiped out centuries ago." This "protective coloration" forces men out of freedom and into responsibility, employment and traps, and therefore provides "an inadequate replacement for a best friend." Feiffer wanted to show a male perspective of sex. It is appealing, he wrote; men "want it, run after it" until "they realize that a woman comes with it."[13] Similarly, Jonathan "traffics" with women but the sexual revolution of the late sixties, free love, ironically complicates simple scoring. "It's not as easy getting laid as it used to be," he laments.

Sandy has moved on, but his evolution irritates Jonathan much the same as the younger generation's sexual politics did Feiffer. Sandy has missed the point of knowledge. The sexual revolution may have made the experience of sex easier for men and women "to get along," but as Feiffer countered, it did not necessarily mean there was broader awareness. Jonathan's best friend Sandy falls short of the film's expectations. "You're a schmuck, have always been," Jonathan derides Sandy. The film agrees, for what does hippie "free love" have to do with it now, and invites viewers to believe that Sandy is a sell-out. It is the brutality of reality—the crisis—not the kindness of another fantasy that gives a man his freedom, Feiffer believed. Sandy, the voice of feminist moralism with whom we should identify if indeed the film is to succeed as a critical comment on men's behavior toward women, is, as Jonathan describes, "a schmuck." The Feiffer predicament of desire and need emanates through Jonathan, who is somehow justified in his brutally cold opinion of women because he declares to the camera what had been previously taboo for the mainstream venue.

Even though Jonathan is the prototype of what feminists were protesting—the chauvinist—he seems powerful, if disturbing. In his forties, with a successful career and a ritzy Manhattan apartment, Jonathan inhibits Sandy and Jennifer from continuing their whimsical relationship. The couple leaves literally in shock after his profane slideshow. Jonathan, therefore, maintains the narrative center of this film and determines the picture's critique of cinematic romanticization.

The ending leaves men and women where Jonathan is—limited and bound to redundant dialogue, programmed scripts, and a two-dimensional point of reference. Both Bobbie and Susan become cultural artifacts, reassigned to the 1950s market of marriage. Cindy and Jennifer represent the cultural present, but both are flattened into negative portrayals of seventies women. Thus, the film's critique of romance through the travesties of Johnathan betrays its task of convincing viewers that he is brutal by inviting viewer sympathy for his pain and confusion. The film indicts Jonathan's code of masculinity to a point. Early on, the picture sets up the relationship between the viewer and Jonathan. Although he is less than a model, heroic character, he is still the narrative voice and the creator of the Fuerst history of women and of *Carnal Knowledge*, figuratively speaking. Following the "shacking up" agreement, Jonathan faces the camera directly and pledges, "I won't lie to you." "I was a little worried and along came Bobbie," he confesses. "I get one look at the size of the pair on her and I never had a doubt I'd ever be anything but okay again and I was." Jonathan's chauvinism has a powerful draw in part because of Jack Nicholson, the actor who made his mark in *Easy Rider* and received an Oscar nomination for *Five Easy Pieces* (1970). He was fresh in the minds of audiences. While the film does not glamorize him, it does leave a certain draw to his voice as the speaker of men's predicament.

Friends, critics, and guests snickered and snorted in New York theaters and wrote Jules

Feiffer the next day. *Carnal Knowledge* was "perfect"; it was "one of the truest and best things ... ever seen on the screen," "a knockout," "brilliant, blistering, and ... a little evil, but beautiful."[14] By the time the film first appeared in Los Angeles, people were standing in lines for blocks around the theater. Said fans and friends, "It was ... gorgeously written, directed and performed." "Fantastic" and "as funny as you've ever been," "everyone and everything about it was right," "I was on the edge of my seat ... and ... laughed like hell." Liz Smith from *Cosmopolitan* sent her praise directly to Nichols, something she said she had done only one other time.[15]

Friend Marta Orbach wrote Feiffer after viewing the film, saying it "made me remember — quite clearly and for the first time in years ... that being nineteen at the very end of the forties was so painful that I couldn't even bear to remember it in the first person." The film pointed out that Hollywood gave us the exceptions, not the rule, of love, or as Orbach put it, "It is the *only* movie ever made for all the people for whom Sam would never play 'As Time Goes By'... and for all the ladies for whom Paul Henried would *not* light two cigarettes — or one, even [Orbach's emphasis]."[16]

Others, however, found the script and production disturbing. One viewer who "saw it at Hef's house" (*Playboy*'s Hugh Hefner) couldn't "approve of the point of view."[17] "Was I supposed to laugh?" a professor of English wrote Feiffer. "It seemed a sad ... movie. And to Philadelphia audiences ... for I saw it in a silent house" unlike New York audiences who "howled with laughter."[18] One New Yorker was incensed: "I was so upset by the film that I had to leave before the end lest I reveal my agony in the rending howls."[19] Novelist and playwright Rosalyn Drexler accused Nichols and Feiffer of again "blow[ing] up on screen ... the usual stereotypes ... as the real thing: woman as wife-mother figure; woman as vapid female 'Oblomov,' helpless and suicidal; woman as tough, metallic 'bachelor' girl, and woman as prostitute." She railed against the "castrator" image and called the film a "grim satire about depersonalization."[20]

Viewers reacted to Drexler's article, saying that she was the one who missed the point. Explained one writer, it is impossible "to understand how anyone could see the movie and miss the fear and pain experienced by the men, as well as the women."[21] Another writer asked Drexler to sympathize with "the obligation Jonathan feels to be the tough guy" and stop letting her "own apparent hostility [get] in her way."[22] A Harvard graduate student tried to set her straight. "The movie is not about the women," he retorted, "it is about the two men's conceptions of women ... it is about male chauvinism — it is not male chauvinist."[23] Another answered Drexler's title, "when she asks ... whether men really hate women, Feiffer would answer a pointed yes."[24]

A *Cleveland Press* critic described *Carnal Knowledge* as "a Feiffer cartoon come to life" and "a movie that many will find offensive and with reason. It is all about sex but without being sexy in the usual movie manner. In language it is explicit, clinical and yet absolutely real." *Carnal Knowledge* "puts down the sexual revolution and as such is undoubtedly ... a moral film, but ... it leans so heavily on its sensational subject matter that for many, if not most, the point will be lost."[25] Charles Champlin of the *Los Angeles Times* found it "the iciest, most merciless and most repellent major ... motion picture in a long time."[26] One frustrated critic wrote Feiffer a two-page letter asking him to clarify several unanswered points in the film.[27]

This "very male" film, as *The Sun* described it, is an indictment of the independent, heartless man who oppresses women by exploiting their beauty.[28] It is a denunciation of Feiffer's entire generation of chauvinists and, if understood from that perspective, Jonathan represents their battle. At the same time, Feiffer is careful not to replace Jonathan with the younger sentiment that Sandy represents. In the screenwriter's words, "The kids today may have quite a bit of the [sexual experience] without getting very far into [understanding]."[29] Yet, it is not easy to dismiss the hooting and howling and the impact the new visuals of female sexuality had on representing women through the film's voyeuristic style to explore the Feiffer premises. The film's adverse effects on the construction of women's identity cannot be ignored.

Filmmakers faced a challenge in the early 1970s, for "reality" on screen still had to reach a wide audience by avoiding censorship and not yielding to a sexploitation fare that would label a film as just another "dirty" movie. Finding the proper balance for Nichols was tricky because Hollywood now sat in the context of an erotica explosion that had appeared in film theaters across America. As *Look* reported in 1970, "Any adult, mature or otherwise, can find movie houses all over the U.S. that show erotica in color and even 3-D."[30] In New York City small theaters called "mini-cinemas" brought in anywhere from $50,000 to $700,000 gross for films that were shot in three days at an expense of little more than $15,000. With these kinds of returns, many of the small art theaters so successful with European films in the early sixties turned their screens to sexploitation during the seventies.[31]

The minor house insurgency also caused a ground swell of protest against the invasion of sexploitation on the community level. Local groups pressured officials to arrest theater owners for profiting from "prurient interest."[32] One congressman even advocated "the creation of an anti-smut squad." *Look* writers joined the conversation by describing films like *Myra Breckinridge* (1970) and *Beyond the Valley of the Dolls* (1970) as "indefensible garbage."[33] Both minor and major film production of graphic sexuality provoked the question of whose right it was to see whatever sexual acts he or she wishes regardless of the court's recognition of "community" standards. In this delicate balancing act between critical art and sexploitation, the courts also came onto the scene.

Only a few months after its release, several cities refused to advertise Nichols' film. Eight months after the film's initial release, Albany, Georgia, officials arrested movie operator Billy Jenkins with "distributing obscene material," fined him $750, confiscated the film, and put him on a year's probation. However, under Jack Valenti's leadership, Universal, MGM, Warner Bros., Twentieth Century, and others organized an action plan to appeal the Georgia Supreme Court's ruling by requesting the U.S. Supreme Court to make their judgment clearer so as to protect films like *Carnal Knowledge* and define the lines between films like that and "the skin flicks," as Valenti described them. "*Carnal Knowledge*," he added, "is the epitome of a picture that is honest and mature without being obscene." A Supreme Court clarification, as Valenti further explained, would "fasten securely the principle that there is a difference between commerce in ideas and the commercial exploitation of obscene material."[34] The exhibition arm of the industry argued that "Carnal Knowledge's fate in Georgia represents 'a pattern of local prosecution and harassment' typical of responses to the court's decision."[35]

From the time of *Carnal Knowledge*'s production in the fall of 1970 to the summer in 1974, the question of censorship shrouded, publicized, and sold the story's social value. *Carnal Knowledge* therefore sits as the moment in the American film industry where the federal jurisdiction and community control over smut and art clashed. It was rated R, had received critical and popular acclaim, sat on the top ten best movies lists, and did not fit the "smut" definition of the 1966 courts. The lobbying power of the MPAA, the National Association of

Theater Owners, the Directors' Guild, the Authors League proved as much. In less than six months after its ruling on the Georgia case against Jenkins, the U.S. Supreme Court forced a new standard and identified *Carnal Knowledge* as the example of what was not "patently offensive" (Judge Rhenquist's words). The picture's nudity and sexuality were "simply not ... hardcore sexual conduct for its own sake, and for ensuing commercial gain."[36] Nichols had achieved the delicate balance. The film became a guideline from which to distinguish legitimate from hard-core material.

At the same time the picture broke boundaries and the court protected its vulnerability and served the film industries' newfound opportunity, it also created new pressures and new stakes for women. The vision of telling it like it is placed women between a rock and a hard spot. New sensual representation on screen seemed empowering on the one hand and objectifying on the other. Despite official and critical approval of this film as developmentally mature, the film reconstructed a new kind of subordination of women.[37] With critical respect for its artistic merit, the film's liberating quality became its truth. Its intent to subvert, outrage, and offend by defining sex as sex, not moonlit nights, made it current, but the apparent honesty in this film was not as transparent as it seems. As feminists explored the product of women's identity in the age of sex on screen, they recognized that a stereotype still operated the same whether in the "tell it like it is" narrative or the MGM past.[38]

The meaning of sexual liberation for women by the 1970s was still contested. As Drexler and others pointed out above, the sexual revolution often had an inverse side. Even *Cosmopolitan* writers were torn. As one writer complained, "Like faithful puritans, we have ruled our new liberties into existence. Dutifully, we observe the mandate of sexual freedom. You decline to sleep with a man ... what's wrong with you? He demands, suspecting some frightful abnormality like frigidity." Having discovered the joy of sex, young women were also discovering the "doctrinaire" of the new mantra. Sexual freedom, women argued, had neither direct correlation to liberation nor much to do with civil rights and equal treatment in and outside the bedroom. As one *Cosmo* writer observed, "The revolution of the sixties may have turned all the labels inside out, but I don't think it's really chased off this doctrinaire habit of mind."[39]

Sexual zealotry became a double-edged sword. For feminists and traditionalists alike, "free" love also translated into unwanted pregnancies, abandonment, and more desperation for women. Sexual liberation, it seemed, became just another version of the "love' em and leave 'em" philosophy. "We're free spirits, we have the Pill, we learned to achieve orgasm," one writer chided. "Without a shot fired, we have surrendered our inalienable rights to be picky, and I want the right back.... The trouble with a quick hop into bed is that it leaves a woman felling nonexistent except for her primary sexual characteristics" and produces self-contempt since "it is quite hard to esteem yourself just for having been born with standard equipment."[40]

While critics and viewers argued endlessly whether *Carnal Knowledge* was about chauvinism but was not chauvinistic, the unresolved issue was the degree to which screen permissiveness in mainstream fare addressed issues of power in the larger society. If "telling it like it is" depended on exploiting Ann-Margret's sensuality and having actors speaking "men's" language (women as body parts), the film's realism also had a vested interest in those identifying features as current, considering the interest in sexploitation. The close-ups of Ann-Margret's body, especially her attractive bosom, were selling points in press releases. She was already an icon in popular culture, which was one of the reasons for her getting the part.

Despite Bobbie's outcome in the story, Ann-Margret's allure became the focal point of the film's appeal.

By keeping women identified through what the *Cosmopolitan* writer called "standard equipment," *Carnal Knowledge* constructs gender as it deconstructs romance.[41] Obviously, the film indulges Jonathan's "no holds barred" realism to point out the "trouble" with MGM. Yet *Carnal Knowledge* enables what Laura Mulvey calls its own "language of desire" or its new discourse of re-representing the reality between men and women. If the film's deconstruction of Americans' fixation with romance works in countering the MGM past by taking love out of the equation, it ignores its own convention.[42] This film sits as one of the most provocative in the debate over film's role in opening up the conventional romance through raw honesty — its claim of innocence.

For men, the film may have been about the absurdity of the macho image and the rebellion against its impotence or, as one writer noted, "a counterpart to 'The Feminine Mystique.'" Yet, if the film liberated men "from the role of oppressor and exploiter," considering the candor in language and the general sympathy for Jonathan's condition, it treaded insensitively on women's historical suppression and exploited the very thing it was trying to subvert.[43] As one woman confessed, "I walked down the street with tears streaming down my face because I had been bombarded for an hour and a half by every demeaning, ugly word ever used to belittle womanhood." Explaining further that she was as much offended by the audience's "predilection by supportive applause" for Jonathan's demeaning of Bobbie as she was by the scene itself, the writer pointed out that the "jock laughter for the screen words and situations that made man's dreary conquest-urge seem sporty, funny, sexy," only endorsed and perpetuated the myth that "boys will be boys."[44]

The film's central argument is for film to be honest in portraying everyday life and show how men and women really are. In this case, it was how men and women battled and, revolution or not, that had to be shown. Realism on the screen tended to place on audiences the burden of subverting and deconstructing. It can, therefore, be assumed that the risk of using sexism to reveal itself was less dangerous than using racism to combat itself, for in the latter there would have been an element of social action or a call for caution to consider. As it stands, the film's ending returns power and control to Jonathan, who has paid for and therefore controls the script. While it may have been possible for Nichols/Feiffer to present a film about male chauvinism and exploitation, the film's effect is left up to the viewers. Viewers still saw men's experiences from a male point of view but not female. Like the woman who left the theater in tears, what were women's choices in a society where boys could still be boys?

At mid-decade, feminist Robin Lakoff saw a parallel struggle. As she declared, "The woman's movement is but a few years old, and has, I should think, much deeper ingrained hostility to overcome than the civil rights movement ever did." Women's struggle would become "a subject for ridicule," even "among the intelligentsia" where "the black civil rights struggle ... never" was "among those very liberals who were the first on their blocks to join the NAACP." By comparison, the gender struggle "should indicate that social change must precede lexical change: women must achieve some measure of greater social independence of men before Ms. can gain wider acceptance."[45] Had the underlying question to Feiffer been, "do whites really hate blacks?" then how many howls would have been heard in the same New York theaters as viewers watched African Americans reduced to passive stereotypes? If the result had been "nightly riots," the film would have said less about real racial strife in America than it would have about prevailing notions (shared by filmmakers and viewers) about what was safe, in bad taste, and discursively "correct" on the silver screen.

Liberating women from the "standard equipment" syndrome meant "reclaiming [their] bodies from a male-dominated" discourse. The result would be "laying claim to other kinds of agency."[46] Feminists saw the difficulty in women's success through civil rights arguments based on gender. One viewer pointed out in the fall of 1971 that if "a similar film [had] been made purportedly exposing racism rather than sexism, in which the script contained epithets describing negritude with the same insensitivity that femaleness is here dealt with, there would have been nightly riots in the cinemas."[47]

As women were calling for more equal treatment socially, film reconceptualized their screen identity. Cinema adapted women to popular portrayals, as Laura Mulvey explained, "heroines who are spies, investigators, or detectives."[48] Yet, the camera cannot be ignored as a "third eye." The way it portrayed women is its construction of agency not just a reflection of reality. *Carnal Knowledge* was fast opening the screen to different identities than had been produced in the MGM past, but it was also keeping possibilities closed for women.[49]

Jonathan, for example, slyly slips a slide of Susan in his slideshow and Sandy gets the message. Slipping Susan in for a microsecond brings the narrative back to the beginning where, for a few sequences, Susan re-conceptualizes the fantasy that Jonathan and Sandy constructed about her. Her strong voice subverts the romantic ideal by setting the conditions of Sandy's inquiry at the mixer in the beginning sequence of the film. She was the icebreaker, the witty intelligence in her semantics game when Sandy finally suggests, "You ought to be a lawyer." Susan replies, "I'm gonna be a lawyer." Susan at this point represents the eastern intellectual woman in sweaters and tweed skirts who was expected "to pursue fierce intellectual independence" yet remain "well-bred, ladylike."[50]

Yet, Susan disappears a third of the way through the film. Sandy tires of her, his marriage, and suburban living. Her disappearance is critical for the story to resume its commentary because she is the ideal of women seeking to combine traditional roles with a career. She is the new assertion, the new possibility. She offers a chance for fair treatment of women in cinematic representations. She "can tell men their thoughts," as Sandy explains to Jonathan. She is the only woman in the film who keeps Jonathan off balance and promises to unload cinema of its notorious use of women as duplicitous or alluringly dangerous. Either way, with Susan silenced, the chosen conclusion of her life and new persona for women — having it all — interrupts the logic of Jonathan's narrative of discontent. Hence, Susan's disappearance prevents the representation of women's natural progression from college to career and cinema's chance to take women's issues seriously. Once Jonathan seduces Susan and Sandy marries her, she exists only as a frame in the slideshow. Her disappearance suggests mainstream's inability to reconfigure women's lives in narratives on screen. She is reduced, euphemized, silenced, erased, and denied social action. *Carnal Knowledge*'s myth of using sexism to confront the romance fails the film's feminist leanings and works instead to see women's resourcefulness as a destabilizing force not only to men's power but also their very identity, as was shown by Susan's disappearance.

With critical acclaim for his groundbreaking film, Nichols helped to establish what could be done in mainstream film. In this sense, *Carnal Knowledge* confirmed the task ahead for women's liberation and showed that women's rights were still bypassed on screens. The stakes were higher for women in this process of deconstruction than for men, as women in the early 1970s claimed. *Carnal Knowledge* fit in the paradigm of sexual liberation for those who believed to experiment meant to advocate. To break down dominant mores and encourage females' sexual expression meant social advancement. Approval of sexual promiscuity in mainstream magazines and popular bestsellers softened the moral implication for women's sexual behavior. When Liz Smith of *Cosmopolitan*, for example, wrote Nichols personally to congratulate him and Feiffer on producing "one of the best movies ever!" she also railed against women's libbers who detested and pilloried the film while dragging it through the "Women's Lib" mud. "Actually," she wrote, the film is "making the very point they want"— that, like life, "this movie is hateful to and about women" but its unfairness "speaks some awful truth."[51]

When feminism's early task was to point out inequities between men and women by raising consciousness about misogyny, the "awful truth" meant that cinema was guilty. *Time's* critic called both Jonathan and Sandy "fatuous travesties of the American male ... who loath the opposite sex."[52] Roger Ebert acknowledged the film's attempt to expose the inability of the sexes to operate outside of their social constructions. "Men and women," he argued, "fail to find sexual and personal happiness because they can't break through their patterns of treating each other as objects."[53] The *Wall Street Journal* pointed out further that it was "not an exploitation film" but instead "a film about exploitation — that of women by men" and "moreover ... a feminist film." If seen as a feminist film, it is about the male ego, misogyny, and bourgeois sexual dysfunction. It is just as the *Wall Street Journal* critic claimed, "a film about exploitation."[54]

Yet the problem was less what the film showed than what it disguised. Tucked inside the political act, in the loosening of women's sexual mores, lay the issue of authority and empowerment. Women's social agency also depended on demystifying stereotypes. As one activist wrote, "What the camera in fact grasps is the 'natural' world of the dominant ideology." Popular culture has to find "new meanings" not just replacing men's traditional roles with women. New assertions for women "have to be created ... within the text of the film." The third eye is both product and process, not an inert tool.[55]

If the truth about men and women is the narrative's measure of disruption, showing victimization through Bobbie's sensuality, for example, was not enough. She was portrayed as the most endearing and the most emasculated female character in the story — the "victim par excellence" and "the film's most powerful feminine argument."[56] She represents the trouble with the "sexy babe who really just wants to get married."[57] She is the one whom the camera dominates, yet the film is about Jonathan, the representative middle-aged man who may be a chauvinist but still gets to tell the story. He has the final word and holds the final image. Strength and power are measured in sexual performance and key to that is woman's physical perfection, still a conventional frame of reference.[58]

With Sandy and Jennifer out of the picture, viewers return to Jonathan and the space of his defined male authority. He finds only one woman necessary to fulfill his needs, since his potency is now measured by his professional success. She is a Middle Eastern call girl, Louise (Rita Moreno), the one person he can pay and predict. Louise propagandizes his strength and power and returns him to his imagined self. He is young, alive, revitalized, and immersed in the angelic fantasy of Bobbie, when he first saw her as an attractive ice skater in Manhattan. He recalls the first image of her before their sexual involvement. The blinding whiteness of her fur hat and white skating costume dominate the screen. He sinks into the myth of the past and just how he wanted it to be, but Louise interrupts, saying he is "a man who inspires worship because he has no need for any woman." He is lying flat on his back with arms stretched out crucifixion style, looking into nowhere, as he hears "because he has himself."

The camera shows a relaxed, grinning man and then ends with a sinister image of the

era of Bobbie. The blurred vision of a twirling, romantic, sensual skater on the blinding white
ice comes into and out of focus and contrasts to the dark warmth and mystical music of
Louise's apartment. The carnal touch of the present displaces the frigidity of the past and
reiterates the power of the script, the reality of cinematic representation, and the anxiety of
impotent stories and meaningless identities. Louise restores Jonathan's identity according to
the script he has engineered, ordered, and bought. The film, through Louise, affirms "the man"
and his story ceases to be personal. Instead, it becomes the fact about women.

The sixties and seventies in filmmaking provided an unprecedented chance and opportunity for experimentation in film. Films were recognized for those new images of carnal freedom and tests of sexual knowledge, for breaking boundaries and claiming new truths. It was
imagined that telling it like it is would somehow connect to empowerment. Hence, *Carnal
Knowledge* was indeed a test for the possibilities in mainstream film.[59] The picture first set up
the '40s and '50s film conventions as influencing men's and women's dishonestly. Next, it liberated the screen through Jonathan's language and Bobbie's body. Finally, the film held up in
court for its artistic merit. Thus, *Carnal Knowledge* was indeed a test of what realism produced.

In the era of women's liberation with sexual permissiveness and new knowledge on
women's sexual experiences equalizing the playing ground, it makes sense that a film such as
Carnal Knowledge would represent how things really are. The federal government's endorsement and protection made it a privileged work of art. Audiences, filmmakers, and actors came
together in a perfect arrangement. What Nichols was showing and Jonathan telling could seem
influential on the one hand and a measure of the film industry's progress on the other. Just
as Jonathan could have his cake and keep it, too, if sex came without intimacy, so too could
the film make a statement on the state of social relations and indulge in mainstream voyeurism
at the same time.

Yet, art without metaphor and deconstruction without reconstruction are contradictions.
Placed in the context of a *Cosmopolitan* type of construction of women's liberation, *Carnal
Knowledge* was part of the discursive process by which men and women negotiated new identities in response to real-world situations. The discussion Nichols' film invited was the question of representing sexuality as liberation rather than arguing that the sexual revolution was
not really liberating. As women discovered limits to the rhetoric of equality emerging out of
the civil rights activity of the previous decade, they began to question the very construction
of gender identity and its relation to social power as produced in places like the media. If, as
Teresa de Lauretis claims, "the movement of ... film actually inscribes and orients desire," then
the desire to be brutally honest in *Carnal Knowledge* is also what gives it license to ignore the
subjugating nature of its own visual exploitation.[60] Feiffer and Nichols' treatise fits the standard female masochist and male sadist model where the female body is etched and inscribed
by men, that is, sexualized and gendered — routed, rerouted, and put back on track.

Before achieving any measure of independence and equality, women had to negotiate
social change by imagining and advocating new identities outside of the traditional discourse
of ladyhood, Madonna, sex-kitten, and even the stereotyping of feminists during the early
seventies. With the Code breakup, the new ratings system, and the experimental trend in
filmmaking well underway by the production of *Carnal Knowledge*, moving pictures faced
no obstacles on their way to sexualizing women on screen. The industry immersed itself
in the context of sexual verity and turned to women to imagine what it might look like in
mainstream features. With the help of *Cosmopolitan* and Helen Gurley Brown's "swinging con-

temporary chick" audience, as one writer put it, it would seem exhilarating to crush "old standards ... under the heels of the advancing young."[61] Perhaps the kind of knowledge audiences consumed was not new information but just carnal visuals; maybe *Carnal Knowledge* is really just another "dirty" movie, despite Academy endorsement, federal sanction, and critical acclaim of the Feiffer/Nichols team.

Three months after *Carnal Knowledge* was released, Norman Lear debuted his soon-to-be-famous *All in the Family*. The television artist gave Archie Bunker, its main character, full rein to represent the bigot in America, the voice of protest against the myriad cultural and social changes. Again the generations meet — Archie and son-in-law Meathead. Archie put America back on course by teaching "the little one" (his daughter Gloria) and her husband the truth about their generation's antiestablishment assumptions.

In the debut of the series, Archie and his wife Edith walk through the door. "I'm sorry, Archie," Edith apologizes to her husband. "How was I to know?" she asked. "I thought it was a religious picture — Cardinal Knowledge," she tells him. "One of the dirtiest pictures I ever seen," he said to her. If cinema seemed too preoccupied with carnality, then Archie and Edith would save American living rooms from it. *All in the Family* defined America's moral standing by using the film as both a contrast to convention and an endorsement of the film as a "now movie" because the television series was a satire of Archie's misguided notions. Making peace with cultural changes meant imagining the working-class Bunkers as the last best place to guard convention and then mocking the convention they protected. This playful incongruity between cardinal and carnal knowledge placed Nichols' film in conversation with other cultural exchanges about generation and gender debates.

Yet, popular culture had passed the likes of the Bunkers. Social change throughout the coming decades brought more complexities. Archie's discomfort did not end with the battle of the sexes and generations. He was asked to make room for a new model of America. This time it would be a multicultural story where groups mingled and narratives changed. While Archie was concerned with dirty movies, Hollywood was quickly turning the tables a bit further. This time a new discourse of ethnicity gained widespread notice. The larger culture turned to new questions about Americanness and the portrayal of American history.

Filmmakers who wished to engage in the debate reimagined the representation of history within a national narrative of westward movement. Arthur Penn rewrote the West and liberated Native Americans from nearly a hundred years of cinematic bondage as the varmints of western lore. He brought Dustin Hoffman back as a white man of the nineteenth century who lived over a hundred years to tell the real story of the West. A daunting feat, it would take a *Little Big Man* to stand up and deliver the next treatise about another romance of the Hollywood kind.

ETHNICITY

CHAPTER X

Forever Native

Penn's New Authentics in *Little Big Man*

Turn the damned thing on; this is how it was.
— Jack Crabb in *Little Big Man*

It is 5:30 A.M. Arthur Penn rises, sips coffee, and leaves his Montana rental for the *Little Big Man* film set. There, cowboy and Indian extras tiptoe across "prickly pear cactus" and move toward "mock villages" set up on the Crow Indian Reservation and at a local ranch. Penn hoists his tortoise-shell glasses off his head and yells, "Cut. Let's do it again." The production crew tips over covered wagons and positions burnt tipis. Makeup artists prepare their actors and actresses for the retakes. Actor Dustin Hoffman, who portrays the main character Jack Crabb, takes a break in his portable trailer, reading *The Village Voice* and *The New Republic*.[1]

At the end of the day, Penn ships the takes to Hollywood and awaits their return. Back at the screening room in Billings, some of the cast join editor Dede Allen for a preview of earlier clips. After screenings Penn returns to his Montana house and sips martinis while perusing *The New Yorker*, *Time*, *Newsweek*, and other eastern newsprint. "I am very sympathetic to the young now," he tells a *New York Times* reporter. "I am very fixed at that point emotionally," and he takes a call from Arlo Guthrie's manager, who tells him that his account of the hippies, *Alice's Restaurant*, is a smashing success.[2]

While the Guthrie movie mesmerized audiences across the country, Penn set up cameras in eight Montana locations. He was fixed emotionally on the victims of frontier history, not the victors. Shot on local ranches, on reservations, and in Montana towns, Penn's rendition represented the way the West *was* instead of the way it was imagined. At least, that was the idea behind the project. In an attempt to take the Western into the seventies and beyond, Penn revised the celluloid construction of the Hollywood Indian by converting Thomas Berger's *Little Big Man*, published in 1964, into a manifesto for Indian empathy. The noble savage and the bloodthirsty villains of captivity narratives would be replaced by New Age authentics in the "tell it like it is" mode of cinema.

For Penn, social activism, Westerns, and Montana were a natural fit. Where better to stage this revision than the territory itself because, most likely, as the director said, "It just doesn't get any better. Montana is the real thing." Having just discovered Montana after vacationing there and listening to local rancher Earl Rosell and Billings mayor Willard Fraser talk about the "Treasure State's" magnificent scenery, Penn saw potential for a successful blend between story and scenery. The Montana location would enable him to revise cinematic representations and help historically subordinated groups become agents in narratives on screen.[3] Montana offered a real look — a big screen, as it were — for an updated image of Native Americans.

The Penn crew raised its cameras toward the Montana landscape in the context of the multicultural debates about America. It was a diverse model that best described the changes from the sixties. His film registered that social mix, beginning with the casting of a Canadian actor and longshoresman, Chief Dan George, in the supporting role of Old Lodge Skins, the Cheyenne patriarch. This role was personal for George. "I wanted to show that an Indian, if he had talent, could play an Indian better than a white," the chief said, "simply because he was playing his own nationality." He finally found his chance to "get things right."[4] To complete the picture of authenticity, Crow Indians filled in as extras. With an authentic chief in a starring role and young Crows on horses, this project revised the mainstream screen and protested the cinema's victimization of American Indians. If an activist perspective could help reconstruct positive screen roles for Native Americans, then perhaps it would improve civil liberties and social relations in America, too.

Showing America as an oppressor to a 1970 audience was not daring, but asking Indians to play themselves in major roles to deconstruct American history was. The effect was nothing short of a new cultural dimension for Westerns, the West, and Indians. Yet while the film's consciousness-raising successfully advanced a multicultural polemic, *Little Big Man* committed one significant crime. Just what Penn was producing was not quite clear. Was it reshaping the past by opening up the stereotypes or merely creating new ones that imposed a different kind of subjugation?[5] On Penn's set in Montana territory, one man held the answer.

Jack Crabb is the 121-year-old survivor of the Battle of Little Big Horn. As the film opens, a history graduate student (William Hickey) has come to the veterans' hospital to interview Jack. "I am more interested in the primitive lifestyle of the Plains Indians" and their "way of life," he condescends. "The tall tale about Custer" or another Old West "adventure" story that Crabb is about to tell has no credence in history, the interviewer explains. Jack takes control of the interviewer's tape recorder, and the camera preps audiences to hear the truth. "You turn that thing on and shut up," he scolds and his story begins. The camera and recorder take viewers back to the nineteenth century when Pawnees ambushed Jack Crabb's westward-moving family. Jack and his sister Caroline (Carole Androsky) were subsequently taken to a Cheyenne village to be taught the "primitive" way of life.

Jack is the mobile, resourceful, postmodern character — a jack of all trades — who crosses cultures with ease. He is the child of a homesteader, an Indian captive, adopted missionary son, husband, storeowner, gunslinger, paramour, and the revisionist voice of Western history on film. His unfettered ability to move between worlds emancipates viewers from Westerns past as he turns minister and gunslinger alike into caricatures. Crabb spans the entire period of American cinema, ends in a veterans' elderly care facility, and is a career find for a budding historian.

Hoffman gives a stellar performance as the vessel through which these identities pass and through which strands of antiwar and adversarial counterculture wisdom tie together. Yet the critical component of Hoffman's significance as a point of reference is in legitimating the

Arthur Penn brought "on-location" realism to *Little Big Man* (1970), intending to de-Hollywoodize the Western; the two actors, Dustin Hoffman (as Jack Crabb) and Chief Dan George (as Old Lodge Skins), show the thin line between representation and "telling it like it is" (Photofest).

Native American. "Now you just sit there and you'll learn something," Crabb tells the interviewer. "I knowed General George Armstrong Custer for what he was and I also knowed the Indians for what they was." If the graduate student and viewer are ready, Crabb's story will provide the raw evidence in the search for truth about the American West. "My name is Jack Crabb, and I am the sole white survivor."

To begin, Penn reacquaints viewers with traditional cinematic images. The film opens to a slow pan of the desolate, dry plains of the West. Viewers see from a low angle torched wagons and dead bodies. Jack picks up his narrative in voice-over and takes viewers back a hundred and eleven years. "My family crossin' the Great Plains was wiped out by a band of wild Indians," he explains. The "murderin' varmints," as he calls them, were the Pawnees. The story then shifts. It is the present in film time and the moment after destruction. Young Jack (Ray Dimas) and sister Caroline eye the destruction, mourn the death of their parents, and then run for cover under a tattered tarp. Audiences suspect a traditional narrative when they see a lone warrior, Shadow that Comes in Sight (Ruben Moreno), riding toward them. Shadow flings the tarp back and terrifies the children. "Bye, Jack," Caroline says. "I'll see you in heaven." Appearing in war paint, Shadow threatens their lives with a raised tomahawk, then empathizes, and saves both children.

Indian representation in this first sequence deliberately imitates old Hollywood and then introduces its critical stance with the sympathetic Shadow. As he takes his captives into camp, the three of them ride past an Indian garbage dump and the reversals continue. Jack's sister Caroline is terrified that she will be raped but Crabb as narrator explains, "Poor Caroline never did have no luck with men." Caroline escapes the Cheyenne and the story focuses on Jack, who is adopted by the patriarch of the group, Old Lodge Skins, his new "granddaddy," and learns the way of tribal life.

Dustin Hoffman enters the screen after the first few sequences as a teenager, and the film begins its most memorable revision. With long, dark braids, bare torso, beaded choker, and buckskin pants, Hoffman rides his pinto into battle. He is part of the procession of Cheyenne who are fighting the U.S. military following a massacre of women and children at another Indian camp. Hoffman brings his star power and iconic authority onto the screen in what one critic noted as "memorable delicacy, humor, and humanity."[6] Hoffman's humane persona legitimates the film's remorse over the clash between westward movement and Indian people. Jack's adoptive family provides the means for the film's social commentary while serving as the narrative authority who determines the value of what they say and do. "I wasn't just playing in it. I was living in it," he explains. His grandfather, Old Lodge Skins, compliments Hoffman's popular persona and together they begin the process of de–Hollywoodizing the feature screen.

The elderly Jack Crabb sets the moral tone of the film when he explains that the Cheyennes call themselves the Human Beings. The camera then takes viewers into the world of Old Lodge Skins, who makes clear that Jack was not born a Human Being since he was white. Yet, when the young boy lives the code of Human Beings by killing a Pawnee, he is converted and named. "His name shall be Little Big Man," the one whose body was small but "his bravery ... big," Grandfather officially declares. Jack the teenager enters Old Lodge Skins' tipi and the training begins. Of course, Crabb's character is pure fiction, but the inclusion of a fictitious white survivor in the Custer history of the Battle of Little Big Horn is exactly what makes Penn's version of history appealing and problematic. Crabb's imperative — "this is how it was" — breaks new ground because his story affirms the value of Indian perspective. At the same time, his authority to speak for Native Americans presumes an innocence that fosters a new "good" image to counter the Hollywood of negative portrayals.

Grandfather instructs Jack that "whites are the enemy" because their world is a place without a center. Jack rides with the Human Beings to war against those adversaries. Sequences show military raids, rifles against bows and arrows, and Old Lodge Skins' people being threatened. In the early scenes, the film encourages sympathy by dehumanizing the white world. During one of the military raids, for example, Jack is mistaken for a Cheyenne. He is about to be slaughtered but yells, "God bless George Washington; God bless my mother," and points out, "Indians wouldn't say that kind of stuff." The soldier who is about to kill him wipes paint off Jack's face and he is saved. Soon adopted into the household of Minister Silas Pendrake (Thayer David), he begins passing from one identity to the next throughout the coming episodes.

The paint-wiping scene advances the plot and also reveals the film's form of revisionism. Paint has been smeared on Jack's face to disguise his origin. Washing it off allows him to cross back into white society where the narrative indicts everyone from preachers to snake oil salesman to icons of the Western. Cleansing Jack's color symbolically erases his identity and implies it is something on the surface, suggesting identity can be acquired, cleaned away, and determined by choice. This short scene exemplifies the belief circulating in the larger society that Americans are multicultural and diverse. At the time of the film's release, protest against the American past included questioning the assimilation process that forced ethnicity to recede from view in favor of the "American way." The aim was to supplant the "assimilated" persona with a "truer," more authentic model. The criticism over Hollywood's role in ignoring diverse

Little Big Man, a.k.a. Jack Crabb, the title character of Arthur Penn's 1970 film, crosses between two societies by merely wiping paint off his face and yelling "God bless George Washington!" (Photofest).

identities at the time was directed toward the industry's overemphasis on a generic American rather than on the real portrayal of a diverse society. Countering the assimilationist model by revising the Western made sense because of the genre's ubiquity.

By the time Penn began production on the movie, literary works humanizing Native Americans had already been circulating. Readers could access stories about Crazy Horse and Sitting Bull and read romantic adventures about Native Americans. Thomas Berger added to the changed discourse with his novel *Little Big Man*; others followed by the 1970s with such titles as *Custer Died for Your Sins* and *Bury My Heart at Wounded Knee*. Film saw its revisionist strain with John Ford's *Cheyenne Autumn* in 1964 when Ford created a sympathetic view of Indians that viewers welcomed. "For once in a western [*sic*]," one film critic explained about Ford's product, "all the Indians looked like Indians," even if Sal Mineo and Ricardo Matalban played the lead roles.[7]

Such authors and filmmakers believed their works were "telling it like it is" and, in turn, advocating change in the larger society. Educators joined the conversation about a more just society. Education departments at universities developed new curricula during the latter sixties to teach empathy for "the other America," as one teaching guide labeled it. Popular books replaced traditional reading lists in high school English classes and teachers argued that the proper image for America should be a mosaic or tapestry where people mix but can still be distinct, rather than disappear in a melting pot. Two popular books, *When the Legends Die* and *Laughing Boy*, were widely taught and circulated as "knowledge" about Ute and Navajo life, respectively. In the first book, the main character changes from Bear's Brother to Thomas Black Bull to Killer Tom Black to Thomas Black to Tom Black Bull. He is the "recalcitrant 'problem teenager' in the reservation school who clings to the old ways" and finally comes to terms with himself and his heritage. According to these books, Indian heritage must be preserved. "When the legends die, the dream ends," the book claims. Other updated literary characters were "pure Navajo, untouched by the white world," as the teaching unit for *Laughing Boy* explained. By contrast, the teenage girl, who "has been severely damaged by her contact with whites," exemplifies the consequences of modernity. In these scenarios, the white world is alien and a threat. The discovery of identity in these stories brought the successful balance between the old world and the new.[8]

The ideal in these methods of activism was to adjust the view of society. Teaching materials explained that these resources could help "blacks, whites, Indians, Orientals, Mexicans, European immigrants ... to blend ... without destroying their separate cultures." Many well-meaning instructors pointed out "the dream ... gone awry" and made students aware of ghettoes, reservation life, and inner city poverty.[9] Prospective teachers took bibliographies and new media listings compiled by Educational Media Centers into high schools. Students watched and critiqued film and read and discussed popular novels and other material, hoping to envision and understand experiences so they could help forge new social relations. Social activism was advanced by many Native Americans themselves through Red Power organizations such as the American Indian Movement (AIM), created in 1968. This group saw the American government as a danger to native lifestyle and culture.[10] Other activists employed less militant methods and pressed courts to prohibit the misappropriation of Indian identity. The most obvious were sports team titles where the names of "The Chiefs" or "Redskins" typecast cultures.

Constructing new reference groups was one answer to changing social relations and altering the process of assimilation. Another was deconstructing icons by forging new narratives in mainstream cinema. To revise popularized myths and images oftentimes meant adjusting the meaning of conventional heroes who symbolized the purpose of American history. Like Berger before him, Penn addressed changing attitudes toward the American past and called for a more fair treatment of minority populations by adjusting the treatment of Native Americans in popular literature and film. The solution for Penn's project, at the same time, meant flipping the coin and dismantling any notion of heroism among the American troops moving United States borders into the West. One historical figure in American frontier history, George Custer, was a likely subject because he had long fascinated historians and popular culture enthusiasts.

As early as 1948 in *Fort Apache*, John Ford reinterpreted the Custer persona. By the late 1960s, Custer was cast as an arrogant egotist signifying the problem with America itself. This "once ... symbolic leader," as one historian wrote, "came to represent the supposed 'moral bankruptcy' of Manifest Destiny."[11] The meaning of the real Custer took on large implications in *Little Big Man* because Penn's portrayal further facilitated what the book had begun. Custer functioned as the sacrificial offering for the representation of an adversarial perspective. This long-lived legend was about to be profaned in American popular culture once again.

The legend of Custer has been one of the most intriguing topics in the history of the American West because Custer's death and defeat in the centennial year of 1876 was controversial from the beginning. Was the battle to be understood as a gallant last stand or a moment of panic under Custer's command? Custer's defeat, as historian Richard White noted, was "hugely symbolic and a major shock." It was difficult for many "to imagine a warrior culture defeating a modern army."[12] The thirty-six-year-old lieutenant colonel already "had star power [and] media awareness" and almost instantaneously became a dashing character for popular culture.[13] The mystery shrouding the battle lent itself to stories of heroism and sacrifice for a nation into the middle of the twentieth century.

Penn took up the Custer legend where Berger and Ford left off. He treated Custer (Richard Mulligan) as a megalomaniac by first casting Native Americans in positive roles opposite Custer and his military. The proper noun Human Beings, for example, signifies a specific identity defined through particular moral attributes and authentic cultural traits. The result, as one writer explains, is that viewers see "the Cheyenne as ... a flourishing tribe with a defined culture."[14] Custer's negative portrayal completed the narrative's logic because the commander represents the savage side of the American past, the wrongdoings of the federal government, and the danger of military power forging its control at the expense of various tribes during westward expansion. Penn broke ground in cinematic historiography by rendering a more poignant depiction of Indians in Westerns, contrasted to a brash American military.

When Penn placed a tribal leader in a leading role and filmed Native Americans in indigenous landscapes, the effect was nothing less than a sign of film's power to change attitudes and influence beliefs. Charles Champlin of the *Los Angeles Times*, for example, noted that unlike "other recent films" about the tragedy of confrontation, Penn's was different. *Little Big Man* showed "the Indians as men and women and children ... rather than as a Culture or a Historical Force," he said. The film "states the tragedy of the confrontation more eloquently and powerfully ... and more effectively indeed than any film I can remember seeing."[15] Roger Ebert of the *Chicago Sun–Times* chimed in: "It is the very folksiness of Penn's film that makes it, finally, such a perceptive and important statement about Indians, the West, and the American Dream."[16] Likewise, Chief Dan George felt he helped erase the stigma of violence perpetuated through Hollywood and the popular culture for Native Americans. As he argued, "movies always showed the Indians as warlike and in reality we are a peaceful people."[17] Custer as the demon and an Indian chief as the source of truth resonated with many in the wake of anti–Vietnam protests.

By the time of the film's release, historical revisionism included a similar change. The language that described frontier history in the historical record, activists pointed out, carried prejudicial attitudes. The use of such words as *battle* when the U.S. Cavalry won and *massacre* when Indian warriors did was a privileged point of view. The description of westward movement as "Manifest Destiny" was also called into question. Such a belief was not necessarily just or liberating from a Sioux or Cheyenne point of view. A new history had to include a revised rendition of the West that took into account devastation as part of the making of a republic. That meant reassessing the idea of progress, the value placed on the wilderness, and the clash of tribal lifestyle with the right to homestead and speculate. It was the process of modernization itself that could be critiqued and reimagined on screen.

Institutionalizing ethnicity through education, literary works, film, and language led to a change in the meaning of American identity. In a multicultural model, red power, black power, euro-ethnic power, and other labels replaced generic, melting-pot America. With popular pressure to preserve minority identity, it made sense when viewers heard the chief complain to Jack that the white man, whom "he cannot get rid of," has always been in "unlimited supply." Compared to "a limited number of Human Beings," Old Lodge Skins tells Crabb, the solution is clear. It is "them" or "us." This approach is reflected in Jack's experience outside the security of the tribe.

Like the grandfather, the film wants to reconstruct a better America than the melting-pot version by establishing the social difference between Indian human beings and white swindlers. "A world without Human Beings has no center to it," Jack remembers as he encounters chaos in the white world. He is adopted by Minister Pendrake (Thayer David) and his wife. His life with the Pendrakes shows a contradictory white society. He is literally bathed in Christian love by a seductive Louise Pendrake (Faye Dunaway) who explains that it is her "Christian duty" to cleanse him and give the child "important religious instruction" about sin and temptation. Louise introduces Jack to the world of lust when he spots her with her lover during her "Wednesday shopping" day. Later, the reverend whips proper behavior into Jack and almost drowns him to save him at his baptism. Jack eventually leaves the religious zealots and takes up with a charlatan, Mr. Merriweather (Martin Balsam), who takes Jack in as a sidekick in the Merriweather show. Jack acts the part of the invalid cured by Merriweather's magic potion. They are eventually tarred, feathered, and run out of town.

The next critique of a society without a center playfully denunciates the TV cowboy, a powerful symbol of American identity in popular culture. Jack reunites with sister Caroline, who outfits him with Gene Autry-style gear. She teaches him to twirl his gun and complete his personal development by becoming a sharpshooter, since a man "ain't complete without a gun." Now the "Soda-Pop Kid"— with black hat, shirt, and bolo tie— he enters the world of Wild Bill Hickok and the manly space of the saloon. Mistaken as a Hollywood villain, he functions as a caricature that de-values the myth of the West as the place for masculine regeneration. Jack sits next to Wild Bill Hickok, the symbol of the western gunslinger, but does a bad job of following his orders and so parodies the century-old icons. As the Soda-Pop Kid, Jack reduces to a caricature the masculinity as it was once represented in the Western.

When Jack Crabb returns to the real Human Beings, he discovers the final travesty of the white world. Grandfather was blinded. Jack rants and raves over this transgression. "Do you hate them?" Jack hysterically screams at the chief. "Do you hate the white man now?" As the revisionist voice and the man who can negotiate all cultures, Jack finally separates himself from a purely assimilated white heritage. He disassociates with his familial ties introduced at the beginning of the film and justifies the narrative's "them or us" revisionism. Jack's ranting turns the plot toward its last episode, the Battle of Little Big Horn. The film leaves audiences with a final sequence that reevaluates the force of westward expansion and the histories that have told about it. The last sequences also carry the paradox of multiculturalism.

Jack's separation from his heritage just before the battle absolves him of responsibility from the past and present. If he relinquishes historical responsibility by becoming Little Big Man instead of Jack, he also frees himself from guilt over the current social conditions. With Grandfather blinded and at the mercy of fate on the battlefield, the film encourages identification with Jack's position and enables both viewers and Jack to recognize the condition for social issues and solutions as being outside themselves. Like Penn, Jack counters stereotypes by replacing them with symbolic goodness, with uppercase Human Beings. By contrast, Jack shows how those who are not Human Beings are a burlesque. The good Indian/bad whites duality is centrally located in the one historical component of the film: Custer and the sequences of the Battle of Little Big Horn. The battle concludes the film's position on social activism and finalizes the meaning of Jack's credibility.

The film ends with Custer standing in the midst of battle — silly, stupid, and megalomaniacal. It is chaos, with women, children, and a blind grandfather dodging the fray. The Last Stand in this film shows Custer ranting and raving amidst those flying arrows and shooting guns. Satanic looking, with blond hair flying and in military uniform, Penn's Custer represents the vanity of leadership that understood the West as an empty space to fill. A vainglorious Custer, following Crabb's denunciation, finalizes the film's revision and the narrative's truth. Brutal conquest, not settlement, had been his mission.

The battle scene confirms Jack Crabb's harangue against an American history not of his doing. The ending confirms Grandfather's words, "If things keep trying to live, the white man will rub them out; that is the difference." Humanizing Indianness when cinematic characters were historically denigrated as "murdering varmints" in Westerns was imperative for the film to take its stance against America's narrative of Manifest Destiny and advance its revisionist stance for social change. Yet, what it accomplishes is not clear.

When New York and Los Angeles viewers applauded *Little Big Man* at the respective openings in December 1970, they approved of new perspectives on American history. New Yorker Judith Crist, for example, contended, "It strikes new ground in its concepts and new perceptions in its subtleties." Crist celebrated its "sense of time and place and ... vitality of its moral era." She concluded, "its concern for humanity approaches universal truths that transcend skin color."[18] Others praised Penn for directing "with an astounding freshness."[19] The trade applauded Penn for "shattering a great many myths about the Old West and its people" and for handling the subject with "sentiment that is genuine."[20] The picture was endorsed as "the best of a new wave of films sympathetic to American Indians."[21]

Parodying the Western's icons allowed the film to label the Cheyenne and eventually all Indian tribes except the Pawnees as Human Beings. Exchanging bad images for good also advanced a new direction and identity suited to the interest in a new model of American identity. When young people from the Crow nation filled in as extras, their presence made a heritage seem appealing. In addition, the film broke ground in cinematic history by casting Chief Dan George as a central figure in the story about Native Americans. Audiences saw close-ups of his deep facial lines and penetrating and piercing eyes. His strong, muscular features, as he often stood tall in fur and feathers while the camera panned the landscape, completed the impression of him as an insightful character. The chief was both the comic and the quintessential surefooted, wise, trustworthy elder, always ready to teach. Yet, as in the initial sequence that begins with stereotypical portrayals of old Westerns to undo those same images, the film's "authenticity" betrays its activist argument.

While many cheered Penn as a "ground-breaker," others accused Penn of pandering. "And you know who the bad guys are this year," *Show* writer Shelley Benon teased. *Variety's* staff asked if the film's "attempt to right some unretrievable wrong via gallows humor" might just "avoid the polemics."[22] Still others complained about the plot's "emotional confusion" and "diffuse" nature.[23] *The New Yorker* took issue with the "offensively simple way" the film belittled non–Indians and portrayed American history as one of "misleading ... genocide."[24] Even Custer's portrayal "becomes personal rather than social" because he is flatly portrayed as maniacal rather than the bearer of federal policy or carrier of a cultural philosophy. Finally, there is "a cheapness in Penn's conception" reflected in the ease with which "we identify with the Indians because they are nice," complained a *Film Quarterly* critic.[25] The revisionist project was clearly limited.

Critics picked up on the trouble with flipping the stereotypes and protested the simplistic duality between white and native, but the underlying issue in the film's discursive role at the time was the way it reestablished cultural roots as an essential part of social change.[26] Similar to characteristic discourse of diversity in the early 1970s, such as educational materials mentioned earlier, *Little Big Man* argued against assimilation and replaced that with an essentializing process. Just when it seemed authenticity would lead to empowerment, the result was a reductive and simplified Indian identity that remained forever native, primitive, and interesting.

The film uses the power of Chief Dan George's authenticity to advance its argument. Cinema proved a difficult place to elevate the social standing of Native Americans because of its visual power. At the same time, he is an actor, dramatizing a familiar story. The difficulty of having it both ways (actor and nationality representative) appears in the film when Old Lodge Skins speaks what one critic called "Hollywoodese." He greets his long-lost Jack with a line straight out of old Hollywood — "to see you again makes my heart soar like a hawk." The literary hawk and the chief represent the natural world, antimodern and authentic. At the same time, Old Lodge Skins juxtaposes authentic nature with New York humor. After a failed attempt to die, Grandfather shakes his head and gives in. "Sometimes the magic works and sometimes it doesn't," he jests. As Canby of *The New York Times* quipped, the screenwriter "never quite gets the hang of how Indians should talk in English meant to represent Cheyenne."[27]

By contrast, the tagline teases viewers into believing that Jack Crabb is "The Most Neglected Hero In History Or A Liar Of Insane Proportion." In that line, Penn's film promotes a psychology that hides its own fiction. It is a clever way of filling in the one missing link in historical accounts of the Battle of Little Big Horn because Jack has the final say about what actually happened ... or maybe not. It is enticing to identify with the "Human Beings." Thus, Indian as an idea of humanity with roots but no modern history served the need to imagine oneself as righteous protector of the future. The film recalls the history student taping Jack's story, for instance, and allows for Crabb's indignation over the American treatment of Indian tribes to be the final thought. The taping of Jack's voice permits him to denounce the western past and exempt him from guilt in the demise of the other. The responsibility of that meaning goes to the viewers, to the receivers of that information. It is neither Jack nor the historian who is responsible for the present, just the telling. To grant the Indian humanity is to authorize the film's valued stance. Even in his literal and figurative mask, Crabb (like the promotion) shores up the retelling as activism.[28] Since there is no definitive account of the Battle of the Little Big Horn, the central catalyst for the plot, the film itself escapes implication.[29]

It is easy enough to see how using "real" people and places in *Little Big Man* glosses over the construction of labels. However, one more example shows the film's inconsistency in the new discourse about diversity. *Little Big Man* empowers men but fails to include women specifically in the revisionist project. Jack Crabb falls immediately in love with the fifteen-year-old Sunshine (Aimee Eccles) who is having her baby in the bushes. She suffers alone during delivery by biting on a leather strap and doesn't even yell out. "I couldn't take my eyes off that girl and her baby," Jack remembers. Together they forge a life at the Cheyenne camp where Crabb enjoys the strength of Sunshine. She exemplifies the clarity of condition and identity — both sure and stable. She is the younger generation (the *Laughing Boy* model) who teaches viewers how to identify and embrace the cultural traits of the Human Beings rather than rebel against them. Similarly, Old Lodge Skins' wife, Snake Woman, serves the men's expectations and quietly assumes the role of Indian "squaw." Like stand-up comedians, Crabb and Lodge Skins banter. "Grandfather, I have a white wife," Jack confessed at one point to the chief. "Does she cook and does she work hard? Does she show pleasant enthusiasm when you want her?" Grandfather inquires. When Jack answers yes, Old Lodge Skins replies, "That surprises me.... I tried one of them once but she didn't show any enthusiasm at all," he jokes; but "my new wife Snake Woman cooks dog very well." The question remains whether it is the image or the laugh audiences take with them. As one woman commented at the time about the film, "It is increasingly offensive to the extent of your own confusion. The violence might have paid off if the humor had been complementary."[30] Instead, the picture's Human Beings are synonymous not only with nativeness but also with patriarchal authority, with the men. The Cheyenne women rarely speak and are relegated to gender-specific roles.

Crabb and Old Lodge Skins, the patriarchs, exemplify the contradiction in activists who "followed their cultural ancestors in playing Indian to find reassuring identities in a world seemingly out of control."[31] In this sense, Chief Dan George helped serve up a misguided cliché. He was both primitive Cheyenne and "every Indian" at the same time.[32] Despite Jack's eleven-some identities and the Pawnees as the "varmints," the persona that was interchangeable was the Indian, albeit an identity reduced to nineteenth-century signifiers, static and fixed. Moreover, since Crabb is the only credible person from "white" society, the film locates the story's central value in him as the original witness.[33] Hoffman's character helps these people tell their stories, but he is the voice of experience. As historian Joan Scott has written, "What could be truer ... than a subject's own account of what he or she has lived through?" "I was there," Jack reminds the audience. Despite Chief Dan George's commanding presence in the film, Jack remains the authority, the outsider/insider who carries validation, who can be believed or not. Whether he appears as a Human Being with paint smeared on his face or cleanses the mask off to save himself, in both cases he is the story. He forever remains the veteran, a valued elder in the respectable Veterans Hospital. It is his narrative (not the Chief's), his emplotment, his truth "as the origin of knowledge," as the person who "was there."[34] A reverse assimilation of sorts, "white-into-Indian" gave choices to the likes of Jack Crabb, the mobile individualist. The reverse was not possible. With Jack's endorsement, Native Americans were returned to a romantic notion of primitiveness.

Certainly Penn's work can serve as an allegory for activism against colonial oppression and appalling social relations, and for that reason there is an argument for historical authenticity in films that dealt with a historical subject by locating cameras on site. Historians and filmmakers constantly compete for recognition of historical accuracy.[35] In this case, the addition of "real Indians," the collapse of white history into one man's narrative, the humanizing of Indian personae as male, and the circulation of these seemingly emancipatory components set in the Montana landscape takes the film beyond allegorical meaning. The "realism" adds to the problem of commodifying victimization by changing representations on screen and then claiming that the "intrinsic" value of culture is enough to confront social problems. The new kind of "cultural reference" that *Little Big Man* fostered (from American to ethnic) raises questions about the use of ethnicity as a new kind of identity, as a thing but not as a process.[36]

Little Big Man added a new mythology to the landscape of the West. The new ideal seemed to begin with rewriting history by adding real Indians in real locations to update old narratives, but the turn to Indianness in this film demonstrates the concern of symbolic power versus historical process. Philip Deloria cautions against "the ways in which a contradictory notion of Indianness, so central to American quests for identities, changed shape yet again in the context of [the] postmodern crises of meaning." As Deloria further explains, "Whenever white Americans have confronted crises of identity, some of them have inevitably turned to Indians." He points out that constructing Indianness as a repository for truth and authentic identity played out "not only in communes, but in politics, environmentalism, spirituality, and other pursuits." The sixties and seventies style of "Indianness," he argues, "allowed counterculturalists to have it both ways." For Indian people, he continues, "reinterpreting those symbols and launching protests of their own, Indianness became a potent political meeting ground."[37]

Since one could practice getting back to the natural world by living in a tipi at a commune or buying an authentic Navajo blanket, building a log cabin by a river in Montana, or just by purchasing a ticket to *Little Big Man*, what was being consumed and appropriated was important. "Nineteenth-century" Indian imagery merged with activism, but what got lost in the metamorphosis was the use of the symbolic as a stand-in for social action. The appropriation of ethnicity as a thing involved several layers of essentializing when the intent was to free cultures from popular pigeonholes. Similarly, what appeared to give respect and dignity to people was their nativeness, as Deloria has argued, that served to mitigate the larger culture's own fears. The dilemma in addressing the problem of stereotyping by making the story "more real" in the "tell it like it is" mode of Montana landscape and Indian primitiveness concealed the very reality it meant to confront. Penn's verisimilitude, like popular curricula and novels, may have appeared to produce more human and kind identities, but they still read as stereotypes, fixed and stable.[38] What once seemed a resource had become a curse.

Similar to the larger society, *Little Big Man* helped convert the Hollywood Indian of the nineteenth century to the victims and protestors of the twentieth. Fiction allowed filmmakers to have it both ways, to say something powerful but not be held entirely responsible. "Authentic" actors played Sioux and Cheyenne, but anyone could play Jack Crabb, icon or not, and could be believed or not. The most popular actor for the younger generation at the time, Dustin Hoffman helped sell that malleability. His movement and mobility were reflected off authentics' stability. Hoffman retained his representation as an actor, but the chief—like the extras — corresponded to themselves. Actor/character/person blended, as if seamlessly the same — on and outside the screen similarly. As one writer put it about *Little Big Man* in a letter to the editor, "I left the theater wondering how accurate its portrayal of Indian life was" and so picked up Mari Sandoz' *These Were the Sioux* which, "like the movie makers ... treats Indian culture with the greatest respect, and makes us see the beauty of their 'primitive' way of life. I now have an even greater admiration for 'Little Big Man.'"[39]

The beauty of primitiveness completed a New York resident's imagined America with the help of Jack Crabb, Sandoz, and Penn, never mind the tug of war about to besiege real Indian people over such issues as water and fishing rights, real estate development, tribal adaptation, or casino tourism. Shot on location for authenticity, the landscape was less a metaphor for America than a location, deterministic of an essentalized identity and a place for reification. The film kept Native Americans on location, remaining natural and forever native (though not vanishing). Penn's cultural construction of identity tied Indianness to the ideological role of geography. Indianness got at once deemphasized and reinstated, kept outside history and recognized in everyday life and practice as it appeared on the screen. The film therefore defined and assigned cultural value by exposing the problems in ways Indianness can be romanticized out of view. Flipping the coin fails to open the dynamic historical process in a shared history. In some ways the film turns Penn's phrase, "It doesn't get better than this," into a sinister premonition for Indian representation in historical narratives of the West.

Cinematic revisionism of the Old West began with critical looks at the Western's stereotypes. Similarly, *Little Big Man* set the standard for what audiences should expect from a new, more "enlightened" Hollywood. Real people played Indian in real spaces to show historical accuracy. Yet, what was intended to serve as a positive outreach from Hollywood to Native American cultures ironically reintroduced new victimization. The authentic, the native, the real became further irreducible, essential, and primitive, all in the name of "telling it like it is," with a little star appeal. As Deloria commented, *Little Big Man*'s Indians "are funny, smart, and sexy."[40] Dustin Hoffman returned to the screen as an American Indian and framed the preferred view of the native past and proper attitudes toward it in the present. Grandfather appealed to those in search of a wise, surefooted leader. These representations helped viewers work through a vision of America imagined as changed, more open and humane, just and liberated.

The construction of Indianness on screen contained its own politics. Penn's film has the same "native imprints" as did the trend toward "primitivism" in earlier times.[41] He has no answer for contemporaneous Native Americans who were more inclined toward modernity.[42] The reality of Native Americans is subject to forever being the primitive. As Deloria argues, oftentimes the primitive Indian became more valued than "real native people."[43] The film's rendition of the good Indian gave credence to the preservationist, both native and academic, who often denied the complexity of current social issues and the historical reasons for the clash of values and beliefs. The result is "victim history," remarked an Albuquerque, New Mexico, director of the American Indian Graduate Center. Well-meaning advocates for social reparation "sell our kids short when we treat them as victims," he continued. "Get over the trauma," he admonished when explaining that misguided thinking has objectified American Indians by promoting "multigenerational trauma" and excusing individuals from "responsibility for themselves" as agents in the present.[44]

Penn's film is very much referenced today and applauded similarly as in 1970 for its intent to de–Hollywoodize Native Americans. Vincent Canby helped set the trend of victimizing while humanizing when he placed *Little Big Man* on "The Ten Best" films list. "Mr. Penn's film is a tough testament to the contrariness of the American experience as survived by 120-year-old Jack Crabb.... The movie attempts to take its horrors seriously by making them comic, and winds up in some confusion. But this sort of confusion is more important than the achievements of lesser movies."[45] In January 1994 the film was shown at the Sundance Film Festival in two locations and marketed as exemplary. "If Penn was looking for an American metaphor for the topsy-turvy sixties," one ad said, "he could scarcely have found a better one than Thomas Berger's portrait of the western frontier at the end of the nineteenth century." The tragi-comedy of "a society in transition with its values in an uproar" makes unique use of Crabb's perspective from inside the tribe: "Here he learns Indian philosophy and how to be a 'human being,'" it continued.[46]

Later in 1996, the novel and film were praised at the San Francisco Film Festival. The novel was spoken about "as a rueful reappraisal of the American West." Berger "saw the corruption and conniving of the frontier and the brave attempt by Native Americans to hold on to their identity" and following Penn's success with *Bonnie and Clyde*, he "won studio support." The writer lamented, "it was not until 1970 that the picture opened." It clearly brought into view "the portrait of the American military and their abuse of the Cheyenne and the Sioux ... as inevitably ... a metaphor for Vietnam." The writer argued, "As time passes, it's easier to see *Little Big Man*'s tragedy as the helpless offshoot of wayward American energy and the great stew of history made by idiots, scoundrels and liars."[47] The film appeared at the 1999 USA Film Festival on April 23 and was touted as a "masterpiece from Arthur Penn," still "retain[ing] its power to shock and amuse after nearly three decades."[48]

One ethnohistorian cautioned viewers about the way film continues to be a source of knowledge about heritage and identity. "We cannot dismiss the stereotypes as unimportant film portrayals," he warns, "because hundreds of millions of people the world over have acquired their beliefs about North American Indians through motion pictures." Part of the group are "American Indians [themselves who] draw heavily from these films in constructing their *own* views of their cultural heritage [text italics]." For the millions of viewers who consumed *Little Big Man* as "new, now, and real," what attitudes and beliefs the film advanced added a word about social change and persistence in the belief that there exists an essence to Indianness.[49] The intent was to decode stereotypes through films such as *Little Big Man*. Those images disassembled the Westerns' cumulative knowledge about Indian cultures and helped build a new reality and thus circulate new information about Indianness. Long-lived films, as well as festival revivals of them, typified the way American feature films solved social issues and maintained cultural legitimacy.

With eyes watching the world through the lens of multiculturalism, independents and film school graduates entered Hollywood politically aware of these social efforts. Eager for cinematic acclaim, one young filmmaker took advantage of the multicultural turn in America and moved film in yet another direction, away from the experimental and adversarial style of sixties experimentation. Between 1972 and 1974, the University of California at Los Angeles film-school graduate Francis Ford Coppola brought American film back to a golden age, more conventional than experimental with *The Godfather Part I* and *Part II*. Coppola revalidated the importance of a formulaic romantic tragedy by forcing viewers once again to reassess the construction of Americanness. This time it was the question of how heritage figured into the American cult of individualism and the legacy of America for third- and fourth-generation European ethnics intent on rediscovering their past and reclaiming their heritage.

In the spirit of diversity and the seventies "mosaic" America, Euro-Americans contested, comprehended, invented, and flaunted culture and heritage. New faces began new traditions. Coppola's moneymakers placed the Pacinos, the De Niros, and other New York ethnics squarely in the center of the screen. Coppola brought Italian voices in sync with Hollywood's gangster tradition by taking a hard look at ethnic families from an insider's point of view four years before Alex Hailey popularized the famous roots movement with his book *Roots* in 1976. The result was an offer Hollywood learned not to refuse.

CHAPTER XI

The Godfather *Films as America*

KAY ADAMS: It made me think of what you once told me: "In five years the
Corleone family will be completely legitimate." That was seven years ago.
MICHAEL CORLEONE: I know. I'm trying, darling.
— *The Godfather: Part II*

For decades Italian Americans objected to representations of themselves as criminals in
American cinema. From *Little Caesar* (1930) to *The Untouchables* television series, the image
was the same. Italians were gangsters and violent, swarthy men who talked out of the corners
of their mouths. It seems odd, then, that two Italian Americans, Francis Coppola, a filmmaker, and Mario Puzo, a novelist, would produce yet another portrayal of Italians as gangsters. At a glance, *The Godfather* films seem exploitative and manipulative. Don Corleone's
(Marlon Brando) patriarchal family reverts to traditional attitudes, with women playing sub-
servient roles and sons following the orders of fathers. Seemingly, it would be difficult to ignore
the feminist challenge to male-dominant narratives at the time. Likewise, young people who
imagined their generation as honest and forthright were rebelling against an overbearing pater-
nalism that limited their lifestyle choices. Yet, when Don Corleone spoke, audiences
applauded.

The Godfather films unequivocally tapped into a yearning for more than gangster drama
or a return to patriarchal tradition. The generation seeking distance from traditional American institutions by popularizing such films as *The Graduate, Alice's Restaurant*, and *Easy Rider*
looked to its roots for new moorings in ethnic values and identities by the 1970s. The release
of *The Godfather* films paralleled the resurgence of ethnic advocacy in the United States and
joined the critical conversation about the meaning of the Southern and Eastern European
immigrant surge between 1880 and 1924. Placed in the cultural debates of the 1970s, *The Godfather* pair inscribed Italians with a new subjectivity in film. The results were two blockbusters
that spoke about ethnicity with a wide audience.

Godfathers I and *II* helped reconstruct and reinvent American Italianness just as third-
generation Southern Europeans entered colleges and professional fields in record numbers.
Obliquely, both films imprinted an immigrant narrative into American cinematic history by
retelling the pertinence of the American Dream, the meaning of work, the importance of success, and especially the ethnic dimension of the immigrant story. Boomer ethnics turned to
a new kind of empowerment that was once denied their grandparents. Primarily, younger
generations widened the assimilation paradigm and enjoyed a new identification process. *The*

The Godfather (1972) **family photo (Photofest).**

Godfather films spoke to that change. In their attempt to present Italianness from an "insider's" point of view, the films were provincial and universal at the same time for a reason. Engaging the well-known and liked gangster story, the films achieved a delicate balance between the conventions of the genre and an immersion in ethnic culture.

Similar to the *The Graduate* in 1967, the ticket lines at the theaters for *The Godfather* stretched for blocks. Hustlers capitalized on the popularity and sold places in line for $20.00. By the end of the first-week run, the film brought in nearly a half-million dollars. Critics saw Coppola's *Godfather* pair as "a primary example of ... progressive film[s]."[1] New York film critic Pauline Kael declared *The Godfather* "one of the two or three best films ever made at a Hollywood studio." In her estimation it was "the work of a major artist."[2] *Time* called it "an Italian-American Gone with the Wind," so effective "that [it] seems to have everything."[3] The 1973 and 1975 Academy Awards echoed the same critical opinion. *The Godfather* received three awards from its ten nominations. It won Best Picture, Best Actor, and Best Screen Play. Two years later, Coppola's *The Godfather: Part II* collected six awards from its eleven nominations. This time Coppola walked away with Best Producer and Director. *Part II* was the only sequel to surpass its precursor in box office gross and win Best Picture. The pair was the only crime drama to win the same Oscar twice.[4]

The young filmmaker's success signaled a change in American film.[5] In 1969, Coppola was working with experimental cinema and his new independent company Zoetrope in San Francisco. By 1974 he had created three classics with major studios.[6] Given these successes compared to his experimental projects, he was well on his way to becoming Hollywood's charismatic filmmaking hero. *The Godfather*'s creation and success meant to many that the experimental sixties had succeeded in reshaping the feature film industry. As film scholar Jon Lewis put it, the film is "a legendary American *auteur* picture — one that is generally and justifiably credited with starting the so-called auteur renaissance in the 1970s."[7] Producer and director Roger Corman claimed it was *The Godfather* that brought together "the American genre film and the European art film." As Corman remarked, "Beautiful, realist, revolutionary, *The Godfather* stepped outside the boundaries of the traditional in both form and story." Coppola synthesized European cinema and Hollywood convention. In Corman's opinion, he "eclipsed and conquered the mainstream."[8] It gave experimental magic an American home and ethnic voices a new sound.

Zoetrope and his *Godfather* films earned Coppola the reputation as "the patriarch of the 'Auteur Renaissance' in Hollywood." The 1972 and 1974 releases became two of Francis Coppola's most memorable films and earned their director the title, "godfather of the blockbuster." Film critic Nick Browne even described Coppola as the "linch-pin of the notable change in a post–1960s' studio system." His "personal artistic vision," Brown continued, showed what "could be, and might even be necessary to, the foundation of enormous financial success, one that inaugurated the Hollywood blockbuster syndrome."[9] These studio pictures set the standard for the seventies style moneymaker dominated by the younger generation of filmmakers. Where the experimental trend defined Coppola's 1960s projects (*Rain People*, for example), the conventional story line marked his seventies undertakings.

Getting Paramount to sign the initial project, however, took some coaxing. The studio had recently been stung by another Mafia picture, *The Brotherhood*, released in January 1969, starring Kirk Douglas, and the last thing executives wanted to risk was another gangster failure. With Douglas at the helm, company and reviewers alike agreed that the *Brotherhood* "had all the makings of a hit." Unfortunately, no one went. Paramount's financial loss meant that if Kirk Douglas (in black hair and shaggy mustache) could not pull off a hit in a popular genre, then why should the studio risk making the same mistake twice? As one critic observed, "the prospect that *The Godfather* could be the financial triumph and cultural phenomenon it became had all the potential of a ticket in a billion-dollar lottery."[10]

Burt Lancaster production executives approached producer Robert Evans and offered to make *The Godfather* provided Lancaster starred. Evans refused because he believed him wrong for the part. Well-established filmmakers such as Fred Zinnemann and Richard Brooks turned down the initial project because "they thought it was just a big commercial project about gangsters and didn't see it as a film with redeeming social or any other value."[11] Others were worried "about being associated with a potentially incendiary ethnic picture."[12] Peter Bart suggested Paramount try Francis Coppola as the director and Evans took advantage of the opportunity so he could avoid the Lancaster deal. Coppola's appeal as an Italian American attracted Paramount since executives saw him as a cover against accusations of stereotyping and defamation. His name and identity would ensure protection.[13]

Coppola himself was not initially interested. He shied away from sensational feature films with tight Hollywood control, believing an Italian "Carpetbagger" style crime drama would cheapen his artistic career. By the spring of 1970, however, Hollywood seemed attractive, especially since he was in financial trouble with Zoetrope, his independent film studio in San Francisco. Coppola conceded. He would make the movie if he could take it in a direction different from that in *The Brotherhood*. Rather than "a film about organized gangsters" it would be "a family chronicle" and a critique of "capitalism in America."[14] Coppola brought an artistic dimension to the genre with notable framing, composition, and juxtaposition. His skill, as Roger Corman noted, was "gritty" and "elegant," realistic and beautiful. No longer would art and blockbuster seemed an oxymoron. The ethnic eye "confirm[ed] the place of artistry in American gangster cinema."[15] First, Coppola helped convert Puzo's bestseller *The Godfather*, a book about the Mafia, into a family story about power, loyalty, conflict, and regeneration. Coppola's talent and visionary cinematic capabilities blended with his desire "to make this an authentic piece of film about gangsters who were Italian, how they lived, how they behaved, the way they treated their families, celebrated their rituals." Clearly, this filmmaker understood the power of film and its global reach. If ever there was a chance to test that, it was now. In collaboration with Mario Puzo, who was in the midst of worldwide fame, Coppola agreed that the film would be "about more than the Mafia." The story would address the "conflicts in American culture" and center on "a powerful man who builds a dynasty through crime — but he wants his son to be a senator, a governor." The larger task was to make it "about the very nature of power. What it does to you. Who survives."[16]

The Godfather set connects to and departs from the traditional gangster genre. The urban criminal was typically romanticized as a tragic hero during the thirties in such films as *Little Caesar* (Melvyn LeRoy, 1930), *The Public Enemy* (William Wellman, 1931), and *Scarface* (Howard Hughes, 1932). The classic gangster was a self-reliant, big-city criminal, the individualist resisting conformity who is eventually gunned down on city streets. In the conventional ending, the gangster's death restores law and order and reaffirms "community morality."[17] *The Godfather*, on the other hand, invites viewers to ignore the criminal element in the Corleones and identify with them.

Rather than respect for the law, a private, personal code of honor determines the worth of the characters in *The Godfather*.[18] The convention Coppola was after had to do with making the subtle switch from characters who played Italian gangsters to people who personalized Italian codes on screen. Coppola insisted on Italian actors, but Paramount disagreed. It was the generic Italian executives wanted. Better still, why not transform a Ryan O'Neil or a Robert Redford into a Northern Italian? Coppola pressed to put Al Pacino in the lead role as Michael Corleone, a second-generation Sicilian American, but when Pacino auditioned, what executives saw was a short Italian with a big nose. "He was too short, 'too Italian,' and so low-key that on first appearance he seemed listless" to those involved. As casting director Fred Roos remembered, "He wasn't a star, which was not pleasing to the executives at that time." Even Evans was unimpressed. "Why the hell are you testing Pacino again? The man's a midget," he complained. Mario Puzo's Michael "was supposed to be the American in the family. He had to look a little classy, a little Ivy League."[19]

Coppola fought for his ideas, eventually convincing the studio he was right. As he noted, "When I read *The Godfather*, whenever I would see the character of Michael, I saw Al's face." Pacino's features were not Hollywood's idea of star material even in the multicultural seventies, but he had performed on Broadway and had talent. Italians — unmelted and authentic — would bring the film in line with contemporary taste for novelty and candor.[20] Pacino himself recognized the importance of Coppola's vision. Later he commented, Coppola's "tenacity ... got me in there."[21] It was Evans who eventually agreed, "He's Italian, he's as written."[22]

By the fall of 1970, the idea of authenticity turned into a marketable commodity. At a press conference in September, the studio exploited the idea of Italians playing themselves. "We're going to cast real faces, people who are not name; nor are we going to have Hollywood Italians." Producer Evans explained, "We would rather go with unknowns than big-name actors and actresses" because "we want it to be authentic." Everybody who was remotely interested applied for parts. A multitude of hopefuls wrote letters. "I'm an unknown." "I'm dark-haired." "I weigh 235 pounds." "My father is the Godfather in Cleveland, and he can make things easy for you." "If you are looking for an unknown who has never done any acting, I might fill the bill. Granted I'm no Ali MacGraw, but what do you expect for an Italian?" Even flashy San Francisco attorney Melvin Belli alerted management he was available. Some "sent a picture of themselves holding a pizza saying they would be perfect for a part," as executive producer Al Ruddy remembered. Others auditioned in full "mafia" regalia. James Caan remembers, "They talked in deze and doze."[23]

Those who had fashioned themselves into Hollywood Italians were typically turned down — except for one onlooker in Little Italy, Lenny Montana. Montana, an ex-professional wrestler, attracted executives and got the part of Luca Brasi. Another unknown, Gianni Russo, played Carlo Rizzi after Ruddy saw a video tape Russo sent.[24] Coppola's wish to do something different depended completely on his "very conscious decision" to pay attention to "the details." As he commented, "I've almost never seen a movie that gave any real sense of what it was like to be an Italian-American."[25] In Coppola's words, viewers should "feel what these people were feeling."[26] With an "insider's" eye, Coppola turned the sights, smells, sounds, and textures of Italianicity into a major film. In his words, it was "the biggest home movie in history."[27]

No doubt, viewers received a little taste of Coppola's Italian American family. He took audiences to a wedding, a funeral, a baptism, a grandfather's garden, and family meals with the Coppola family producing, directing, scoring, and acting in the film. Francis's Italian-American father, Carmin Coppola, collaborated with Nino Rota on the soundtrack. Talia Shire, Coppola's sister, played Connie and Francis' daughter and sons played extras. As Talia remarked, both films were "textured or perfumed in a way with the memories of our Italian American family."[28] The effect worked for one film commentator, who enthused the film was "one of those rare experiences that feels perfectly right from beginning to end — almost as if everyone involved had been born to participate in it."[29] Film scholar Vera Dika agreed, "*The Godfather* brings to us, like perhaps no other film before it in American film history, the notion of 'authenticity' when presenting Italian Americans as an ethnic group."[30]

Like Robert Altman, who had his cast and crew live in tents in the rainy Northwest to internalize the sensation of frontier times, Coppola prepped his troop with "character-reinforcing tools" such as "thin Italian cigars ... prop pistols, Italian wine and food, cooking utensils, silverware, newspapers, and other personal items." They met for dinners as the Corleone family at local restaurants. Coppola believed these outings would "inspire the spark of character development."[31] He indeed enlightened his cast and took the crew in that direction. This provocative director "knew the way these men ate their food, kissed each other, talked. He knew the grit."[32]

The movie's co-screenwriter and the book's author, Mario Puzo, also knew the "grit." As the second-generation son of Italian-born parents noted, during his childhood in the "heart of New York's Neapolitan ghetto," Hell's Kitchen, he "never heard an Italian singing." Nor were "the grown-ups ... charming or loving or understanding." Those he remembered "seemed coarse, vulgar, or insulting." Puzo's novel responded to "all the clichés of lovable Italians, singing Italians, happy-go-lucky Italians" and therefore the Hollywood that constructed them. As he commented, "I wondered where the hell the moviemakers and story writers got all their ideas from."[33]

If the ethnic touch was to function as more than a simplistic reference point, it had to start with a definition of place. High on Evans' and Coppola's list of demands was on-location shooting in New York. Set designer Dean Talouvaris had a keen eye for creating an Italian American neighborhood. His crew constructed the "urban village," the "Little Italy" of the immigrant generation. The neighborhood was essential to Coppola's focus on the Italian family drama as an American story told through an ethnic eye. The texture of those neighborhoods in the film displayed the lifestyle of Europeans' pre-suburb exodus from the city and the "grip ... of ... family."[34] Little Italy on Mott Street served as Mulberry Street in the film and Bruno Tattaglia's nightclub in the Edison Hotel hosted Luca Brasi's murder.[35]

Representing the gangster's domestic life was not new in film, but personalizing Italian culture was. Typically, in classic tradition the gangster-loner shows a "deep devotion to family" by projecting that value onto a sidekick. This "every-man" sort of character eventually "abandons the gangster in favor of traditional society."[36] Such a split is not central to *The Godfathers'* personae because of both films' dependence on ethnic identity.

Part I establishes that fact instantly. *The Godfather* opens with a father-to-father plea: "I believe in America," a mustached Amerigo Bonasera (Salvatore Corsitto) tells Don Corleone who is receiving guests asking for his family's help. "America has made my fortune. And I raised my daughter in American fashion but I taught her never to dishonor her family," Bonasera continues. "She found a boyfriend, not an Italian." In traditional fashion, Bonasera asks for the Godfather's help to avenge the brutal beating and rape of his daughter by two American boys. "I went to the police like a good American," Bonasera explains. The "boys were arrested" and sentenced, but the judge "suspended the sentence." The opening scene

The ethnic neighborhood in *Godfather: Part II* (1974) was essential for the film's focus on ethnic America (Photofest).

locates Bonasera's peripheral position within dominant society and justifies the Corleone means of violence as retribution, as a form of resistance. "Murder is justice" for the ethnic outsider, as filmmaker Roger Corman pointed out, because America failed them and not the reverse.[37]

The Corleones offer Bonasera friendship and a promise of help, but Don Corleone leaves business behind to enjoy himself as father of the bride. He dances with his daughter, Connie Corleone, then his wife (Morgana King), and later toasts to his godson, the Hollywood star Johnny Fontaine (Al Martino). He insists on a family photo that includes everyone. Mother, father, brother, children, bridal party, and friends surround bride and bridegroom. The portrait captures the depth and width of the Corleone extended family with twenty-some people posing for *Godfather* audiences. From the beginning, the film characterizes Don Corleone as an endearing elderly man who runs a tight Mafia family but who will play with his grandchild, stop at grocery stands to buy fruit for his family, and pass fatherly wisdom to those around him. He counsels his godson. "Spend time with your family?" Vito asks. "Because the man who doesn't spend time with his family can never be a real man." The wedding places the family at the center of the story of power. Connie Corleone, Vito's only daughter, marries Carlo Rizzi and the film indulges in an Italian-style "backyard" celebration at the Corleone estate. In several camera pans of the guests, viewers see them enjoying homemade wine, Italian delicacies, and traditional folk music of mandolins, clarinets, and accordions. They dance and sing to handclapping, clink glasses until the bride and groom kiss, drop money into the wedding basket, and gather for the wedding-cake march. Children and adults, family and friends mingle and participate.

The early scenes define the Corleone identity as Italians first. They are godfather, husband, grandparent, brothers, sons, daughters, and mothers, the ethnic family that gathers for special occasions and believes in America. The film's story is not the Don's story but the struggle of his family to realize the vision of both passing on tradition and seizing the opportunity for a new future. The film therefore moves beyond the formulaic model of the gangster film and invites audiences to connect with the characters first as Italian Americans, ordinary and unique, defiant and human.

In its ethnic imprint, the Corleone family contrasted to a 1970s trend of family restructuring. Known as Zero Population Growth (ZPG), this movement sought to reconstruct perceptions and to influence attitudes about family size. Promoters distributed buttons and other paraphernalia with the words "STOP AT TWO." Middle-class American men and women had to justify (to themselves and others) having children. To some, this new development seemed like "procreative inhibition," as *Life* labeled it, but to others the notion of limited families seemed liberating. When childbearing became a choice, regeneration no longer sufficed as reason enough for reproduction. As one proponent argued, having children "to please … parents, or perpetuate your name or image" is not doing "the rest of [society] a favor." Popular psychology urged against the "oversized" household. Doctors informed the public that "children from small families are, on the whole, more intelligent, more creative, more independent, taller, more energetic and healthier mentally and physically — all because the parents have the leisure and resources to take good care of themselves as well as their children."[38]

Juxtaposed with ZPG, this old-fashioned Italian clan accentuates heritage, ancestral loyalty, and succession. A new cast with Italian names and a screen alive with the texture of Little Italy brought, as one critic remarked, "a true Italian-American voice, an insider's view, as it were" to the mainstream screen.[39] The shift from a generic "Brotherhood" to an inside voice of heritage established a subject position, a point of connection with which ethnic groups in general could identify. Whether through experience in everyday practice or memory and stories about the immigrant-American past, identification brought the turn-of-the-century Southern European rural lifestyle into present dialogue about ethnicity. The films raise issues in the 1970s about the ways millions of immigrants wrestled with the balance between integration into American culture and maintenance of local customs. Most of these groups were unschooled and untrained for modern America. As Italian American writer Mary Ann Vigilante Mannino noted, many immigrants from Italy "came into direct contact with an opposing culture, the enlightenment-centered Anglo-American social mores that frame the dominant American ethos." Direct contact also portrayed the experience of other European ethnics.[40]

The Godfather had to pass through the eye of the assimilationist model to construct the new shape of ethnicity. The film revealed the fact that the end product of an inclusive society is not necessarily "dignity, or satisfaction, or moral pride, or political potency." Coppola added the personal touch of ethnic families to a "WASP sense of reality, stories, and symbols."[41] Adjustment to that representation occurred after antiestablishment stirrings of the late sixties and early seventies promoted a fuller realization of the ideals of autonomy and individualism. Coppola countered that emphasis on the individual with a more appropriate model stressing tradition. American society was imagined as a kaleidoscope, tapestry, and multilayered design with interwoven entities, each contributing a strand here and a color there.

A story about gangsters certainly provided the dramatic conduit and ethnicity clearly contributed an original element to the formula picture. Ultimately, however, Coppola's turn to classic narrative structure tied ends together. With the focus on the family established, the story brings Michael Corleone into the center. The favored son, the third-born Corleone played by Sicilian American Al Pacino, is not the rugged individual of urban crime dramas. He is the ideal core, the family's hope, the reason the film moves beyond Coppola's "home movie" and introduces the classic theme of power.

Michael is an American soldier, educated at Yale, dating an Anglo-American woman, and being groomed for higher aspirations than the family business. "Senator Corleone; Governor Corleone," his father tells him, but, in the tradition of Sophocles and Shakespeare, Michael is dealt another fate. Coppola will create a character with the trappings of a classic, tragic hero to provide the narrative transition into the critical commentary on the underbelly of the American dream.

Connie's wedding provides the space within which to begin constructing Michael as the subject of the narrative and a representative of Italian culture in contemporary society. Through Vito's eyes, viewers first see Michael escorting Kay Adams (Diane Keaton) to the family function. As Vito peers through the blinds in his office, he watches Michael walk in between the cars in the parking lot into the crowd at Connie's wedding. The young Corleone appears in his army uniform and sits secluded from the family, courting Kay, his beautiful, fair-haired girlfriend.[42] Kay asks Michael about his family. After resisting for a few minutes, Michael relents and tells the story of his father helping Johnny Fontaine by making a Hollywood director Jack Woltz (John Marley) "an offer he couldn't refuse." Kay is stunned when she learns that meant "either his brain or his signature would be on the contract." Michael comforts her, "That's my family, Kay. It's not me."

This sequence singles out Michael's position in the family. In the midst of festivities, he and Kay are literally separated from the Corleones while Michael establishes his version of who he is. He does not appear in a tuxedo but in a military uniform. Before he sees his

In *The Godfather* (1972) Kay (Diane Keaton) is Michael's (Al Pacino) measure of legitimacy in America (Photofest).

parents and siblings, Michael shows Kay he is interested in her alone. Fredo (John Cazale), the oldest brother, interrupts the intimate moment, meets Michael's girlfriend, kisses Kay on the cheek, and figuratively brings her into the family. Yet it will not be the calm, endearing model of the time-honored American family. The issues are different, the experiences worlds apart.

Though the film begins in the early 1950s and Michael Corleone is second generation, he functions as a voice for third-generation–Southern Europeans who attended universities, spoke English instead of the native language, dressed fashionably, fell in love with the dominant culture, and selectively disconnected themselves from ethnic identity without severing ties. The assimilation process often proved that cultural conversion was the logical conclusion to the immigrant generation's search for a better life. By contrast, a multiculturalist focus meant developing a sense of "ethnic belonging," something that would provide "a person's sense of reality," as sociologist Michael Novak explained it. One approach encouraged telling stories in "the symbols that move him."[43] Thus, many immigrant descendants in the seventies reconciled Americanization by "returning" to the past — telling family stories, recording oral histories, and renewing interest in the immigrant experience. College campuses created ethnic studies departments in colleges, promoted folklore classes, and encouraged students to write grandparents' stories and fill libraries with records of immigrant experience. The new design of interlocking bits and pieces constructing new Americana clearly meant ethnic identity could newly be imagined as an advancement in one's life, not a dilemma.[44]

Like many descendants, Michael's burden is to prove to the larger society that Italians are smart enough to attend Ivy League schools, loyal enough to serve in the military, and assimilated enough to marry successfully outside the group. Similarly, Michael Corleone separates from his roots and negotiates his life as an American with ethnic ties. His struggle throughout the film will be "to achieve one goal: to become legitimate," as one writer put it.[45]

Yet, legitimacy proves to be a double-edged sword because it involves much more than graduating from college or attracting an educated, sophisticated American woman. He is pulled into the crime world against his will and thus begins the process of reinventing both his family and himself. The film follows two plot lines at this point, one placing the Corleones within a Mafia struggle for power and the other following Michael's personal battle with his designated purpose. Michael walks into his father's hospital room where the senior is recovering from multiple gunshot wounds after an assassination attempt on his life. Intending just to visit, Michael discovers a set-up and moves quickly to save his father's life. Father and son are alone and Michael pledges, "I'm with you now, I'm with you." He rubs his father's head, kisses his hands, and Vito tearfully smiles back. It is a bittersweet moment, for they both know fate has short-circuited opportunity. Vito accepts Michael as the proper successor to the family business. Unlike the irrational, temperamental older son Santino (James Caan), the younger one is the respected, clean hero, who has "never been busted," as one policeman in the film put it.

The visit at the hospital successfully deflects the murder of his father and Michael begins to gain authority within the Corleone organization. He spars with his brother Sonny when they try to decide what to do with the most powerful syndicate head, Sollozzo (Al Lettieri), nicknamed the Turk after his dealings in the Turkish drug business. Sollozzo has called a meeting with Michael but Sonny doubts his brother's capabilities. "Hey, what are you gonna do? Nice college boy, huh?" Sonny ridicules Michael. "Didn't wanna get mixed up in the family business?" and "now you wanna gun down a police captain because he slapped you in the face a little bit?" Sonny derides his brother and ridicules the naiveté with which it appears Michael has entered into the pact. "What, do you think this is the army where you shoot 'em a mile away? You gotta get up close.... Blow their brains all over your nice Ivy League suit."

Michael proves his worthiness by devising a plot to kill both Solozzo and the corrupt police captain McCluskey (Sterling Hayden). He looks straight into Sonny's eyes and tells him, "It's not personal, Sonny. It's strictly business." Michael explains that the Solozzo operations would not be gratuitous killings. He would get both the crime head and the corrupt cop at one time. "I'm talking about a cop that's mixed up in drugs," he argues. "I'm talking about a dishonest cop, a crooked cop who got mixed up in the rackets and got what was coming to him." The young son's insularity dissolves and he becomes Vito's progeny.[46]

The Corleone henchmen have decided to go along with Michael's plan to root out Solozzo and send Michael on the assassination assignment. In one of Pacino's stellar moments in the film, Michael alone meets the Turk and McCluskey at Louis' Restaurant in the Bronx. Solozzo immediately engages Michael by brushing McCluskey aside and speaking directly to Michael in Italian. While the Irish police captain eats his Italian meal, Michael listens to Solozzo, answers with a few words here and there, but what Michael understands is not clear since this scene provides no subtitles. Solozzo's intent to bond through language suggests the distance between Michael's generation and the older one. Corleone's lack of fluency in Solozzo's discussion separates more than connects the two. Michael excuses himself, retrieves a planted gun, calmly returns, and shoots McCluskey and Solozzo in cold blood while the two eat their dinner.

Once Michael accepts the burden of the family, he dominates the film's narrative. Here the film becomes a national story that transcends ethnic references. Through Michael, the film follows classic themes of power and succession similar to medieval epics and classical tragedies. To America's families — the Vanderbilts, Kennedys, Rockefellers — Coppola adds the Corleones. The classical turn surprised the studio.[47] As Coppola said, "I knew they were not happy with what I had done. The kind of classic style that I chose in rushes maybe didn't impress them but I just wanted to survive it."[48]

Following the Sollozzo scene, Michael flees to Sicily. In contrast to Michael's previous scene in the night setting of Louis' Restaurant, the pure, bright countryside is breathtaking. The wide-angle, long shot shows off goat herders taking their flocks through the hillsides of Italy. The camera offers a panorama of the rocky hills dotted with rock and plaster, red-tile-roofed huts. Michael walks with two bodyguards up the narrow paths and into the village called Corleone perched on the side of a mountain. For a twenty-minute sequence, viewers see village pathways, men in black vests and wool caps, tavernas serving homemade wine. They hear Italian in this simple, beautiful place.

While in Sicily for over a year, Michael immerses himself in the intimacy of peasant life, *La Via Vecchia*, the "ancient" society or, in the words of one writer, the "ways of behaving, of thinking, and of organizing one's life." Villagers help fill in for Michael the images and behaviors of his heritage. They show him his father's compatriots and embrace this American as one of theirs. Viewers hear him speak Italian while they read subtitles. Away from America,

This way to Corleone, the old country, where Michael discovers his roots and Americans can find personal strength in heritage (photo courtesy of the author).

Al Pacino as Michael Corleone (shown here with Franco Citti as Calo) in *The Godfather* (1972) learns the ways of "La Via Vecchia" in Sicily (Photofest).

he retrieves a new sense of genealogy and Sicilian history. "This pastness," as one writer explains, is defined by "the diction and the gestures of the characters ... either by speaking Italian in the dialect of southern Italy, or when in America, an English often marked by the accents of the recent immigrant."[49] Michael has returned to his roots, newly empowered by the strength of a heritage built on collective identity. Sicily also transplants passion into Michael's heart and awakens him to beautiful Appolonia (Simonetta Stefanelli), the tavern owner's daughter. He approaches her father according to the code of the village and seeks permission to court his daughter. He begins his negotiation in Italian but frustrated with his lack of fluency, he turns to one of his bodyguards, Fabrizio (Angelo Infanti) to translate. The father and villagers alike require Michael to meet all concerned parties before he receives approval. Michael marries Appolonia, but danger follows and the young bride is killed soon afterwards.

Michael's old-world education allows him to mediate between La Via Vecchia and Americanization. He returns to New York more clearly connected to Sicily and his ancestor's history. During Michael's stay in Corleone, Sonny has been betrayed and murdered. Vito calls the families together and demands a stop to the feuding. He clarifies the Corleone position on the drug trade that threatens the Mafia code of honor and draws a line between drugs and acceptable organized crime. In contrast to the other syndicates, Vito refuses to let the sinister gangsterism of drugs contaminate his family. The drug argument allows the narrative to separate old-world ethics from new forms of American greed.

The last image of Don Corleone is as an elderly man, dressed in a faded, plaid flannel shirt and forties-style khakis. He and Michael are alone near the estate gardens. Vito sadly recognizes his failed mission. "I never wanted this for you," he tells Michael. "I work my whole life — I don't apologize — to take care of my family, and I refused to be a fool, dancing on the string held by all those big shots." In a close-up of the two faces, Vito continues, "I don't apologize ... but I thought that, that when it was your time, that you would be the one to hold the string.... Well, it wasn't enough time, Michael. It wasn't enough time." Shortly there-after Don Corleone dies in his garden while playing with his grandson, Anthony (Anthony Gounaris). This vulnerable father with gray stubble and crumpled clothing personalizes the Corleones and emphasizes their cultural place in American history. *The Godfather* prepares the way for a story that ends tragically, thus commenting on the possibility of ruin in the immigrant hope of a better life.

In one of Coppola's most artistic moments, during another family gathering — the bap-tism of Connie's son — brutal executions of the rival Mafiosi take place in restaurants, stair-wells, and other public places while Michael serves as the baby's godfather. Viewers see close-ups of a priest's hands administering the holy sacrament of baptism, sprinkling and anointing the baby. Juxtaposed with the family gathered in church, Corleone hit men pre-pare machine guns, grip handguns, and execute rival mobsters. In Eisenstein-like juxtaposi-tion and intercutting, sound overlays image. Viewers hear baptism water and a baby cry during the ceremony of rebirth as they watch men shoot rivals in the eye, the throat, and in between revolving hotel doors. "Do you renounce Satan," the priest asks Michael, "and all his works?" "I do," Corleone responds as two hit men machine-gun a couple in bed. Michael's ordered brutality, set in Coppola aesthetics of beauty in violence, is justified because he is fighting for the old order. Tessio (Abe Vigoda) is about to betray him. To maintain the Corleones' sense of order in an organization built on a code of loyalty, Michael officially begins his reign.

Michael is not the pathological gangster who is unaware of the nature of his own vio-lence. The baptism/execution sequence states definitively Michael's legitimate ownership of his position as the Corleone head and identifies his struggle as valiant by comparison to the impurity of Mafia activity threatening his family. He inherits his father's duty. He will pro-tect what Vito created and is justified in doing so by what one writer called "the masculinist ethic in defense of family."[50] In that system of loyalty, "Fathers 'do what they have to do' to grant their sons a better life; sons inherit the mantle to defend the achievements and the honor of their fathers." The emotional bond and financial security guarantee succession, but repro-ducing the organization requires replenishing the family.[51]

The film closes with a powerful demonstration of an important issue about America and ethnicity. Michael has returned to Kay, who confronts him over his involvement in the vio-lent killing of Connie's husband Carlo. When she asks, "Is it true?" Michael's patronizing reply — "this one time, this one time you ask me about my affairs" — defines their separation, and when he answers "no," he is like a father who keeps information from a child affection-ately and indicates she has intruded into a traditional space, exclusive to men. Kay hugs Michael, leaves the room, and in a point of view shot watches Michael. Hands shake, men hug, and the door closes. He has shut Kay out of his world and the camera zooms to Kay's agonized look. The film invites empathy for her judgment of Michael. She is the objective observer, the third perspective. Through her, viewers learn that Michael is duplicitous in his method of keeping Kay out of the business. Here, he enters into a narrative that will objec-tify him and thrust him into a trajectory of descent. As he closes the doors in front of Kay, he entices interest in the conflict and drama of his new role as the don. Like Kay, we are excluded from family business and at once believe in and distrust Michael.

In *The Godfather: Part II*, Vito's struggle for family "success" turns into Michael's personal project. Coppola rectified the prequel's glamorization of Michael.[52] *Part II* begins with Coppola's intent to build and then destroy the power of the Corleone family. The narrative flows as two parallel stories, one the sequel and the other the preface to the first film. The preface fills in Vito Corleone's life from the time he was a ten-year-old boy witnessing the murder of his mother to his immigration to America and his evolution into the Godfather. Vito (Robert De Niro) is the Italian immigrant who stops at nothing to protect his family from New York street violence. The story of a young man's success weaves in and out of Michael's reign as the family Godfather, covering the early 1900s to 1959. Coppola contrasts Vito's empowerment with Michael's indulgent and exaggerated American success story.

The opening sequence places a preadolescent Vito at Ellis Island where he sings a village hymn in Italian and gazes at the Statue of Liberty. He establishes the connection to Italian immigration and the impersonal process of quarantine in America. A dissolve shifts viewers' attention to the Corleone Lake Tahoe manor where Anthony (James Gounaris), now ten years old, celebrates his first communion, and the parallel stories begin. On "the lawns of this great estate," hundreds of guests dance to a thirty-piece orchestra, swim in the pool, water-ski on the lake, and drink champagne.

The celebration sanctions Michael's legitimacy according to American standards of wealth. A thirty-piece band at a first communion is impressive, but the Tahoe event also introduces the film's stance on ethnicity and Americanization. Frankie Pentangeli (Michael V. Gazzo), a family friend, a "via vecchia man," arrives and searches for Italian delicacies. He asks Fredo, for example, "Hey, what's with the food? Some kid in a white jacket brings me a Ritz cracker with some chopped liver. 'Canapes,' he says," and Pentangeli replies, "Go get me a salami sandwich and a glass of wine." Later, he leads Michael's mother to the dance floor and chastises the musicians, "Out of thirty professional musicians, not one of you is Italian.... C'mon, give us a tarantella," he yells at them. The band confuses the traditional song with "Pop Goes the Weasel" and Pentangeli leaves the dance floor, disgusted and clearly out of place. The garish party recalls *Part I*'s wedding reception at the Corleone estate in New York when viewers saw close-ups of Italians drinking homemade wine, eating Italian cheese, and dancing to the tarantella.

Pentangeli's objection to the Tahoe lawn party suggests not only that it is a different time but that an acculturation process has taken place between the two films. The Tahoe estate juxtaposed with Vito's immigration cubicle represents the inverse side of success, portending the real American story, one that is a bittersweet product of gains and losses. On one side, Vito's view of America from a small square window reinforces the belief in the land of opportunity. On the other, the flashy, extravagant lawn party inserts the sequel's new critical perspective. Where ethnicity and its specific sense of tradition and custom defined the Corleone family within a larger society, by *Part II*, wealth overpowers their identity.

The story begins and ends in Nevada, a western state contrasting to New York's ethnic neighborhood filled with diverse languages, businesses, and surnames that once reflected the degree of ethnic identity in Vito's community. This "village-centered Southern Italian culture" provided a means of cultural identification and relationship. By contrast, Lake Tahoe is the contemporary West, a resort built with new money. Houses are secluded in mountainscapes. Here, Michael is a loner, outside the community of ethnics. He has been handed a complex destiny: to construct a world where the power he has amassed legitimates and protects his family while not destroying the core of what means most — all without the support system of ethnic culture. Halfway through the story, the agitated son turns to his silent mother and asks "if ... father ever feared he would lose his family by being strong for it," and she replies, "times are changing." In amassing wealth, he honored his ethical duty to protect the family business, but the task changes from a clear defense against enemies outside the family to combating enemies within. By the movie's end, he is abandoned and betrayed by two brothers and his new wife Kay. Corleone wealth brings agency and legitimacy, but this elusive empire becomes the site of personal and familial destruction.

In *Part II* profit and gain shape and pervade American society. Nevada's U.S. Senator Pat Geary (G. D. Spradlin) is a common hood who makes casino deals with the mob. Michael's road to success is contingent on these connections. Through the senator, the film links the Mafia to everyday business practices, making ruthlessness a normal part of enterprise. Brutality, business, and violence are synonymous in the real world of money. *The Godfathers* portray an ironic version of making it in America. Like *Easy Rider*, the films show that the dream costs.[53] Michael justifies his father's activities to Kay by comparing Vito to senators, businessmen, and other officials. Kay replies that Michael is naïve since these officials do not kill people. Michael's answer — "Who's being naïve?" — argues that the corruption of the gangster is part of a larger force that stems from the abuses within a system of free enterprise that markets "cars and cigarettes and pollution," as Marlon Brando put it.[54]

Violence, on the other hand, justifies violence in another way. Since these films revisit the gangster genre in the post–Code era, aesthetic innovation gives the film its agency as a subversive tool. Visually, the extreme violence — an ice pick jammed through Luca Brasi's hand, a bloody horse head in between silk sheets, a woman stabbed and mutilated in bed — is justified. If the realism of brutality exists in the "legitimate" world and the film uses the Mafia as metaphor for American capitalism, brutality exaggerated represents that part of the American dream that has been hidden. The gangster of popular culture, not the businessman, held mythic power in American cinema. Generally, the "animus against business and commerce" at the time, as one commentator suggested, precluded the "legitimate businessman ... from serv[ing] as the hero of any such story." Gangster brutality is offset "by virtue of their worldly success: they are self-made men with the will, the daring, the energy ... to claw their way to the top."[55]

Yet not all violence is equal and *The Godfather* narrative qualifies the Corleones within that context. Violence operates as the form of justice in a corrupt world and creates an aura of glamour around the family. All the rough edges have been smoothed over in the appearances of Brando, Pacino, and Caan compared to the other Mafiosi, those *via vecchia* men. Their masculine appeal allows the narrative to submerge Corleone gangsterism in contrast. They are gangsters who happen to be Italian. The Mafia characters are Italian gangsters. Differentiating between the Corleones and the Mafia "others," the story defines Vito's family as the modern Italian Americans. Rival syndicate heads, Barzini (Richard Conte) and Tataglia (Tony Giorgio), for instance, have stronger features — bushy eyebrows, scarred faces, large noses — and the hit men are overweight, dumb fools and extremely violent. The Corleone henchmen also contrast to Michael and Vito, who exude control, patience, planning, and a Hollywood machismo. Similarly, Connie's husband Carlo is the Italian American "outsider" opportunist who abuses his wife and betrays the honor of the code protected by Vito early in *Part I*.[56] "You played with my sister; do you think you could fool a Corleone?" Michael mocks Carlo just before the latter's ordered strangulation.

The split between the glamorous Corleones and the Mafia "others" represents the American system ("I believe in America") that ignores its own corruption. Michael's struggle to exude "masculinity and power" but maintain control in a seemingly fair and virtuous way explains why he orders violence. At the same time, as one writer puts it, "aggression against and assimilation within the system proceed together in redefining the culture of the organization." If adding Italianness from an insider's point of view subverts "cultural prejudice," building an anticapitalist argument by othering the Mafia was also essential to set up the contrast. The separation between the Mafia and the Corleones makes a generic *Brotherhood* the point of departure for ethnic identity. It allows *The Godfather*'s family to appear legitimate within the logic of anticapitalism. The differentiation enables Vito's family to perform violent acts symbolically on long-held derisive attitudes and beliefs about Italians. The Corleones sit somewhere between the brutes of the old-world Mafia and the generic rendering of a Kirk Douglas type of casting.

The Corleones, not the Mafia "others," are America. They represent the process of Americanization, shifting from the paradigm of defacing names, disavowing ethnicity, and appropriating the whiteness of popular culture. In the assimilation model, as writer Mannino explained, immigrants were "accustomed to seeing themselves through the lens of the dominant culture." Skin color and other physical features defined social location and distinguished Southern from Northern Europeans. As the third-generation writer observed: "Italian/Americans ... [were] barred ... from certain churches, schools, neighborhoods, and clubs before the Civil Rights Act of 1964." The dominant culture's fixation with skin color spilled over to distaste of custom. Italians were "identified ... as coming from an inferior race." Thus, Mannino continued, "A specific Italian/American may find herself treated as a white American by some and as a black American by others." A derogatory term such as "black dago" reflected the contrasting image of Italians to the prevailing Anglo celebration of blondness and whiteness.[57] The likeness was both absorbed and resisted by the descendants of immigrants. As sociologist Michael Novak observed, "Many still carry the marks of changing the names, of 'killing' their mother tongue and renouncing their former identity, in order to become 'new men' and 'new women.'"[58] Exaggerating Italianness through the Mafia characters functions as an avowal of the history of ethnic derision. Affirming that history is a necessary first step to de-stigmatizing ethnic identity and creating a sense of renewal.

On the one hand, the Mafia as the "others" offers a way for the Corleones to construct themselves as powerful, ethnic, and glamorous. At the same time, the Mafia as an allegory of violence in America recalls the days of "dago" derision and justification for revenge.[59] The film's treatment of Italianicity and Michael's nightmare fifties affluence confront both the perception of Italians that Hollywood helped create and the role of assimilation in repressing cultural identity in the larger society. In short, "othering" works both ways. The Mafia allows Italianicity to escape its derisive days by dividing the group into the good and bad. This division allows for a positive rendition of ethnic identity if seen in the context of a cautionary tale about the meaning of Michael's success.

The film's warnings work through Vito's parallel story of immigration. Sicily is juxtaposed with Lake Tahoe. These contrasting places construct an American narrative at a time when Americans argued that identity recovery was an important process of ethnic regeneration. Where baby boomers likely grew up with parents concealing ethnic affiliation, they now found cultural uniqueness empowering. As Novak contended, "The new ethnicity ... is a movement of self-knowledge on the part of members of the third and fourth generation."[60]

The 1970s afforded Euro-ethnics an opportunity for self-definition, no longer expected to "melt" themselves into Americanness, as something disembodied and detached. Ethnic Americans began wearing pins and buttons, displaying bumper stickers and nationalistic flags, or otherwise negotiating new terms of cultural identity. "Italian Power," "Kiss Me, I'm Greek," "Polish is Beautiful," and "For Italians Only" were forms of marketing ethnic legitimacy and ways of expanding the meaning and range of Americanness. One's ancestral affiliation and non–American inheritance appeared not only normal but symbolic of Americanism. Southern and Eastern European immigrants (Jews, Poles, Italians, Greeks, Slavs, Armenians, Croatians, Serbs, Czechs, Slovaks, Lithuanians, Estonians, Portuguese, and others) helped engender social and cultural changes during these years with the reinvention of what was called "ethnic pride." Popular culture embraced instead of denied ethnic food, dress, jewelry, and other identifying features.

To claim this ancestry without embarrassment meant taking a clear step toward understanding "the inner history of this migration" and "the aspirations and fears of some seventy million Americans."[61] By bringing the "peasant" family into view on location in Sicily, *Part II* dramatizes a way of life once disparaged in America. The return to the past through the film's narrative of Vito as a young boy recasts the importance of the immigrant experience. The ancient society became part of the newly desired balance for many descendants. The challenge for many, once in American society, was to ensure regeneration and reproduction of ethnic culture in such diversity and also to retain personal authority on American terms. A new tradition began in the 1970s where Americans emphasized reconnecting rather than breaking with the past. Michael's return to the immigrant country reconciles for the third and fourth generations what the primary part of Italian (hence ethnic) recovery is. From ethnic denial to ethnic ideal, identity is not something to "get over."

Both films add to ethnic regeneration by filling in the past through a nostalgic rendition of the Sicilian village. As a way to imagine a journey into the world of grandparents' homelands, the Sicily sequences make the immigrant country beautiful and necessary. In the slow pace, the bright daylight, and the country lifestyle, the films create a standard of taste for the expansive space of Sicily in contrast to the claustrophobic streets of Little Italy and dark interiors of the Tahoe estate. Descendants return to the premodern village to seek roots and enjoy leisurely travel. In the book, the Sicilian scenes informed readers of the origins of Vito's Mafia connection and the motivation for revenge. In the film, the peasant past operates as what historian Joan Scott calls an "originary" moment.[62] In the narrative of family history, Sicily functions as an aesthetic magnet, a form of roots assertiveness, a way of reimagining Hollywood Italians as Italian authentics.

For the immigrant generation, the ethnic neighborhood manifested a sense of belonging. As sociologist Richard Alba pointed out, it had the "capacity to concentrate the institutions and cultures of an ethnic group, thereby keeping alive the sentiments and loyalties associated with ethnicity in adult residents and socializing a new generation to ethnic ways." By the third generation, however, after the flight to suburbs, identity construction depended less on living in concentrated neighborhoods. Identification for those in more assimilated areas had to flow from other sources — going to ethnic restaurants, festivals, churches, or to the "old country." These "undeniable embodiments of ethnicity," Alba continues, serve the purpose of "rekindl[ing] some of the memories and feelings of those whose identities have weakened or lapsed." *The Godfather* provided a similar kind of travel and allowed viewers a glimpse at, as if passing through, an ethnic neighborhood, thus encouraging an emotional attachment.[63] The neighborhood tour provided essential details from Southern European experience in America, imagined on screen as the way it was for immigrants.

The view of the neighborhood from a theater seat resonated as part of what the new ethnicity sanctioned for third and fourth generations in comparison to what second generations often experienced. As Alba contended, "The reassessment of ethnicity ... produced not simply a rediscovery of significant existing aspects of American society, but a different image of what American society *should* be." Ethnic agency, seventies style, became "a valid form of self-expression under the threat of obliteration by the cultural hegemony implicit in the melting pot." Many saw, as Alba continued, "hold[ing] on to their particular traditions and differences" as a right.[64] Set in a seventies milieu of diversity rather than previous ones of assimilation, understanding ethnicity as a right also implied identity was a choice rather than an evolutionary flow of inheritance and ancestry. This shift changed the source of cultural knowledge. Ethnicity could be consumed and identity acquired. In this fashion, ethnic consumption easily became subject to the trappings of what Philip Deloria described for Native Americans as "cosmopolitan multiculturalism," that is, "a license for *anyone* to choose an ethnic identity ... regardless of family, history, or tribal recognition" [Deloria's italics].[65]

The *Godfather: Part II* participates in the play between ethnic self-expression and cultural consumption, that is, wearing the mask of stereotypes, in a similar way. On the one hand, the Mafia as "other" extricates Italianness from its Hollywood background because those who play these characters exude traditional practices closer to the ethnic family of ancestry than "cosmopolitan" multiculturalism. They are the *ancien regime*. Their characters have entered the discourse of multiculturalism by reviving traditional identity. At the same time, the Mafia "authentics," the *via vecchia* men, recycle a persona. Tattaglia, Clemenza, Pentangeli, and others performed Italianness for viewers' consumption. What they produced is both the recognition of the value of old ways and a new category for Hollywood use. They represent both the true identity and the mask of Italianness.

Michael, on the other hand, signifies Americanness and mediates Italianness. Expressing ethnicity for Michael means returning to the cultural source of knowledge that filled in heritage and ancestry, a key component to the seventies multiculturalism. This new awareness helps him fulfill his role as family patriarch and his duty to create stability. Michael also defines essential Americanness — Ivy League schools, marriage outside Italian boundaries, making money. The story of American success is the sequel to Vito's struggle. Wealth, not family or culture, has given the young Corleone his power and mobility, but wealth also overshadows the "ancien" system of succession. Both family identity and monetary stability depended on a patriarchal system for regeneration in conventional cultures. Passing on lineage in the family, like passing on the organization of crime through service and loyalty, gave Italianness and the Mafia their social structure. Both the ethnic family and the Mafia ethic of honor and loyalty centered on reproducing the "hereditary status." Passed through the bond especially of father and son, this "patriarchal foundation," as one critic explained, "and the associated paradigm of masculinity — of silence, honor, and protection — governed the relations of men and women in the family."[66]

The masculine ethic of protection so motivates Michael in *Part II* that he orders the murder of his brother, Fredo, upon discovering his betrayal. "You're nothing to me now," Michael shouts at Fredo. "You're not a brother. You're not a friend. I don't want to know you or what you do. I don't want to see you at the hotels. I don't want you near my house. When you see our mother, I wanna know a day in advance so I won't be there. You understand?" It is raining. Michael is inside his Lake Tahoe mansion and looks out onto the lake where Fredo is slain in a rowboat.

It was necessary to sacrifice Fredo for the good of Michael's position and protection of the honor code, but by the end of the film, Michael "fires" his Irish step-brother, Tom Hagen (Robert Duvall). Tom is the faithful family consigliere and Vito's adopted son. Steadfast and loyal in his legal protection of the family during the reign of both father and son, Tom resists the young don's next request. "You're gonna come along with me in these things I have to do or what?" Michael asks Tom. "I'm staying," Tom replies. Michael casts him aside and severs all ties that bind. Unlike Fredo, whose death does not destroy his identity, Michael's dismissal of Tom obliterates the faithful consigliere's legitimacy as a Corleone. In a sense, Michael denies Tom his past, his identity, by becoming his employer at the end of the film instead of his brother.

Michael kills Fredo and dismisses Tom, but he has to face a larger problem. For ethnicity and therefore the code to be collective, passing tradition on through stable processes is key. The ancient code assured succession because it predetermined who belonged. The American tradition of choice and independence, however, spoiled the conditions of lineage. Michael's form of Italianicity by the end of *Part II* is nothing like his father's. Compared to Vito's paternal benevolence, Michael is the calculating professional, intent on absolute power, exploiting even his brothers. Vito's family resembled the norm for many ethnics in America where the father was the "head" of the household. Michael's American rendition complicates that model by suggesting male power can also be abusive. Similar to Puzo's memories of male violence in the larger Italian community, the film deromanticizes Vito's "immigrant" America by showing the result of the Corleone rise to power. Michael has forsaken the possibility of regeneration of the family by destroying its cohesive unit.

Kay holds the key to Michael's irrevocable exchange of power for family. Unlike Vito's wife, Kay refuses to subject her children to the violence of the Mafia and divorces her husband. Michael forbids Kay to see their young children and he again shuts the door in her face when she unexpectedly appears in Tahoe. Divorce and estrangement are clear enough, but the question of how to ensure the life of the family in view of Michael's power, wealth, and impersonalized existence persists. He sits alone in the Tahoe winter, centered in the narrative, a gangster, and the credits role. Undoubtedly, he has achieved financial success, the American necessity for mobility. Michael Corleone controls the syndicate but the history and turn of events qualify that triumph. A decorated soldier, an underdog ethnic, has also become a ruthless murderer.

Identifying with Michael encourages recognizing the inherent tragedy of the American struggle, balancing personal success with ties that bind. By contrast, the Pentangelis and the Tattaglias help shape the Corleone Americanness but also expose an underlying truth about what the film's critique of American society accomplishes. Michael has become America. He is the capitalist, a corporate executive whose power works best single-handedly. Both films shroud the narrative of American immigration with a cautionary gloom. Protecting the unit that guarantees succession — the family — is extremely important to organized crime. The Mafia are also there to remind Michael that old ethnicity, family belonging, is not a choice. It is different from a "cosmopolitan multiculturalism." It is rooted in ancestry, loyalty, and collective agreement, not voluntary consent. Michael Corleone's world has become a spectacle of contemporary desolation. It is a frozen landscape of mansions in forests overlooking winter lakes. *Part II* represents both the secularization and objectification of Vito's hope.

Michael represents loss, not gain. It is an exemplary "death of the subject."[67] Michael is denied an inner life.

The film critiques capitalism by showing that its highly individualistic competitiveness destroys the individual and therefore the family. At the same time, from the vantage point of multicultural discourse, autonomy destroys the individual if the culture is lost. Thus, the death of the subject as the final objectification must be positioned within American tradition that has privileged the individual's freedom as the central subject and the governing claim to triumph over outside forces. American film has been mostly a cinema of the individual, promoting the value of autonomy and individualism. These films do something different if seen through ethnic perspectives. Obliquely they encourage identification with the collective ideal through the downfall of Michael, Connie, and Sonny. Despite and because of their fall, the family, as a "mediating structure for society" and a "guarantee" for passing heritage on, is reinforced.[68] Ambition and success cost Vito's children their family but not their identity born into Italianness. Two primary Corleones remain at the end of *Godfather II*, Connie and Michael. Kay, Tom, and other "disloyal" and "unfit" members have been banished. "Michael," Connie tells him, "I'd like to stay close to home now if that's all right." The Mafia "others" constantly remind viewers of the cultural identity lost with the second generation. They serve as the "authentic" by contrast and offer the romantic viewer a way back to heritage. They also serve as a reminder that the past can teach.

When Paramount's 1969 *The Brotherhood* found no audience waiting in line, it was not the genre, the plot, or even the interest in Italian gangsters that failed to bring in millions. Clearly by 1972 the "ethnic inflections" of Pacino and Talia Shire in *The Godfather* films contrasted deeply with the "whiteness" of a Kirk Douglas (even in a black mustache) and the "Brotherhood." [69] That several powerful directors turned the first project down speaks even more highly for the assumptions of the time. Not only could many of them not envision Italians playing the parts, they also skipped over the ethnic imagination to which Coppola spoke so well with his final product. *The Godfathers* were vibrant, urban, and romantic. They brought the "unmeltable ethnics" into the kaleidoscopic, multidimensional seventies, offering an alternative to the assimilation process that leads to denial of cultural identity. Ethnic eyes could immerse themselves into recovery and American success symbols of power and wealth at the same time. If seen as a caution against that fate, the films allowed the subject to be not destroyed but reborn.

Coppola's "home movie" prepared the way for a 1970s hope of regeneration. His films revitalized the value in the ties that bind if seen as a cautionary tale. These films brilliantly reconciled both conservative and liberal views of American society. On the conservative side, the films offered a means for preserving these ideals. As one critic commented, "They are not destroyed because they are inadequate per se; family ties, social mobility, quest for security, male companionship, and even religious values all relate and correspond to real universal human needs for community, love, respect, support, appreciation." On the liberal side, it is the "the social institution ... upon which the Corleones relied to provide and protect these values [that] withered before the irrational, destructive forces of capitalism, the main goal of which is profit, not the meeting of human needs."[70]

Such ideological significance in representing an extended family with authority resonated with one film critic at the time. "I think the film affected me so powerfully even after several viewings," he commented, "because it presents and plays on most of the now-threatened bourgeois values — family ties, social mobility, the quest for security and respectability in a competitive world, the friendship between men engaged in the same work, the importance of religion, and individualism — which I was taught to believe in and respect." His enthusiasm grew not from identifying as an Italian but as a member of "a large, newly urbanized, upper-middle-class Pennsylvania German family whose religion was Mennonite." Like the family in *The Godfather*, he was "surrounded by relatives" in his formative years. This "positive and comfortable" experience stayed "deep inside" and its ideals "remain[ed] intact," even though he left the family in his early adult years.[71]

Ethnicity, therefore, functioned as a way to negotiate the 1960s "free spirit" identity and the 1970s fondness for roots. This kind of multicultural discourse encouraged mutual appreciation rather than the generation gap. Group identity, not autonomy, was the aim. Distrusting anyone over thirty now seemed disingenuous. Reevaluating the integrity of authority and reassessing the meaning in profound individuality led to questioning the result of autonomy. A common answer was a mediated identity, a reconciliation based not on renouncing one's cultural heritage but on transcending parochialism. A subtle but important shift showed the process of subjectification as one that forms the individual out of the group rather than the reverse.

The Godfathers measure the distance American society had come from the time when immigrants appeared as "alien" creatures, carriers of disease, or threats to American society. The progressive aspect of the films lies in their Italian revival — in sanctioning speaking, looking, acting, and individuating as American and ethnic success. *The Godfather I & II* change the position, the image, and the kind of Italian American that movies had constructed. They also speak to seventy years of social angst fed by language repression and the treatment of differences as contemptible. Instead of skin color, foodways, and personal lifestyle as something to despise, they were now celebrated as examples of American diversity.[72]

The Coppola pair, some have argued, "can be seen as an inflated wish for [the singular, white, male subject's] reconstitution, and it has been the Italian-American criminal, with its connotation for a nostalgic form of power, that has been utilized to construct this fantasy." During "this particular construction of ethnicity ... white racial and ethnic purity was being seriously threatened by nonwhite peoples." Thus the fantasy is the wish for exclusive control through "an all-white militant group."[73] Italian American men hold the reins of power in these films. Their incorporation into American society as part of the wealthy elite adds an ironic twist to the American dream and the defining features of multiculturalism. The question is whether the nature of dominance for white ethnics during this period is also a nostalgic wish for self-glorification and uninhibited power.

At a glance, the way both films treat women seems to confirm that argument. Italian American women in this film are either silent or psychotic. Vito's wife in *Part II*, for instance, is a figurehead. She speaks occasionally to her children in both films ("times are changing"), but her role closely compares to stereotypical renditions of women in aprons who take care of children. Moreover, Connie represents women in an abusive marriage. Instead of rebelling against that form of subservience, by *Part II*, she shuns her role as mother, wife, and daughter. Glamour and allure hide her self-hatred. Connie sweeps into the Tahoe celebration (a week late, her mother tells her), "rushing through tables, waving an arm jangling with gold jewelry, and carrying several gift-wrapped packages." At her side she brings "a blond and wrinkled-handsome escort named Merle" (Troy Donahue), a "pimp" according to Michael.[74] Connie's exaggerated glamour represents the inverse side of autonomy and raises the question of paternal benevolence. Her attraction to Merle is neither an act of defiance nor a statement of independence but a sign of poor judgment or an inability to desire anyone but abusive, controlling men. Rather than being a resourceful woman, Connie literally falls onto her knees in *Part II,* begging for Michael to be her keeper. "I think I did things to hurt myself," Connie tells Michael in their moment of reconciliation, "so that you'd know that I had hurt you." Her return humanizes Connie and brings her back to a functional role within the family and keeps her dependent on Michael's protection at the same time.

By contrast, Vito's mother (Maria Carta) at the beginning of *Part II* embodies the ideal center of the family. She desperately tries to avenge her husband's death by pulling a knife on his murderer while trying to save her son. This characterization echoes portrayals of female ancestors as strong, resourceful, and in the words of one writer, exuding "a zest for life" and the strength to "triumph over adversities." In America, Michael's duty to the Mafia family is based on a patriarchal control keeping women outside its core. Only one woman has a measure of choice. Kay, a New England WASP, is the nonethnic who desires the dark-haired Italian. For Michael she is both "remedy" and obstacle. Kay's "outside" status signifies the guarantee of passing, especially for children to enter the dominant culture.[75] Yet, a contemporary relationship based on mutual understanding comes with Kay. When that does not materialize, she aborts her pregnancy and divorces Michael. This film selectively characterizes Kay's "outside" status as her means of agency. While the films personalize the power to speak from the inside, combating former ethnic stereotypes by contrasting the Corleones to the Mafia men, their power to reconstruct ethnicity is limited to Puzo's deconstructed singing Italian and *The Brotherhood*'s gangsters. A film extending the same critical comment to ethnic domination of women would have to wait.

Obliquely, the films decode a final image. In the famous horse-head scene in *Godfather I,* filmmaker Jack Woltz, who refused to give a movie role to Vito's godson, wakes up to the bloody head of his prize racehorse buried between the sheets of his bed. By targeting the Hollywood producer of the classic age, this scene speaks specifically to the violence of the cinematic past that collapsed Italian culture into stereotypes. If, as Lester Friedman and others have written, producers and directors "buried their immigrant roots, as they ruled over one of American's largest and most influential industries," their "ferocious, even pathological embrace of America," their reinvention of the "idealized America" that would require "one ... to cast off 'foreignisms,' religious observances, names, and traditions," came back to haunt them in the image of Woltz, a Jewish filmmaker. Severing old stereotypes meant confronting Hollywood head on (no pun intended).[76]

At the same time, culture is sometimes a stronger determinant of politics than economics. If so, then ethnic visualization (like ethnic resurgence outside of film) had a power and a price. Ethnicizing the gangster genre through the grittiness of gangster and Italian culture in New York City obviously risked making Italianicity generic and stereotypical or emboldened and imposing, both consumables ready for the marketplace. Italians from Coppola's and Puzo's points of view narrowed representations of the ethnic to the city streets, idealizing ethnicity at the same time it empowered viewers with new authority of ethnic identity. City Italians and Mafia men, as if the complete authentic Italians, led viewers out of and into contradictions.[77] Visualizing ethnicity in the two films proved appealing and socially empowering. The new reality of cultural roots legitimized by the celebrity appeal of Brando, Pacino, and Caan generated a new resource of distinctiveness. Noticing ethnicity on screen, however, ultimately deepened the impact of Hollywood and its culture of production.[78]

Mutual appreciation of cultural difference had an exchange rate, a cultural advantage for many immigrants' offspring. With the turn to multiculturalism in the 1970s, to be able to celebrate the past and turn ancestors' struggles into a success story suggests agency and privilege.[79] As some critics have suggested, if ethnic grievances were over legitimacy, their struggle was less economic and political than social. Those who aspired to and experienced the American dream by graduating from college and entering into the political, entrepreneurial, and professional realm, experienced a more open and less contentious environment. The expression of a collective identity was possible because ethnic Europeans were able to claim a different history and status from racialized groups such as African Americans. Celebrating ethnicity to shed oppressive social conditions became an opportunity for a new avowal of whiteness in relation to multicultural discourse emanating from a separation of race. Thus, Southern and Eastern European descendants asking for self-respect vis-à-vis the past seemed to some disingenuous and ironic.[80] It would be difficult to claim the harsh history of oppression and pine for the past at the same time.

Ethnic revival was caught in the space between liberation from a derogatory image and romanticizing immigrant experience by presenting it as quaint. The challenge was to take advantage of the current popularity of ethnic pride without preying on the cultural space of others or reinventing another pigeonhole. At the same time, to be meaningful, the new ethnicity needed to be more than just an appreciation of food, language, and appearances. Awareness was valuable only if the result was collective reinvigoration and if there was a recognition of cultural identity as a "life-support" rather than a "colonizer." The new ethnicity had to be founded on the knowledge of others, the "liberty from assault," and a release from the "stigma of foreignness." Rather than "melting," disappearing, and subordinating family identity, the new ethnicity needed to offer cultural reclamation. If diversity were to become the dominant model of American society, then living it (without self-glorification) was "crucial for mutual understanding."[81] A new ethnicity that did not answer real issues would soon turn up an empty vessel.

Coppola's films encouraged ethnic identification by posing a narrative that affirmed rather than denied culture, experience, custom, practice, and heritage. The filmmaker and the novelist implanted a possibility for ways that archetypes and traditions in American narratives could include ethnicity.[82] Through reaffirmation one could legitimate personal identity within a collective ancestry and American experience without deferring to either one. Ethnic resurgence during the 1970s redefined the conditions of whiteness. Its makeup changed. Rather than just sliding into a unified dominant group, third-generation ethnics weighted it with their own objections and additions.

The 1970s regeneration of ethnicity seemed like a refuge at a time when Americans in general were coming to terms with Watergate and the end of the Vietnam War. Puzo placing the endearing Corleones in bookstores across America in the late sixties offered exciting drama, but Coppola's 1970s screen magic made the ethnic presence specific and memorable. Through images of Sicily and its village-scapes that defined cultural identity, the film placed, as one writer put it, "Vito and Michael Corleone ... among the best loved and most well known in the history of American film."[83] These elements helped interrogate the "bleached" Burt Lancaster image of dominant culture. Looking too Italian was finally acceptable, intriguing, and fascinating. If expressing ethnicity drew popular interest, Michael's story of destruction tapped into popular desire for humanizing cultures through family imagery. Michael's tragedy expands and exploits the popular desire for multiculturalism as a cure for the ills of American society at the time. This alternative imagination addresses the pattern of cultural denial and rejection experienced by immigrants by legitimizing heritage. If nothing more, the attempt to move from Hollywood Italians to Italians in Hollywood conveyed a sense of "dignified difference" by mere public endorsement of the films.[84]

Coppola has forever made an Italian crime family a part of American identity. *The Godfathers* combined the experimental with the classical, the romantic with realistic, and broke box office records set by Robert Wise's family picture *The Sound of Music* nearly a decade earlier. Compared to Wise's 1965 cast with Julie Andrews, Christopher Plummer, Richard Haydn, Eleanor Parker, Ben Cartwright and others, Coppola's line-up — Al Pacino, Robert De Niro, Richard Casagliano, Al Martino, Alex Rocca, Tony Giorgio, Salvatore Corsitto, Franco Sitti, Blachard Caragliano, and others — makes the cultural significance of his pair of pictures difficult to ignore. The Corleone family sat as an unlikely contender for attention from those

While accepting their Oscars for *The Godfather: Part II* (1974), the Coppolas show that filmmaking is a family affair. From left (in back): Francis Ford Coppola, wife Eleanor Coppola, mother Italia Coppola, and father Carmine Coppola; from left (in front): son Roman Coppola and unidentified. (©AMPAS/ABC/Photofest).

who grew up on *Leave it to Beaver, Ozzie and Harriett, Donna Reed, Father Knows Best*, and other such serials promoting functional relationships in a relatively democratic household where children had rights. To find the extended, ethnic family in familiar American ideals took the 1970s social context of multiculturalism. Popular films such as *The Graduate* and *Love Story* critiqued family inconsistencies, but they did not redraw the basic unit of the family established in the well-known television programs.

The turn to multiculturalism in the broader society offered American film a chance to examine the effects and meaning of assimilation in relation to immigrant cultures and experiences. If empowerment once meant accommodating Anglo-hegemony and melting ethnic cultures into dominant identities, *The Godfathers'* popularity suggests ethnic inflections tapped into rapidly changing attitudes and values about being American. These films both widened and narrowed the scope in imagining American identity. Playing "the ethnic factor" in the gangster genre proved a delicate balance between innovative embellishments and engrained stereotypes. Together with its sequel, *Part I* helped define a paradigm shift toward diversity as the appropriate ways of understanding American society. Coppola's films inscribed a new subjectivity for Italians in the midst of rising numbers of immigrant descendants' college attendance. How these offspring negotiated cultural identity conveys the degree to which American society had changed from the 1960s. Placed in the 1970s era of multiculturalism, the result for both films was an appeal across the spectator spectrum. The films changed ethnic engagement and helped viewers negotiate a different America. During the process, questions of gains and losses, identification, and "othering" surfaced. As American icons, *The Godfathers* helped make ethnic identity "completely legitimate" while warning about unbridled success.

Coppola's *The Godfather* changed forever the amount of money a film could gross. In just six months it earned twice as much as *Love Story* in the same amount of time and four times *Airport*'s half-year run in 1970.[85] To film critic Andrew Sarris, the film manifested "probably the first reasonably talented and sensibly adaptable directorial talent to emerge from a university curriculum in film-making."[86] Coppola was now conspicuous. The young Italian American confirmed that a college-trained filmmaker could make it big.[87]

The 1970s brought experimental films such as Peter Bogdanovich's *The Last Picture Show* (1971), Stanley Kubrick's *A Clockwork Orange* (1971), and Bob Fosse's *Cabaret* (1972) into the million-dollar box-office earnings range.[88] Later moneymakers, including *The Exorcist* (1973), broke *The Godfather*'s box office record and *The French Connection* won best picture of 1974. Despite being crowd pleasers, however, none of these films acquired the cultural status of *The Godfathers*. By December 1974, with *Part II*'s release, it was clear that a new Hollywood had taken shape.

At the 1975 Academy Awards ceremony, it was "The Francis Ford Coppola Family Hour." With *The Godfather: Part II* collecting six Oscars of eleven nominations, the "family" dominated the Dorothy Chandler Pavilion stage that night. Coppola and his father each received an award as did the film for Best Picture and Robert De Niro for Best Actor.[89] Indeed, Hollywood no longer dealt in the same abstract way with ethnicity. Real people walked to the center of the stage as the Coppolas claimed the Corleone success.

Sight & Sound's Top Ten films poll in 2002 listed *The Godfather* as "one of the enduring works of American cinema."[90] The American Film Institute's best one hundred American films list placed *The Godfather* as number three and *The Godfather: Part II* number thirty-two. The gangster story that swept critics and viewers off their feet became a cultural icon.

What Coppola once worried may cheapen his artistic career and take him from San Francisco to Hollywood permanently turned him into the cinematic renaissance man. Not only did the visionary filmmaker convert a bestseller into a cultural emblem, but better than anyone at the time, he understood the power of the experimental trend. While not forsaking the potential to entertain, he brought the "now movie" in line with the traditional story of power and success. On many levels, Coppola's projects exemplify the changes in the industry between 1965 and 1975. *The Godfather* films confirmed that the studio system was now composed of both university- and industry-trained directors. With their new visual style, these films demonstrated the worth of the new ratings system. The post–Code era allowed filmmakers the creative chance to visualize the gritty elements of everyday life. Coppola also showed that unknown faces — Italian at that — could make the screen come alive. Like Nichols, Penn, and Altman, Coppola chanced the unproven cast. His foresight gave Pacino the break of a lifetime and satisfied viewers' taste for the "authentic" image. These details, along with exceptional timing, jump-started careers and transported film into its next artistic zone.

Generated in part by Coppola's blockbuster success in *The Godfather* in 1972, the "world of the contemporary cinema" emerged. Those experimentalists on college campuses took the high road through mainstream film, popularizing classical narratives in ways that set the standard for content and taste for the upcoming Generation X. The college-trained group such as Martin Scorsese developed sophisticated narratives for the audiences seasoned on probing the complex underbelly of contemporary America. Outside the film-school circle, another boomer with a knack for the visual, Steven Spielberg, drew viewers back to the family picture. His 1975 spectacle *Jaws* led the next generation of blockbusters forward with the particular kind of electronic experimentation the film offered. More interested in classic stories than the experimental element, Spielberg fashioned myth into the language of American film. Coppola's colleague and collaborator George Lucas further drew the era that brought the independent experimentalists — the *Easy Rider*s, the *Alice's Restaurant*s — into classic stories of good and evil. Once more filmmakers adjusted the lens for an America that had changed. Antigenre and traditional story makers lined their cameras up, side by side, and prepared for the next view of the promise that is the agency of film.

Conclusion

Cinematic Anarchists Go Generic

The Seventies movies meant so much to young people.... The kids who said "Wow!" when they came out of a movie and couldn't say any more were expressing some deep feeling. The kids who come out of *Twister* may say "Wow!" but it isn't the same "Wow!" It's a special-effects "Wow!"
— Pauline Kael interview

As *The Godfather: Part II* swept the Academy Awards and played in theaters around the world, a rookie director, twenty-nine-year-old Steven Spielberg, completed production near Martha's Vineyard of a film that defined the contemporary blockbuster for decades. The *Jaws* project began in early 1974 and opened a year later in June at 409 theaters around the country. Bringing in over seven million dollars during its first weekend, the project earned six times *The Godfathers*' combined initial run. With other big-budgets — *The Exorcist* (1973), *The Sting* (1973), and *The Towering Inferno* (1974) — indeed the experimental era of the "Now Movie" deferred to a new New Hollywood.[1]

Some saw the beginning of a new golden age; others saw a red flag. Next to the low-budget experiment of *Easy Rider*, these big films seemed like sell-outs. Peter Biskind praised the monumental directors of the seventies, but disputed "the cultural revolution of that decade." Real change, he claimed, "like the political revolution of the '60s, ultimately failed." Writer-director Leonard Schrader, Paul's older brother, found that "this group of people started to make really interesting films, and then just took a toboggan ride into the gutter. How the hell did that ever happen?" Like Schrader and Biskind, Peter Bogdanovich lamented the change. To him, the new industry verified that the experimentalist moment had caved in to the American system of wealth. After *Jaws*, filmmakers forgot how to make the artistic movie. "They're no longer interested," he lamented.[2]

As in the larger society, evolution, not revolution, was possible. Artistry eclipsing economics demanded too much of American viewers and the industry. Within those limitations, however, something had happened. There was a transfer of artistic power from the producer to the director, a new status for independent filmmaking, a rising interest in the artistic potential of the feature, and new content for mainstream cinema. The years 1965–1975 witnessed the end of the old studio structure and the censorship code system and the development of

204

a ratings classification. By the end of the 1960s, the industry redefined itself with new chief Jack Valenti and a national organization promoting quality cinema, the American Film Institute. These foundational changes were generated partially by members of a younger generation who saw film as their art. Interested devotees formed film societies, took film education courses in college, and developed regional film festivals. Accomplishments between 1965 and 1975 confirmed the status of cinema as "the art that matters."[3]

Subverting convention by picking up a camera seemed a promising form of activism for sixties experimentalists. Film, like a social movement or piece of legislation to reconfigure American society, had the potential to change minds. From the local film society to the campus classroom to the annual film festival, film's agency appeared promising. At the very least, it would provide consciousness-raising, helping "people to think and feel their relationship to their conditions of existence" as film educator Christopher Faulkner put it. "The most important knowledge we can take away from the cinema," he argued, "must be knowledge of our social existence[s]."[4]

In this environment, it was not the big name but the *unusual* story that engaged viewers. They expected "something new and something different," Richard Zanuck remarked.[5] The "amorphous under-30 audience," as film historian Diane Jacobs described them, showed "it was tired of the costume drama and the safe situation comedy."[6] Other writers noted, "The self-styled new film generation never thinks of movies as an 'industry' but idealistically as 'the language of today.'"[7] Only a few years before that such an idea would have been "a crass outrage," a *Saturday Review* pundit declared.[8] With boomer enthusiasm, film earned the status in America as the preferred art form and the place to invest the most artistic vitality at hand. Encouraged by the creative freedom within the industry by the late 1960s and spurred by the antiestablishment sentiment, the young showed their passion for revolutionizing the role of film in American society.

The fervent interest in a cinema of change helped cast a shadow on the musical extravaganza, the bedrock of studio Hollywood. Before 1965, the industry invested in the family epic, the musical, and the spectacle picture. Producers controlled the filmmaking process and directors worked as technicians. Gradually, American viewers showed that the European art film, the auteur cinema, had widespread support in theaters across the country. Twentieth-Century–Fox's *Cleopatra* (1963) should have been the warning sign, with its extensive losses. The industry was slow to respond, however, and thought it still had a lively market when *The Sound of Music* (1965) broke box office records. With the dissolution of the censorship code and changing social mores, however, Hollywood awoke to the value of an experimental film such as *Easy Rider*. Captain America's ride made it clear to filmmakers that Hollywood would no longer be haunted by the ghost of the "zillion million" spectacle or "some ancient Egyptian queen on a cruddy barge," as one *Look* writer commented.[9]

Experimentation with mainstream film brought a star image better matched to the tastes and identities of the under-thirty audience. By the time Francis Coppola collaborated with Mario Puzo, audiences had seen the new "rough hewn" talent of Hoffman, Fonda, Hopper, Ross, Christie, and Guthrie.[10] Added to those were Pacino, De Niro, and Duvall. Few knew any of these actors before the improvisation period in filmmaking. Audiences interested in watching stars of a different kind helped the industry turn the corner toward a fresh film business. Together they became forces in Hollywood.

Changes in the infrastructure along with new attitudes toward film ultimately altered the exhibition arm of the industry. Exhibitors at the time confirmed that content, not geography, determined audience choice. They reorganized advertising enticements and targeted the new composition of film markets based on ratings categories.[11] The classification of films established in the latter sixties and early seventies helped guide specific interests for marketers. The R-rated film became a solid money maker and improved the chance for Hollywood's mainstream big-budget film to broaden its appeal. Generally, exhibitors refused to show the X-rated film and newspapers declined space for advertising. In 1971, the industry added another category: PG (Parental Guidance) for the adolescent group. The PG markets sat alongside the R-rated class, and Eisenstein-like aesthetics integrated with Hollywood drama. By 1975, as one film historian noted, "the full impact of the movie ratings system was clearly established."[12]

The body of pictures considered in this study characterizes the development of film as the art that mattered and the place where experimental enthusiasm met commercial success. During this period, both filmmakers and viewers imagined themselves as producers of something called the "Now Movie." Filmmakers arrived in Hollywood politically aware of the culture debates circulating throughout America and eager to challenge the traditional boundaries of film. Collectively, they examined popular notions about the generation gap, counterculture wisdom, feminist insights, and ethnic self-advancement. Each film in this study questioned incongruities in the American promise of equality, whether embedded in generational and gender hegemony or patriarchal dominance and Anglo-centered identity. In one way or another, these films made the contradictory nature of American society "intelligible" rather than cohesive. They each promoted "telling it like it is" to represent youth, men, women, and ethnic cultures. For the role they played in satisfying taste in cinematic changes, they earned an iconic place in American culture. The aesthetic, intellectual, social, and experimental components of these films exhibited the extent to which they were agents in social change. In the way they framed the world, these pictures tested the "boundaries to power and to perception — that is, to representation."[13] In the years 1965–1975, between the hope for film to be an agent in social change and raising commercial success to new levels, Hollywood made its contemporary move.

The ten films of this study spoke to a number of contentious issues and offered remedies for American ailments. Each picture voiced the concerns of a particular group. *The Graduate* spoke for a younger generation that found the consumer culture of American society dehumanizing. In *Alice's Restaurant*, folk singer Arlo Guthrie took viewers from the East to the West and back again to Alice and Ray Brock's lively Vermont commune. *Easy Rider* tapped into Americans' fondness for the West. With their Harleys, Wyatt and Billy replaced the classic Western hero bikers on the road again. *Midnight Cowboy* tested the Western's legacy and its influence on the construction of male identity. *M*A*S*H* deconstructed American power and exceptionalism and unequivocally dismissed the American military while conjuring conventional roles for women. When feminism asked hard questions of patriarchy in the larger society, *McCabe and Mrs. Miller* rewrote the Western yet again to allow room for women and changing notions of masculine identity. Just as it seemed a woman could be represented as strong and capable in mainstream film, *Carnal Knowledge* appeared to remind audiences that nothing had changed between men and women.

A new film model challenged the dominant Anglo culture of autonomy during the multicultural debates.[14] *Little Big Man* brought real Indians to the screen to portray themselves and undo decades of stereotypes. In the process, the film played with new pigeonholes for Native Americans on screen. With the emphasis on ethnic belonging and the family, *The Godfather* showed audiences that "ethnic heritage ... often plays an integral if rarely examined role in creative activity."[15] Two years later, *The Godfather: Part II* filled in the story of immigration from the turn of the century and commented on the downside of assimilation and success. These two films brought the gangster genre back to Hollywood with contemporary flair.

These films redefined the individual's place in America by imagining new social roles, displaying new attitudes, and forming new perceptions of lifestyle and the young's rejection of tradition for autonomy. Showing the changes taking place in America at the time, these moving pictures marked the shift in the industry's focus from a generic adult audience to a specific young-adult with distinct interests. In *The Graduate*, Benjamin and Elaine leave their families and carve a new path for their generation. In *Alice's Restaurant*, Arlo Guthrie shows the limits of the counterculture family and departs for a life on the road, autonomous from even the idealistic hope of the hippie commune. The classic statement of 1960s autonomy comes through *Easy Rider* and the cyclists' journey away from ties that bind. Finally, Mrs. Constance Miller enters western territory alone to stage her independence in *McCabe and Mrs. Miller*. These and other films taught viewers to cherish separation and self-sufficiency. *The Godfather* films joined the conversation and showed that the much revered American individualism was not obvious for families bound to heritage and bent on preserving a culture threatened by the melting pot.

Penn, Altman, and Nichols claimed a new authority as voices for a younger audience that called for alternative renderings and resolutions of social strife through new representations of generation and gender. Hopper and Fonda — closer in age and sensibility to boomer audiences — pushed film further into experimental territory and Coppola incorporated old with new by asking how to widen the scope of Anglo-centered distinctiveness for Italian Americans. From *The Graduate* to *The Godfather*, these films showed that meaning is open, not fixed and preset or entirely predictable. Their meaning lies in what Christopher Faulkner labels "the contradictory or the heterogeneous." This in-between space, the unoccupied gaps, "is itself the enabling condition — and not the antithesis — of any projected 'unity.'"[16] At a time when Americans saw film as the space for imagining a new society and when the "heterogeneous" and the "contradictory" emerged out of conventional culture, film indeed seemed "now," "new," and "real." This set of films dramatized the meaning-making process celebrated through new images of generation, gender, and ethnicity because of, not in spite of, their noticeable incongruities. These films could ask hard questions about gaps, gendered hierarchies, and repressed desires of identification and still make money.

It was not by filmmaking alone that the "cinematic ferment" of the sixties resulted in a mature film age by the mid-seventies. The next generation of filmmakers asked film to be personal and filmmaking spontaneous. It was the experience, not the message, that mattered. Young viewers saw their lives reflected more closely in Benjamin Braddock's impulsive freeway race to find Elaine than in Maria's story of destiny in *The Sound of Music*. "Telling it like it is" governed the camera's work and, as one professor said, "Instead of resisting change and bottling it, film intensifie[d] the experience of change, humanizing it in the process."[17] In answer to the new spirit of viewing, the films' constructions, their fictions, and social life manifested the ways people debated, negotiated, and imagined their relationships at a historical moment of social volatility when American youth were engaged in common antiestablishment protest.

The success of the films speaks for the claims of audiences that cinema could raise consciousness and therefore alter society. Film incorporated social experimentation into cinematic subject matter with help from the active engagement of audiences. As one historian claimed, "The issues raised have demanded new perspectives on society, new analyses, new urgencies for self-examination."[18] Audiences and directors agreed on film as one avenue of activism for internalizing pressing social concerns.

Independent production and experimentation were encouraged in the early 1970s. At that time, independents made up 30 percent of the movie market, but retreated with the rise of mythic-style narratives in the following years. Interest in European cinematic art waned, and viewers attracted to art films lost their influential voice. Classic stories scripted the new New Hollywood that advanced the next series of films.[19]

Splitting two decades into late and early years highlights the fundamental change made in the industry and in audiences' taste for film. The grouping also shows the period of time that created culture divisions among Americans. The latter years of radical protest contrasted to the idealistic reform of the early ones. The early seventies highlighted the struggles for resolution of explosive social issues. The gender debates, the *Roe v. Wade* decision, the controversy over Vietnam, generational conflict, affirmative action, and other legislation challenged the nation in new ways. Debates ensued about Americanness and belonging. It seemed to be a nation of individuals with little sense of community. Yet a unified America, a time of consensus, was a fantasy. As Christopher Faulkner tells us, cohesiveness "can never be more than imagined, fictive, rhetorical." Rather, "continual tension" and "instability" are "the motor and dynamic that tests the limits (and potentialities) of social and personal identity."[20] The seventies reorganized American society after cultural beliefs, attitudes, and values had already shifted to left of center. Since the films in this study have taken on symbolic meaning as representative of America, they unmistakably show how far shifts could go at the time and how deeply those years implanted social dividing lines.

In reconfiguring Hollywood or the larger society, new contradictions emerged. By and large, whether experimental or conventional genre, film at this time showed and told experiences from white perspectives. Race, in the atmosphere of experimentation, failed to claim significant space. Filmmakers and writers for the most part addressed issues more of generation, gender, and ethnicity than of race.[21] African American producers and directors had not yet gained an inside voice in the industry. Race obviously appeared on screen, but safe narratives dominated the screens at the time.[22] Films dealing with racialized experience advanced the civil rights agenda as a subject of narratives starring African Americans and receiving both Academy notice and popular acclaim.[23]

Considering the active engagement of audiences who believed film to be an agent in social change, the reasons for absent images rest on questions of discourse and domination. What did succeed, however, was the incorporation of black actors into conventional narratives. Charismatic detective John Shaft, played by Richard Roundtree, for example, triggered a successful entertainment series of formula films with black actors as heroes. The success of *Shaft* sparked the development of films appropriately labeled "blaxploitation" that placed blacks in the lead roles of classic detective, spy, private eye, and other formula stories. The cleverness of these twists opened a market for those interested in seeing the silver screen through the lens of "soul," as the popular reference went. *Shaft*'s success marks the extent of possibilities for the popular film to subvert and reconstruct society, but the films in this study also measure the distance between the safe zone and the provocative, the unusual, and the unacceptable. Within the discursive limitations in what proved to be popular lies the work of film as a cultural battleground and an agent between 1965 and 1975.[24]

The early 1970s showed that experimental success could not sustain an industry. In time, a new set of filmmakers combined art with the potential for commercial success. These directors were "creatures of their own times," as film historian Jeanne Basinger put it. They were "comfortable with the big screen and the small, educated to have high artistic goals, but comfortable in the world of commerce."[25] The Academy and critics had to catch up once again with the stirrings of viewers and accept the return of the good, common hero, the average "little guy" in the film that marked a turning point and brought the foundational years into a contemporary Hollywood. Spielberg's *Jaws* showed that the industry, audiences, and assumptions about the art and function of film were reconfigured during the sixties and again by 1975. Seasoned as a television director, Steven Spielberg shaped a provocative classic narrative about good and evil and confirmed what Coppola's pictures suggested earlier. Spielberg in 1975 "proved that genre films, skillfully directed in a traditional style, had returned."[26]

By Spielberg's entrance into the business, the tensions, anxieties, and fears that terrorized everyday Americans were imagined as a mechanical fish rather than an institution. The studio-trained enthusiast was an iconoclast of a different sort. Spielberg's anti-antiestablishment art rescued vacationing tourists. His 1970s "everyman" helped displace the antiestablishment idol. Spielberg's "influences" themselves came from within. "I was truly more of a child of the establishment than I was a product of USC or NYU or the Francis Coppola protégé clique." His heroes were locals who saved the town from Jaws, the shark in the depths of the deep eastern sea. Bringing up the rear of the film-school generation, Spielberg represented that part of the boomers more interested in conventional genres. The switch brought directors and producers of the blockbusters personal wealth unsurpassed by the previous generation in the business. Studio and censorship changes shifted the Hollywood infrastructure to accommodate historic conditions and the needs of filmmakers and audiences. Producer Richard Zanuck, for example, exceeded his father's entire career earnings with the *Jaws* receipts, video reproductions, and tie-in products.[27]

The blockbuster success did not mean that all filmmakers turned away from the artistic film. Changes in the industry made it possible for the social commentary pictures to succeed alongside the entertaining extravaganza of *Jaws*. The Academy recognized its investment in feature films as art. Cinema as a language of social change surfaced in the industry's choice of winners for the 1975 Oscars. Spielberg was sure he would win Best Director, but he was not even nominated. Instead, the Academy chose Milos Forman for *One Flew Over the Cuckoo's Nest* and decided *Jaws* was more notable for sound, music, and editing. Popular features challenged the success of the antigenre strain and offered a "celebration of renewal," a resolution for "the social order and its salvation," to use the words of Fredric Jameson.[28]

The iconoclasts continued to make the unusual film. Robert Altman tried to rouse viewers with *Nashville* (1975), a story of a rock star who pursues a Tennessee housewife. Arthur Penn offered to deconstruct the detective genre with *Night Moves* (1975). Both films' low box office grosses made critics such as Pauline Kael rail against the thought that "there's no audience for new work." Yet, *Jaws* was new and had an audience. As pundit Peter Biskind said it, "'Us' is no longer narrowly and tendentiously defined as the hip counterculture, but is expansive and inclusive, a new community comprised of just about everyone." Biskind conceded that Spielberg's film "transcended the political and demographic divisions between the *Easy Rider* counterculture audience and Nixon's ... middle-Americans."[29]

By 1975, the blockbuster shared its fame with new technology, offering Americans other options for screening enjoyment. Technology and computers guided the silver screen and the new cameras of success. The world of electronics not only changed production for the feature film but also redefined viewing habits. Sony helped viewers stay home and have their feature films, too. The company introduced Betamax, a cassette recorder for TV in 1975 and initiated the video-age in filmmaking and viewing. Time, Incorporated, added the concept of pay television with the Home Box Office (HBO) channel, which offered subscribers uncut and uninterrupted movie viewing. Ted Turner purchased MGM and its film vaults.[30] The cable business, as *Variety* predicted, would be "the next great big-money market for Hollywood, which will dovetail perfectly in complementing profile with the theatre-going demographic studies."[31] Paying to watch movies in living rooms and renting a copy led the American film business promptly into its multinational, corporate era.

Like the films in this study, we remain much in the framework of the debates from the 1960s that developed into the 1970s multiculturalism, political correctness, and personal politics. All pertain to different levels of understanding and desire for redefinition of social, economic, and political structures in America and all were outgrowths of critical moments in 1960s social protests. The challenges required everyone to think about and respect change. Pro-civil rights, pro-gender equality, pro-ecology, demands for sexual freedom, and other once-radical notions were mainstreamed during this time. As one historian observed, "We are fundamentally a different culture, facing fundamentally different questions" because of the cultural environment developing during these years.[32] This narrative, as historian David Farber writes, cannot seem to "go gently into the night," even as aging baby boomers made room for their younger siblings.[33] American film's visual nature, reproductive capabilities, and highly developed industrial system have influenced the meaning of modern experience. The impact goes deeply into the American imagination and the period under question is part of the medium's potency. Changes in the industry, the break-up of the code era, and audience interest in European art films moved filmmaking into a new direction.

The enthusiasm for the artistic potential for commercial film coming out of campuses has become a legend for those remembering this era as foundational. *New Yorker* writer David Denby, nearly three decades later, pined yet again for those golden experimentalists. Why, he asked, would viewers fail to resist the phony exterior of another exploitation movie? Denby hankered for the critical eye of the college audience, those who saw themselves as the movie generation. Looking back nostalgically on the sixties and seventies in response to the unexpected success of independent director Nia Vardalas' *My Big Fat Greek Wedding* (2002), Denby wondered, "If filmmakers were able to find an older audience with this film, couldn't they also find that audience with a stronger movie?" In reality, what Denby wished promoters would discover was a "different audience." Yearning for that counterculture moment, Denby asked, "What happened, for instance, to the college kids who were courted so assiduously in the late sixties and early seventies? When movies were aimed at them, directors and writers were encouraged to take risks, and American mainstream filmmaking entered its most creative period." As Denby continued, "The college audience has ceased to exist in Hollywood's mind as a vanguard of taste."[34]

The boundary breakers of a time past, however, were most likely in the driver's seat. Making films and looking backward as much as forward, they no doubt noticed that even if it were true that today "practically everyone goes to college," it would not guarantee the same dynamic between filmmaker, viewer, and critic. Denby hoped the fault was with the filmmakers who failed to see that "maybe millions are waiting for new subjects and moods — waiting for a little attention."[35] Yet it is more complicated than imagining an audience. It has to do with an attitude about what film can be, a new technology of moveable equipment that supplies the creative interest, and a social energy molded out of movements and intent.

Popular film is a valuable resource for understanding what was at stake for Americans at the time. Film and all of its complex aesthetics, storytelling, industry, presences, and absences means looking at a narrative's discursive make-up positioned within its role in mass entertainment. Generation, gender, and ethnicity frame what mattered in the debate over America, its people, and its social issues. As visualized stories constructing Americanness, these films serve the memory of the sixties and seventies. They relay the possibilities and limitations in advancing film as an art form, commercial success, and an agent in social change. Likewise, contemporary film, the new New Hollywood, found ways to resist and restore images of the cinematic past.

To answer why film mattered is to return to the year 1915 when D. W. Griffith proclaimed that American cinema would soon be the primary vehicle for educating audiences. Like a history book, film would serve as a window onto the past, with each frame revealing events as they must have been and speaking to a present time vividly and completely.[36] Unlike books, however, film is a hybrid of stage entertainment, literature, art, photography, history, and technology and shares those traditions but creates something new out of them. The commercial industry took Griffith's hope beyond the margins of a visualized history and crossed popular, academic, and entrepreneurial boundaries. Not quite the primer Griffith had imagined, film at the very least is still a chronicle and a record. Depending on the lens, history ambiguously appears in feature films and confirms cinema's role as both an agent and a window treatment at once covering, enhancing, and decorating the past for the present. Reflective and affective, commercial features are part of the play with images believed to be the power in the agency of film.

Chapter Notes

Introduction

1. Joseph J. Mangano, *Living Legacy: How 1964 Changed America* (Lanham, MD: University Press of America, 1994), 170.

2. One of the motivations behind this project is to test the limits of the feature film as a piece of evidence from a historian's point of view. This project does not focus on the historical film or the "costume drama" that chooses specific historical subjects for narrative material but the feature film that operates as a form of mainstream entertainment and is recognized by the industry through the Academy's nominations and awards. The feature may contain historical references such as *Alice's Restaurant* does, but does not intend to pass as historical drama. Analyses of specifically historical films characterize the review section in *American Historical Quarterly* and *Journal of American History*. Most often, the reviewer is concerned with film as it parallels "but cannot duplicate the methods or findings of" written history within the discipline as historian Robert Rosenstone points out. The film in this view functions as a mode of history similar to "serious works of visual history." Unlike many studies of historical films, this project does not begin with the fact or fiction of a film. To the contrary, the concern is with the construction of fiction that does not consciously engage in the discourse of history but is historical because it engages in discourse of the 1960s and 1970s and can be treated as a visual record of what existed in the dynamic between cameras and audiences for a new generation of filmmakers from 1965 to 1975. The historical film is the focus of such important works as Robert A. Rosenstone, *Visions of the Past: The Challenge of Film to Our Idea of History* (Cambridge and London: Harvard University Press, 1995); Tony Barta, ed., *Screening the Past: Film and the Representation of History* (Westport, CT, and London: Praeger, 1998); Mark C. Carnes, ed., *Past Imperfect: History According to the Movies* (New York: Henry Holt and Company, 1995).

3. For example, the Pantages in Los Angeles was built in the summer of 1930 for $1.25 million. Part of the Fox Theater chain, it seats 2700 spectators.

4. Douglas Gomery, *The Hollywood Studio System* (New York: St. Martin's Press, 1986), 1.

5. Cinema of Third World Countries, for example, may use film as a "powerful tool of oppositional movements" against Hollywood's influence. For ways film studies can teach resistance reading of film, see Robert Sklar and Charles Musser, eds., *Resisting Images: Essays on Cinema and History* (Philadelphia: Temple University Press, 1990), 9.

6. Anthony Schilacci, "Film as Environment," *Saturday Review* 51 (28 Dec. 1968): 10.

7. David E. James, *Allegories of Cinema: American Film in the Sixties* (Princeton: Princeton University Press, 1989), 350.

8. The musical held on for another few years with *Dr. Dolittle* and *Camelot*, but after 1968 Hollywood largely abandoned it. Musicals also fared poorly in Europe, the market that provided a large percentage of revenues for successful pictures. When *Bonnie and Clyde* received nine nominations and *The Graduate* seven, it was clear that a new kind of movie had registered itself with American viewers.

9. Ronald Bergan, *The United Artists Story* (New York: Crown Publishers, 1986), 1. See also Lis Pontecorvo, "The Raw Material: Film Resources," in *The Historian and Film*, ed. Paul Smith (Cambridge, London, New York, and Melbourne: Cambridge University Press, 1976), 16.

10. Stephen Greenblatt, "Culture," in *Critical Terms for Literary Study*, ed. Frank Lentricchia and Thomas McLaughlin (Chicago and London: University of Chicago Press, 1990). As Greenblatt explains, "The concept of culture gestures toward what appears to be two opposite things: *constraint* and *mobility*" (ibid., 225). Culture both regulates and guarantees movement. Film is therefore a way to "come to terms with the governing patterns of culture" (ibid., 229). See also Stephen Greenblatt, "The Circulation of Social Energy," in *Shakespearean Negotiations* (Berkeley and Los Angeles: University of California Press, 1988), 1–20, for an explanation of the way an artistic work maintains social prominence and becomes an important means of transferring culture.

11. In Stephen Greenblatt's terms, culture is a "regulator and guarantor of movement," a means of "passing on order." To the degree that it recycles core American beliefs, values, and ideals, film guarantees cultural identity and regulates its parameters. Stephen Greenblatt, "Culture," 228.

12. Christopher Faulkner, "Teaching French National Cinema," *Cinema Journal* 38.4 (Summer 1999): 88–93.

13. Hayden White, "AHR Forum," *American Historical Review* 93.5 (Dec. 1988): 1198. Quote is from Faulkner, "Teaching French National Cinema," 90.

14. Homi Bhadha defines cultural passage as the "recreation of the self in the world of travel, the resettlement of the borderline community of migration." Though film offers a different kind of travel, it still functions as a migration of sorts when viewers leave feeling as if they have participated in the world presented on the screen before their

eyes. Homi Bhadha, *Location of Culture* (London and New York: Routledge), 9.

15. *See* Joseph J. Mangano, *Living Legacy*, 1–2.

16. Douglas T. Miller, *On Our Own: Americans in the Sixties* (Lexington, MA: D.C. Heath and Company, 1996), 181.

17. Godfrey Hodgson, *America in Our Time: From World War II to Nixon What Happened and Why* (New York: Vintage Books, 1976), 3.

18. William O'Neill, *Coming Apart: An Informal History of America in the 1960's* (New York: Quadrangle, 1971); Hodgson, *America In Our Time*; Alan Matusow, *The Unraveling of America: A History of Liberalism in the 1960s* (New York: Harper and Row, 1984).

19. David Halberstam, "Farewell to the 60s," *McCalls* 97.4 (Jan. 1970), 85.

20. Dominick Cavallo, *A Fiction of the Past: The Sixties in American History* (New York: St. Martin's Press, 1999).

21. *Village Voice*, 23 Dec. 1967, p. 22.

22. David R. Colburn and George E. Pozzetta, "Race, Ethnicity, and Political Legitimacy," in *The Sixties: From Memory to History*, ed. David Farber (Chapel Hill and London: The University of North Carolina Press, 1994), 121.

23. Peter Biskind and Susan Sontag in Peter Biskind, *Easy Riders, Raging Bulls: How the Sex-and-Drugs-and-Rock 'N' Roll Generation Saved Hollywood* (New York: Simon and Schuster, 1998), 17.

Chapter I

1. William Tusher, "Hollywood 1967," *The Film Daily Yearbook of Motion Pictures* 50 (1968): 90; Vincent Canby, "Jack Warner, 75, Resigns Top Job: Move Makes Darryl Zanuck the Last Tycoon," *The New York Times*, 25 July 1967. The Big Five (Paramount, RKO, Warner's, Loews, Inc., and Twentieth-Century-Fox) controlled production, film processing, music publishing, and other movie-related interests by 1929. William Tusher, "Window on Hollywood," *The Film Daily Yearbook of Motion Pictures* 49 (1967): 90, 92. William Tusher, "Hollywood 1967," 90.

2. Tusher, "Window on Hollywood," 94.

3. "Theatrical and TV Producers Unite Under a Single Hollywood Roof," *Variety* 234.7 (8 Apr. 1964): 5. By the mid–1950s, a large segment of television production had moved from New York to Los Angeles. The timing was right by the 1960s for such a unification to take place effectively. With Los Angeles turning into the dominant region for television production by then, the industry integrated well into the development of consumerism and a rising popular culture.

4. "Producers Unite in Movie-TV Group," *The New York Times*, 29 Mar. 1964. The movie companies consisted of Allied Artists, Columbia, Disney, M.G.M., Paramount, Fox, Universal, U.A., Warners, and the television sector consisting of Bellmar Enterprise, Amigo Productions, Bing Crosby Productions, Calvada, Daystar, Desilu, Mayberry Enterprises, and others. The former organizations included the Association of Motion Pictures and the Alliance of Television Film Producers.

5. "Movie Producers Reporting Gains," *The New York Times*, 5 July 1964. See also Peter Bart, "Expansion Begun by Movie Studios," *The New York Times*, 21 Apr. 1965. *New York Times*' specials writer, Peter Bart, remarked, "The expansion programs are in contrast to the aura of economic gloom that pervaded the major studios as recently as two years ago when at least one studio, 20th-Century-Fox, was all but closed down."

6. Tusher, "Window on Hollywood," 92, 94. Universal Studios' employment pool rose from 200 to 3,000 potential recruits by mid-decade, for instance. Peter Bart,

"Hollywood Watching Economics as Well as the Esthetic Things: Picture-Making is Said to be on a More Businesslike Basis Than Before — Quality I Replacing Quantity," *The New York Times*, 5 July 1964.

7. Leonard Sloane, "At the Movies: Big Costs, Revenues, TV Sales," *The New York Times*, 23 Oct. 1966. Television stations had always bought films from studios but, as Peter Bart reported, what made the current market different was that "movies started to dominate TV schedules." Peter Bart, "TV-Film Accords Arousing Doubts: Golden Goose Looks Like a Trojan Horse to Some," *The New York Times*, 7 Jan. 1966.

8. Leonard Sloane, "Paramount Pictures Joins Gulf and Western," *The New York Times*, 20 Oct. 1966.

9. Leonard Sloane, "At the Movies." See also Leonard Sloane, "Paramount Pictures."

10. Tino Balio, *United Artists: The Company that Changed the Film Industry* (Madison: University of Wisconsin Press, 1987), 197. On the 1st of January, MCA, Inc. (producer and distributor), merged with Decca Records and on May 25, 1966, Universal Pictures became Universal Studios, Inc., a subsidiary of MCA. Among the other divisions were MCA Music, Universal Film Exchanges, Universal International Films, Decca Distributing, and Universal Television. M-G-M owned Robbins Music Corporation, Variety Music, Inc., Miller Music Corporation, the Big 3 Music Corporation and Pine Ridge Music, Inc. Twentieth-Century-Fox controlled Surrey Music Corporation, Twentieth Century Music Corporation, and Movietone Music Corporation. Warners owned Music Publishers Holding Corporation and Warner Brothers Records. *The Film Daily Yearbook of Motion Pictures* 49 (1967): 716, 721, 724. By 1966 United Artists had made two million dollars on the soundtrack for *A Hard Day's Night*. The cost of the film was $580,000. M-G-M's royalties from the *Doctor Dolittle* soundtrack and sheet music helped the company recover the $11 million in production costs for the film. Music rights from *The Magnificent Seven* brought United Artists a "six figure" sum for using a few bars from the film on the Marlboro ads running on TV and radio. As Vincent Canby reported, "Film music … has now also become a significant source for recurring profits." Vincent Canby, "Music is Now Profit to the Ears of Filmmakers," *The New York Times*, 24 May 1966.

11. Paramount advertisement in *The Film Daily Yearbook of Motion Pictures* 51 (1969): 879.

12. Balio, *United Artists*, 197, 198, 201.

13. Leonard Sloane, "Advertising: Movies Termed Unusual Breed," *The New York Times*, 18 Sep. 1966. Good marketing generally brought in three-fourths of the ad budget at first-run theaters, which usually meant New York. Press-screenings provided the media with lead-time to prepare the promotional story. VIP screenings sought endorsements from leading figures in the educational, political, and religious arenas. These tactics all garnered in-group sales from official endorsement. When film news coincided with a real news event, like debuting a film on a holiday or by using the premiere as a charity benefit, the film gained more advertising ground free of charge. As Tino Balio explained, United Artists, for example, used charities and premieres "to ennoble the picture and perhaps to neutralize any unfavorable critical opinion." Balio, *United Artists*, 216.

14. Balio, *United Artists*, 202. The 1960s' marketing strategies followed earlier advertising practices that placed the star as the main draw in advertising a film but in an exaggerated way that typically de-centered the studio and allowed the construction of celebrity status to take on a life of its own outside studio dominance.

15. Peter Bart, "Better Breaks for New Talent: Film Industry Discovers that the Famous Old Stars Are not

Worth Their Weight in Box Office Gold," *The New York Times*, 18 Oct. 1964. Bart's list of disappointments includes Frank Sinatra, Audrey Hepburn, Laurence Olivier, Kirk Douglas and even Marlon Brando. Peter Bart, "Hollywood Watching Economics."

16. Peter Bart, "A Prisoner of the System?" *The New York Times*, 23 Oct. 1966.

17. Sloane, "Advertising." Companies turned to intense advertising campaigns to bring the film and the new faces to the viewers. For just a first-run or "road show" engagement, marketing ranged from $500,000 to $3,000,000 for one picture. Likewise, for pre-opening promotion a New York showing alone could cost $100,000 to $150,000. Multiply that by twenty-some pictures a year and several companies and the total advertising expenses reached into the hundreds of millions, making the film business a billion-dollar-a-year industry. Promotion included expanding coverage in trailers, posters, displays and other forms of publicity.

18. In the early years, the bulk of capital lay in the exhibition end of the business, not in the production. The Big Five had developed a complex distribution system to keep their control intact. The system obliged important producers to negotiate with the studios for distribution. Even independent theater owners preferred the majors because they produced the biggest stars and thus had the most potential for box office sales. During the 1943–1944 season, before the big slump in movie going, the Big Five received around 75 percent of film rental revenue in the United States, the Little Three (United Artists, Columbia, and Universal) took in 20 percent, and the rest 5 percent. See Douglas Gomery, *The Hollywood Studio System* (New York: St. Martin's Press, 1986), 12, 21. Films were released exclusively to theaters in cities with large audience potential and high incomes. See also Balio, *United Artists*, 212.

19. See Garth Jowett, *Film, The Democratic Art: A Social History of American Film* (Boston: Little, Brown, 1976), especially pages 275–281; the *United States v. Paramount Pictures* (334 U.S., 131); Gregory D. Black, *The Catholic Crusade Against the Movies, 1940–1975* (Cambridge, UK: Cambridge University Press, 1997). He explains, "This case struck down the vertical integration of production, distribution, and exhibition that had been the economic foundation for the glitter and glamour of Hollywood." Even though the Big Five only "directly controlled about 2,800 theaters out of the roughly 17,000 in the United States," their monopolistic practice lay in their capacity to restrict first-run features (of which they produced 90 percent) to play only in the theaters they controlled. As Black has shown, "These theaters playing first-run features were responsible for the majority of film rentals." The Big Five partitioned the American markets according to "spheres of influence," with Paramount dominating 50 percent of the Southern theaters, Fox controlling the West Coast, Warners in the Mid-Atlantic, RKO in New York and New Jersey and Loew's in the premiere place, New York City. Black describes the aspect of monopoly: "Using traditional economic techniques, the majors fixed prices, pooled profits, set how long theaters could play a feature, agreed to exhibit one another's films, and forced independent theater owners to take all the films produced by a studio or take none (block booking)." Black, *Catholic Crusade*, 69. See Murray Smith for a critique of the assumptions that the injunction period reorganized the kinds of products coming from Hollywood and undermined its oligopolistic nature. Whether this period ultimately created new forms of industry organization is certainly up for debate. Still, the opportunities and changes that were created for theater owners and specific individuals of Hollywood played a decisive role in the direction film as an aesthetic product took

during the 1960s. Murray Smith, "Theses on the Philosophy of Hollywood History," in *Contemporary Hollywood Cinema*, ed. Steve Neale and Murray Smith (London and New York: Routledge, 1998), 3–20. National General Corporation (National Theatres and Television, Inc.) assumed Fox's Film Corporation in 1952. Theater operations and film production together in 1950 brought Fox $9.5 million. After separation, it took the company until 1954 to come close to that figure with its approximate $8,000,000 in earnings that year. See *The Film Daily Yearbook of Motion Pictures* 49 (1967): 716, 717 and "Fox Film Sets Earnings Mark," *The New York Times*, 27 Mar. 1964.

20. See Jowett, *Film, The Democratic Art*, 428–429.

21. Howard Thompson, "Double Feature: Shows and Shops," *The New York Times*, 7 Mar. 1964. Many center contractors put up the $250,000 cost for theaters, built them, and then leased them to exhibitors.

22. "The King of Intermissions," *Time* 86 (9 July 1965): 93–94.

23. "Theaters Adapt to Suburban Life: Follow Growth Pattern by Avoiding Downtown Sites," *The New York Times*, 19 Jan. 1964.

24. Loews was essentially in hotels; Stanley Warner in Playtex; and AB-Paramount in radio, TV, real estate, CATV, and savings and loans.

25. *Business Week* 2115 (14 Mar. 1970): 29. Locations included Bartow and Tampa, FL; Muskogee, OK; and Saginaw, MI.

26. Paul Leglise, "The Hidden Face of the Cinema Pt. III: An Audience of 12,000,000,000," *UNESCO Courier* (Feb. 1963): 26–27.

27. "Theaters Adapt to Suburban Life." Fire code regulations were also responsible for eliminating the balcony, since it was typically the smoking area. Renovated theaters with balconies presented the added responsibility to theater owners of prohibiting smoking.

28. Hollis Alpert, "Something New in Movie Communication," *Saturday Review* 45 (9 June 1962): 54, 55. As Alpert reported, by June 1962, "a two-decker theatre known as Cinema I and Cinema II...open[ed] its double doors and double box office on Manhattan's Third Avenue which, not so many years ago, was a dank, dark street covered over by an elevated connection between the Bowery and the Bronx." Cinema I seated 700 and Cinema II 300 viewers. Don Rugoff chose the newly transformed "mid–East Side" to showcase a double-decker, the kind with an intimate setting where "coffee is served in the lounge and Ingmar Bergman and Michelangelo Antonioni are served on the screen." Rugoff's plan included "[book] displays, hi-fi listening areas, and an art gallery." He saw the specialized theater as a "compact cultural center" and if New York State would have permitted, he would have served the artsy sophisticates sherry.

29. Ernest Callenbach, "Temples of the Seventh Art," *Sight and Sound* 35 (Winter 1965): 14, 12.

30. Ibid.

31. For details on rulings, see Black, *Catholic Crusade*, 66–73. From 1907, when progressive reformers in Chicago forced theaters to obtain permits for screenings, censorship boards nationwide voiced municipal concerns over movies' social influence. In 1915 the United States Supreme Court sanctioned the constitutionality of an Ohio law that required official approval of all films prior to their exhibition in Ohio theaters, but no national censorship code was created.

32. The Production Code of 1930 specified over thirty standards of production. These standards scrutinized topics that were either forbidden or, if used, to be filmed with discretion. Those in question included "crimes against the law," "adultery," "seduction and rape," "white slavery,"

"miscegenation," "vulgarity," "profanity," "indecent dance movement," "ridicule of any religious faith," "respect for national feelings," and "repellent subjects" such as cruelty to animals and children, hangings, prostitution, and others. The code's "Preamble" recognized "the high trust and confidence which have been placed in [motion picture producers] by the people of the world and which have made motion pictures a universal form of entertainment." Hence, producers accepted their role as entertainers who were also subject to the public trust and to "the life of a nation." See Jowett, *Film, the Democratic Art*, for a complete copy of the Code in Appendix IV, p. 468, and "Production Code Administration," *The Film Daily Yearbook* 49 (1967): 616.

33. William Tusher, "Window on Hollywood," 92.

34. Father Daniel Lord, contributor to PCA's code, and well-known lay Catholic Martin Quigley based the role of censor on the shared belief that "entertainment films should reinforce religious teachings that deviant behavior, whether criminal or sexual, cost the violator the love and comforts of home, the intimacy of family, the solace of religion, and the protection of law." Father Lord, Quigley, and Protestant colleagues saw movies as "twentieth-century morality plays that illustrated proper behavior to the masses." In Father Lord's words, the industry had a "special Moral Responsibility" and that meant that film could not be considered the same as a book or a newspaper because of its universality. For that reason, "movies had to be more restricted ... because they were persuasively and indiscriminately seductive. Whereas audiences of books, plays, and even newspapers were self-selective, the movies had universal appeal." Between enticing the viewer with movie palace interiors, glamorous stars, and film itself, Hollywood produced "irresistible fantasy." Because of film's pervasive, sensual nature, the Legion's code determined that "no picture should lower the moral standards of those who see it." Black, *Catholic Crusade*, 13. For a discussion of criticisms of the League from professors, screenwriters, racial groups and others, see Paul W. Facey, *The Legion of Decency: A Sociological Analysis of the Emergence and Development of a Social Pressure Group* (New York: Arno Press, 1974), especially 2, 178.

35. In 1964, for example, the Catholic League issued 16 "C's" — the largest number since the Legion's inception. Thirteen of those were domestic films. In December, American Bishops issued a report "in preparation for Pledge Sunday," to encourage American Catholics "to renew their pledge of support to the Legion by boycotting theaters that present 'objectionable' films."

36. Black, *Catholic Crusade*, 3. At the same time the code system gained strength, filmmakers declared First Amendment violations and insisted that cinema be subject to freedom of speech just as printed media was. In the mid–1950s, United Artists (a maverick production company to begin with) released two American films without Code Seals: Otto Preminger's 1953 *The Moon is Blue*, a film about adultery, and, in 1955, *The Man with the Golden Arm*, a story about drug addiction starring Frank Sinatra.

37. Ibid., 5, 220. American moviegoers spent an estimated $10,000,000 on one foreign film, *Zorba the Greek*, and one American art film, *The Pawnbroker*, by 1966. Peter Bart, "The Excitement Is All From Europe," *The New York Times*, 3 Apr. 1966.

38. See Jowett, *Democratic Art*, 465–472.

39. Ronald Gold, "Jack Valenti Seeks New Ways," *Variety* 243.2 (1 June 1966): 1, 52–53. Valenti was offered a $125,000 salary plus expenses.

40. For a full discussion on this film's role in breaking down the censorship codes, see Leonard J. Leff, "A Test of American Film Censorship: *Who's Afraid of Virginia Woolf?*" in *Hollywood as Historian: American Film in a*

Cultural Context, ed. Peter Rollins (Lexington: The University Press of Kentucky, 1983), 214, 216, and 211–229. *Who's Afraid of Virginia Woolf* was released in 1966.

41. See Richard S. Randall, *Censorship of the Movies: The Social and Political Control of a Mass Medium* (Madison: University of Wisconsin Press, 1968). As mentioned earlier, challenges to the industry had been fought along individual lines with *The Moon is Blue* (1953), *The Man With the Golden Arm* (1956), and *The Pawnbroker* (1964). By the time *Virginia Woolf* challenged censorship strictures, the issues went beyond the case of an individual film. The concerns were now understood on the social and cultural level. The PCA had bent the rules only a few years earlier with films such as *Hud* (1963) when they allowed "bitch" and "bastard" in the script, but the PCA stood firmly against *Virginia Woolf*. See Leff, *Virginia Woolf*, 214. Yet, as a Broadway play, the script had the New York intelligensia's endorsement and that in itself revealed the unevenness of the Code restrictions on film. The stage had updated itself; it was time for film to do the same.

42. Leonard J. Leff, "A Test," 226. See also "Catholic Office's A-4 Rating To 'Woolf'; Industry's own Seal Still Not Bestowed," *Variety* 243.2 (1 June 1966): 7.

43. "'Virginia Woolf' to Be Shown As a 'For Adults Only' Film," *The New York Times*, 26 May 1966. The clause was "the first ever adopted by Warner Brothers" because, as Mr. Warner noted, "we do not think it is a film for children." See also "Catholics Define 'Woolf' Attitude," *Variety* 243.2 (1 June 1966): 7.

44. Vincent Canby, "'Virginia Woolf' Given Code Seal: Industry's Censors Exempt Film from Speech Rules," *The New York Times*, 11 June 1966.

45. Martin Quigley, Jr., son of the prominent coauthor of the Code Martin Quigley, declared the Code obsolete in an editorial on July 6, 1966, entitled, "The Code is Dead," in the *Motion Picture Herald*. For reference to this editorial in the Academy of Motion Picture Arts and Sciences clip file, see footnote #48 in Leff, *Virginia Woolf*, 227.

46. Vincent Canby, "Filmmakers Show Less Fear of Catholic Office: 5 Movies Condemned in Year but are Released With Tag 'For Mature Audience,'" *The New York Times*, 13 Oct. 1967.

47. Another court sanction in the 1950s authorized the distribution of *The Miracle*, an Italian film, by declaring it a "significant medium for the communication of ideas." This sanction helped open ways for future questionable aspects of sexual depictions on screen, thereby further defining film's social value. See Leff, "A Test," 228.

48. Vincent Canby, "Czar of the Movie Business," *The New York Times*, 23 Apr. 1967.

49. Tusher, "Hollywood 1967," 96.

50. Gomery, *The Hollywood Studio System*, 24. See also Balio, *United Artists*, for an explanation of United Artists' encouragement of independents. The "independent" trend began in 1951 with the new management team of Arthur B. Krim and Robert S. Benjamin, who reorganized a near-bankrupt United Artists (UA) in February of that same year and changed the company policy from merely distributing to financing independent films. This pacesetter company "started a revolution in the motion picture industry" by redefining the relationship between the distributor-financier-producer-artist (quoted in Balio, *United Artists*, 3). With industry restructuring and Code break-up, the 1960s made UA's support of independents more possible, but ultimately, opportunity for independents, via UA or not, could hardly have occurred without the Big Five's substantial loss of control with the PCA break-up. Censorship for the Big Five indirectly served as a control of first-run production and exhibition. As Gregory Black has explained, "The

majors had agreed they would neither produce nor play in any theater under their control, a film that did not carry the industry PCA seal." First-runs were virtually inaccessible to independents without going through the PCA process. Black, *Catholic Crusade*, 69.

51. Tusher, "Hollywood 1967," 96. In 1967 Jack Valenti held a press conference in New York to unveil a new Production Code which contained the category SMA (Suggested for Mature Audiences). This new form of categorizing film led to the movie ratings of 1968 but also marked a time that Hollywood clearly defined poetic license as the highest significance of film. The SMA structure opened the doors for a new film audience and allowed for experimentation of visual taste for the mainstream screen. For a sample of Valenti's New Production Code, see *Film Daily Yearbook* 49 (1967): 627–628.

52. Peter Biskind, *Easy Riders, Raging Bulls: How the Sex-Drugs-and-Rock 'n' Roll Generation Saved Hollywood* (New York: Touchstone Book Published by Simon and Schuster, 1998), 29.

53. Joseph Gelmis, *The Film Director as Superstar* (Garden City: Doubleday and Co., 1970), ix.

54. Peter Bart, "An Ambition: To Make a Movie No One Else Would," *The New York Times*, 30 Jan. 1996.

55. Balio, *United Artists*, 3 and chapter 6.

56. Peter Bart, "Can Our New Directors Steal the Show Away from Europe's?" *The New York Times*, 25 Dec. 1966. Jack Valenti had also created the new category SMA.

57. Peter Bart, "Hollywood Has Warm Welcome For an Influx of New Directors," *The New York Times*, 11 June 1965.

58. Quoted in Gelmis, *The Director as Superstar*, xi, xii.

59. Ibid., xv.

60. Peter Biskind, *Easy Rider, Raging Bulls*, 14, 15, 20, 21, 22.

61. Ibid., 20.

62. Vance King, "Hollywood 1968," *Film and Television Daily* 51 (1969): 91; Biskind, *Easy Rider, Raging Bulls*, 15.

63. King, "Hollywood 1968," 91.

64. Peter Biskind, *Easy Rider, Raging Bulls*, 14–17.

65. Robert Osborne, *70 Years of the Oscar: The Official History of the Academy Awards* (New York, London, and Paris: Abbeville Press, 1999), 187.

66. Gelmis, *Director as Superstar*, xx.

67. Maurice Rapf, "Can Education Kill the Movies?" *Action* 2.5 (Sep.–Oct. 1967): 10.

Chapter II

1. Hollis Alpert, "Something New in Movie Communication," *Saturday Review* 45 (9 June 1962): 54–55. *A Room at the Top*, for example, attracted 5 million viewers, giving substantial notice for the art film to Hollywood exhibitors and producers. As reported, *Room at the Top* "which went far beyond the art house patronage ... was the most important breakthrough for an English film made in the American market since the 1930's." Martin Quigley, Jr., and Richard Gertner, *Films in America, 1929–1969* (New York: Golden Press, 1970), 269. When art film success coincided with studio failures of trusted genre moneymakers, Hollywood executives started to ask why. *Cleopatra*, for example, almost cost Fox its theatrical future. One industry official perceptively understood that European art films seemed to gain attention and therefore "set ... the pace" while Hollywood was "making the same pictures over and over again." By mid-decade, industry loyalists could no longer ignore the profits made by films such as *Goldfinger* and *Cassanova '70*. The European challenge more than anything framed the paradox of Hollywood and

its claim to be the center of the film industry at a time when excitement for European material was at an all-time high. Peter Bart, "Europe's Successes Worry Hollywood," *The New York Times*, 20 Sep. 1965. Interest in the art film indicated the industry might also take advantage of "the potential market for quality pictures," but, as director George Stevens pointed out, Hollywood's "trickle" of serious pictures had "all but stopped." Peter Bart, "The Excitement Is All From Europe," *The New York Times*, 3 Apr. 1966.

2. James I. Limbacher, "Film Societies Reply to Exhib Fears: 16-Millimeter Shows Divert No Biz," *Variety* 237.7 (6 Jan. 1965): 27, 51.

3. The hope of earlier societies' wish for preservation was fulfilled when later society members created the public research archive at the University of Wisconsin in Madison.

4. Founding officers of AFFS included Director Fred Goldman of the Exceptional Films Society in Philadelphia, University of California at Berkeley Professor Cameron McCauley, film critic and writer Gideon Bachman, and Ernest Callenbach, editor of *Film Quarterly* in early 1960s. Approximately 735 societies were involved in the AFFS by 1963. Phillip Chamberlin, "What About Film Societies?" *Journal of the Screen Producers Guild* 11.5 (Sep. 1963): 37.

5. Gideon Bachman, "Change or Die," *Film* 28 (Mar.–Apr. 1961): 17.

6. Anthony Hodgkinson, "What Is a Film Society For?" *Film Society Review* 3 (Apr. 1967): 24.

7. Limbacher, "Film Societies Reply," 51.

8. Chamberlin, "What About Film Societies?" 36–38.

9. Hollis Alpert, "Onward and Upward with the Institute," *Saturday Review* 50 (24 June 1967): 50.

10. Bachman, "Change or Die," 17.

11. Hodgkinson, "What Is a Film Society For?" 26.

12. Bachman, "Change or Die," 17.

13. Membership ad in *Film Society Review* 1 (Sep. 1965): 23. Officers included Chairman of the Board Jack Ellis from Northwestern and officers Anthony Hodgkinson from Boston University, Arthur Knight from USC, Colin Young, Jr., from UCLA, and David C. Stewart from Dartmouth.

14. John Thomas, "The Big Picture," *Film Society Review* 1 (Oct. 1965): 5.

15. Arthur Mayer, "Motion Picture Courses in American Universities: A Report by an Old Instructor," *The Journal of the Producers Guild of America* 19 (Mar. 1967): 26.

16. Chamberlin, "What About Film Societies?" 37.

17. David L. Parker, "Projection Room — A University Film Series," *Journal of the University Film Producers Association* 19.1 (Fall 1967): 26–29. Jack C. Ellis, "The Little Ivy-Covered Giant," *The Journal of the Producers Guild of America* 19 (Mar. 1967): 20. Membership of campus and non-campus film societies totaled an estimated 2.5 million by mid-1966. The number of campus societies had increased from two hundred to approximately four thousand from 1950 to 1967. Bart, "The Excitement Is All From Europe"; David C. Stewart, "Movies and Colleges: Some Notes on the Fall of an Ivory Tower," *Journal of University Film Producers Association* 19.1 (1967): 17; David C. Stewart, ed., *Film Study in Higher Education* (American Council on Education: Washington, DC, 1966), 6 and Appendix C; Molly Wilcox, "Film Education: The National Picture," *Filmmaker's Newsletter* 2.2 (Dec. 1968): 1.

18. Jack C. Ellis, "The Big Picture," *Film Society Review* 1 (Jan. 1966): 5.

19. *The Daily Utah Chronicle*, 27 Sep. 1968.

20. Professor Rob Yeo, Chair Department of Film, University of Wisconsin — Milwaukee, telephone interview by author, Dec. 3, 2002. Professor Yeo was an undergraduate student during the late 1960s when he directed the college film series.

21. Robert Gessner, "Bachelors of Pix Biz," *Newsweek* 25 (2 Apr. 1945): 86. From the early 1950s to the 1965–1964 school year, campuses witnessed a 47-percent increase in degree-oriented film courses. The number of production courses increased by 64 percent. History and criticism courses doubled; audio-visual grew by 26 percent. Numbers are taken from the American Council on Education report from 1965. See David C. Stewart, "Movies and Colleges," 17; and Ellis, "The Little Ivy-Covered Giant," 20.

22. Raymond Spottiswoode, "Eyewitnessing the World of the 16 mm. Motion Picture," *The Saturday Review* 32 (8 Jan. 1949): 36.

23. Haig P. Manoogian, "New Spirit in Young Film-makers," *The Journal of the Producers Guild of America* 9.1 (Mar. 1967): 23. As professor Manoogian noted on p. 23, "A college film society holding weekly showings of specialized films gained such popularity that the showings became a course, and then a course or two became a program." Likewise, at Dartmouth in 1964, two hundred undergraduates petitioned Provost John Masland for a film course and the administration responded by instituting one in the English Department in the spring of 1965, taught by Arthur L. Mayer. Maurice Rapf, "Can Education Kill the Movies?" *Action* 2.5 (Sep.–Oct. 1967): 11. The petition read, "We, the undersigned, request that the faculty of Dartmouth College consider offering a full credit course in the history and appreciation of motion pictures. We feel that the motion picture is a legitimate art form of great significance in our society, and that it deserves serious study in a liberal arts college." *Film Daily* gave it front-page coverage as "The first motion picture course to be conducted by film-makers and motion picture executives at an Ivy League college." David C. Stewart, "Men and Movies at Dartmouth," *Journal of the University Film Producers Association* 18.2 (Winter 1966): 7. Students who became more serious about their future in film gravitated to those centers of film study — NYU, USC, and UCLA — which in turn became more cohesive and consistently produced solid programs for study and production.

24. Terry Anderson, *The Movement and the Sixties: Protest in America from Greensboro to Wounded Knee* (New York: Oxford University Press, 1995), 95.

25. Lawrence E. Dennis and Joseph F. Kauffman, *The College and the Student: An Assessment of Relationships and Responsibilities in Undergraduate Education by Administrators, Faculty Members, and Public Officials* (Washington, DC: American Council on Education, 1966). The council, in cooperation with the President's Commission on Academic Affairs, convened in 1965 to address improvements for "the student in higher education." Their primary concerns included the proper use of the college, a clearer definition of the role and responsibilities of the student, and the changing college social environment.

26. See Willis Rudy, *The Campus and A Nation in Crisis: From the American Revolution to Vietnam* (Cranbury, NJ: Associate University Presses, Inc., 1996) for a discussion on the history of campus insurrection in America. Max Lerner discussed the 1960s campus as "the convergence point of the major revolutionary forces of our time." Max Lerner, "The Revolutionary Frame of Our Time," *The College and the Student* (1966), 8. Lerner's article addressed impact of these forces on the changes in curriculum and the college system.

27. Although the numbers of radicals and conservatives who joined in the debate over American social and political issues were relatively small, their publications coming from organizations such as Young Americans for Freedom and Students for a Democratic Society indicate the depth of interest. Both organizations published material debating the meaning of America. Their dialogue was representative of the active political discourse of the time. A revealing source documenting the conversation about the young's discontent is Irving Kristol, "What's Bugging the Students?" in *The Troubled Campus, Writers, Educators, and Students Confront the Question, What's Wrong in the Colleges and Universities*, ed. *Atlantic Monthly* (Boston and Toronto: Little, Brown and Company, 1965), 6.

28. Stanley Rothman and S. Robert Lichter, *Roots of Radicalism: Jews, Christians and the New Left* (New York: Oxford University Press, 1982), 9.

29. Manoogian, "New Spirit in Young Film-makers," 23.

30. Ellis, "The Big Picture," 7.

31. Mayer, "Motion Picture Courses in American Universities," 26.

32. Bernard Kantor, "Film Study in Colleges," *The Journal of the Producers Guild of America* 19 (Mar. 1967): 3.

33. Film societies at the time sent their notes to Dartmouth, where affiliates made up packets and sent them to AFFS members. Because the college was relatively isolated, its residents provided a following for the local theater, "The Nugget." As David C. Stewart reported, the theater "enjoyed a virtual commercial monopoly on collegiate movie-going in Hanover for fifty years." Thirty-three films screened in one season brought a total of nearly 28,000 in attendance. Stewart, "Men and Movies at Dartmouth," 8.

34. Robert Steele, "Film Scholars at the New York Film Festival," *Film Comment* 2 (Fall 1964): 41–43.

35. Stewart, *Film Study in Higher Education*, 15; and George C. Stoney, "Breaking the Word Barrier," in ibid., 84.

36. Wilcox, "Film Education," 8.

37. "The Student Movie Makers," *Time* 91.5 (2 Feb. 1968): 78. In Lexington, MA, Yvonne Anderson, according to the *Time* article, ran an extracurricular workshop for five-year-olds and up.

38. The University Film Producers Association was founded in 1947. Comprised largely of those faculty involved in teaching and research, the Association served as a "central source of information on film instruction and film production by educational institutions" and sought "to assist ... those members in recognized educational institutions engaged in the teaching of the arts and sciences of motion pictures production techniques, film history, criticism, and related subjects." Stewart, *Film Study in Higher Education*, 152–153.

39. Shirley Clarke, "Teaching Filmmaking Creatively," *Journal of the University Film Producers Association, A Quarterly* 17.3 (Spring 1965): 8. Clarke co-managed the Film-makers Distribution Center, which was established to meet demands for viewing independent films at theaters. James Lithgow, "Filmmakers' Distribution Center," *Filmmakers' Newsletter* 2.6 (Apr. 1969): 10.

40. Colin Young, "Films are Contemporary: Notes on Film Education," *Arts in Society* 4.4 (Winter 1967): 29, 32. As Young stated, "The class is more important as an audience than as a class in the traditional sense." Ibid., 28.

41. Edward Fischer, "Film Studies Are Coming — Ready or Not," *Journal of University Film Producers Association* 14.4 (Fall 1965): 25.

42. Northwestern had ten graduate students in 1966–1967, compared to zero ten years prior. See Kantor, "Film Study in Colleges," 4; and Ellis, "The Little Ivy-Covered Giant," 20, 21.

43. "Center for Advanced Film Studies Established in California," *Filmmakers Newsletter* 2.8 (June 1969): 4.

44. Stewart, "Movies and Colleges," 28, 17.

45. Mayer, "Motion Picture Courses in American Universities," 26.

46. *The Daily Utah Chronicle*, 27 Sep. 1968.

47. Ibid.

48. Ellis, "The Little Ivy-Covered Giant," 21.

49. Kantor, "Film Study in Colleges," 8.

50. Alvin Fiering, "Film at Boston University," *Film Society Review* 1 (Feb. 1966): 16.

51. Laurent Tirard, *Moviemakers' Master Class: Private Lessons from the World's Foremost Directors* (New York and London: Faber and Faber, 2002), 59.

52. "The Student Movie Makers," 78.

53. Aljean Harmetz, "The American Film Institute," *Show* 1.5 (20 Aug. 1970): 16.

54. Anthony Schilacci, "Film as Environment," *Saturday Review* 51 (28 Dec. 1968): 14.

55. http://www.cinema.sfsu.edu/curricframe.html. Accessed 22 Nov. 2002.

56. David C. Stewart, "The Movies Students Make," *Harper's* 231 (Oct. 1965): 68.

57. Young, "Films are Contemporary," 32; and Colin Young, "Film at UCLA," *The Journal of the Producers Guild of America* 19 (Mar. 1967): 11. Student filmmaking required a considerable amount of money and, as film programs grew, outside companies contributed funds to promising students. The Louis B. Mayer Foundation awarded five grants at $3,000 each to UCLA. Others included appropriations to USC (the Disney Foundation, M.C.A., The Directors Guild, Johnson Wax-Red Skelton Scholarship, and individual donors). In 1965, the Screen Producers Guild awarded Martin Scorsese's "It's Not Just You, Murray," produced at NYU, "best student film made in America." Student films were also sent to universities overseas where they were shown and discussed. Stewart, "The Movies Students Make," 70.

58. Parker, "Projection Room," 29.

59. Young, "Film at UCLA," 9.

60. Darrell Loo, "Student Film Making Hits University," *The Daily Utah Chronicle*, 27 Sep. 1968.

61. Jackson Burgess, "Student Film-Making," *Film Quarterly* (Spring 1966): 33.

62. At mid-decade USC and UCLA had a combined film study and production enrollment of approximately 316 undergraduates and graduate students. Peter Bart, "Hollywood Scholars: College Groups Try For Improvement In Screen Teaching Techniques," *The New York Times*, 2 Aug. 1964.

63. Part of what prevented students from getting Hollywood jobs was the union structure in Hollywood, which controlled admission and therefore employment. From the late 1950s, few students had gone from the UCLA film school directly to Hollywood (although, in countries around the world, a degree in film from UCLA might result in the opposite). At the same time, by 1965, an estimated $400 million a year was spent on educational and industrial filmmaking. As a result, the non-theatrical fare drew "some 70 percent of U.S.C.'s film students." Ibid.

64. Kantor, "Film Study in Colleges," 5.

65. Manoogian, "New Spirit in Young Film-makers," 23.

66. Young, "Films are Contemporary," 31, 32.

67. Loo, "Student Film Making Hits University."

68. See Young, "Film at UCLA," page 9, for a list of thirty-some professionals involved at the time with the UCLA program. See also Mayer, "Motion Picture Course," page 27, for a list of the prominent campus educators, and Kantor, "Film Study in Colleges," page 5, for the experimental program between USC and Universal.

69. Burgess, "Student Film-Making," 33.

70. Stewart, "The Movies Students Make," 71, 72.

71. Larry Cohen, "The New Audience: From Andy Hardy to Arlo Guthrie," *Saturday Review* 52 (27 Dec. 1969): 9.

72. Wilcox, "Film Education," 2.

73. Hollis Alpert, "The Falling Stars," *Saturday Review* 51 (28 Dec. 1968): 16.

74. See Richard Maltby, "'Nobody Knows Everything': Post-classical Historiographies and Consolidated Entertainment," in *Contemporary Hollywood Cinema*, ed. Steve Neale and Murray Smith (London and New York: Routledge, 1998), 27. Maltby provides a discussion on the marketing strategies Hollywood employed with well-known sponsors to market a film's saleability before release.

75. Ibid.

76. *Saturday Review* dedicated its annual movie issue on Dec. 28, 1968, to "The Now Movie." Articles were written mainly by film specialists under thirty.

77. Stewart, "The Movies Students Make," 72.

78. Philip Chamberlin, "The Big Picture," *Film Society Review* 1 (Dec. 1965): 29.

79. AFI received over $5,000,000 in funding from foundations and government, corporate, and private sources; the institute is located in Washington, DC, and offers scholars and independents an educational resource. George Stevens, Jr., director of AFI in 1968, explained to *Saturday Review* that the AFI serves the purpose of helping thousands of young people to mature in their film production, not to create another Hollywood. Washington added one more filmmaking site to the dominance of New York and Los Angeles. Richard L. Coe, "Support for New Talent," *Saturday Review* 51 (28 Dec. 1968): 22–23. See also Alpert, "Onward and Upward with the Institute," 50; and Stewart, "Men and Movies at Dartmouth." The Institute also developed an advisory committee made up of university professors and department chairs from Ohio, Stanford, Temple, New York, UCLA, and USC. This committee helped with the development of educational material, study programs, and funding. The representatives of the academic community worked hand in hand toward their common goal with the leading people in the film industry who sat on the Institute's Board. "The American Film Institute," *Dialogue in Film* 2.1, n.d.

80. Robert Geller and Sam Kula, "Toward Filmic Literacy: The Role of the American Film Institute," *Journal of Aesthetic Education* 3.3 (July 1969): 99.

81. Coe, "Support for New Talent," 22–23.

82. "The American Film Institute," 16, 17.

83. Aljean Harmetz, "Custodian for Cinema Culture," *Show* (Aug. 1970): 16.

84. George Stevens, Jr., "Remarks of George Stevens, Jr. on his Appointment as Director of the American Film Institute," *Journal of the University Film Association* 20.1 (1968): 6.

85. The United Nations became involved by conducting an educational session on the impact of the "projected image" versus the "printed word" and considered several ways to "protect them [young people] against the barrage of visual impressions to which they are being subjected increasingly." The most important solution suggested was "the development of screen education." Mayer, "Motion Picture Courses in American Universities," 27. The Television Information Office released results from a survey showing that "a very substantial portion of the total television audience watching feature films these days has a college education." Stewart, "Movies and Colleges," 18.

86. Arthur Knight, "Engaging the EyeMinded," *Saturday Review* 51 (28 Dec. 1968): 18.

Chapter III

1. Edgar Z. Friedenburg, "Calling Dr. Spock!" *The New York Review of Books* 10.6 (28 Mar. 1968): 27.

2. Paul Clark, L.B. Press-Telegram, 10 Jan. 1993. Production folder, Margaret Herrick Academy of Motion Picture Arts and Sciences Library, Beverly Hills, CA.

3. Martin Quigley, Jr., and Richard Gertner, *Films in America, 1929–1969* (New York: Golden Press, 1970), 328.

4. Peter Bart, "Mike Nichols, Moviemaniac," *The New York Times*, 1 Jan. 1967. Godard had dramatized contemporary youth but his films did not get much notice in the United States. Francis Ford Coppola had also produced *You're a Big Boy Now* (1966), which dealt with a similar theme of generation.

5. The film was later rated PG.

6. Nadine M. Edwards, "The Graduate, Hilarious Romp Beautifully Done," *Hollywood Citizen-News*, 22 Dec. 1967.

7. William Tusher, *The Film Daily Yearbook of Motion Pictures* 50 (1968): 96.

8. William Wolf, "The Graduate," *Cue* 36 (23 Dec. 1967): 57.

9. Paul Seydor, "The Graduate Flunks Out," reprinted in *Film Society Review* 5–6 (Jan. 1969–1970): 36.

10. *Life* ran a four-part series on "the individual in our mass society." The editors framed the subject as the struggle to maintain an identity and "make a difference." A lead article featured images of adult commuters caught in their world of mass technology, streamlined buildings, and impersonal air terminals or bus stations, and dodging about chaotically in front of glass and steel buildings. The theme carrying the subsequent parts is the young's positive impact on society through their myriad "involvement" programs. Bayard Hooper, "Challenge for Free Men in a Mass Society" and "Modern Society's Growing Challenge: The Struggle to Be an Individual" *Life* 62.16 (21 Apr. 1967): 60. Author Bayard Hooper argued, "for many, the forces of society have become so vast and encompassing that its goals seem too obscure to fathom, too complex to pursue." The "emptiness and anonymity in modern life are a direct result of technological advances and affluence." Young people turned to social work as a way of helping to stop a drifting society. "Comfort is not enough," one young college student said. "The Search for Purpose: Among the Youth of America, a Fresh New Sense of Commitment," *Life* 62.17 (28 Apr. 1967): 66.

11. W. H. Ferry, "Forward," in *Students and Society: A Report on a Conference* (New York: Center for the Study of Democratic Institutions, 1967), 2.

12. Frederick Richman, "A Disenfranchised Majority, Extracts from a Paper," *Students and Society*, 4–5.

13. Daniel Sisson, "The Dialogue: Youth and Society," in *Students and Society: A Report on a Conference* (New York: Center for the Study of Democratic Institutions, 1967), 40–41.

14. George R. Bach, "We Can Close the Generation Gap," *Ladies Home Journal* 85.1 (Jan. 1968): 36.

15. Ibid., 36, 95.

16. The Institute of Group Psychotherapy in Beverly Hills and Marathon were the two mentioned. Ibid., 36.

17. "Robert F. Kennedy, What Our Young People Are Really Saying," *Ladies Home Journal* 85.1 (Jan. 1968): 96.

18. Russell Lynes, "Cool Cheer or Middle Age," *Look* 31.21 (17 Oct. 1967): 45–46.

19. Frank Bardacke, "Discussion," in *Students and Society: A Report on a Conference* (New York: Center for the Study of Democratic Institutions, 1967), 8.

20. Hollis Alpert, "Mike Nichols Strikes Again," *Saturday Review* 50 (23 Dec. 1967): 24.

21. Sandra A. Lonsfoote, "Making Out 'The Graduate,'" Letter to the Editor, *Saturday Review* 51.30 (27 July 1968): 19.

22. Pauline Kael, "Review," http://www.geocities.com/hollywood/8200/gradkael.htm.

23. David Brinkley, "What's Wrong with the Graduate," *Ladies Home Journal* 85.4 (4 Apr. 1968): 79.

24. Phyllis N. Braxton, Letter to the Editor, *Saturday Review* 51.30 (27 July 1968): 19.

25. John Simon, "Movies into Film 1967–1970: The Graduate," Feb. 1968, 1971, http://www.geocities.com/hollywood/8200/gradfilm.htm.

26. Pauline Kael, *Going Steady: Film Writings 1968–1969* (New York and London: Marion Boyers, 1994), 280, 281, 124, 127.

27. Senator Jacob K. Javits, "Politics Or Pix — You Gotta Make Your Audiences Believe," *Variety* 252.13 (13 Nov. 1968): 31, 157.

28. Joseph McBride, ed., *Filmmakers on Filmmaking: The American Film Institute Seminars on Motion Pictures and Television*, vol. II (Los Angeles: J. P. Tarcher, Inc., 1983), 33.

29. Personal Interview, Susan Parker. Feb. 2001, Salt Lake City.

30. Miriam Weiss, Letter to the Editor, "Movie Mailbag: She Identifies with 'Graduate,'" *The New York Times*, 9 June 1968.

31. Hollis Alpert, "'The Graduate' Makes Out," *Saturday Review* 51 (6 July 1968): 14–15.

32. *The New York Times*, full-page ad, 26 Nov. 1967, and subsequent advertisements.

33. Stuart Byron, "Rules of the Game," *Village Voice* 27.2 (6–12 Jan. 1982): 48. Embassy's publicity vice president at the time explained that one likely candidate was Chris Connelly of *Peyton Place*.

34. Joseph Morgenstern, "A Boy's Best Friend," *Newsweek* 71.1 (1 Jan. 1968): 63.

35. McBride, *Filmmakers on Filmmaking*, 30.

36. Jeff Lenburg, *Dustin Hoffman: Hollywood's Anti-Hero* (New York: St. Martin's Press, 1983), 22.

37. David Zeitlin, "A Swarthy Pinocchio Makes a Wooden Role Real," *Life* 63.21 (24 Nov. 1967): 113.

38. Byron, "Rules of the Game," 48.

39. Peter Biskind, *Easy Riders, Raging Bulls: How the Sex-Drug-and-Rock 'n' Roll Generation Saved Hollywood* (New York: Touchstone book Published by Simon and Schuster, 1998), 34.

40. Betty Rollin, "Of Wit," *Look* 32 (2 Apr. 1968): 74.

41. Bart, "Mike Nichols, Moviemaniac." Production Notes from Margaret Herrick Academy of Motion Picture Arts and Sciences Library, Beverly Hills, CA, 8.

42. Douglas Brode, *Dustin Hoffman* (Secaucus, NJ: Citadel Press, 1983), 8.

43. David Zeitlin, "A Swarthy Pinocchio," 114.

44. Ibid. 16.

45. Stanley Kauffmann, "Stanley Kauffmann on Films," *The New Republic* 157.26 (23 Dec. 1967): 37. That same year Gene Hackman helped extend the star image to include the casual midwestern look through the Academy-Award-winning *In the Heat of the Night*.

46. Byron, "Rules of the Game," 48.

47. Brode, *Dustin Hoffman*, 10.

48. Charles Webb, *The Graduate* (New York: The New American Library, 1963), 68, 69, 41.

49. *The Graduate*, Script 45.

50. Kauffmann, "Stanley Kauffmann on Films," 22.

51. In the early 1960s, surfing as a sport was married to surf music. Its radical element came from promoting a loose, laid-back lifestyle in contrast to eastern sophistication and its fast-paced, everyday life. Surf music's mild form of cultural anarchism did not move beyond the "hot rod" and "woodie" form of good times.

52. Part of film's challenge in the decade's early years was

to compete with the potency of music as a young person's market. Because of rock music's appeal as an expression of dissent, filmmakers appropriated music and incorporated rock music into cinematic narratives, broadening the appeal of the feature film by associating it with music's rebellious flair. Certainly the 1950s Elvis and early 1960s Beach Blankets films used music to incorporate teen culture, but the post–1966 filmmakers' application of music in film disseminated music for both common consumption and as way to advance the social role of music and film as a forms of protest.

53. "See 'The Graduate' Again for the First Time Now!" in the press kit at Margaret Herrick Academy of Motion Picture Arts and Sciences Library, Beverly Hills, CA. It described Sunset Strip as "a hazardous undertaking because of the 'tripping' hippies who populate that area when the stars come out and the smog goes to rest for the night." "See 'The Graduate,'" 2.

54. Bart, "Mike Nichols, Moviemaniac."

55. *The Graduate* Script directions, 54.

56. *The Graduate* Script, 61.

57. She is the transgressor of what Michel Foucault calls "conjugal and parental obligations." Michel Foucault, *The History of Sexuality: An Introduction*, trans. Robert Hurley (New York: Vintage Books, 1990), 121.

58. William Herndon, Letter to the Editor, *The New York Times*, 21 Jan. 1968.

59. Hollis Alpert, "Mike Nichols Strikes Again," 24.

60. Joseph Morgenstern, "A Boy's Best Friend," 63.

61. Andrew Sarris, "Films," *Village Voice* 13.11 (28 Dec. 1967): 33.

62. Because Ben has already established the honesty of his agenda and because of Hoffman's new appeal as the young adult with inner strength, the film encourages viewers to accept his authenticity. A helpful essay on the construction of celebrity status and the power of star strength is Richard Dyer, "Heavenly Bodies: Film Stars and Society," in *Film and Theory*, ed. Robert Stan and Toby Miller (Malden, MA: Blackwell Publishers, 2000), 613.

63. John Simon and Pauline Kael. Kael "because so many people are beginning to treat 'youth' as the ultimate judge—as a collective Tolstoyan clean old peasant." http://www.geocities.com/hollywood/8200/gradfilm.htm.

64. The phrase is Michel Foucault's in *The History of Sexuality*.

65. David Zeitlin, "A Swarthy Pinocchio," 113. While the zoo confrontation and the shower scene both suggest shifting symbols of youth and screen images from the golden boys to eastern New York ethnics through the Hoffman persona, it was clearly not an indication of ethnic acceptance in the larger society. Early in the story at Ben's graduation party, a guest admires Ben's car and comments on "the little red Wop job." Certainly the intent was to show a "self-satisfied, middle-class person who would be bigoted enough to use such an expression." In the book the word does not appear. Moreover, the Italian League requested to have the reference to Wop removed from the script and film copies. Despite the MPPA's Code censoring "words or symbols contemptuous of racial, religious or national groups" if "used so as to incite bigotry or hatred," the word remained. Embassy justified the word's inclusion by explaining that it did not denigrate "people of Italian descent" but advanced the narrative's stance against bigotry. Code words are from *Film Daily Yearbook of Motion Pictures* (1967), 626. The Americans of Italian Descent spokesman, Joseph Jordan, explained to Embassy, "We have been besieged by telephone calls and letters from many of our members and friends who are appalled at the slur in the movie, *The Graduate*, which we would like to believe was unintentional. I refer to the line spoken by one of the

actors to Dustin Hoffman, 'That's a beautiful red wop job [car] you have out there,' referring to an Italian-make car, which may not be a verbatim quote but certainly does use the word *wop*." "Italian Descenters Hit 'Graduate' 'Slur,'" *Film and TV Daily*, 16 May 1968. Ignoring arguments from the Italian Defamation League and the censorship code suggests the language was not explosive enough to threaten receipts.

66. Susan Parker interview.

67. Sarris, "Films," 33.

68. Kaufmann, "Stanley Kaufmann on Films," 37. Note: In classic literary structure, the interruption of weddings is typically to expose to the protagonists an imposter minister, a bigamist bridegroom, or some legal problem that satisfies conventional morality.

69. Alpert, "The Graduate Makes Out," 32.

70. Webb quoted in ibid.

71. Webb and Nichols both quoted in ibid. See also Anthony F. Macklin, "Benjamin Will Survive...." *Film Heritage* 4.1 (Fall 1968): 3.

72. Seydor, "The Graduate Flunks Out," 42.

73. Brode, *Dustin Hoffman*, 64.

74. Weiss, "Movie Mailbag."

75. Byron, "Rules of the Game," 48.

76. Friedenburg, "Calling Dr. Spock!" 27.

77. Kael, *Going Steady*, 126. See also Tom Milne, "Films," *The [London] Observer*, 11 Aug. 1968; "Movies," *McCall's* 95.1 (Apr. 1968); Simon, "Movies into Film."

78. Seydor, "The Graduate Flunks Out," 40.

79. Eric Harpuder, Letter to the Editor, *The New York Times*, 21 Jan. 1968.

80. Bart, "Mike Nichols, Moviemaniac."

81. Gary Dauphin, "Plastic Fantastic," *Village Voice* 42.7 (18 Feb. 1997).

82. Kaufmann, "Stanley Kaufmann on Films," 22.

83. Friedenburg, "Calling Dr. Spock!" 27.

84. Ibid., 26.

85. Ibid., 25.

86. It was the move from the privacy of the daughter's room to the hotel to the red convertible that enabled Hoffman's character to reveal his true self, his genuineness, and thus speak for a generation's ideas about what is real.

87. Simon, "Movies into Film."

88. Seydor, "The Graduate Flunks Out," 38.

89. Weiss, "Movie Mailbag."

90. See Janet Staiger for a discussion on reception theory and ideal representations. Janet Staiger, *Interpreting Films: Studies in the Historical Reception of American Cinema* (Princeton: Princeton University Press, 1992).

91. Kauffmann, "Stanley Kaufmann on Films," 37. Especially noticeable were the juxtapositions, jump cuts, noir interiors, low angles, and perspective visualizations through rainy windows, foliage, and chain link fences and around objects such as statues and pillars.

92. Biskind, *Easy Riders, Raging Bulls*, 34, 10.

93. McBride, *Filmmakers on Filmmaking*, 32.

94. Kael, "Review."

95. Ella Taylor, "Boomer Reunion, The Graduate turns 30," *L.A. Weekly* (7 Mar. 1997): 33.

96. Susan Lydon, "Movies: The Graduate," *Rolling Stone* 1.5 (10 Feb. 1968): 14.

97. Other award-winning films critiqued social reality, but they typically stayed safely within the parameters of already popularized views. *Guess Who's Coming to Dinner?* and *In the Heat of the Night*, for example, not only cast celebrities, but they also cast them as ideal, resourceful, articulate, and intelligent characters during the civil rights movement's mainstream activism and prior to overt militancy. Both films, in a sense, recycled what was already legitimized politically by that time. The social reconciliation of

racial strife was by no means congenial, but the change in attitude had already circulated in friendly articles about interracial issues. When Peggy Rusk, the daughter of Georgia-born Secretary of State Dean Rusk, married a black college student in the fall of 1967, *Ladies Home Journal* engaged in the debate about public acceptance of interracial marriages. As Mrs. Medgar Evers wrote in April 1968, "I envy my children's color-blindness and the color-blindness of their many white friends. I know that they are right, that their attitudes are those of a hopeful future." Though the strongest display of racial strife was yet to come in the final years of the 1960s with militant revolution, the view from 1967 looked promising. "Peggy Rusk: First Pictures of Her Interracial Marriage," and Mrs. Medgar Evers, "A Distinguished Negro Mother Asks: Why Should My Child Marry Yours?" *Ladies Home Journal* 84.4 (Apr. 1968): 80–81.

98. Alpert, "The Graduate Makes Out," 32.
99. Dauphin, "Plastic Fantastic."
100. Lenburg, *Dustin Hoffman: Hollywood's Anti-Hero*, 35.
101. Robert Windeler, "Study of Film Soaring on College Campuses," *New York Times*, 18 Apr. 1968.

Chapter IV

1. Sharon McCormick, "Alice's Restaurant," *Filmex* (3 Apr. 1976): 55.
2. "Reviews, Alice's Restaurant," *Digest, Motion Picture Herald* (13 Aug. 1969).
3. Ibid.
4. As Stuart Hall has explained, "All meanings are produced within history and culture. They can never be finally fixed but are always subject to change, both from one cultural context and from one period to another. There is thus no single, unchanging, universal 'true meaning.'" Stuart Hall, "The Work of Representation," in *Representation: Cultural Representations and Signifying Practices*, ed. Stuart Hall (London, Thousand Oaks, New Delhi: Sage Publications, 1997). Penn's most compassionate representation of Alice is helpful for understanding the limitations of the counterculture in 1969.
5. Axel Madsen, "Reaching the Tribes," *Sight and Sound* 39.1 (Winter 1969/1970): 33.
6. Stephen Farber, "End of the Road?" *Film Quarterly* 23.2 (Winter 1969–1970): 3.
7. Ernest Callenbach, "Editor's Notebook: American New Wave?" *Film Quarterly* 23.2 (Winter 1969–1970): 1.
8. Ernest R. Barea, Letter to the Editor, *The New York Times*, 2 Nov. 1969.
9. Callenbach, "Editor's Notebook," 1.
10. Deac Rossell, "Arlo Guthrie's 'Alice's Restaurant,' becomes Arthur Penn's newest movie," *Boston After Dark*, 27 Nov. 1968; "Hillard Elkins Plans Show, 'Real People' in 'Alice's,'" *Hollywood Reporter* (6 Feb. 1969): 38.
11. Venable Herndon, "Alice's Restaurant," *Hollywood Citizen-News*, 22 Aug. 1969.
12. Paul D. Zimmerman, "Alice's Restaurant's Children," *Newsweek* 74.13 (29 Sep. 1969): 101–106.
13. Rossell, "Arlo Guthrie's 'Alice's Restaurant,'" 16.
14. Roland Gelatt, "SR Goes to the Movies, Arlo as Arlo" *Saturday Review* 52.35 (30 Aug. 1969): 35.
15. Rossell, "Arlo Guthrie's 'Alice's Restaurant,'" 17.
16. Zimmerman, "Alice's Restaurant's Children," 106.
17. *Time* estimated some 300,000 young people in America had actually dropped out of their middle-class environment while many others entertained aspects of the burgeoning counterculture during the summer of 1967. Though this group was small on all counts, the counter-

culture phenomenon extended past sheer numbers and went widely and deeply enough to be tagged a subculture or, as *Time* put it, a "permutation of the middle-class American ethos from which it evolved." "The Hippies: Philosophy of a Subculture," *Time* 90.1 (7 July 1967): 18.
18. Michael Kazin, *The Populist Persuasion: An American History* (Ithaca and London: Cornell University Press, 1995), 139, 145, 1, 142. See also Brent Ortega Murphy and Jeffery Scott Harder, "1960s Counterculture and the Legacy of American Myth: A Study of Three Films," *Canadian Review of American Studies* 23.2 (Winter 1993): 57.
19. Advertisements for *Alice's Restaurant* in *Village Voice* 14.44 (14 Aug. 1969): 26 and 37, and (21 Aug. 1969): 38.
20. Edwin Miller, "Spotlight! The Hollywood Scene," *Seventeen* (Feb. 1969): 54.
21. Susan Braudy, "Kids are Groovy, But Adults Are Not," *The New York Times Student Weekly* (9 Sep. 1969): Special News Report Section II.
22. Ibid.
23. Herbert I. London, *Closing the Circle: A Cultural History of the Rock Revolution* (Chicago: Nelson-Hall, 1984), 76.
24. Braudy, "Kids are Groovy."
25. Philip French, "Alice's Restaurant," *Sight and Sound* 39 (Winter 1969–1970): 44.
26. Zimmerman, "Alice's Restaurant's Children," 101.
27. Miller, "Spotlight! The Hollywood Scene," 54.
28. Ibid.
29. London, *Closing the Circle*, 73.
30. When guitars went electric and music went industrial, the two types of music became antithetical. Bob Dylan, the early guru of the folk movement, was booed offstage when he walked on with his electric guitar. On the other hand, one promoter was forced to close a rock show in Detroit because Peter, Paul, and Mary were part of the show. The schism between rocker and folk singer marked splits in advocacy in the larger society at the time. Ibid., 76.
31. French, "Alice's Restaurant," 44.
32. Advertisements for *Alice's Restaurant* in *Village Voice*, 38.
33. The film added to his fame already established through the twenty-five to thirty concerts a year, at a minimum of $6,000 a concert. Arlo had also already amassed wealth with his 260-acre spread in Massachusetts. A second home and fame awarded through music and film by the end of the decade made Arlo's famous refrain, "you can get anything you want" a bit more sinister. Zimmerman, "Alice's Restaurant's Children," 101–106.
34. Miller, "Spotlight! The Hollywood Scene," 42.
35. The Free Print Shop provided the space for the main means of communication. A well-known example of communal publication is *Kaliflower*, a small magazine that was circulated every Thursday to three hundred people. The Shop organized messengers to hand-deliver the publication by posting it on a plywood board situated in a designated communal space. Any free messages or free ads for the deliverer were attached to a bamboo rod on the board. The messengers typically returned from their intercommunal travels with stories and information for the content of future publications on intercommunal life. *Kaliflower* functioned as an important means of intercommunal communication and also a mode of developing newsworthy stories, feeding subsequent publications. When the members felt the publication "compromised ideals of staying small, local and anonymous," the staff suspended its production. "Diggers" (Mar. 1967–Mar. 1969 MS 4008 *The Friends of Perfection Collections*), donated by Sutter Street Commune, known also as the Scott Street Commune. In Folder 1, Special Collections at North Baker Research Library, California Historical Society, San Francisco, CA.

36. *Kaliflower* 1.4 (15 May 1969) MS4008, Box 1, Folder 1, Special Collections at North Baker Research Library, California Historical Society, San Francisco, CA.

37. "Miscellaneous File," MS3159/6 (n.d.), Special Collections at North Baker Research Library, California Historical Society, San Francisco, CA.

38. "Miscellaneous File," MS3159/5, Special Collections at North Baker Research Library, California Historical Society, San Francisco, CA. These words come from the Manifesto of "The Resurgence Youth Movement of California," reissued in 1967 from the originally published one in 1964 in Manhattan.

39. Stan Smith, "Hippy Identity Within Self," *Utah Daily Chronicle*, 2 Oct. 1967, p. 4.

40. Communication Company Folder, MS3159/3, Special Collections at North Baker Research Library, California Historical Society, San Francisco, CA.

41. "Miscellaneous File," MS3159/5 (15 Mar. 1968), and *Free City News* in Folder MS3159/4 (1967–1968), Special Collections at North Baker Research Library, California Historical Society, San Francisco, CA.

42. Murphy and Harder, "1960s Counterculture," 9.

43. Zimmerman, "Alice's Restaurant's Children," 104.

44. George W. Favre, "Hippiedom and the Neighbors," *Christian Science Monitor* 7 (Nov. 1967).

45. Smith, "Hippy Identity Within Self," 4.

46. *Free City News* (1967–1968), MS3159/4, Special Collections at North Baker Research Library, California Historical Society, San Francisco, CA (quoted as appeared, all in capital letters).

47. "Time to Forget," Digger Papers (Mar. 1967–Mar. 12, 1969), Folder MS 3159/1, Special Collections at North Baker Research Library, California Historical Society, San Francisco, CA.

48. Paul Warshow, "Easy Rider," *Sight and Sound* 39.1 (Winter 1969/1970): 35.

49. *Kaliflower* 1.4 (15 May 1969), MS4008, Box 1, Folder 1, Special Collections at North Baker Research Library, California Historical Society, San Francisco, CA.

50. Gelatt, "SR Goes to the Movies," 35.

51. Zimmerman "Alice's Restaurant's Children," 104.

52. Farber, "End of the Road?" 10.

53. Favre, "Hippiedom and the Neighbors."

54. "The Hippies: Philosophy of a Subculture," 20.

55. Favre, "Hippiedom and the Neighbors."

56. As Pierre Bordieu has pointed out, "most of the types of discourse which have been or are produced in support of the 'people' come from producers occupying dominated positions in the field of production. And ... the more-or-less idealized 'people' is often a refuge against failure or exclusion." Idealizing the free spirit mocked class struggle because rebellion took place in culture through lifestyle instead of politics and resistance. Thus when counterculture discourse replaced work with freedom, peace, and love, it earned "symbolic capital" that mocked "the people" not for bigotry but for their social value. Pierre Bordieu, "The Uses of the 'People,'" *In Other Words: Essays Towards a Reflexive Sociology*, trans. Matthews Adamson (Stanford: Stanford University Press, 1990), 151.

57. Barea, Letter to the Editor, *New York Times*.

58. Zimmerman, "Alice's Restaurant's Children," 102.

59. Stephen Mintz and Randy Roberts, *Hollywood's America: United States History Through Its Films* (St. James, NY: Brandywine Press, 1993), 268. Because the counterculture was largely a white, middle- and upper-middle-class phenomenon, its kind of grassroots differed from the middle-class world long represented by such directors as Frank Capra. Capra's characters created a middle-class world that validated the importance of America. Their belief that "America is the last, best hope of mankind" is exactly the premise that films like *Alice's Restaurant* question but do not replace. The Capra world "celebrate[d] the characteristic institutions of ... marriage, the family, the neighborhood, the small business" in middle-class style. Therefore, the form of "populism" that hippie ethos imparts aligns itself more with the Steinbeck types of "little guy" than with the independent American seeking legitimacy. Capra's senators, career girls, and other libertarians "distrust power" but seek to "preserve the basic integrity of their political and social institutions." Certainly there is an antimaterialism strain in Capra's films that the counterculture shares, but the end result of that argument is the opposite of the anti–middle class themes that run through counterculture ethos. Contrary to *Alice's Restaurant*, Capra's characters offer "a way of looking at middle-class life which does not make it seem banal, sterile, and purposeless, and which invests it with vitality and style." John Raeburn, "Introduction," in *Frank Capra: The Man and His Films*, ed. Richard Glatzer and John Raeburn (Ann Arbor: University of Michigan, 1975), ix, xi, xiii.

60. "The Current Cinema," *The New Yorker* (9 Sep. 1969): 96.

61. Zimmerman, "Alice's Restaurant's Children," 102, 106.

62. The second part of this sentence refers to Fredric Jameson, "Reification and Utopia in Mass Culture," in *Signatures of the Visible* (New York and London: Routledge, 1992), 24–25; and Frederic Jameson, *Geopolitical Aesthetic: Cinema and Space in the World System* (Bloomington: Indiana University Press, 1992), xii — xiv.

63. Murphy and Harder, "1960s Counterculture."

64. Herndon, "Alice's Restaurant."

65. Bordieu, "The Uses of the 'People.'" Popular uses of the people are most profitable in the political world because politicians and others can show the "history of struggles within progressive parties or workers' unions." In academic discourse the idea of "workerism" has maintained a symbolic effect that confirms the value of experience. Thus, when political activists (many of whom were students of intellectuals) formed organizations such as the SDS spoke to and for the working class they assumed the right to. In Bordieu's words, intellectuals "set themselves up as holders of a sort of pre-emptive right over the 'people.'" Intellectual refinement also allows laying claim as protectors while concealing the "break with the 'people' that is implied by gaining access to the role of spokesperson." Ibid., 152. Like the intellectual, the counterculturalists "always presuppose a certain cultural capital." Their task was to de-anesthetize the broad middle class, but to do so meant to de-value their experience and especially the importance of work. Repression would hardly resonate from self-proclaimed revolutionaries whose struggle seemed more rhetorical than everyday. Ibid., 155, 151–154.

66. Madsen, "Reaching the Tribes."

67. Thomas Frank, *Conquest of Cool: Business Culture, Counterculture, and the Rise of Hip Consumerism* (Chicago: University of Chicago Press, 1997), 15, 108.

68. As Fredric Jameson has argued, "The commodity production of contemporary or mass culture has nothing whatsoever to do, and nothing in common, with older forms of popular or folk art." Jameson, "Reification and Utopia in Mass Culture," 15.

69. Zimmerman, "Alice's Restaurant's Children," 101–106.

70. Claudia Dreifus, "Arlo Guthrie," *Progressive* 57.2 (Feb. 1993): 32.

71. Jack Slater, "'Alice' Still Food for Thought," *Los Angeles Times*, 1 July 1981. Slater's comments pertained to the many enthusiastic responses about what the movie meant from the audience who was discussing the film and

sharing memories about it. The film was shown at the Royal in Los Angeles for the Common Cause 1981 Summer Film Festival.

72. Barbara Bannon, Sundance Film Festival Catalogue. The film played Monday Jan. 24, 1993, at 9:30PM at Park City Library Center.

73. McCormick, "Alice's Restaurant," 55.

74. Braudy, "Kids Are Groovy," Section II.

75. Zimmerman, "Alice's Restaurant's Children," 104, 106.

76. Ibid., 104.

77. Rossell, "Arlo Guthrie's 'Alice's Restaurant.'"

78. Zimmerman, "Alice's Restaurant's Children," 106.

79. *People Magazine* (Sep. 26, 1994).

80. Michael Quinn, "Alice's Church," *Time* 139.9 (2 Mar. 1992): 37.

81. Ned Zenman and Lucy Howard, "Arlo Go Home," *Newsweek* 119.7 (17 Feb. 1992): 8.

82. Warshow, "Easy Rider," 35.

Chapter V

1. Peter Biskind, *Easy Riders, Raging Bulls: How the Sex-Drug-and-Rock 'n' Roll Generation Saved Hollywood* (New York: Touchstone Book Published by Simon and Schuster, 1998), 42.

2. Production notes, Core Collection, Margaret Herrick Academy of Motion Picture Arts and Sciences Library, Beverly Hills, CA.

3. *Hollywood Reporter*, 9 Nov. 1990.

4. For an example of how viewers identified with the Western, see Jane Tompkins, *West of Everything: The Inner Life of Westerns* (New York and Oxford: Oxford University Press, 1992).

5. Emanuel Levy, *All About Oscar: The History and Politics of the Academy Awards* (New York and London: Continuum, 2003), 186, 188. For many years, Westerns provided "the 'bread and butter'" of filmmaking. During the golden 1950s, the genre produced over 30 percent of Hollywood production. Yet, not one of the "a-grade" pictures won an Oscar. In fact, only three out of seventy-four Best Picture awards have gone to Westerns. Neither Howard Hawks nor John Ford, masters of the trade, even received nominations for what are now considered masterpieces: *Red River* (1948) and *Stagecoach* (1959), respectively. Westerns that satirized the genre (*Blazing Saddles*, 1974) or reexamined its merit (*Unforgiven*, 1992) drew Academy interest. The Academy's preference for the more personal, biographical, and social-problem pictures rather than the Western (a white Protestant narrative) has dominated Academy standards and taste for artistic achievement. As John Ford once said, "I don't think a lot about honors, but I think it's demeaning to the Westerns that I have received honors for other films and none for my Westerns," in Ibid., 186.

6. Lee Clarke Mitchell, *Westerns: Making the Man in Fiction and Film* (Chicago and London: The University of Chicago Press, 1996), especially chapter 1. The West has long been a location and an idea in American popular culture. On physical terms the components that shaped the West in the imaginations of many included land ownership, conservation, adventure, economy, extraction, openness, and especially modernization, with its freeways, sprawling cities, and fashion malls. In ideological terms, the West has been a region for arguing and living rugged individualism, connecting oneself in general to an aesthetics that combines veneration of the landscape with entertainment and identity.

7. An early script has a helicopter chasing the two characters, but they successfully evade it. The script also begins with the story of Wyatt and Billy working a local circus. The opening scene shows them getting paid for their last performance and then quitting "to prepare for their long journey." Script #27 in *Easy Rider* File, Special Collections, Margaret Herrick Academy of Motion Picture Arts and Sciences Library, Beverly Hills, CA.

8. Charles A. Reich, *The Greening of America: How the Youth Revolution Is Trying to Make America Livable* (New York: Random House, 1970), 64, 68, 71.

9. Ray-Ban sunglasses were a popular brand sported in the sunglasses craze at the time. For the theme of search for America see the production notes and press book, Core Collection, Margaret Herrick Academy of Motion Picture Arts and Sciences Library, Beverly Hills, CA.

10. "Hippie?" *The Haight-Ashbury Maverick* I.8 (1967): 2 (reel #8, University of Utah).

11. Fredric Jameson, *Signatures of the Visible* (New York and London: Routledge, 1992), 9.

12. Thomas Frank, *The Conquest of Cool: Business Culture, Counterculture, and the Rise of Hip Consumerism* (Chicago: University of Chicago Press, 1997), 15.

13. Script #27 in *Easy Rider* File, Special Collections, Margaret Herrick Academy of Motion Picture Arts and Sciences Library, Beverly Hills, CA.

14. For an earlier version of this essay, see Elaine M. Bapis, "*Easy Rider* (1969): Landscaping the Modern Western," in *The Landscape of Hollywood Westerns: Ecocriticism in an American Film Genre*, ed. Deborah A. Carmichael (Salt Lake City: University of Utah Press, 2006).

15. Tom Milne, "Easy Rider," *Sight and Sound* 38.4 (Autumn 1969): 211. Similar to what Walter Benjamin argued about the panorama, this film displaced temporal and spatial properties by offering the urban spectator an illusion of travel. As Benjamin remarked, "The city-dweller … attempts to introduce the countryside into the city. In the panoramas the city dilates to become landscape…." Likewise the film brought the rugged outdoors into the city and thus restructured the relation of the viewer to both landscapes and time. Quoted in Anne Friedberg, "The Mobilized and Virtual Gaze in Modernity: Flaneur/Laneuse," in *The Visual Culture Reader*, ed. Nicholas Mirzoeff (London, New York: Routledge, 1998), 259.

16. "A Summer of Love," (n.d.) file MS3159, no. 5, Special Collections at North Baker Research Library, California Historical Society, San Francisco, CA.

17. Milne, "Easy Rider," 211.

18. Quoted in Paul Warshow, "'Easy Rider,'" *Sight and Sound* 39, no.1 (Winter 1969/1970): 36.

19. Ibid., 36–37.

20. "Movies," *Playboy* 16.9 (Sep. 1969): 42.

21. Stephen Farber, "End of the Road?" *Film Quarterly* 23.2 (Winter 1969–1970): 7. *Variety* also picked up on this notion early in the film's career when it noted, "Peter Fonda has come to bear much the same relationship to the motorcycle picture that John Wayne has to the Western — the rugged, handsome, prototype hero…." "Easy Rider" *Variety* 254.18 (14 May 1969). See, too, William Wolf, "New Films," *Cue* 38 (19 July 1969): 72.

22. Paul E. Martin, "Happier Now," Letter to the Editor, *The New York Times* (23 Nov. 1969).

23. Script #27 is more literal. One of the teenage girls challenges the deputy's treatment of the three bikers. "You probably don't realize that Jefferson Davis had long hair and Robert E. Lee and Daniel Boon" (68, 69). A second man decries the association and distinguishes between historically revered characters and the counterculture representatives on the bike: "Don't you mention their names in the same breath with a bunch of dirty Yankee queers" (79). Script #27 in *Easy Rider* File, Special Collections, Margaret

Herrick Academy of Motion Picture Arts and Sciences Library, Beverly Hills, CA. The total sum of the scenes left out equals the impact and value of hair at the time as a tool of negotiation and resistance; hence, the importance of cultural signifiers as historical explanations.

24. "Acid, Pot Users Describe Psychedelic Trips," *The Daily Utah Chronicle* 76 (29 Sep. 1967): front page. David L. Westby, *Clouded Vision: The Student Movement in the United States in the 1960s* (Lewisburg, PA: Bucknell University Press, 1976). Charles Perry, et al., "Summer of Love," *Edging West* 8 (July/Aug. 1996): 40–43. Dennis M. Cox, subscriptions manager of *Edging West*, hung out in the Haight at age 17 during the famous Summer of Love.

25. Tom Burke, "Will *Easy* Do it for Dennis Hopper?" in Nancy Hardin and Marilyn Schlossberg eds., *Easy Rider Original Screenplay* (New York: Signet, New American Library, 1969), 14. Elizabeth Campbell, "Rolling Stone Raps with Peter Fonda," in ibid., 26–35.

26. Warshow, "Easy Rider," 36.

27. Dennis Hopper in Burke, "Will *Easy* Do it for Dennis Hopper?" 17. Script #27 explains the ending as two "red-neck CRACKERS of forty/fifty, one of them wearing a hunting jacket, the other a cap with a hunting license pinned on it" and "the 2nd CRACKER yells out to Billy, 'Hey, Boy! You gonna get a hair cut … or you rather have your head blowed off?'" The gun discharges as "the wheel hits something, jolting the truck, and causing the gun to go off" but the truck then doubles back and the passenger "fires both barrels, point blank, just as they pass" Wyatt (88). This literal explanation confirms openly what the film does visually. Portraying Wyatt and Billy as victims links race to hair, hair to tolerance. Script #27 in *Easy Rider* File, Special Collections, Margaret Herrick Academy of Motion Picture Arts and Sciences Library, Beverly Hills, CA.

28. Haskell Wexler's *Medium Cool* (1969), a documentary about Chicago 1968, for example, gives a virtual tour of white activists being rebuffed by hostile black militants.

29. Warshow, "Easy Rider," 37.

30. Ibid., 35–37.

31. In the script, Billy and Wyatt establish their position outside the intolerance circle by befriending a pack of black cyclists who "lend them some gasoline" and share a joint. The moment is intense, with suggestions of antagonism and the possibility of violent confrontations, but "the sequence ends with Wyatt and Billy pulling off into a desert Gas Station [sic], exchang[ing] waves with the Black Cyclists [sic] who continue on in the distance." Script #27 in *Easy Rider* File, Special Collections, Margaret Herrick Academy of Motion Picture Arts and Sciences Library, Beverly Hills, CA.

32. "From Method to Madness: Dennis Hopper," *Pacific Film Archive* (June 1988).

33. Production notes, Core Collection, Margaret Herrick Academy of Arts and Sciences Library, Beverly Hills, CA.

34. Warshow, "Easy Rider," 38.

35. Ibid., 36.

36. Fredrick Jameson has explained that "works of mass culture cannot be ideological without at one and the same time being implicitly or explicitly Utopian as well: they cannot manipulate unless they offer some genuine shred of content as a fantasy bribe to the public about to be manipulated." The bike's role as a means of freedom and identity construction is dependent on the ideological role given to open space in Westerns and the "fantasy fulfillment" they provide by becoming the modern horse. The Harley becomes the modern horse because it solves the problem of men moving freely in a contemporary time. Fredric Jameson, "Reification and Utopia in Mass Culture," in *Signatures of the Visible* (New York and London: Routledge, 1992), 29.

37. Ibid.

38. Farber, "End of the Road?," 7–8.

39. Stanley Kaufmann, "Easy Rider," *New Republic* (2 Aug. 1969): 22.

40. Andrew Sarris, "From Soap Opera to Dope Opera," *The Village Voice* (14 Aug. 1969): 35. This review was a response to a review in the *New York Times* by Richard Goldstein, who blasted Sarris for his critical view of the film.

41. "Col's 'Easy Rider' Takes Two Awards," *Hollywood Reporter*, 29 May 1969.

42. Press book, Core Collection, Margaret Herrick Academy of Motion Picture Arts and Sciences Library, Beverly Hills, CA.

43. "'Easy Rider' Wins Award," *Los Angeles Times*, 29 Dec. 1969.

44. Roland Gelatt, "Those Under-Thirties Again," *Saturday Review* 52.28 (12 July 1969): 20.

45. Farber, "End of the Road?" 7–8.

46. Press book, Core Collection, Margaret Herrick Academy of Motion Picture Arts and Sciences Library, Beverly Hills, CA.

47. *Hollywood Reporter*, 19 Sep. 1969.

48. Brent Ortega Murphy and Jeffery Scott Harder, "1960s Counterculture and the Legacy of American Myth: A Study of Three Films," *Canadian Review of American Studies* 23.2 (Winter 1993): 57.

49. Quoted in Burke, "Will Easy Do it for Dennis Hopper?" 17–18.

50. Robert Christgau, "Easy Rider's Soundtrack," in *Easy Rider Original Screenplay*, ed. Nancy Hardin (New York: Signet, New American Library, 1969), 23.

51. Press book, Core Collection, Margaret Herrick Academy of Motion Picture Arts and Sciences Library, Beverly Hills, CA.

52. The production notes from Columbia Films, Core Collection, Margaret Herrick Academy of Motion Picture Arts and Sciences Library, Beverly Hills, CA.

53. Beth Gardiner, "Fonda Raises Money with 'Easy Rider' Bike Rally," *Entertainment Today* (22 Oct. 1999). In Core Collection, Margaret Herrick Academy of Motion Picture Arts and Sciences Library, Beverly Hills, CA. The ride supported a charity to raise money for seriously ill children while promoting Columbia's *Easy Rider* DVD.

54. Peter Fonda, "On the Road Still, Riding Solo, Free and Easy," *New York Times*, 27 June 1998. "The first bike I customized was the one I rode in 'Easy Rider,' which became an international icon," Fonda told the *Times*. "I had faith that the film would be successful but was not sure how successful. I took delight that at the least I had designed myself a very cool and unique chopper. For the movie I bought four Los Angeles Police Department motorcycles at auction, for $500 apiece. Two were for Dennis Hopper to ride and two for me. I came up with a redesign for them and did the work with the help of several friends.… We burned one of the bikes in the film, and, sadly, the other three were stolen before we finished production.…"

55. Mark Ehrman, "Leather, Bikers and Celebs Mean Just One Thing," *Los Angeles Times*, 18 July 1994; Fonda, "On the Road Still, Riding Solo, Free and Easy."

56. Bobos comes from David Brooks' "Bourgeois Bohemians" in *Bobos in Paradise: The New Upper Class and How They Got There* (New York: Simon and Schuster, 2000). In his book, Brooks offers "comic sociology" about how the sixties' adults live today with wealth and authority.

57. Kate Maddox, "From 'Easy Rider' to Breezy Pitcher," *tele.com* 6.5 (5 Mar. 2001): 18.

58. *Forbes*, 167.5 (26 Feb. 2001): 97.

59. Quotes are from http://www.ezrider.co.uk/Easy-

Rider/easy_rider.html and http://members.tripod.com/
~TazRidereasyrider.html; many others can be found at Easy
Rider.com.

60. http://www.canoe.ca/JamMoviesF/Fonda-peter.
html.

61. Untrammeled freedom, a masculine trait in general,
is like an unconscious representation. As Fredric Jameson
writes about such "cognitive or allegorical investments ...
it is only at that deeper level of our collective fantasy that
we think about the social system all the time, a deeper level
that also allows us to slip our political thoughts past a liberal and anti-political censorship." Fredrick Jameson, *The
Geopolitical Aesthetic: Cinema and Space in the World System* (Bloomington and Indianapolis: Indiana University
Press, 1992), 9.

Chapter VI

1. Ralph Graves, "Bridging Two Worlds," *Life* 67.2
(11 July 1969): 1; "Dusty and the Duke," *Life* 67.2 (11
July 1969): 36.

2. Graves, "Bridging Two Worlds," 1.

3. "Dusty and the Duke," 40.

4. As sociologist Victor J. Seidler says, "The disown-
ing of masculinity weakens men, rather than helping to
focus our feelings and thoughts." Victor J. Seidler, *Rediscovering Masculinity: Reason, Language and Sexuality* (Routledge: New York and London, 1989), 178.

5. Jane Tompkins, *West of Everything: The Inner Life
of Westerns* (New York and Oxford: Oxford University
Press, 1992).

6. Ann Fabian, "History for the Masses: Commercializing the Western Past," *Under an Open Sky: Rethinking
America's Western Past*, ed. William Cronon, George Miles,
and Jay Gitlin (New York: W. W. Norton, 1992).

7. Joan Wallach Scott, "Gender: A Useful Category of
Historical Analysis," *Feminism and History*, ed. Joan Wallach Scott (Oxford: Oxford University Press, 1996), 163.

8. "John Wayne Explains the Meaning of 'True Grit,'"
press book, Margaret Herrick Academy of Motion Picture
Arts and Sciences Library, Beverly Hills, CA.

9. Production notes, Special Collections, 3, 5; "John
Wayne Explains the Meaning of 'True Grit,'" press book,
Margaret Herrick Academy of Motion Picture Arts and
Sciences Library, Beverly Hills, CA.

10. As Seidler says, "Since we inherit an identification
of masculinity with reason, there is a strong connection
between masculinity and our sense of morality ... and
morality is supposed to be universal if it is anything." Seidler *Rediscovering*, 191.

11. John J. O'Connor, "On Film: A Lonely Hustler,"
The Wall Street Journal, 27 May 1969.

12. Page 1 of program notes, Special Collections, Margaret Herrick Academy of Arts and Sciences Library, Beverly Hills, CA.

13. Seidler argues that "the liberalization of attitudes
has often rendered pain invisible, as men pretend to live
out conceptions of themselves which have very little reality in their experience. This makes it crucial to maintain
a dialectic between our experience and the conceptual terms
in which we would seek to know it." Seidler, *Rediscovering*, 195.

14. Leonard Quart, "I Still Love Going to Movies: An
Interview with Pauline Kael," *Cineaste* 25.2 (Spring 1996):
10, 13.

15. Page 2 of program notes, Special Collections, Margaret Herrick Academy of Motion Picture Arts and Sciences
Library, Beverly Hills, CA.

16. Dotson Radar, "The Cowboy as Hustler," *Interview*

1.2 (1969). In Core Collection, Margaret Herrick Academy
of Motion Picture Arts and Sciences Library, Beverly Hills,
CA.

17. As Seidler points out, "When we question our inherited conceptions of masculinity we are challenging moral
traditions which have identified masculinity with moral
superiority." Seidler, *Rediscovering*, 194.

18. "Dusty and the Duke," 42.

19. Rader, "The Cowboy as Hustler."

20. "John Wayne Explains the Meaning of 'True Grit,'"
press book, Margaret Herrick Academy of Motion Picture
Arts and Sciences Library, Beverly Hills, CA.

21. Wayne quipped to a reporter that he always saw
himself as a progressive liberal before the sixties.

22. Seidler writes, "Feminists have argued that men
know who they are because they live in a society and culture that is made in their own image. But this can be to
mistake the institutional power which heterosexual men
undoubtedly have in the larger society to define the reality of others for the lived personal experience of men themselves." If "work is more than a source of dignity and pride"
then it has become "the very source of masculine identity
so that without work ... it is as if men cease to exist at all."
Seidler, *Rediscovering*, 150, 151, 152.

23. Seidler argues, "Through sharing a vulnerability,
people have come to a renewed understanding of the
sources of personal strength. In sharing themselves with
others, they have ceased to feel ashamed and refused to feel
guilty for themselves. This marks a profound political
transformation of the personal that had one of it sources
in the struggles against the Vietnam War. This is a tradition men often find hard to understand." Seidler, *Rediscovering*, 151.

24. Ian Buruma, "John Schlesinger," *Preview* (Dec./Jan.
2006), page 94 of Special Collections, Margaret Herrick
Academy of Motion Picture Arts and Sciences Library, Beverly Hills, CA.

25. Roger Ebert, "Midnight Cowboy," *Chicago Sun-
Times*, 5 July 1969.

26. Ibid.

27. Joseph Gelmis, *Newsday*, 26 May 1969.

28. Jan Dawson, "Midnight Cowboy," *Sight and Sound*
38 (Autumn 1969): 212.

29. Gene Phillips, "John Schlesinger: Social Realist,"
Film Comment 5.4 (Winter 1969): 62.

30. Ian Buruma, "John Schlesinger."

31. Stanley Kaufmann, "Midnight Cowboy," *New
Republic* (June 7, 1969): 33.

32. Vincent Canby, "Midnight Cowboy," *The New York
Times*, 26 May 1969.

33. Evan Carton, "Vietnam and the Limits of Masculinity," *American Literary History* 3.2 (Summer 1991): 296.

34. In Seidler's words, "Sexual politics was threatening
because it sought to connect our intellectuality with our
personal lives. Often it is a deep fear of the personal, of
vulnerability and intimacy, that unites men who would
otherwise have sharp political disagreements." Seidler,
Rediscovering, 183.

35. Rick Mitchell, "After 'Midnight,'" Letter to the Editor, *Los Angeles Times*, 6 Mar. 1994.

36. Douglas Soesbe, Letter to the Editor, *Los Angeles
Times*, 6 Mar. 1994. The X rating for the film was dropped
in 1971 in favor of an R rating. The program for the
twenty-fifth anniversary release of the film explained
that the change to an R rating was "an indication of how
swiftly the implications of the initially neutral X rating
were skewed negatively." "25 Years with Midnight Cowboy," Special Collections, Margaret Herrick Academy of
Motion Picture Arts and Sciences Library, Beverly Hills,
CA.

37. Owen Gielberman, "Midnight Cowboy," *Entertainment Weekly* (Mar. 4 1994): http://www.ew.com/ew/article/0,,301325,00.html.

38. Desson Howe, "Midnight Cowboy," *Washington Post*, 15 Apr. 1994.

39. http://www.indiatravelite.com/accommodations/monarchooty.htm; http://www.urbandecay.com/products/NailEnamel/MidnightCowboyNailpolish.cfm.

40. Jonathan Wellemeyer, "Intelligence Squared U.S. Hollywood and the Spread of Anti-Americanism" 6 Jan. 2007. http://www.npr.org/templates/story/story.php?storyId=6625002.

41. Anderson Cooper and Elvis Mitchell, "Live from the Headlines" 6 Aug. 2006, CNN interview transcript, http://transcripts.cnn.com/TRANSCRIPTS/0308/06/se.04.html.

42. http://www.emanuellevy.com/article.php?articID=6782.

43. J. Hoberman, "Blazing Saddles," *Village Voice* (29 Nov. 2005): online.

Chapter VII

1. *M*A*S*H*, Core Collection, Margaret Herrick Academy of Arts and Sciences Library, Beverly Hills, CA.

2. John Walker, "Cannes: The Prizewinners," *Arts Guardian London*, 18 May 1970.

3. Russ AuWerter, "A Conversation with Robert Altman," Core Collection, Margaret Herrick Academy of Motion Picture Arts and Sciences Library, Beverly Hills, CA.

4. "Patton," *Variety* (21 Jan. 1970).

5. George C. Scott, "Why Patton?" Twentieth-Century-Fox Film Production Manual, reprinted in *New Guard* 10.8 (Oct. 1970).

6. Letter dated Dec. 28, 1968; Ring Lardner, Jr., Folder 21, Special Collections, Margaret Herrick Academy of Motion Picture Arts and Sciences Library, Beverly Hills, CA.

7. Letter from Dick Hornberger to Ring Lardner, Jr., Dec. 22, Ring Lardner, Jr., Folder 21, Special Collections, Margaret Herrick Academy of Motion Picture Arts and Sciences Library, Beverly Hills, CA.

8. Jan. 7, 1969, Ring Lardner, Jr., Folder 21, Special Collections, Margaret Herrick Academy of Motion Picture Arts and Sciences Library, Beverly Hills, CA.

9. Page 6 of Ring Lardner Script, Special Collections, Margaret Herrick Academy of Motion Picture Arts and Sciences Library, Beverly Hills, CA.

10. Maurice Yacowar, "Actors as Conventions in the Films of Robert Altman," *Cinema Journal* 20.1 (Fall 1980): especially 23–24.

11. Derek Prouse, "Casualties of War," *The Sunday Times*, 17 May 1970.

12. Ring Lardner, Jr., to Dick Hornberger, Jan 31, 1970; Ring Lardner, Jr., Folder 21, Special Collections, Margaret Herrick Academy of Motion Picture Arts and Sciences Library, Beverly Hills, CA.

13. Letter to Ring, July 8, 1970, Ring Lardner, Jr., Folder 21, Special Collections, Margaret Herrick Academy of Motion Picture Arts and Sciences Library, Beverly Hills, CA.

14. Dilys Powell, "War Games," *The London Times*, 24 May 1970.

15. William Johnson, "M*A*S*H," *Film Quarterly* 23.3 (Spring 1969), 38.

16. Walker, "Cannes: The Prizewinners."

17. William Johnson, "M*A*S*H," 38.

18. Aljean Harmetz, "The 15th Man Who Was Asked To Direct 'M*A*S*H' (and Did) Makes a Peculiar Western," Core Collection, Margaret Herrick Academy of Motion Picture Arts and Sciences Library, Beverly Hills, CA.

19. "Cannes Chief Raps Award to 'M.A.S.H.'" Ring Lardner, Jr., Folder 25, Special Collections, Margaret Herrick Academy of Motion Picture Arts and Sciences Library, Beverly Hills, CA.

20. Thomas Quinn Curtiss, "M*A*S*H Wins Top Picture Award at Cannes Festival," *International Herald Tribune*, 18 May 1970, and *Daily News*, 18 May 1970.

21. John Fairbairn, "First Ever Round-the-Clock London Showing for Cannes Festival Winner," A News Special, M*A*S*H*: Twentieth-Century-Fox, Special Collections, Margaret Herrick Academy of Motion Picture Arts and Sciences Library, Beverly Hills, CA.

22. Leaflet, May 20, 1979, Ring Lardner, Jr., Folder 25, Special Collections, Margaret Herrick Academy of Motion Picture Arts and Sciences Library, Beverly Hills, CA.

23. Powell, "War Games."

24. "Cannes Chief Raps Award to 'M.A.S.H.,'" *Daily News*, 18 May 1970; Ring Lardner, Jr., Folder 25, Special Collections, Margaret Herrick Academy of Motion Picture Arts and Sciences Library, Beverly Hills, CA.

25. "What is the Price of Your Entertainment?" Ring Lardner, Jr., Folder 22, Special Collections, Margaret Herrick Academy of Motion Picture Arts and Sciences Library, Beverly Hills, CA.

26. Ibid.

27. First quotes from Harmetz, "The 15th Man Who Was Asked"; second quote from Walker, "Cannes: The Prizewinners."

28. Judy Klemesrud, "Feminist Goal: Better Image at the Movies," *The New York Times*, 13 Oct. 1974.

29. Betty Friedan in Klemesrud, "Feminist Goal." Second quote from Betty Friedan, "Unmasking the Rage in the American Dream House," *The New York Times*, 31 Jan. 1971.

30. Molly Haskell in Klemesrud, "Feminist Goal."

31. Ibid.

32. Friedan, "Unmasking the Rage in the American Dream House."

33. Thomas Quinn Curtiss, "M*A*S*H: Laughter is the Only Remedy," *International Herald Review*, 13 May 1970.

34. *Newsweek*, 7 Dec. 1970.

35. Ellen Willis, "Misogyny," Letter to the Editor, *The New York Times*, 7 Feb. 1971.

36. Letter from Dick Hornberger to Ring Lardner, Jr., Jan. 9, 1969, Ring Lardner, Jr., Folder 21, Special Collections, Margaret Herrick Academy of Motion Picture Arts and Sciences Library, Beverly Hills, CA.

37. Publicity Folder for *M*A*S*H*, Core Collection, Margaret Herrick Academy of Motion Picture Arts and Sciences Library, Beverly Hills, CA. Richard Corliss, "I Admit It, I didn't Like 'M*A*S*H,'" *The New York Times*, 22 Mar. 1970.

38. Corliss, "I Admit It, I Didn't Like 'M*A*S*H.'"

39. Press book for *M*A*S*H*, Core Collection, Margaret Herrick Academy of Arts and Sciences Library, Beverly Hills, CA.

40. Corliss, "I Admit It, I Didn't Like 'M*A*S*H."

41. Klemesrud, "Feminist Goal."

42. Harmetz, "The 15th Man who Was Asked."

43. Guy Flatley, "So Truffaut Decided to Work his Own Miracle," *The New York Times*, 27 Sep. 1970.

44. Stanley Penn, "Focusing on Youth: A New Breed of Movie Attracts the Young, Shakes up Hollywood," *The Wall Street Journal*, 4 Nov. 1969.

45. Klemesrud, "Feminist Goal."

46. Judy Gerstel, "Robert Altman a Misogynist? He Just Tells the Truth About Women," *Knight Rider/Tribune News Service*, 11 Nov. 1993.

47. Penelope Mortimer, "A Lovable Satire," *The Observer Review*, 17 May 1970.

48. *Denver Rocky Mountain News*, 9 Nov. 1997.

49. Pauline Jelinek, "Army Closes MASH," *The Outlook*, 12 June 1997, World Section.

50. Melody Parker, "Korean War Vets Lend Authenticity to 'M*A*S*H Production," *Waterloo Courier*, 29 Sep. 2006.

51. Diane Jacobs, *Hollywood Renaissance* (London, Brunswick, and New York: A. S. Barnes and Co., 1977).

52. Ira Mothner, "Now Faces," *Look* 3 (Nov. 1970): 77.

53. Jacobs, *Hollywood Renaissance*, 67, 68.

54. Ibid., 70.

55. Since then films such as *Apocalypse Now, Platoon, Good Morning Vietnam*, and *Full Metal Jacket* have shaped the dominant discourse on Vietnam. War representation for that period through these films fostered a new war veteran genre that highlights the experimentalist skeptic.

56. Editor's note, *New Guard* 10.8 (Oct. 1970): 3; Ronald Docksai, "George S. Patton: A Magnificent Anachronism," *New Guard* x, no. 8 (Oct. 1970): 7.

Chapter VIII

1. "Hollywood: The Year You Almost Couldn't Find It," *Look* 3 (Nov. 1970): 40, 51, 52. Fletcher Knebel, "Hollywood: Broke and Getting Rich," *Look* 3 (Nov. 1970): 50.

2. Production notes, Core Collection, Margaret Herrick Academy of Arts and Sciences Library, Beverly Hills, CA.

3. "The After M*A*S*H of Robert Altman," *Where It's At* (Aug. 1971): 12, 13. His studio biography officially described him as such. At the time, Altman's production company operated out of an apartment building near UCLA.

4. Page 1 of production notes, Core Collection, Margaret Herrick Academy of Motion Picture Arts and Sciences Library, Beverly Hills, CA.

5. Sara Evans, *Personal Politics: The Roots of the Women's Liberation in the Civil Rights Movement and the New Left* (New York: Vintage Books, 1979); toward the end of the decade, Sara Evans published her findings about radical women's experience in *Personal Politics*. As she noted, even in organizations such as the New Left, many female activists played waitresses and secretaries throughout the Civil Rights movement.

6. Daniel Yankelovich, *The New Morality: A Profile of American Youth in the 70s* (New York: McGraw Hill, 1974). The CBS survey taken in 1969, "Generations Apart," supplied Yankelovich with the information about sixteen- to twenty-five-year-olds. Yankelovich conjectured that once the non-college sector converted political resistance into personalized forms of lifestyle changes, rebellion marked the 1970s as the time of integration of the new morality. Yankelovich noted that "sweeping changes in sexual morality, work-related values, a changing climate of mistrust of our basic institutions, and other challenges to traditional beliefs and values" were common thoughts among young people, but the 1970s also witnessed a "gap *within* the generation" with cultural issues overshadowing radical politics for many young people. Ibid., v–vii, 3–4.

7. By this time African-American women protested against feminism as a "white women's movement" with the publication of Toni Morrison's criticism in the *New York Times*. Control of a woman's body became the central issue for many in the 1970s wave of women's liberation. On the radical side were women who believed that reproduction was a fundamental right of women; birth and abortion were exclusively up to women to decide. On the conservative side, organizers in 1970 led the protest against abortion with the National Right to Life group. The duration of the debate attests to the complexity of the issues and the multi-voiced nature of women's liberation. What seemed to be about women in the 1970s has evolved into cross-gender issues, involving economics, class, race, religion, and popular culture.

8. Beth Bailey, *Sex in the Heartland* (Cambridge and London: Harvard University Press, 1999), 8, 9; and Beth Bailey, "Sexual Revolution(s)," in *The Sixties: From Memory to History*, ed. David Farber (Chapel Hill and London: The University of North Carolina Press, 1994), 254–255.

9. Beth Bailey observes that "portraying the sexual revolution as the product of a few extremists, somehow unattached to the world the rest of us lived in, is a political act." Bailey argues that "while the revolution was built of purposeful assertions and acts, often on the part of self-proclaimed outsiders, it was possible because of the recasting of American society during and after World War II." Through "national media," for example, American citizens negotiated that change. Film was part of that forum of debate among the generations. "This," as Bailey claimed, "was not a foreign 'national' culture. It was *their* culture…. The sexual revolution was not a simple, two-sided contest between the proponents of freedom and the forces of repression." She explained that "the set of changes we call the sexual revolution was thoroughly part of American culture, born of widely shared values and beliefs and of major transformations in the structure of American society." Bailey, *Sex in the Heartland*, 5–10.

10. Allan Fromme, "Masturbation, A Doctor's Report," *Cosmopolitan* 169.6 (Dec. 1970): 98.

11. Helen Gurley Brown, "Step into My Parlor," *Cosmopolitan* 168.5 (May 1970): 6.

12. Robin Lakoff, *Language and Woman's Place* (New York, Evanston, San Francisco, London: Harper and Row, 1975), 30.

13. Production notes, Special Collections, Margaret Herrick Academy of Arts and Sciences Library, Beverly Hills, CA.

14. *McCabe and Mrs. Miller* Script and production notes, Special Collections, Margaret Herrick Academy of Arts and Sciences Library, Beverly Hills, CA.

15. Ibid.

16. Ibid., 2, 5, 2.

17. Ibid., 2.

18. Marty Weisman Collection, Special Collections, no date; Margaret Herrick Academy of Arts and Sciences Library, Beverly Hills, CA. Letter from Kevin Genther, Studio Publicity Director for Warner Brothers Studios in Pasadena, California 91505 in production notes, Margaret Herrick Academy of Motion Picture Arts and Sciences Library, Beverly Hills, CA.

19. Gerald A. Browne, "The She-Man — Today's Erotic Hero," *Cosmopolitan* 168.3 (Mar. 1970): 50.

20. Letter to publication editors from Kevin Genther, Studio Publicity Director for Warner Brothers Studios in Pasadena, CA, 91505, Special Collections, Margaret Herrick Academy of Motion Picture Arts and Sciences Library, Beverly Hills, CA.

21. *McCabe and Mrs. Miller* Script, Special Collections, Margaret Herrick Academy of Motion Picture Arts and Sciences Library, Beverly Hills, CA.

22. Squamish is the setting for Bear Paw, the mining company town.

23. Lakoff, *Language and Woman's Place*, 27.

24. Production notes, Margaret Herrick Academy of

Motion Picture Arts and Sciences Library, Beverly Hills, CA.

25. Joan Wallach Scott, *Feminism and History* (Oxford and New York: Oxford University Press, 1996), 2.

26. Page 37 of *McCabe and Mrs. Miller* Script, Special Collections, Margaret Herrick Academy of Motion Picture Arts and Sciences Library, Beverly Hills, CA.

27. Anne Koedt, "Politics of the Ego: A Manifesto for N.Y. Radical Feminists," in *Radical Feminism*, ed. Anne Koedt, Ellen Levin, and Anita Rapone (New York: Quadrangle Books/The New York Times Book Co., 1973), 379, 381.

28. Ibid., 383.

29. Lakoff, *Language and Woman's Place*, 7, 5, 9, 11, 28.

30. Teresa de Lauretis, *Technologies of Gender: Essays on Theory, Film, and Fiction* (Bloomington and Indianapolis: Indiana University Press, 1987), 2–3.

31. Robert Merrill, "Altman's McCabe and Mrs. Miller as a Classic Western," *New Orleans Review* (1990): 84.

32. Page 3 of production notes, Special Collections, Margaret Herrick Academy of Motion Picture Arts and Sciences Library, Beverly Hills, CA.

33. Robert Warshow quoted in Merrill, "Altman's McCabe," 85; second quote is Robert Merrill's in ibid.

34. Diane Jacobs, *Hollywood Renaissance* (London, Brunswick, and New York: A. S. Barnes and Co., 1977), 80.

35. Ibid., 82.

36. As Laura Mulvey has argued, "It is also important to acknowledge that negative aesthetics can act as a motor force in the early phases of a movement, initiating and expressing the desire for change." Laura Mulvey, *Visual and Other Pleasures* (Bloomington: Indiana University Press, 1989), 164.

37. Ibid. The shift from the West of wide open spaces to the rainy climate of the Northwest "initiate[d]" the conversation about the Western genre. Likewise, Mrs. Miller's positive portrayal is the motor force for change, but the shift from her to McCabe as the narrative's "controlling figure" suggests the limits to her as a propelling force for the narrative. See also Christine Gledhill, "Genre and Gender," in *Representation: Cultural Representations and Signifying Practices*, ed. Stuart Hall (London, Thousand Oaks, and New Delhi: Sage Publications, 1997), especially 380–385.

38. In his words, "What is visually produced, by the practices of representation, is only half the story. The other half— the deeper meaning — lies in *what is not being said, but is being fantasized, what is implied but cannot be shown*" (Hall's italics). Hall, *Representation*, 263. While reversing the Western by replacing a male protagonist with a female, the film appears to present a positive portrayal of women. Yet, as Hall points out about reversing stereotypes, it does "not necessarily overturn or subvert it" but could also "mean being trapped in its stereotypical 'other.'" Many critics applauded the reversal, of course, but the reversal did not necessarily "unlock ... the complex dialectics of power and subordination," nor did the portrayal of a strong business woman who runs a prostitution house displace the history of objectification of women. Hall, *Representation*, 274. Laura Mulvey explains that negating expectations "depend[s] on acknowledging the dominant codes in the very act of negation itself." Thus, Altman's intent to undercut the Western depended on the audience's knowledge of the genre. That knowledge allowed the counter-argument to work and fail at the same time. In Mulvey's words, "It could only be through an audience's knowledge of the dominant that the avant-garde could acquire meaning and significance. A negative aesthetic can produce an inversion of the meanings and pleasures it confronts, but

it risks remaining locked in a dialogue with its adversary. Counter-aesthetics, too, can harden into a system of dualistic opposition." Mulvey, *Visual and Other Pleasures*, 164.

39. Pauline Kael, "The Current Cinema, Pipe Dreams," *The New Yorker* (July 3, 1971): 41.

40. De Lauretis, *Technologies of Gender*, 3, 130. As Emanuel Levy writes, "Gainfully employed screen women [in Oscar-winning films] are confined to ... two most prominent professions ... [as] actresses and prostitutes. Emanuel Levy, *All About Oscar: The History and Politics of the Academy Awards* (New York and London: Continuum, 2003), 225. Molly Haskell has remarked, "Prostitution, in which she is remunerated for giving sexual pleasure, and acting, a variant on natural role-playing" shows the hold on women's role as "adapting to others, aiming to please." Molly Haskell quoted in Levy, *All About Oscar*, 225.

41. As historian Beth Bailey has argued, "Who we are became determined less by our geographic communities and more by other sorts of identities ... from cultural categories and institutions of national scope." Film works culturally and nationally as a product and process, an assertion and transformation of identity construction and social relations. Bailey, *Sex in the Heartland*, 6.

Chapter IX

1. "Geniuses at Work," File 7, Box 33, Jules Feiffer Collection, Library of Congress. Note: all references in this chapter to the Jules Feiffer Collection are at the Library of Congress.

2. Hollis Alpert, "Why Are They Saying Those Terrible Things About Us?" *Saturday Review* 54.27 (3 July 1971): 18.

3. Jules Feiffer, notes in Folder 10, Box 33, Jules Feiffer Collection.

4. Jules Feiffer notes on speech about "Bernard the Loser," in Folder 9, Box 55, Jules Feiffer Collection, 6–10. Speech entitled "THE SUNDANCE KID 1965," Folder 9, Box 55, Jules Feiffer Collection, 6–7. Jules Feiffer notes, Folder 10, Box 33, Jules Feiffer Collection.

5. Jules Feiffer, "Writing and Drawing for Fun and Profit," speech given by Jules Feiffer on Jan. 18, 1971, at the 92nd Street YMHA. Box 55, Folder 11, 12, Jules Feiffer Collection.

6. Jules Feiffer, "THE SUNDANCE KID, 1965," Folder 9, Box 55, Jules Feiffer Collection, 6–7. As Feiffer wrote in his notes on page 2, "we numb ourselves to the crises around us" and "we deaden the issues by discussing them" away.

7. Bosley Crowther, "Carnal Knowledge," *The New York Times*, 1 July 1971.

8. "Writing and Drawing for Fun and Profit," speech given by Jules Feiffer on Jan. 18, 1971, at the 92nd Street YMHA. Box 55, Folder 11, Jules Feiffer Collection, 12.

9. Norma Lee Browning, "A Plum for Annie," *Chicago Tribune*, 9 July 1970.

10. "Carnal Knowledge Hailed as a Picture Whose Time Has Come," Publicity Department Avco Embassy Pictures Corporation, Margaret Herrick Academy of Motion Picture Arts and Sciences Library, Beverly Hills, CA.

11. Arthur Thirkell, "Sins and Lovers..." *Daily Mirror*, 17 Sep. 1971.

12. Michelene Victor to Jules Feiffer, n. d., Folder 4, Box 12, Jules Feiffer Collection.

13. Jules Feiffer, "True Confessions," Folder 13, Box 33, Jules Feiffer Collection. Jules Feiffer notes, Box 33, Folder 10, Jules Feiffer Collection.

14. First quote from Marta Orbach in letter to Jules Feiffer, June 20, 1971; second quote from Ellis Amburn in

letter to Jules Feiffer, June 23, 1971; third quote from
Samuel W. Gelfman to Jules Feiffer, June 24, 1971; fourth
quote from Bernard Drew, "Review," July 1, 1971; all in
Folder 4, Box 33, Jules Feiffer Collection.

15. First quote from Lee Philips, letter to Jules Feiffer,
July 2, 1971; second quote from Philip Roth, letter to Jules
Feiffer, July 2, 1971; third quote from Ned Rorem, letter
to Jules Feiffer, July 27, 1971; last quote from Lewis Allen,
letter to Jules Feiffer, Sep. 28, 1971; all in Folder 4, Box 12,
Jules Feiffer Collection.

16. First quote from Marta Orbach, letter to Jules Feiffer, June 19, 1971; second quote from Marta Orbach, letter to Jules Feiffer, June 20, 1971; both in Folder 4, Box
33, Jules Feiffer Collection.

17. Letter to Jules Feiffer, Aug. 26, 1971 in Folder 4,
Box 12, Jules Feiffer Collection.

18. Gerald Weales, English Department, University of
Pennsylvania, letter to Jules Feiffer, Oct. 4, 1971 in Folder
4, Box 12, Jules Feiffer Collection.

19. Kristin Linklater, "Demeaning," Letter to the Editor, The New York Times, 14 Nov. 1971. As Laura Mulvey
writes, realism in film also evokes a new "fetishism" where
"the fetishist becomes fixated on an object in order to avoid
knowledge." Like Jonathan who fetishized the women
through the slideshow, there is a certain sensual satisfaction in reducing experience and women to labels. Mulvey
continues, "The fetishist ... has to abandon the desire to
know the true nature of sexual difference in order to avoid
castration anxiety." Thus, "the fetish" provides stability
and the slideshow turns a threat into an artifact, an object
again. Laura Mulvey, Visual and Other Pleasures (Bloomington and Indianapolis: Indiana University Press, 1989),
xii.

20. Roslyn Drexler, "Do Men Really Hate Women?"
The New York Times, 5 Sep. 1971.

21. Jude Pease, Letter to the Editor, The New York
Times, 3 Oct. 1971.

22. Marcia Cooper, "Glib?" Letter to the Editor, The
New York Times, 3 Oct. 1971.

23. Steven Kovaks, "Misplaced Concern," Letter to the
Editor, The New York Times, 3 Oct. 1971.

24. Jack C. Rossetter, "Feiffer's Answer?" The New York
Times, 3 Oct. 1971.

25. Tony Mastoianni, "Sensationalism Obscures Point of
'Carnal Knowledge,'" Cleveland Press, 3 July 1971.

26. Charles Champlin, "'Carnal' Indicts Sexual Patterns."

27. Michelene Victor, letter to Jules Feiffer, n. d., in
Folder 4, Box 12, Jules Feiffer Collection.

28. Fergus Cashin, "Beastly Men Give Ann Her
Chance," The Sun, 16 Sep. 1971, in Folder 7, Box 33, Jules
Feiffer Collection.

29. Jules Feiffer, "Geniuses at work." Jules Feiffer Collection.

30. Louis Botto, "They Shoot Dirty Movies, Don't
They?" Look 3 (Nov. 1970): 59.

31. As David F. Friedman of the Adult Film Association explained, "Generally, it begins with the successful run
of a sexy, foreign film. Then the theater brings in a foreign
picture with no sex in it, and it falls flat on its face." An
Oregon theater owner had the same experience. "When we
played 'The Battle of Algiers' to almost no business, and
followed it with Brigitte Bardot in 'Mademoiselle
Striptease' and practically filled the place, we began to see
the light." Arthur Knight, "Adult Film Group in Quest to
Gain Respect," Los Angeles Times, 17 Feb. 1974.

32. Judge William J. Rehnquist, "Jenkins v. Georgia,"
Supreme Court of the United States, 418 U. S. 153, June
24, 1974.

33. Botto, "They Shoot Dirty Movies, Don't They?" 60.

34. Don Shirley, "A Plan to 'Erase Confusion,'" The
Washington Post, Times Herald, 2 Aug. 1973. Last quote
from Gregg Kilday, "'Knowledge' Obscenity Ruling to be
Appealed," Los Angeles Times, 3 Aug. 1973. See also The
Authors League of America, Inc., press release and statement
of support in Folder 9, Box 33, Jules Feiffer Collection.

35. Linda Matthews, "Court May Refine Ruling on
Obscenity," Los Angeles Times, 11 Dec. 1973.

36. As Judge Rehnquist wrote, "It would be a serious
misreading of Miller [Miller v. California, 1973] to conclude that juries have unbridled discretion to determining
what is 'patently offensive'" under the document." Rehnquist, "Jenkins v. Georgia."

37. Robin Lakoff, Language and Woman's Place (New
York, Evanston, San Francisco, London: Harper and Row,
1975), 9.

38. Lakoff, Language and Woman's Place; Teresa de Lauretis, Technologies of Gender: Essays on Theory, Film, and
Fiction (Bloomington and Indianapolis: Indiana University Press, 1987); Mulvey, Visual and Other Pleasures.

39. Hillary Collins, "The New Puritanism," Cosmopolitan 168.3 (Mar. 1970): 50.

40. Jane Allerton, "Help Bring Back the Seducer," Cosmopolitan 169.3 (July 1970): 26.

41. Teresa de Lauretis has written that "the construction of gender is ... affected by its deconstruction." De
Lauretis, Technologies of Gender, 3.

42. Mulvey argued that women's bodies in film "organized the discourses of law and medicine into the realm of
representation. Women's struggle to gain rights over their
bodies could not be divorced from questions of image and
representation." Mulvey, Visual and Other Pleasure, ix, xi.

43. David L. Minkow, "Fighting It," Letter to the Editor, The New York Times, 5 Dec. 1971.

44. Linklater, "Demeaning."

45. Lakoff, Language and Woman's Place, 42.

46. Joann Wallace, "Where the Body Is a Battleground:
Materializing Gender in the Humanities," Resources for
Feminist Research, 22 Sep. 2001.

47. Linklater, "Demeaning."

48. Mulvey, Visual and Other Pleasures, xi.

49. Laura Mulvey writes, "Analysis of the representation of femininity in popular culture had to become an
analysis of collective fantasy under patriarchal culture ...
watched through the eyes that were affected by the changing climate of consciousness." It was especially important
to note that "the belief that women's reality could ade-
quately counter male fantasy was not enough." She further
points out how "the sexualized image of woman says little
or nothing about women's reality, but is symptomatic of
male fantasy and anxiety that are projected onto the female
image." Thus, Carnal Knowledge shows just how firmly
secured the "male fantasy" and its "narrow identity" were
in film's construction of women. Socially, this film points
out the ways that positive results for feminism were never
resolved during the 1970s. Mulvey, Visual and Other Pleasures, xiii.

50. "How College Girls Really Are," Life 59.25 (17 Dec.
1965): 66B.

51. Liz Smith, Letter to Jules Feiffer and film review,
June 28, 1971, in Folder 7, Box 33, Jules Feiffer Collection.

52. S. K. "Spiritual Disease," Time (5 July 1971).

53. Roger Ebert, "Carnal Knowledge," Chicago Sun
Times, 6 July 1971.

54. Joy Gould Boyum, "A Case for Fem Lib, in Film,"
Wall Street Journal, 16 Aug. 1971.

55. Quote from Claire Johnston, "Women's Cinema
as Counter-Cinema," in Teresa de Lauretis, Alice Doesn't:
Feminism, Semiotics, Cinema (Bloomington: Indiana University Press, 1984), 4.

56. Boyum, "A Case for Fem Lib, in Film."

57. Liz Smith, Letter and film review, June 28, 1971, in Folder 7, Box 33, Jules Feiffer Collection.

58. De Lauretis *Technologies of Gender*, 11. De Lauretis has pointed out why women "must walk out of the male-centered frame of reference in which gender and sexuality are (re)produced by the discourse of male sexuality." This is because "the male-centered frame of reference" reproduces "gender and sexuality" as if natural and fixed. Other filmmakers made the sexual revolution attractive to mainstream cinema by constructing women as 1970s prostitutes in such films as *The Owl and the Pussycat* (1970) with Barbra Streisand and *Klute* (1971), for which Jane Fonda won an Oscar. More difficult was the balance between sexuality and power, especially since the sexual revolution was still equated with the Hefner vision of flaunting a woman's body parts. Ibid., 13–21.

59. This film was a way to "position women in the symbolic," to use de Lauretis's phrase. De Lauretis *Technologies of Gender*, 11.

60. De Lauretis maintains, "Cinema powerfully participates in the production of forms of subjectivity that are individually shaped and unequivocally social." The power of the carnal in this picture both promotes sexual desire and shaves the romance of sexual engagement away." De Lauretis, *Alice Doesn't*, 8.

61. Hillary Collins, The New Puritanism."

Chapter X

1. Bernard Weinraub, "Arthur Penn Takes on General Custer," *The New York Times*, 21 Dec. 1969.

2. Ibid.

3. Christene Meyers, "Western Movies Turn 100: Montana Takes Star Turn in Film," *Billings Gazette*, 21 Sep. 2003.

4. "The Chief," *Newsweek* (25 Jan. 1971): 80. The associate producer "discovered" George on screen at a San Fernando Valley movie theatre where George played in *Smith!*

5. Rey Chow argues that what seemed emancipatory in the "primitive" also came with its own oppression since film's "visuality" goes "beyond the merely physical dimension of vision." Images function "as a kind of dominant discourse of modernity" and as such contain "epistemological problems that are inherent in social relations and their reproduction." Rey Chow, *Writing Diaspora: Tactics of Intervention in Contemporary Cultural Studies* (Bloomington: Indiana University Press, 1993), 55.

6. Winifred Blevins, "Penn's 'Little Big Man'—Admirable," *Los Angeles Herald-Examiner*, 22 Dec. 1970.

7. Bruce Beresford, "Decline of a Master: John Ford," *Film* 56 (Autumn 1969): 6.

8. *The Other America* (Englewood Cliffs, NJ: Campus Book Club Scholastic Services, 1972).

9. Ibid. Philip Deloria noted, "Difference ... was not to be rejected, but rather embraced. First framed in the early twentieth century, confronted more directly in the post–World War II years, and quasi-institutionalized during the 1970s and 1980s, multiculturalism had become a key idea around which social meanings could be negotiated." Deloria further showed that "the presence of multicultural images and statements ... let Indian players claim a sincere, but ultimately fruitless, political sympathy with native people. Indeed, the New Age's greatest intellectual temptation lies in the wistful fallacy that one can engage in social struggle by working on oneself." Little Big Man was fully immersed in both the embracing of difference and "political sympathy." From both vantage points, the film exhibits the same kind of "wistful fallacy" seen in the strategy of "working on oneself." Philip Deloria, *Playing Indian* (New Haven and London: Yale University Press, 1998), 172, 177.

10. Basically an urban contingency, members confronted the U.S. government at a standoff at Wounded Knee, South Dakota, in 1973 where activists battled for the sovereignty of the Oglala Nation. For a brief overview of the literature about this movement during the 1970s, see the notes in T. V. Reed, "Old Cowboys, New Indians: Hollywood Frames the American Indian," *Wicazo S A Review* (Summer 2001): 75–96.

11. Paul A. Hutton, "From Little Bighorn to Little Big Man: The Changing Image of a Western Hero in Popular Culture," *The Western Historical Quarterly* 7.1 (Jan. 1976), 38. As Hutton wrote in 1976, "Once a symbolic leader of civilization's advance into the wilderness, within one hundred years he came to represent the supposed moral bankruptcy of Manifest Destiny." Ibid., 19.

12. Andrew Curry, "Custer's Bluster," *U. S. News and World Report*, http://www.usnews.com/usnews/doubleissue/mysteries/custer.htm.

13. Quote is from Lorna Thackeray, "The Custer Connection: 'Amazing Disaster' Resonates Still, especially in Big Horn County," *Billings Gazette*, 17 June 2001. Librarian Eric Halverson called Custer "the Michael Jackson of his day." Custer history, legends, and myths have produced thousands of research projects, books, and film for television and theaters. With them have come fierce debates and theories about the history of Little Big Horn, making it a site of contention about the meaning of America. Some twelve hundred books about Custer sit on library shelves and countless television and movie reels in archives. See also Paul A. Hutton, "The Celluloid Custer," *Red River Valley Historical Review* 4.4 (Fall 1979): 20–42, for a review of cinema's treatment of the Indians, and Hutton, "From Little Bighorn to Little Big Man," for an overview of the treatment of the Custer story over time. Custer was an educated writer, self-promoter, and military leader. The press at once editorialized the campaign and politicized its nature.

14. Margo Kasdan and Susan Tavernetti, "Native Americans in a Revisionist Western: Little Big Man," in *Hollywood's Indian: The Portrayal of the Native American*, ed. Peter Rollins and John E. O'Conner (Lexington: University Press of Kentucky, 2003): 121.

15. Charles Champlin, "Tragedy of Indian in 'Man,'" *Los Angeles Times*, ca. 1970.

16. Roger Ebert, "Little Big Man Review," *Chicago Sun–Times*, 1 Jan. 1970.

17. "The Chief," 80.

18. Judith Crist, "Joltin' Joe Never Had it So Good," *New York Times*, 21 Dec. 1970.

19. Paul Yawitz, "Movies," *Beverly Hills Courier*, 8 Jan. 1971.

20. "Little Big Man," *Motion Picture Herald*, 6 Jan. 1971.

21. Jacquelyn Kilpatrick, *Celluloid Indians* (Lincoln: University of Nebraska Press, 1999), 94.

22. Shelly Benon, "Motion Pictures," *Show* (Mar. 1971): microfiche, Core Collection Margaret Herrick Academy of Motion Picture Arts and Sciences Library, Beverly Hills, CA; *Variety*, 1 Jan. 1970.

23. Blevins, "Penn's 'Little Big Man'—Admirable."

24. "The Current Cinema," *The New Yorker* (26 Dec. 1970): 50–54.

25. Dan Georgakas, "They Have Not Spoken: American Indians in Film," *Film Quarterly* 25.3 (Spring 1972): 30.

26. Chow explains that "the visual" is a modern discourse that holds "epistemological problems," which "inform the very ways social difference—be it in terms of class, gender, or race—is constructed." This "cultural

expansionism" emancipates us from the past, on the one hand, but is "also Eurocentric and patriarchal" on the other. Chow, *Writing Diaspora*, 55.

27. Vincent Canby, "Film Seeking the American Heritage," *The New York Times*, 12 Dec. 1970.

28. Postmodernists treated history with skepticism and instead of accepting the traditional historical record, writers chose to revise historical accounts. Thus the history student in this film provides the context for postmodern skepticism of history. When Berger's novel hit the market, writers were in the throes of revisionism. Penn carried this distrust from Berger's novel into his film. Penn's *Little Big Man* reflected the novelists' intent to discount conventional conclusions in historical narratives, except of course those that are being satirized as in the film's rendition of Wild Bill Hickok. He is portrayed as more human but basically presented according to legend. Custer, on the other hand, is the key subject of the film's reversals and mythic deflations. This film offers a reevaluation and an alternative to the official records but no particular commitment to the truth. That is up to how viewers understand the tagline. See Michael Leigh Sinowitz, "The Western as Postmodern Satiric History: Thomas Berger's *Little Big Man*," *CLIO* 28.2 (1999): 129–148, for a discussion on postmodern strains in Berger's novel.

29. Penn's rationality in a revisionist project is similar to academic revisionism, which validates its worth through "objective rationality." In doing so, Chow claims "it erases its own implication in the history of Western cultural hegemony in the name of quantifiable scholarship. Those who share a 'concern with social reality must be accompanied with a close attention to how language works — not so much in the creation of formal beauty as in the concealment of ideology.'" Chow, *Writing Diaspora*, 134, 135.

30. Benon, "Motion Pictures."

31. Deloria, *Playing Indian*, 158.

32. As Chow explains, "Our fascination with the native, the oppressed, the savage, and all such figures is therefore a desire to hold on to an unchanging certainty somewhere outside our own 'fake' experience. It is a desire for being 'non-duped,' which is a not-too-innocent desire to seize control." Chow, *Writing Diaspora*, 53.

33. As Chow explains, the good Indian/bad white division encourages indifference rather than valuing difference because of "the persistently negative critique of dominant culture in total terms." The film's episodic structure literally proved what Chow refers to as the "vicious circle" or "as what Baudrillard calls ... 'reduction of difference' and the facile 'interchangeablitity.'" The reductive identity of the primitive in the film's appropriation of Native American culture is the same as "reduction of difference." Chow, *Writing Diaspora*, 59.

34. Joan W. Scott, "The Evidence of Experience," *Critical Inquiry* 17 (Summer 1991): 777.

35. Mark C. Carnes, ed., *Past Imperfect: History According to the Movies* (New York: H. Holt, 1995).

36. Rey Chow explains that cultural traits are "the first step toward the formulation of a new type of cultural reference." Yet, to stop there is to ignore "social experience which is not completed once and for all but which is constituted by a continual, often conflictual, working-out of its grounds. As Hall puts it, 'The slow contradictory movement from 'nationalism' to 'ethnicity' as a source of identities is part of a new politics.'" Chow, *Writing Diaspora*, 143.

37. Deloria, *Playing Indian*, 157, 156, 159, 158, 163.

38. See endnote #38 in Chapter 6.

39. Helena Schwarz, "Accurate," *The New York Times*, 7 Feb. 1971.

40. Deloria, *Playing Indian*, 161.

41. Chow asks "why are we so fascinated ... with the 'native' in 'modern' times" and she answered, "We turn, increasingly with fascination, to the oppressed to locate a 'genuine critical origin.'" Chow, *Writing Diaspora*, 42, 44.

42. "American Indians Struggling for Power and Identity," *The New York Times*, 11 Feb. 1979. See also Gary Edgerton, "'A Breed Apart': Hollywood, Racial Stereotyping, and the Promise of Revisionism in *The Last of the Mohicans*," *Journal of American Culture* 17.1 (Spring 1994).

43. Deloria, *Playing Indian*, 156, 163, 158. 159.

44. Jodi Rave, "Says Indian Students Deserve More Than Victim History," *The Billings Gazette*, 21 May 2007.

45. Vincent Canby, "Critic's Choice: Ten Best Films of 1970," *The New York Times*, 27 Dec. 1970.

46. The film played on Sunday, January 23, at the Park City, Utah Library Center and Tuesday, January 25, at the Holiday Village Cinema. The quotes are from the program.

47. *Little Big Man*, Core Collection, Margaret Herrick Library Academy of Motion Picture Arts and Sciences Library, Beverly Hills, CA.

48. Ibid.

49. John Price writes, films "were created as entertainment, but they cumulatively built a separate reality about Native cultures.... They ... are difficult stereotypes to correct in university courses on American Indians." John A. Price, "The Stereotyping of North American Indians in Motion Pictures," *Ethnohistory* 20.2 (Spring 1973): 154.

Chapter XI

1. Glenn Mann, "Ideology and Genre in the Godfather Films," in *Francis Ford Coppola's The Godfather Trilogy*, ed. Nick Browne (London: Cambridge University Press, 2000), 128.

2. Jon Lewis, "If History Has Taught Us Anything ... Francis Coppola, Paramount Studios, and *The Godfather* Parts I, II, and III," in Browne, *The Godfather Trilogy*, 26.

3. "The Making of the Godfather," *Time* (13 Mar. 1972): 62.

4. Emanuel Levy, *All About Oscar: The History and Politics of the Academy Awards* (New York and London: Continuum International Publishing Group, Inc., 2003), 159. See also Robert Osborn, *Seventy Years of the Oscar: The Official History of the Academy Awards* (New York, London, and Paris: Abbeville Press, 1999), 220. Only Bob Fosse's *Cabaret* took more awards than *The Godfather* at the forty-fifth Oscars.

5. Browne, *The Godfather Trilogy*, 17.

6. The company's goal was to give creative license to the director. With this company, it seemed possible that independents did not need Hollywood. By loaning filmmakers money based on revenue returns, Zoetrope, it was hoped, would become its own governing industry. By 1972 Paramount and Coppola released *The Godfather* and in 1974 *The Godfather Part II* and *The Conversation*.

7. Lewis, "If History Has Taught us Anything," 29–30.

8. Roger Corman, "The Godfather and The Godfather Part II," *Sight and Sound* (Sep. 2002): 32. It was the occasion of the magazine's "Top Ten" films poll.

9. Browne, *The Godfather Trilogy*, 12, 17.

10. They turned to Al Ruddy because he "could make it cheap." Al Ruddy is quoted in Harlan Lebo, *The Godfather Legacy: The Untold Story of the Making of the Classic Godfather Trilogy Featuring Never-Before Published Production Stills* (New York: Simon and Schuster, 1997), 7.

11. Ibid., 12.

12. Lewis, "If History Has Taught Us Anything," 27.

13. Lebo, *The Godfather Legacy*, 23.

14. Lewis, "If History Has Taught Us Anything," 27.

15. Corman, "The Godfather and The Godfather Part II."

16. Coppla's words in Lebo, *The Godfather Legacy*, 30.

17. Thomas Schatz, *Hollywood Genres: Formulas, Film-making, and the Studio System* (New York: Random House, 1981), 90.

18. Vera Dika, "The Representation of Ethnicity," in Browne, *The Godfather Trilogy*, 93.

19. Lebo, *The Godfather Legacy*, 63, 100.

20. Ibid., 63. As Lebo writes, "On many days in late 1970, Ruddy and his production team would arrive at their offices on the Paramount lot to find a gathering of protestors waiting for them on Melrose Avenue outside the gates. The protestors carried signs that read: INDIANS FOR INDIAN ROLES. MEXICANS FOR MEXICAN ROLES. ITALIANS FOR ITALIAN ROLES." Ibid., 39.

21. From "Coppola's Notebook," *The Godfather Bonus Materials*, produced by Paramount Pictures, 2001. DVD in disk.

22. Lebo, *The Godfather Legacy*, 64.

23. Ibid., 52; San Francisco attorney line is from "The Making of the Godfather," 59.

24. Ruddy's words in Lebo, *The Godfather Legacy*, 26, 25, 52, 92.

25. Coppola quoted in Robert K. Johnson, "Francis Ford Coppola," in *Twayne's Theatrical Arts Series*, ed. Warren French (Boston: Twayne Publishers, 1977), 104.

26. "Coppola's Notebook," DVD.

27. Ibid.

28. Ibid.

29. Tom Koegh; http://www.super70s.com/Super70s/Movies/1974/Godfather; Ronald Bergan, *Francis Ford Coppola: The Making of His Movies* (New York: Thunder's Mouth Press, 1998). Bergen writes, "As befits someone whose films have often concerned themselves with the workings of the family, Coppola's own family occupies a central position in his life. His musician father, Carmine, composed the scores for many of his features. [He and his] brother August (father of Nicolas Cage), to whom he dedicated *Rumble Fish*, have always had a close relationship. His younger sister, the actress Talia Shire, was Connie Corleone in *The Godfather* trilogy; his second son, Roman (named after Polanski), has worked as second-unit director and production assistant on his father's movies, and daughter, Sofia, who appeared in *The Outsiders* and *Rumble Fish*, had a leading role in *The Godfather III*."

30. Dika, "The Representation of Ethnicity," 78.

31. Lebo, *The Godfather Legacy*, 88.

32. Bob Evans quoted in "The Making of the Godfather," 59.

33. Lebo, *The Godfather Legacy*, 1–2.

34. Michael Barone, "Italian Americans and American Politics," in *Beyond The Godfather: Italian American Writers on the Real Italian American Experience*, ed. Kenneth Ciongoli and Jay Purini (Hanover and London: University Press of New England, 1997), 241–246.

35. Lebo, *The Godfather Legacy*, 127.

36. Schatz, *Hollywood Genres*, 93.

37. Corman, "The Godfather and The Godfather Part II."

38. Albert Rosenfeld, "What is the Right Number of Children?" *Life* 71.25 (17 Dec. 1971), 99.

39. Dika, "The Representation of Ethnicity," 79.

40. Mary Ann Vigilante Mannino, *Revisionary Identities: Strategies of Empowerment in the Writing of Italian American Women* (New York: Peter Lang Publishing, Inc., 2000), 1.

41. Michael Novak, *The Rise of the Unmeltable Ethnics: Politics and Culture in American Life* (New Brunswick and London: Transaction Publishers, 1972), 272, 271.

42. Al Pacino in DVD, "Coppola's Notebook."

43. Novak, *The Rise of the Unmeltable Ethnics*, 272, 271.

44. Returning to an "originary" point is of course impossible because going back is part of the process of constructing a new identity. As Mannino quotes Julia Kristeva about writing, the act is a "'semiotic practice that facilitates the ultimate reorganization of psychic space before a postulated maturity.'" Yet Mannino comments, "The Italian/American writer never attains this postulated maturity; she is always rewriting herself," defending "an incestuous love for the nineteenth century peasant culture that their very ability to read and write make it impossible for them to really experience. This incestuous love for the Italy of their grandparents transforms itself into an imaginary identification with it." The result is "'a double language' both loving and despising the Italian peasant culture and the Anglo-American one." Mannino, *Revisionary Identities*, 65.

45. Alessandro Camon, "The Godfather and the Mythology of Mafia," in Browne, *The Godfather Trilogy*, 66.

46. The "Soliticzo" scene secured Pacino's role for good. "They kept me after that scene," he commented. From Coppola's Notebook CD, Scene 26: This is one of the most important scenes because it defines Michael's character. As Coppola said, this scene was an important scene for Al Pacino because it was the one that convinced the studio Pacino was right for the part. More than any other scene, this one showed Michael's negotiation of American society.

47. In Nick Browne's words, "The Coppola aesthetic is ultimately one of 'mise-en-scene' that is to say of acting, blocking, and delivery of dialog. The narrative of *The Godfather* possesses the simplicity of linear development by plausible complication following reliable dramatic laws of action and reaction." Browne, *The Godfather Trilogy*, 2–3.

48. "Coppola's Notebook," DVD.

49. Dika, "The Representation of Ethnicity," 91–92. In her words, "It must be stressed that *La Via Vecchia* is a Sicilian term ... that has a bearing on the rules of comportment for men, women, and the members of the family. It is through the clash of these ways with the encroachments of American society, then, that this film enacts its major codes of Italianicity." Ibid., 88.

50. Browne, *The Godfather Trilogy*, 19.

51. Camon, "The Godfather and the Mythology of Mafia," 60. As Camon remarks, individuating and working for self is "a flagrant violation of the organization's ethics.... Collective interest is inseparable from that of the individuals.... Ultimately, the Mafia's 'family values' are key to its power." Ibid., 60–62.

52. Johnson, "Francis Ford Coppola," 125.

53. Mann, "Ideology and Genre in the Godfather Films," 122, 124. As Mann remarks, "It achieves this success only through a series of compromises that destroy its integrity. The dangers inherent in capitalist impulse surface in Michael's paranoid vengeance." Ibid., 121.

54. Johnson, "Francis Ford Coppola," 114.

55. The quote is from Norman Podhertz, *Commentary*, in "Behind the Mystique of the Mafia," *Time* (13 Mar. 1972): 61.

56. Dika, "The Representation of Ethnicity," 88. As she explains, "La Via Vecchia ... occupies a symbolic central position within the film, dictating the behavior of all its men, and thus defining the limits of masculinity and the limits of culpability as well. The villainous male characters in the film are guilty and punishable to the degree that they deviate from these established codes of honor. In this

way, The Godfather diminishes the characters' association with crime and its squalid realities, and instead foregrounds acts made punishable precisely because they are reactions against the breach of an ancient masculine code." Ibid., 89.

57. Mannino, *Revisionary Identities*, 50–52, 57. As Mannino argues, "Although blatant discrimination against Italian/Americans is illegal, their stereotyped portraits are still current images in popular culture." To be sure, subjectiveness is never without structures of power. The idea of a completely autonomous individual is a fantasy. Thus, recognizing what is possible within the defining features of domination is the problem and the answer for identity construction. The social position of the individual also influences the strategy and negotiating potential in making moves through relations of power. See ibid., 50.

58. Novak, *Unmeltable Ethnics*.

59. Dika tells us that the term *dago* derives from the association of Italians with daggers and "feared as a stiletto-wielding Mafioso." Dika, "The Representation of Ethnicity,"105.

60. Novak, *Unmeltable Ethnics*, 348.

61. Ibid., 351.

62. Joan Scott, "The Evidence of Experience," *Critical Inquiry* 17 (Summer 1991): 776, 777.

63. As Alba's study shows, many of the urban ethnic centers have disappeared since "the outward migration from inner-city ethnic neighborhoods" to the suburbs and the soaring numbers in intermarriages, which complicates choices in lifestyles. Richard D. Alba, *Ethnic Identity: The Transformation of White America* (New Haven and London: Yale University Press, 1990), 254–255.

64. Ibid., 3.

65. Philip J. Deloria, *Playing Indian* (New Haven and London: Yale University Press, 1998), 173.

66. Browne, *The Godfather Trilogy*, 18.

67. Vera Dika points out, "In intellectual circles, this situation has been touted as 'the death of the subject,' the death of individualism as such, and in everyday life it has been experienced as the individual's lessening ability to fully control or understand the world." In Dika, "The Representation of Ethnicity," 97.

68. These films are part of the discursive process that makes the subject though for opposite ends and even reasons.

69. Dika, "The Representation of Ethnicity," 82.

70. John Hess, "Godfather II: A Deal Coppola Couldn't Refuse," *Jump Cut, A Review of Contemporary Cinema* 7 (May–July 1975): 11.

71. Ibid., 10.

72. Philip Deloria says American Indians were "ethnic gifts for a pluralistic American whole" by the late twentieth century. While Native American and immigrant history carry their clear racial and class differences, the 1970s multiculturalism ties them to the same dynamic over consuming and constructing identities. Not the degree but the means of making identities popular and legitimate worked in similar ways. Deloria, *Playing Indian*, 175.

73. Dika, "The Representation of Ethnicity," 96–97.

74. *The Godfather* Script, 23A.

75. Mannino, *Revisionary Identities*, 18. Anthony Tamburri remarks that the women's social roles were passed on generationally. It was expected that daughters would live the lives of mothers and housewives. Anthony Tamburri, *A Semiotic of Ethnicity: In Recognition of the Italian/American Writer* (Albany: State University of New York Press, 1998), 57, 143, 158.

76. Lester D. Friedman, "Celluloid Palimpsets: An Overview of Ethnicity and the American Film," in *Unspeakable Images: Ethnicity and the American Cinema*, ed. Lester D. Friedman (Urbana and Chicago: University

of Illinois Press, 1991), 29, 30. Friedman's take is that Jewish filmmakers wished to "create a new country — an empire of their own ... its myths and values" through film. Film's expansiveness offered a powerful route in which to control the narrative and images in "an overwhelming endorsement of a melting-pot mentality, one that ignores crucial differences in ethnic identities and blends cultural oppositions into a bland conception of Americannness." Ibid., 29, 25. See ibid., 29 for filmmakers Friedman includes.

77. Ethnic resurgence presented the challenge of re-essentializing identity while claiming authenticity, since saying who is more ethnic raises questions of authority and value judgment. Philip Deloria explains the unique difficulty in American popular culture and native societies for the resurgence of Indian identity. "Playing Indian ... has been an intercultural meeting ground upon which Indians and non–Indians have created new identities, not only for white Americans, but for Indians themselves." Deloria, *Playing Indian*, 187.

78. Paul Lyons, *New Left, New Right and the Legacy of the Sixties* (Philadelphia: Temple University Press, 1996), 133. Lyons argues that one of the problems with diversity is that it risked denying a "shared politics, a belief in a potentially common, American interest." For that goal to be recovered, he believed that the middle class had to figure into the equation of multiculturalism. *The Godfather* in a sense supplies a shared politics for middle-class audiences by making ethnicity a vibrant attribute in a traditional drama.

79. Matthew Frye Jacobson, *Whiteness of a Different Color: European Immigrants and the Alchemy of Race* (Cambridge, MA, and London, England: Harvard University Press, 1998). Jacobson objects to Michael Novak's sense that discrimination against ethnics has taken away their dignity based on his grouping of Europeans in the same category of oppression as others. He writes, "'Chicanos, [and] Blacks' ... appear unproblematically in a list of aggrieved Poles, Italians, Greeks, Armenians, and French, as though these latter groups' becoming Caucasian meant nothing in the American milieu. As though, by virtue of their non–WASPness, these groups all occupied the same terrain in American political life." Ibid., 279. Some saw seventies' ethnicity as another form of "pan–white supremacism," a Europeanness based on white privilege. If ethnics negotiated a new distinction of worthiness, founded on a history of oppression then, as Jacobson noted, "Only where whiteness has been rejected out of hand as an insignificant detail can grievances reduce to a matter of 'unworthiness.'" Ibid., 278–279. Yet, Jacobson also argues that "the problem [of race] is not merely how races are comprehended, but how they are seen." The problem of perception describes as much the value of ethnic revival in Coppola's films. Ibid., 9.

80. The same contradiction rests in the popular television serial, *Archie Bunker*, and its theme of "those were the days." An Irish ethnic yearning for the good old days would require a selective memory if he is to emerge as the voice of white authority. Part of the position from which he speaks must include the history of discrimination.

81. Novak, *The Unmeltable Ethnics*, 22, 402.

82. Friedman, "Celluloid Palimpsets," 29, 30.

83. Dika, "The Representation of Ethnicity," 85.

84. The Pacino/DeNiro addition creates a subject-position for Italians. The images of Italians in Hollywood have provided objectified Italians and although film does not offer the socializing tools for regeneration of ethnicity, it does contribute to the meaning of the culture on display. As sociologist Richard D. Alba argues, "Because of the erosion of the structural foundations of ethnicity and the porousness of ethnic boundaries, solidarity is possible only

if ethnic identities are socially recognized." Pacino's popularity therefore was key not to the formation of ethnic identity but to the social legitimacy of his look. Alba, *Ethnic Identity*, 26.

85. After *The Godfather's* successful second run, "NBC-TV paid the highest price ever for an exclusive single showing of the film on network television." Paramount owned over 84 percent of the picture. Lewis, "If History Has Taught Us Anything," 30–35.

86. Andrew Sarris' comment about Coppola in the early days in Andrew Sarris, *The American Cinema: Directors and Directions* (New York: E. P. Dutton and Co., Inc., 1968), 210.

87. Johnson, "Francis Ford Coppola," Forward.

88. See Lewis, "If History has Taught Us Anything," 37–38 for an account of Paramount's Frank Yablans who brought Coppola, Bogdanovich, and William Friedkin under "studio superstructure" by forming the Director's Company (3 Jan. 1973), a "production unit" gave contract and "creative autonomy" at the same time. Yablans optimistically assumed the company would produce a "New" Hollywood but turning power over to the artists was not so easy and the company dissolved. During its lifetime it produced *The Conversation* (Coppola), *Paper Moon* (Peter Bogdanovich), and *Daisy Miller* (Bogdanovich).

89. Original Dramatic Score went to Carmine Coppola, the director's father. He and Nino Rota composed the music.

90. Corman, "The Godfather and The Godfather Part II," 32.

Conclusion

1. Martin Quigley, Jr., *Films in America: 1929–1969* (New York: Golden Press, 1970), 347.

2. Peter Biskind, *Easy Riders, Raging Bull: How the Sex-Drugs-and-Rock 'N' Roll Generation Saved Hollywood* (New York: Touchstone, 1998), 22, 255.

3. "The Art that Matters" is the title of the film section in *Saturday Review*, 27 Dec. 1969.

4. Christopher Faulkner, "Teaching French National Cinema," *Cinema Journal* 38.4 (Summer 1999): 88, 89. Although Hollywood is different from official national cinema, Faulkner's concepts about French film apply to the most dominant entertainment industry in America.

5. Jack Hamilton, "Where, Oh Where Are the Beautiful Girls?" *Look* 3 (Nov. 1970), 62–71.

6. Diane Jacobs, *Hollywood Renaissance* (London, Brunswick, and New York: A. S. Barnes and Co., 1977), 12, 14.

7. Fletcher Knebel, "Hollywood: Broke — and Getting Richer," *Look* 3 (Nov. 1970), 41, 46, 52.

8. "Fiction and Film: A Search for New Sources," *Saturday Review* 52 (27 Dec. 1969): 13.

9. Knebel, "Hollywood: Broke," 51.

10. Jeanine Basinger, *American Cinema: One Hundred Years of Filmmaking* (New York: Rizzoli Books, 1994), 289.

11. Douglas Gomery, *Movie History: A Survey* (Belmont, CA: Wadsworth Publishing Company, 1991), 424, 433.

12. Gregory D. Black, *The Catholic Crusade Against the Movies, 1940–1975* (Cambridge: Cambridge University Press, 1998), 3.

13. Faulkner, "Teaching French National Cinema," 89, 90.

14. Richard Alba, *Ethnic Identity: The Transformation of White America* (New Haven: Yale University Press, 1999).

15. Lester D. Friedman, "Celluloid Palimpsets: An Overview of Ethnicity and the American Film," in *Unspeakable Images: Ethnicity and the American Cinema,* ed. Lester D. Friedman (Urbana and Chicago: University of Illinois Press, 1991), 30.

16. Faulkner, "Teaching French National Cinema," 89.

17. Anthony Schillaci, "The Now Movie," *Saturday Review* (28 Dec. 1968): 10.

18. David L. Westby, *Clouded Vision: The Student Movement in the United States in the 1960s* (Lewisburg, PA: Bucknell University Press, 1976), 17.

19. Richard Maltby, "'Nobody Know Everything:' Post-Classical Historiographies and Consolidated Entertainment," in *Contemporary Hollywood Cinema,* ed. Steve Neale and Murray Smith (New York and London: Routledge, 1998), 33, 32.

20. Faulkner, "Teaching French National Cinema," 90, 89.

21. Speaking about race by opposing Hollywood's rendition of blacks caught the attention of Lawrence Turman (*The Graduate*) and Martin Ritt (*Hud*). *The Great White Hope* (1970) visualized a new relationship between white and black with James Earl Jones as heavyweight champion Jack Johnson and Jane Alexander as his lover. The film addresses the superficial nature of the promises in a multicultural society. Since it made only 20 percent of the production costs in box office revenues, it is safe to say viewers were to connected to other offering such as *M*A*S*H* and *Patton* in the same year.

22. Historians Robert Sklar and Charles Musser in *Resisting Images,* a collection of essays about films "that resist" or are "resistant to hegemonic cinema," argues film's agency lies in the act of opposition. Resistance, they claim, "implies exertion, force, effort." It "means that people have the possibility to act on their own behalf, as opposed to being completely shaped by dominant classes and ideologies." Films that resist "overcome the ideological intentions of conventional texts and criticism." The concept of resistant viewing and filmmaking is an important and necessary one when holding the films in this study next to other narratives dealing with problematic issues such as race. From the lens of race, Hollywood's whiteness even during multiculturalism was still pretty blinding. Robert Sklar and Charles Musser, eds., *Resisting Images: Essays on Cinema and History* (Philadelphia: Temple University Press, 1990), 5.

23. Stanley Kramer and *Guess Who's Coming to Dinner?* in 1965 made the question about civil rights and interracial marriages a foremost topic for the mainstream screen. *In the Heat of the Night* with Rod Steiger and Sidney Poitier won Best Picture for 1967 and *Sounder* was nominated for 1971.

24. While it is not clear how much a film subverts dominant power in everyday life, changes were made and audiences did get heard during the years that bookend this study. All ten films considered, to varying degrees, were perceived as defiant within their historical context. As Teresa de Lauretis has argued, "The cinematic contract that binds each individual spectator to the social technology of cinema is more complex than an exchange of money for pleasure or entertainment. For it produces, as a surplus, certain effects of meaning which are central to the construction of gender and subjectivity." Changing a viewer's "self-representation" explains much of the agency in this body of films if seen through the categories of generation, gender, and ethnicity. Not just a ripe marketing tool for co-opting audiences, film, whether a commercial success or not, was a place of cultural exchange. Teresa de Lauretis, *Technologies of Gender: Essays on Theory, Film, and Fiction* (Bloomington and Indianapolis: Indiana University Press, 1987), 96.

25. Basinger, *American Cinema*, 281.

26. Gomery, *Movie History: A Survey*, 433.

27. Biskind, *Easy Riders, Raging Bulls*, 279, 278, 279; Richard Zanuck quoted in ibid., 278.

28. Frederic Jameson, *Signatures of the Visible* (New York and London: Routledge, 1992), 27. *One Flew Over the Cuckoo's Nest* won Best Picture.

29. Pauline Kael quoted in Biskind, *Easy Riders, Raging Bulls*, 281; ibid., 279.

30. Ibid., 424, 425.

31. "Demographics Favoring Film's Future," *Variety* (3 Oct. 1975): 3, 34.

32. Paul Lyons, *New Left New Right and the Legacy of the Sixties* (Philadelphia: Temple University Press, 1996), 18.

33. David Farber, ed., *The Sixties: From Memory to History* (Chapel Hill and London: The University of North Carolina Press, 1994), 1.

34. "The Current Cinema: Good-Time Girls," *The New Yorker* (23 Sep. 2002): 99.

35. Ibid.

36. From an interview with D. W. Griffith by Richard Barry, *New York Times Magazine* (28 Mar. 1915): 16.

Selected Bibliography

Historical Context

Alba, Richard D. *Ethnic Identity: The Transformation of White America.* New Haven: Yale University Press, 1999.

"American Indians Struggling for Power and Identity." *The New York Times*, 11 Feb. 1979.

Anderson, Terry. *The Movement and the Sixties: Protest in America from Greensboro to Wounded Knee.* New York and Oxford: Oxford University Press, 1995.

Bach, George R. "We Can Close the Generation Gap." *Ladies' Home Journal* 85.1 (Jan. 1968): 36.

Bailey, Beth. *Sex in the Heartland.* Cambridge and London: Harvard University Press, 1999.

"Behind the Mystique of the Mafia." *Time* 99.11 (Mar. 13, 1972): 61.

Bird, Caroline, with Sara Welles Briller. *Born Female: The High Cost of Keeping Women Down.* New York: David McKay Company, Inc., 1968.

Bloom, Alexander, and Wini Breines, eds. *"Takin' It to the Streets": A Sixties Reader.* New York and Oxford: Oxford University Press, 1995.

Braudy, Susan. "Kids Are Groovy, but Adults Are Not." *The New York Times Student Weekly*, 9 Sep. 1969, Special News Report Section II.

Brooks, David. *Bobos in Paradise: The New Upper Class and How They Got There.* New York: Simon and Schuster, 2000.

Browne, Gerald A. "The She-Man — Today's Erotic Hero." *Cosmopolitan* 168.3 (Mar. 1970): 50.

Burner, David. *Making Peace with the 60s.* Princeton: Princeton University Press, 1996.

Cavallo, Dominick. *A Fiction of the Past: The Sixties in American History.* New York: St. Martin's Press, 1999.

Christgau, Robert. "Anatomy of a Love Festival." *Esquire* (Jan. 1968): 61–66, 147.

Clecak, Peter. *Radical Paradoxes: Dilemmas of the American Left: 1945–1970.* New York, Evanston, San Francisco, and London: Harper and Row, 1973.

Davidson, Bill. "The Turned-on, Tuned-in World of Hippie Capitalists." *Cosmopolitan.* 168.5 (May 1970): 155–158.

Dennis, Lawrence E., and Joseph F. Kauffman, eds. *The College and the Student: An Assessment of Relationships and Responsibilities in Undergraduate Education by Administrators, Faculty Members, and Public Officials.* Washington, DC: American Council on Education, 1966.

Dickstein, Morris. *Gates of Eden: American Culture in the Sixties.* Cambridge, MA, and London: Harvard University Press, 1997.

Evans, Sara. *Personal Politics: The Roots of the Women's Liberation in the Civil Rights Movement and the New Left.* New York: Vintage Books, 1979.

Fabian, Ann. "History for the Masses: Commercializing the Western Past." In *Under an Open Sky: Rethinking America's Western Past*, edited by William Cronon, George Miles, and Jay Gitlin. New York: W. W. Norton, 1992.

Facey, Paul W. *The Legion of Decency: A Sociological Analysis of the Emergence and Development of a Social Pressure Group.* New York: Arno Press, 1974.

Farber, David. *The Age of Great Dreams: America in the 1960s.* New York: Hill and Wang, 1994.

_____. *Chicago '68.* Chicago: University of Chicago Press, 1988.

_____, ed. *The Sixties: From Memory to History.* Chapel Hill and London: The University of North Carolina Press, 1994.

_____, and Beth Bailey. *The Columbia Guide to America in the 1960s.* New York: Columbia University Press, 2001.

Favre, George W. "Hippiedom and the Neighbors." *Christian Science Monitor* 7 (Nov. 1967): 3.

Ferry, W. H. *Students and Society: A Report on a*

Conference. New York: Center for the Study of Democratic Institutions, 1967.

Feuer, Lewis S. *The Conflicts of Generations: The Character and Significance of Student Movements*. New York: Basic Books, 1969.

Frank, Thomas. *Conquest of Cool: Business Culture, Counterculture, and the Rise of Hip Consumerism*. Chicago: University of Chicago Press, 1997.

Frasers, Ronald. *1968: A Student Generation in Revolt*. London: Chatto and Windus, 1988.

Gelatt, Roland. "Those Under-Thirties Again." *Saturday Review* 52.28 (July 12, 1969): 20.

Gerberding, William P., and Duane E. Smith. *The Radical Left: The Abuse of Discontent*. Boston: Houghton Mifflin Company, 1970.

Halberstam, David. "Farewell to the 60s." *McCalls* 97.4 (Jan. 1970): 85–92.

Hamalian, Leo, and Frederick R. Karl, eds. *Radical Vision: Essays for the Seventies*. New York: Thomas Y. Crowell Company, 1970.

Hamilton, Jack. "Where, Oh Where Are the Beautiful Girls?" *Look* 3 (Nov. 1970): 62–67.

"Happy Drug World Attracts Hippies and Housewives." *Daily Utah Chronicle*, 29 Sep. 1967, p. 2.

Harlan, Judith. *Feminism: A Reference Handbook*. Santa Barbara, Denver, and Oxford: ABC-CLIO's Contemporary World Issues Series, 1998.

Hayden White, et al. "AHR Forum." *American Historical Review* 93.5 (Dec. 1988): 1198–1227.

"The Hippies: Philosophy of a Subculture." *Time* 90. 1 (7 July 1967): 18–22.

Hooper, Bayard. "Challenge for Free Men in a Mass Society" and "Modern Society's Growing Challenge: The Struggle to Be an Individual." *Life* 62.16 (21 Apr. 1967): 60–64.

_____. "Modern Society's Growing Challenge: The Struggle to Be an Individual." *Life* 62.16 (21 Apr. 1967): 70–73.

Horowitz, David. *The Politics of Bad Faith: The Radical Assault on America's Future*. New York, London, Toronto, Sydney and Singapore: The Free Press, 1998.

"Hot Pants: A Short But Happy Career." *Life* 71.26 (31 Dec. 1971): 14–15.

Howard, Gerald, ed. *The Sixties: The Art, Attitudes, Politics, and Media of Our Most Explosive Decade*. New York: Marlowe and Company, 1995.

Isserman, Maurice. "The Not So Dark and Bloody Ground: New Works on the 1960s." *American Historical Review* 94 (Oct. 1989): 990–1010.

Kazin, Michael. *The Populist Persuasion: An American History*. Ithaca and London: Cornell University Press, 1995.

Kennan, George F. *Democracy and the Student Left*. Boston: Little and Brown, 1968.

Kennedy, Robert F. "What Our Young People Are Really Saying." *Ladies' Home Journal* 85.1 (Jan. 1968): 96.

Kenniston, Kenneth. *Young Radicals: Notes on Committed Youth*. New York: Harcourt, Brace and World, 1968.

Kerr, Clarke. "Higher Education in America and Its Discontents." In *The University in Transition*, edited by Festus Justin Viser. Memphis: Memphis State University Press, 1971.

Knebel, Fletcher. "Hollywood: Broke — and Getting Richer." *Look* 3 (Nov. 1970): 50–52.

Koch, Stephen. "Fiction and Film: A Search for New Sources." *Saturday Review* 52 (27 Dec 1969): 12–14, 38.

Koedt, Anne, Ellen Levin, and Anita Rapone, eds. *Radical Feminism*. New York: Quadrangle Books/The New York Times Book Co., 1973.

Kristol, Irving. "What's Bugging the Students." In *The Troubled Campus, Writers, Educators, and Students Confront the Question, What's Wrong in the Colleges and Universities*, edited by *The Atlantic Monthly*. Boston and Toronto: Little, Brown and Company, 1965.

Lakoff, Robin. *Language and Woman's Place*. New York, Evanston, San Francisco, London: Harper and Row, 1975.

Leary, Timothy. *The Politics of Ecstasy*. New York: Putnam, 1968.

London, Herbert I. *Closing the Circle: A Cultural History of the Rock Revolution*. Chicago: Nelson-Hall, 1984.

Lukas, Anthony J. *Don't Shoot—We Are Your Children!* New York: Random House, 1968.

Lynd, Alice. *We Won't Go: Personal Accounts of War Objectors*. Boston: Beacon Press, 1968.

Lynes, Russell. "Cool Cheer or Middle Age?" *Look* 31.21 (17 Oct. 1967): 45–49.

Lyons, Paul. *New Left, New Right, and the Legacy of the Sixties*. Philadelphia: Temple University Press, 1996.

Mangano, Joseph J. *Living Legacy: How 1964 Changed America*. Lanham, MD: University Press of America, 1994.

Miller, Douglas T. *On Our Own: Americans in the Sixties*. Lexington, MA: D. C. Heath and Company, 1996.

Miller, James. *Democracy Is in the Streets: From Port Huron to the Siege of Chicago*. Cambridge and London: Harvard University Press, 1987, 1994.

Millett, Kate. *Sexual Politics*. New York: Avon, 1971.

Morgan, Edward. *The '60s Experience: Hard Lessons About America*. Philadelphia: Temple University Press, 1991.

Novak, Steven J. *The Rights of Youth: American Colleges and Student Revolt, 1798–1815*. Cambridge and London: Harvard University Press, 1977.

Novaks, Michael. *The Rise of the Unmeltable Ethnics: Politics and Culture in American Life*, 2nd ed. New Brunswick and London: Transaction Publishers, 1972.

Oglesby, Carl, ed. *The New Left Reader.* New York: Grove Press, Inc., 1969.

Osborne, John. "Intellectuals and Just Causes." *Encounter* (Sep. 1967): 3–4.

The Other America. Englewood Cliffs: Campus Book Club Scholastic Services, 1972.

Perry, Charles, et al. "Summer of Love." *Edging West* (July/Aug. 1996): 40–43.

"Playboy Interview: Mike Nichols." *Playboy* (June 1966): 63.

Rave, Jodi. "Says Indian Students Deserve More Than Victim History." *The Billings Gazette*, 21 May 2007.

"The Real Change Has Just Begun." *Life* 68.1 (9 Jan. 1970): 102–106.

Rehnquist, Justice William H. "Jenkins v. Georgia, Supreme Court of the United States" 418 U.S. 153 (24 June 1974).

Reich, Charles A. *The Greening of America: How the Youth Revolution Is Trying to Make America Liveable.* New York: Random House, 1970.

Rorabaugh, W. J. *Berkeley at War: The 1960s.* Berkeley: University of California Press, 1989.

Rosenfeld, Albert. "What Is the Right Number of Children?" *Life* 71.25 (17 Dec. 1971): 97–99.

Roszak, Theodore. *The Making of a Counter Culture.* Berkeley, Los Angeles, and London: University of California Press, 1969.

_____. "The Summa Apologica." *New Politics* 5 (Fall 1966): 257–269.

Rothman, Stanley, and S. Robert Lichter. *Roots of Radicalism: Jews, Christians, and the New Left.* New York and Oxford: Oxford University Press, 1982.

Rudy, Willis. *The Campus and a Nation in Crisis: From the American Revolution to Vietnam.* Cranbury, NJ: Associate University Presses, Inc., 1996.

Savran, David. *Taking It Like a Man: White Masculinity, Masochism, and Contemporary American Culture.* Princeton: Princeton University Press, 1998.

Schuth, Howard W. "The College Milieu in the American Fiction Film." Ph.D. dissertation, Ohio State University, 1972.

Schuth, Wayne H. *Mike Nichols.* Boston: Twayne Publishers, 1978.

"The Search for Purpose: Among the Youth of America, a Fresh New Sense of Commitment." *Life* 62.17 (28 Apr. 1967): 66.

Smith, Stan. "Hippy Identity within Self." *Daily Utah Chronicle*, 2 Oct. 1947, 4.

Taber, Robert A. *From Protest to Radicalism: An Appraisal of the Student Movement in the*

New Left: An Anthology. Boston: Beacon Press, 1966.

Thackeray, Lorna. "The Custer Connection: 'Amazing Disaster' Resonates Still, Especially in Big Horn County." *Billings Gazette*, 17 June 2001.

"This Was the Year That Kids Cooled It." *Life* 71.26 (31 Dec. 1971).

Tyler, Parker. *Underground Film: A Critical History.* New York: Grove, 1969.

Unger, Irwin, and Debi Unger. *The Movement: A History of the American New Left.* New York: Harper and Row, 1974.

_____ and _____, eds. *The Times Were A Changin': The Sixties Reader.* New York: Three Rivers Press, 1998.

Valenti, Jack. "The Movie Rating System: How It Began, Its Purpose, How It Works, The Public Reaction." New York and Washington DC: Motion Picture Association of America, n.d.

"We're Scared of Our Kids: A Journal of Readers' Poll." *Ladies' Home Journal* 85.1 (Jan. 1968): n.p.

Westby, David L. *Clouded Vision: The Student Movement in the United States in the 1960s.* Lewisburg: Bucknell University Press and London: Associated University Presses, 1976.

Yankelovich, Daniel. *The New Morality: A Profile of American Youth in the 70s.* New York: MacGraw Hill, 1974.

Visual Media

"Coppola's Notebook." *The Godfather: Bonus Material.* Produced by Paramount Pictures, 2001. DVD, 2001.

Flashing on the Sixties: A Tribal Document. Produced by Lisa Law and Alton Walpole, directed by Lisa Law, 60 min. Flashback Productions, 1990. Videocassette, 1990.

Gimme Shelter: The Rolling Stones. Produced and directed by David Maysles, Albert Maysles, and Charlotte Zwerin, 91 minutes. A Maysles Films Inc. Production, 1970. Videocassette, 2000.

Medium Cool. Produced by Tully Friedman and Haskell Wexler, directed by Haskell Wexler, 111 min. Paramount Pictures, 1969. Videocassette, 1994.

Monterey Pop. Produced by Joe Adler and John Phillips, directed by D. A. Pennebaker, 98 min. Pennebaker, 1968. Videocassette, n.d.

Woodstock. Produced by Michael Richards, directed by Michael Wadleigh, 60 min. Virtue Films, 1970. Videocassette, 1995.

Woodstock. Produced by Bob Maurice, directed by Michael Wadleigh, 225 min. Warner Brothers, 1994. Videocassette, 1994.

Film Culture and Film Industry

"The After M*A*S*H of Robert Altman." *Where It's At* (Aug. 1971).

Alpert, Hollis. "The Falling Stars." *Saturday Review* (28 Dec. 1968): 15–17.

———. "Onward and Upward with the Institute." *Saturday Review* 50.25 (24 June 1967): 50.

———. "Something New in Movie Communication." *Saturday Review* (9 June 1962): 54–55.

———. "Why Are They Saying Those Terrible Things About Us?" *Saturday Review* 54.27 (3 July 1971): 18.

"The American Film Institute." *Dialogue in Film* 2.1, n.d.

"Art House Boom." *Newsweek* 59.11 (28 May 1962): 102.

Bachman, Gideon. "The American Federation." *Film* 17 (Sep.-Oct. 1958): 24.

———."Change or Die." *Film* 20 (Mar.-Apr. 1961): 17.

Balio, Tino. *United Artists: The Company That Changed the Film Industry*. Madison: Wisconsin Press, 1987.

———, ed. *The American Film Industry*. Madison: University of Wisconsin Press, 1985.

Barry, Iris. "The Film Library and How It Grew." *Film Quarterly* 22.4 (Summer 1969): 19–27.

Bart, Peter. "The Excitement Is All from Europe." *The New York Times*, 3 Apr. 1966.

———. "Europe's Successes Worry Hollywood." *The New York Times*, 20 Sep. 1965.

———. "Hollywood Scholars: College Groups Try for Improvement in Screen Teaching Techniques." *New York Times*, 2 Aug. 1964.

Barta, Tony, ed. *Screening the Past: Film and the Representation of History*. Westport, CT, and London: Praeger, 1998.

Basinger, Jeanine. *American Cinema: One Hundred Years of Filmmaking*. New York: Rizzoli International Publications, 1994.

Benon, Shelly. "Motion Pictures." *Show* (Mar. 1971), microfiche, Core Collection, Margaret Herrick Academy of Motion Picture Arts and Sciences Library; Beverly Hills, CA.

Beresford, Bruce. "Decline of a Master: John Ford." *Film* 56 (Autumn 1969): 6.

Bergan, Ronald. *Francis Ford Coppola: The Making of His Movies*. New York: Thunder's Mouth Press, 1998.

———. *The United Artists Story*. New York: Crown Publishers, 1986.

Bernard, Weinraub. "Arthur Penn Takes on General Custer." *The New York Times*, 21 Dec. 1969.

Billingsley, K. L. *The Seductive Image: A Christian Critique of the World of Film*. Westchester, IL: Crossway Books, Good News Publishers, 1989.

Bingham, Dennis. *Acting Male: Masculinities in the Films of James Stewart, Jack Nicholson, and Clint Eastwood*. New Brunswick: Rutgers University Press, 1994.

Biskind, Peter. *Easy Riders, Raging Bulls: How the Sex-Drugs-and-Rock 'n' Roll Generation Saved Hollywood*. New York: Touchstone, 1998.

Black, Gregory D. *The Catholic Crusade Against the Movies, 1940–1975*. Cambridge: Cambridge University Press, 1998.

Botto, Louis. "They Shoot Dirty Movies, Don't They?" *Look* 3 (Nov. 1970): 59–60.

Boyum, Joy Gould, and Adrienne Scott. "A Case for Fem Lib, in Film." *Wall Street Journal*, 16 Aug. 1971.

——— and ———. *Film as Film*. Boston: Allyn and Bacon, 1971.

Braxton, Phyllis N. Letter to the Editor. *Saturday Review* 51.30 (27 July 1968): 19.

Breakwell, Ian, and Paul Hammond, eds. *Seeing in the Dark: A Compendium of Cinemagoing*. London: WBC Print (Bristol) Ltd., 1990.

Browne, Nick, ed. *Francis Ford Coppola's The Godfather Trilogy*. London: Cambridge University Press, 2000.

Browning, Norma Lee. "A Plum for Annie." *Chicago Tribune*, 9 July 1970.

Burgess, Jackson. "Student Film-Making." *Film Quarterly* 19.3 (Spring 1966): 29–33.

Buruma, Ian. "John Schlesinger." *Preview* (Dec/Jan 2006).

Buscombe, Edward, and Roberta E. Pearson, eds. *Back in the Saddle Again: New Essays on the Western*. London: British Film Institute, 1998.

Business Week (14 Mar. 1970): 29.

Byron, Stuart. "Rules of the Game." *Village Voice* 27.2 (6–12 Jan. 1982): 48.

Callenbach, Ernest. *Sight and Sound* 35 (Winter 1965): 12–17.

———, ed. "Editor's Notebook: American New Wave?" *Film Quarterly* 23.2 (Winter 1969–1970): 1–2.

Campbell, Elizabeth. "*Rolling Stone* Raps with Peter Fonda." In *Easy Rider Original Screenplay*, edited by Nancy Hardin and Margaret Schlossberg. New York: New American Library, 1969.

Canby, Vincent. "Critic's Choice: Ten Best Films of 1970." *The New York Times*, 27 Dec. 1970.

Carnes, Mark C., ed. *Past Imperfect: History According to the Movies*. New York: Henry Holt and Company, 1995.

Carton, Evan. "Vietnam and the Limits of Masculinity," *American Literary History* 3.2 (Summer 1991): 294–318.

Cashin, Fergus. "Beastly Men Give Ann Her Chance." *The Sun* (16 Sep. 1971). Box 33, no. 7. Jules Feiffer Collection, Library of Congress, Washington, D.C.

"Center for Advanced Film Studies Established in

California." *Filmmakers Newsletter* 2.8 (June 1969): 4.

Chamberlin, Phillip. "Philip Chamberlin: The Big Picture." *Film Society Review* 1 (Dec. 1965): 28.

_____. "What About Film Societies?" *Journal of the Screen Producers Guild* 11.5 (Sep. 1963): 35–38.

"The Chief." *Newsweek*, 25 Jan. 1971, p. 80.

Christgau, Robert. "Easy Rider's Soundtrack." In *Easy Rider Original Screenplay* by Peter Fonda, Dennis Hopper, and Terry Southern, edited by Nancy Hardin, 22–25. New York: Signet, New American Library, 1969.

Clark, Paul. "L. B. Press-Telegram," 10 Jan. 1993. Production folder, Margaret Herrick Academy of Motion Picture Arts and Sciences Library, Beverly Hills, CA.

Clarke, Shirley. "Teaching Filmmaking Creatively." *Journal of the University Film Producers Association, A Quarterly* 17.3 (1965): 6–14.

"Cannes Chief Raps Award to 'M.A.S.H.'" *Daily News*, 18 May 1970.

"The Code Is Dead." *Motion Picture Herald*, 6 July 1966.

Coe, Richard L. "Support for New Talent." *Saturday Review* 50 (28 Dec. 1968): 22–23.

Cohen, Larry. "The New Audience: From Andy Hardy to Arlo Guthrie." *Saturday Review* 52 (27 Dec. 1969): 11.

"Col's 'Easy Rider' Takes Two Awards." *Hollywood Reporter,* 29 May 1969.

Cooper, Anderson, and Elvis Mitchell. "Live from the Headlines." 6 Aug. 2006. CNN interview transcript, http://transcripts.cnn.com/TRANSCRIPTS/0308/06/se.04.html.

Cooper, Marcia. "Glib?" Letter to the Editor. *The New York Times*, 3 Oct. 1971.

Corman, Roger. "The Godfather." *Sight and Sound* 12.9 (Sep. 2002): 32.

Crist, Judith. "Joltin' Joe Never Had it So Good." *New York Times*, 21 Dec. 1970.

Crowther, Bosley. "Mike Nichols, Winner 'Best Director,' N.Y. Film Critics Award, Graduating with Honors," *The New York Times*, 3 Jan. 1967.

"The Current Cinema: Good-Time Girls," *The New Yorker*, 23 Sep. 2002, p. 99.

Curtiss, Thomas Quinn. "M*A*S*H Wins Top Picture Award at Cannes Festival." *International Herald Tribune*, 18 May 1970.

"Damone Drops Role in 'Godfather' Film." *New York Times*, 5 Apr. 1971.

Dauphin, Gary. "Plastic Fantastic." *Village Voice* 42.7 (18 Feb. 1997).

"Demographics Favoring Films Future." *Variety* (3 Oct. 1975): 3, 34.

Denby, David. "The Moviegoers." *The New Yorker* (6 Apr. 1998): 94–98.

Dent, Maggie. "A Film Society Takes Root in Chapel Hill." *Film Comment* (Summer 1962): 46.

Docksai, Ronald. "George S. Patton: A Magnificent Anachronism." *New Guard* 10.8 (Oct. 1970): 7–12.

Downing. "Music Hall: Still the No. 1 Hit." *Business Week*, 25 Dec. 1965, pp. 44–49.

Dreifus, Claudia. "Arlo Guthrie." *Progressive* 57.2 (Feb. 1993): 32–36.

Drexler, Roslyn. "Do Men Really Hate Women?" *The New York Times*, 5 Sep. 1971.

Dumazedier, Joffre. "The Cinema and Popular Culture." *Diogenes* (Fall 1960): 103–113.

Dworkin, Martin S. "Seeing for Ourselves: Notes on the Movie Art and Industry, Critics, and Audiences." *The Journal of Aesthetic Education* 3.3 (July 1969): 45–55.

Dyer, Richard. *Heavenly Bodies: Film Stars and Society.* New York: St. Martin's Press, 1986.

"'Easy Rider' Wins Award." *Los Angeles Times*, 29 Dec. 1969.

"'Easy' Rides Record for Columbia in This Area." *Hollywood Reporter*, 17 Sep. 1969.

Edgerton, Gary. "'A Breed Apart': Hollywood, Racial Stereotyping, and the Promise of Revisionism in *The Last of the Mohicans*." *Journal of American Culture* 17.1 (Spring 1994).

Ehrman, Mark. "Bikers and Celebs Mean Just One Thing." *Los Angeles Times,* 18 July 1994.

Ellis, Jack C. "The Big Picture." *Film Society Review* 1 (Jan. 1966): 7.

_____. "The Little Ivy-Covered Giant." *The Journal of the Producers Guild of America* 19 (Mar. 1967): 19.

Evers, Mrs. Medgar. "A Distinguished Negro Mother Asks: Why Should My Child Marry Yours?" *Ladies' Home Journal* 84.4 (Apr. 1968): 80–81.

Faulkner, Christopher. "Teaching French National Cinema." *Cinema Journal* 38.4 (Summer 1999): 88–93.

Fells, George. "What Ever Became of the Common Scolds?" *Look* 3 (Nov. 1970): 90–93.

Ferretti, Fred. "Corporate Rift in 'Godfather' Filming." *New York Times*, 23 Mar. 1971.

Fiering, Alvin. "Film at Boston University." *Film Society Review* 1 (Feb. 1966): 16.

"Film at the Boston University." *Journal of the University Film Producers Association* 13.4 (Summer 1961): 4.

"Film Editor: Dede Allen." *Look* 3 (Nov. 1970): "M."

"Film History for Exhibitors: A Winnowing of 'Box-office's' Winnowing of 50 Years' Headlines." *Films in Review* 21 (Oct. 1970): 473–477.

Fischer, Edward. "Film Studies Are Coming — Ready or Not." *Journal of University Film Producers Association* 14.4 (1965): 16–18.

Flatley, Guy. "So Truffaut Decided to Work His

Own Miracle." *The New York Times*, 27 Sep. 1970.

Fonda, Peter. "On the Road Still, Riding Solo, Free and Easy." *The New York Times*, 27 June 1998.

Forbes 167, no. 5 (Feb. 26, 2001): 97.

French, Warren, ed. *Twayne's Theatrical Arts Series*. Boston: Twayne Publishers, 1977.

Friedan, Betty. "Unmasking the Rage in the American Dream House." *The New York Times*, 31 Jan. 1971.

_____. "What Makes These Characters Desperate?" *The New York Times*, 19 Dec. 1971.

Friedman, Lester D. "Celluloid Palimpsets: An Overview of Ethnicity and the American Film." In *Unspeakable Images: Ethnicity and the American Cinema*, edited by Lester D. Friedman. Urbana and Chicago: University of Illinois Press, 1991.

Gardiner, Beth. "Fonda Raises Money with 'Easy Rider' Bike Rally." *Entertainment Today*, 22 Oct. 1999.

Gaskin, Stephen. *Amazing Dope Tales and Haight Street Flashbacks*. Summertown, TN: The Book Publishing Company, 1980.

Gelatt, Roland. "Those Under-Thirties Again." *Saturday Review* 52.28 (12 July 1969): 20.

Geller, Robert, and Sam Kula. "Toward Filmic Literacy: The Role of the American Film Institute." *Journal of Aesthetic Education* 3.3 (July 1969) 99–100.

Gelmis, Joseph. *The Film Director as Superstar*. Garden City, NY: Doubleday, 1970.

_____. "Midnight Cowboy." *Newsday*, 26 May 1969. In *Film Facts: A Publication of the American Film Institute*, edited by Ernest Parmentier. Vol. XII, No. 8: 171.

Georgakas, Dan. "They Have Not Spoken: American Indians in Film." *Film Quarterly* 25.3 (Spring 1972): 26–32.

Gerstel, Judy. "Robert Altman a Misogynist? He Just Tells the Truth About Women." *Knight Ridder/Tribune News Service*, 11 Nov. 1993.

Gessner, Robert. "Bachelors of Pix Biz." *Newsweek* 25 (2 Apr. 1945): 86.

Glatzer, Richard, and John Raeburn, eds. *Frank Capra: The Man and His Films*. Ann Arbor: The University of Michigan Press, 1975.

Gold, Ronald. "Ex-LBJ Aide's Film Vision." *Variety* 243.2 (1 June 1966): 1, 52.

_____. "Jack Valenti Seeks New Ways." *Film Daily*, 1967.

Gomery, Douglas. *The Hollywood Studio System*. New York: St. Martin's Press, 1986.

_____. *Movie History: A Survey*. Belmont, CA: Wadsworth Publishing Company, 1991.

_____. *Shared Pleasures: A History of Movie Presentation in the United States*. London: British Film Institute, 1992.

Gordon, Stanley. "Voight: Fresh Eye on Hollywood." *Look* 3 (Nov. 1970): 78.

"'Graduate' Nearing $ Million Income." *Hollywood Citizen-News*, 6 July 1968.

"'Graduate' Rates A-4 from Catholics, Recent B's Include 'Brain,' 'Dark of Sun,' 'Ambushers' Condemn Swedish '491.'" *Variety* 250.2 (Jan. 10, 1968).

Graves, Ralph. "Bridging Two Worlds." *Life* 67.2 (11 July 1969): 1.

_____. "Dusty and the Duke." *Life* 67.2 (11 July 11 1969): 36–45.

Greenberg, Caren. "Carnal Knowledge: A Woman Is Missing." *Diacritics* 5 (Winter 1975): 57–60.

Griffith, D. W. "Interview with D.W. Griffith by Richard Barry." *New York Times Magazine* (28 Mar. 1915): 16.

Hamilton, Jack. "Where, Oh Where Are the Beautiful Girls?" *Look* 3 (Nov. 1970): 62–71.

Hardin, Nancy, and Marilyn Schlossberg, eds. *Easy Rider Original Screenplay*, by Peter Fonda, Dennis Hopper, and Terry Southern. New York: Signet, New American Library, 1969.

Harmnetz, Alijean. "The American Film Institute." *Show* 1.5 (20 Aug. 1970): 16.

_____. "Custodian for Cinema Culture." *Show* 1.5 (Aug. 1970): 16.

Harpuder, Eric. Letter to the Editor. *The New York Times*, 21 Jan. 1968.

Haskell, Molly. *From Reverence to Rape: The Treatment of Women in the Movies*, 2nd ed. Chicago and London: The University of Chicago Press, 1973, 1987.

Hayden, Tom. *Reunion: A Memoir*. New York: Random House, Inc., 1988.

Herndon, William. Letter to the Editor. *The New York Times*, 21 Jan. 1968.

Hess, John. "Godfather II: A Deal Coppola Couldn't Refuse." *Jump Cut, A Review of Contemporary Cinema* 7 (May-July 1975): 1–11.

Hoberman, J. "Blazing Saddles." *Village Voice* (29 Nov. 2005). http://www.villagevoice.com/film/0538,hoberman2,68001,20.html.

Hodgkinson, Anthony. "What Is a Film Society For?" *Film Society Review* (Apr. 1967): 24–29.

"Hollywood: The Year You Almost Couldn't Find It." *Look* 3 (Nov. 1970): editor's page.

"How College Girls Really Are." *Life* 59.25 (17 Dec. 1965): 66B.

Hutton, Paul A. "The Celluloid Custer." *Red River Valley Historical Review* 4.4 (Fall 1979): 20–42.

_____. "From Little Bighorn to Little Big Man: The Changing Image of a Western Hero in Popular Culture." *The Western Historical Quarterly* 7.1 (Jan. 1976): 19–45.

"Italian Descenters Hit 'Graduate' 'Slur.'" *Film and TV Daily*, 16 May 1968.

Jacobs, Diane. *Hollywood Renaissance*. London,

Brunswick, and New York: A. S. Barnes and Co., 1977.

James, David E. *Allegories of Cinema: American Film in the Sixties*. Princeton: Princeton University Press, 1989.

Javits, Senator Jacob K. "Politics or Pix — You Gotta Make Your Audiences Believe." *Variety* 252.13 (13 Nov. 1968): 31, 157.

Jelinek, Pauline. "Army Closes MASH." *The Outlook*, 12 June 1997, World Section.

Johnson, Robert K. "Francis Ford Coppola." In *Twayne's Theatrical Arts Series*, edited by Warren French. Boston: Twayne Publishers, 1977.

Jowett, Garth. *Film, The Democratic Art: A Social History of American Film*. Boston: Little, Brown, 1976.

Joy, Daniel F. "Editor's note." *New Guard* 10.8 (Oct. 1970): 3.

Kael, Pauline. *Going Steady: Film Writings 1968–1969*. New York and London: Marion Boyers, 1968, 1969, 1970, 1994.

Kantor, Bernard R. "Film Study in Colleges." *The Journal of the Producers Guild of America* 19 (Mar. 1967): 3–5, 8.

Kasdan, Margo, and Susan Tavernetti. "Native Americans in a Revisionist Western: Little Big Man." In *Hollywood's Indian: The Portrayal of the Native American*, edited by Peter Rollins and John E. O'Conner. Lexington: University Press of Kentucky, 2003.

Kauffmann, Stanley. "Stanley Kauffmann on Films: Midnight Cowboy." *New Republic*, 23 Dec. 1967, pp. 20–33.

Kelly, Karin, and Tom Edgar. *Film School Confidential: The Insider's Guide to Film Schools*. New York: The Berkeley Publishing Group, 1997.

Kilday, Gregg. "'Knowledge' Obscenity Ruling to Be Appealed." *Los Angeles Times*, 3 Aug. 1973.

Kilpatrick, Jacquelyn. *Celluloid Indians*. Lincoln: University of Nebraska Press, 1999.

King, Vance. *The Film Daily Yearbook of Motion Pictures* 53 (1969): 90.

"The King of Intermissions." *Time Magazine*, 9 July 1965, pp. 93–94.

Klemesrud, Judy. "Feminist Goal: Better Image at the Movies." *The New York Times*, 13 Oct. 1974.

Knebel, Fletcher. "Hollywood: Broke — and Getting Richer." *Look* 3 (Nov. 1970): 50–52.

Knight, Arthur. "Adult Film Group in Quest to Gain Respect." *Los Angeles Times*, 17 Feb. 1974.
_____. "Engaging the Eye-Minded." *Saturday Review* 51 (28 Dec. 1968): 17–22.

Koch, Stephen. "Fiction and Film: A Search for New Sources." *Saturday Review* 52 (27 Dec 1969): 12–14, 38.

Kosnett, Jeff. "Easy Rider It's Not." *Kiplinger Personal Finance Magazine* 46.9 (Sep. 1992): 13.

Kovaks, Steven. "Misplaced Concern." Letter to the Editor. *The New York Times*, 3 Oct. 1971.

Laurent, Tirard. *Moviemakers' Master Class: Private Lessons from the World's Foremost Directors*. New York and London: Faber and Faber, 2002.

Lebo, Harlan. *The Godfather Legacy: The Untold Story of the Making of the Classic Godfather Trilogy Featuring Never-Before Published Production Stills*. New York: Simon and Schuster, 1997.

Leglise, Paul. "The Hidden Face of the Cinema, Pt. III: An Audience of 12,000,000,000." *UNESCO Courier* (Feb. 1963): 26–27.

Lehman, Peter, ed. *Masculinity: Bodies, Movies, Culture*. New York and London: Routledge, 2001.

Lenburg, Jeff. *Dustin Hoffman: Hollywood's Anti-Hero*. New York: St. Martin's Press, 1983.

Loo, Darrell. "Student Film Making Hits University." *Daily Utah Chronicle*, 27 Sep. 1968.

Levy, Emanuel. *All About Oscar: The History and Politics of the Academy Awards*. New York and London: Continuum International Publishing Group, Inc., 2003.

Lonsfoote, Sandra A. "Making Out 'The Graduate.'" Letter to the Editor. *Saturday Review* 51.30 (27 July 1968): 19.

Lichtenstein, Grace. "'Godfather' Film Won't Mention Mafia." *The New York Times*, 28 Mar. 1971.

Limbacher, James. "Film Societies Reply to Exhib Fears: 16-Millimeter Shows Divert No Biz." *Variety* 237.7 (8 Jan. 1965): 51.
_____. "Forever Faithful Film Fans." *Variety* 233.7 (8 Jan. 1964): 15, 52.

Linklater, Kristin. "Demeaning." Letter to the Editor. *The New York Times*, 14 Nov. 1971.

Lithgow, James. "Filmmakers' Distribution Center." *Filmmakers' Newsletter* 2.6 (Apr. 1969): 10.

Livingston, Guy. "Levine Tells His Home Burg 'Graduate' Hits $44,000,000, Might Reach $120 Mil." *Variety* (W), 24 July 1968.

Loo, Darrell. "Student Filmmaking Hits University." *The Daily Utah Chronicle*, 27 Sept. 1968.

Lynch, Dennis F. *Clozentropy: A Technique for Studying Audience Response to Films*. New York: Arno Press, 1978.

Lynes, Russell. "After Hours: Flicks for the Fastidious." *Harper's Magazine* (June 1968): 24.

Macklin, Anthony F. "Benjamin Will Survive...." *Film Heritage* 4.1 (Fall 1968): 1–6.

Maddox, Kate. "From 'Easy Rider' to Breezy Pitcher," *tele.com* 6.5 (5 Mar. 2001): 18.

"The Making of the Godfather." *Time Magazine* (13 Mar. 1972): 62.

Maltby, Richard. *Harmless Entertainment: Hollywood and the Ideology of Consensus*. Metuchen and London: The Scarecrow Press, Inc., 1983.

Manoogian, Haig P. "New Spirit in Young Filmmakers." *The Journal of the Producers Guild of America* 9.1 (1967): 23.

Martin, Paul E. ""Happier Now." Letter to the Editor. *The New York Times*, 23 Nov. 1969.

Mastoianni, Tony. "Sensationalism Obscures Point of 'Carnal Knowledge,'" *Cleveland Press*, 3 July 1971.

Matthews, Linda. "Court May Refine Ruling on Obscenity." *Los Angeles Times*, 11 Dec. 1973.

Mayer, Arthur. "Motion Picture Courses in American Universities: A Report by an Old Instructor." *The Journal of the Producers Guild of America* 19 (Mar. 1967): 25–27.

Mayer, Michael. *Foreign Films on American Screens.* New York: Arco, 1965.

McBride, Joseph. *Filmmakers on Filmmaking: The American Film Institute Seminars on Motion Pictures and Television.* Los Angeles: J. P. Tarcher, Inc., and Boston: Houghton Mifflin Co., 1983.

Merrill, Robert. "Altman's McCabe and Mrs. Miller as a Classic Western." *The New Orleans Review* (1990): 79–86.

Meyers, Christene. "Western Movies Turn 100: Montana Takes Star Turn in Film." *Billings Gazette*, 21 Sep. 2003.

Minkow, David L. "Fighting It." Letter to the Editor. *The New York Times*, 5 Dec. 1971.

Mintz, Steven, and Randy Roberts. *Hollywood's America: United States History Through Its Films.* St. James, NY: Brandywine Press, 1993.

Mitchell, Lee Clarke. *Westerns: Making the Man in Fiction and Film.* Chicago and London: The University of Chicago Press, 1996.

Mitchell, Rick. "After 'Midnight.'" Letter to the Editor. *Los Angeles Times*, 6 Mar. 1994.

"Modern Movies: No Kids, No Popcorn." *World Journal Tribune* (17 Oct. 1966): 13.

Mothner, Ira. "Now Faces." *Look* 3 (Nov. 1970): 73–77.

"Movie Theaters Stage Comeback." *The New York Times*, 5 July 1964, Part III.

Mulvey, Laura. *Visual and Other Pleasures.* Bloomington and Indianapolis: Indiana University Press, 1989.

Neale, Steve, and Murray Smith, eds. *Contemporary Hollywood Cinema.* London and New York: Routledge, 1998.

"Newsweek Extra: The 100 Best Movies." *Newsweek*, Summer 1998.

Nichols, Bill. *Ideology and the Image: Social Representation in the Cinema and Other Media.* Bloomington: Indiana University Press, 1981.

"Not so Sad Sack." *Time Magazine* (27 July 1962): 65.

"The Now Movie: SR's Annual Report on the Cinema." *Saturday Review* 50 (28 Dec. 1968), full issue.

Obst, David. *Too Good to Be Forgotten: Changing America in the '60s and '70s.* New York, Chichester, Weinheim, Brisbane, Singapore, and Toronto: John Wiley and Sons, Inc., 1998.

"On Wednesday," *Variety* 191 (8 Apr. 1964): 5.

Ortega Murphy, Brent, and Jeffery Scott Harder. "1960s Counterculture and the Legacy of American Myth: A Study of Three Films." *Canadian Review of American Studies* 23.2 (Winter 1993): 57.

Osborn, Robert. *Seventy Years of the Oscar: The Official History of the Academy Awards.* New York, London, and Paris: Abbeville Press, 1999.

"Paramount Repudiates Italo-Am Group vs. 'Godfather.'" *Variety* 62.6 (24 Mar. 1971): 1, 21.

Parker, David L. "Projection Room — A University Film Series." *Journal of the University Film Producers Association* 19.1 (1967): 26–29.

Parker, Melody. "Korean War Vets Lend Authenticity to 'M*A*S*H' Production." *Waterloo Courier*, 29 Sep. 2006.

Peary, Danny, ed. *Close-ups.* New York: Workman Publishing, 1978.

Pease, Jude. Letter to the Editor. *The New York Times*, 3 Oct. 1971.

"Peggy Rusk: First Pictures of Her Interracial Marriage." *Ladies' Home Journal* 84.4 (Apr. 1968): 80–81.

Penn, Stanley. "Focusing on Youth: A New Breed of Movie Attracts the Young, Shakes Up Hollywood." *The Wall Street Journal*, 4 Nov. 1969.

"Peter Fonda." *Biography* 4.7 (July 2000): 22.

Phillips, Gene. "John Schlesinger: Social Realist." *Film Comment* 5.4 (Winter 1969): 58–63.

Pintoff, Ernest. *The Complete Guide to American Film Schools and Cinema and Television Courses.* New York: Penguin Group, 1994.

Pontecorvo, Lis. "The Raw Material: Film Resources." In *The Historian and Film*, edited by Paul Smith. Cambridge, London, New York, and Melbourne: Cambridge University Press, 1976.

Powell, Dilys. "War Games." *The London Times*, 24 May 1970.

Price, John A. "The Stereotyping of North American Indians in Motion Pictures," *Ethnohistory* 20.2 (Spring 1973): 153–171.

Prince, Stephen, ed. *Sam Peckinpah's The Wild Bunch.* Cambridge: Cambridge University Press, 1999.

Program Notes. *Cinema Texas* 22.1 (25 Jan. 1982).

Prouse, Derek. "Casualties of War." *The Sunday Times*, 17 May 1970.

Quart, Leonard. "I Still Love Going to Movies: An Interview with Pauline Kael." *Cineaste* 25.2 (Spring 1996): 8–13.

Quigley, Martin, Jr. *Films in America 1929–1969.* New York: Golden Press, 1970.

Quinn, John W. "Hypo for the B.O. Ardently Probed at Show-a Rama." *Variety* (25 Mar. 1964): 13.

Radar, Dotson. "The Cowboy as Hustler." *Interview* I.2 (1969).

Rapf, Maurice. "Can Education Kill the Movies?" *Action* 2.5 (Sep.–Oct. 1967): 11.

Rawlinson, Dustin. "A World Survey of Training Programs in Cinema." *Journal of University Film Producers* 14.4 (1962).

Reed, T. V. "Old Cowboys, New Indians: Hollywood Frames the American Indian." *Wicazo S A Review* (Summer 2001): 75–96.

"Richard Hornberger, Author of Original M*A*S*H book." *Denver Rocky Mountain News*, 9 Nov. 1997.

Rollins, Peter, ed. *Hollywood as Historian: American Film in a Cultural Context.* Lexington: The University of Kentucky Press, 1983.

Rose, Ernest. "Problems and Prospects in Film Teaching." *Journal of the University Film Association* 21.4 (Summer 1969): 98.

Rosenstone, Robert A. *Revisioning History: Film and the Construction of a New Past.* Princeton: Princeton University Press, 1995.

_____. *Visions of the Past: The Challenge of Film to Our Idea of History.* Cambridge and London: Harvard University Press, 1995.

Rossetter, Jack C. "Feiffer's Answer?" *The New York Times*, 3 Oct. 1971.

Rubin, Joan Alleman. "The Student and Film." *Mademoiselle* (Mar. 1966): 172.

Sarris, Andrew. *The American Cinema.* New York: Dutton, 1968.

Schatz, Thomas. *Hollywood Genres: Formulas, Filmmaking, and the Hollywood Studio System.* New York: Random House, 1981.

Scherle, Victor, and William Turner Levy. *The Films of Frank Capra.* Secaucus, NJ: The Citadel Press, 1977.

Schickel, Richard. "Days and Nights in the Arthouse." *Film Comment* 28 (May–June 1992): 32.

Schilacci, Anthony. "Film as Environment." *Saturday Review* 51 (28 Dec. 1968): 11–14.

Scott, George C. "Why Patton?" Twentieth Century–Fox Film Production Manual, reprinted in *New Guard* 10.8 (Oct. 1970): 9.

Selvin, Joel. *Summer of Love: The Inside Story of LSD, Rock and Roll, Free Love and High Times in the Wild West.* New York: Cooper Square Press, 1994.

Shirley, Don. "A Plan to 'Erase Confusion.'" *The Washington Post, Times Herald*, 2 Aug. 1973.

Sinowitz, Michael Leigh. "The Western as Postmodern Satiric History: Thomas Berger's *Little Big Man.*" *CLIO* 28.2 (1999): 129–148.

Sklar, Robert, and Charles Musser, eds. *Resisting*

Images: Essays on Cinema and History. Philadelphia: Temple University Press, 1990.

Soesbe, Douglas. Letter to the Editor. *Los Angeles Times*, 6 Mar. 1994.

"Something New in the Motion Picture Theatre." *Closeup* 10.2 (June 1933): 154–157.

Spottiswoode, Raymond. "Eyewitnessing the World of the 16 mm. Motion Picture." *The Saturday Review* 32 (8 Jan. 1949): 36.

Stan, Robert, and Toby Miller, eds. *Film and Theory.* Malden, MA: Blackwell Publishers, 2000.

Steele, Robert. "Film Curriculum." *Journal of the University Film Producers Association, a Quarterly* 13.4 (Summer 1961): 10–11.

_____. "Film Scholars at the New York Film Festival." *Film Comment* 2 (Fall 1964): 41–43.

Stevens, George, Jr. "Remarks of George Stevens, Jr., on His Appointment as Director of The American Film Institute." *The Journal of the University Film Association* 20.1 (Spring 1968): 6.

Stewart, David C., ed. *Film Study in Higher Education.* Washington, DC: American Council on Education, 1966.

_____. "Men and Movies at Dartmouth." *Journal of Film Producers Association* 18.2 (1966): 5–8.

_____. "The Movies Students Make: A New Wave on Campus." *Harper's Magazine* (Oct. 1965): 66–72.

Stokes, Melvyn, and Richard Maltby. *Identifying Hollywood's Audiences: Cultural Identity and the Movies.* London: British Film Institute, 1999.

"The Student Movie Makers." *Time Magazine* 91.5 (2 Feb. 1968): 78.

Taylor, Ella. "Boomer Reunion, The Graduate Turns 30." *L.A. Weekly* (7–13 Mar. 1997): 33.

"Theatrical and TV Producers Unite Under a Single Hollywood Roof." *Variety* 234.7 (8 Apr. 1964): 5, 20.

Thomas, John. "The Big Picture." *Film Society Review* 1 (Oct. 1965): 5.

Tirard, Laurent. *Moviemakers' Master Class: Private Lessons from the World's Foremost Directors.* New York and London: Faber and Faber, 2002.

Tompkins, Jane. *West of Everything: The Inner Life of Westerns.* New York and Oxford: Oxford University Press, 1992.

Tubbs, Gordon H. "Films and Education." *The Film Daily Yearbook of Motion Pictures* 49 (1967): 634.

_____. "Tomorrow's Film-makers Need Your Help Today." *The Film Daily Yearbook of Motion Pictures* 51 (1969): 637–638.

Tusher, William. "Hollywood 1967." *The Film Daily Yearbook of Motion Pictures* 50 (1968): 92–94.

_____. "Windows on Hollywood." *Film Daily Yearbook of Motion Pictures* 49 (1967): 90–94.

"Twice As Many Drive-In Theaters?" *Business Week* (1 Jan. 1949): 44–45.

Valenti, Jack. "Badge of Honor." *The Film Daily Yearbook of Motion Pictures* 52 (1969): 78.

_____. "Letting the Public Know." *The Film Daily Yearbook of Motion Pictures* 52 (1968): 80.

"Valenti Meets Manhattan Press." *Variety* 243.1 (25 May 1966): 18.

Van Dyke, Willard. "The Role of the Museum of Modern Art in Motion Pictures." *Film Library Quarterly* 1.1 (Winter 1967–1968): 36–38.

"Wall Street Analysis of Film Grosses." *Variety* 176.10 (16 Nov. 1949): 10.

Weiss, Miriam. "Movie Mailbag: She Identifies with 'Graduate.'" Letter to the Editor. *The New York Times*, 9 June 1968.

Wellemeyer, Jonathan. "Intelligence Squared U.S. Hollywood and the Spread of Anti-Americanism." National Public Radio, 6 Jan. 2007. http://www.npr.org/templates/story/story.php?storyId=6625002.

White, Hayden, et al. "AHR Forum." *American Historical Review* 93.5 (Dec. 1998): 1186–1227.

Wilcox, Molly. "Film Education: The National Picture." *Filmmaker's Newsletter* 2.2 (Dec. 1968): 1.

Wilinsky, Barbara. *Sure Seaters: The Emergence of Art House Cinema*. Minneapolis and London: University of Minnesota Press, 2001.

Williams, Linda, ed. *Viewing Positions: Ways of Seeing Film*. New Brunswick, NJ: Rutgers University Press, 1995.

Willis, Ellen. "Misogyny." Letter to the Editor. *The New York Times*, 7 Feb. 1971.

Windeler, Robert. "Study of Film Soaring on College Campuses." *The New York Times*, 18 Apr. 1968.

Wood, Robin. *Hollywood from Vietnam to Reagan*. New York, Chicester: Columbia University Press, 1986.

"'Wop' Looks in to Stay; Embassy Reply to Italo Body Defends Its Use." *Variety* 251.1 (22 May 1968).

Wright, Derek. "The New Tyranny of Sexual 'Liberation.'" *Life* 69.19 (6 Nov. 1970): 4.

Wright, Will. *Six Guns and Society: A Structural Study of the Western*. Berkeley, Los Angeles, and London: University of California Press, 1975.

Yacowar, Maurice. "Actors as Conventions in the Films of Robert Altman." *Cinema Journal* 20.1 (Fall 1980): 23–24.

Yawitz, Paul. "Movies." *Beverly Hills Courier*, 8 Jan. 1971.

"Yes, Mr. Ruddy, There Is a...." Editorial. *The New York Times*, 23 Mar. 1971.

Young, Colin. "Film at UCLA." *The Journal of the Producers Guild of America* 19 (Mar. 1967): 11.

_____. "Films Are Contemporary: Notes on Film Education." *Arts in Society* (Winter 1967): 32.

Zeitlin, David. "A Homely, Non-hero, Dustin Hoffman, Gets an Unlikely Role in Mike Nichols' The Graduate." *Life* 63.21 (24 Nov. 1967).

_____. "A Swarthy Pinocchio Makes a Wooden Role Real." *Life* 63.21 (Nov. 24, 1967): 113.

Zenman, Ned, and Lucy Howard. "Arlo Go Home." *Newsweek* 119.7 (17 Feb. 1992): 8.

Movie Reviews

"The After M*A*S*H of Robert Altman." *Where It's At* (Aug. 1971): 12–15.

Alpert, Hollis. "'The Graduate' Makes Out." *Saturday Review* 51 (6 July 1968): 14–15, 32.

_____. "Mike Nichols Strikes Again." *Saturday Review* (23 Dec. 1967): 24.

_____. "Why Are They Saying Those Terrible Things About Us?" *Saturday Review* 54.27 (3 July 1971): 18.

"Arlo Guthrie's 'Alice's Restaurant.'" *Boston After Dark* (27 Nov. 1968): 16.

Barea, Ernest R. Letter to the Editor. *The New York Times*, 2 Nov. 1969.

Bart, Peter. "Mike Nichols, Moviemaniac." *The New York Times*, 1 Jan. 1967.

"Bets and Bawds." *Playboy* 18.9 (Sep. 1971): 103–105.

Biuliano, Charles. "Alice's Thanksgiving." *Boston After Dark*, 3 Dec. 1969.

"The Blame." *Hollywood Reporter*, 18 Oct. 2001.

Blevins, Winfred. "Around LA." *Los Angeles Herald-Examiner*, 1 Aug. 1971, D-1, E- 5.

_____. "McCabe: Evidence of Greatness." *Herald Examiner Entertainment*, 1 Aug. 1971.

_____. "Penn's 'Little Big Man'—Admirable." *Los Angeles Herald-Examiner*, 22 Dec. 1970.

Brinkley, David. "What's Wrong with the Graduate." *Ladies' Home Journal* 85 (4 Apr. 1968): 79.

"Britain's Censor Gives 'Easy Rider' X Rating, No Cuts." *Variety* (20 June 1969).

Canby, Vincent. "Film" Seeking the American Heritage." *The New York Times*, 12 Dec. 1970.

_____. "'McCabe': How to Demythologize the West." *Los Angeles Times*, 1 or 7 Aug. 1971.

_____. "Midnight Cowboy." *The New York Times*, 26 May 1969.

"The Case Pays Off for Eye in the Sky." *Hollywood Reporter*, 18 July 1994.

Chamblin, Charles. "No Easy Road in Interpreting 'Easy Rider.'" *Los Angeles Times*, 2 Dec. 1969, Part IV.

_____. "Tragedy of Indian in 'Man.'" *Los Angeles Times*, 22 Dec. 1970.

Clark, Paul. L. B. Press-Telegram, Jan. 10, 1993.

Cohen, Larry. "?Ful Film: ?er Fails," *Hollywood Reporter*, 25 June 1971.

"Col's 'Easy Rider' Set for Edinburgh." *Hollywood Reporter*, 18 Aug. 1969.

Corliss, Richard. "I Admit It, I Didn't Like 'M*A*S*H.'" *The New York Times*, 22 Mar. 1970.

Corman, Roger. "The Godfather and The Godfather Part II," *Sight and Sound* 12.9 (Sep. 2002): 35.

Crowther, Bosley. "Carnal Knowledge." *The New York Times*, 1 July 1971.

_____. "Film: Tales Out of School, The Graduate Arrives on Local Screens." *The New York Times*, 22 Dec. 1967.

"The Current Cinema." *The New Yorker*, 9 Sep. 1996.

"The Current Cinema." *The New Yorker*, 26 Dec. 1970.

"The Current Cinema: Pipe Dream." *The New Yorker*, 3 July 1971, pp. 40–41.

Curtiss, Thomas Quinn. "M*A*S*H: Laughter is the Only Remedy." *International Herald Review*, 13 May 1970.

Dargis, Manohla. "Born to Be Wild." *L.A. Weekly*, 15 July 1994.

Dauphin, Gary. "Plastic Fantastic." *Village Voice*, 18 Feb. 1997.

"David Foster Buys 'McCabe.'" *Hollywood Reporter*, 17 July 1968.

Dawson, Jan. "Midnight Cowboy." *Sight and Sound* 38.4 (Autumn 1969): 211–212.

Dreifus, Claudia. "Arlo Guthrie." *Progressive*, 57.2 (Feb. 1993): 32.

"Easy Rider." *Box Office*, 21 July 1969; Margaret Herrick Library of Arts and Sciences, Core Collection for "Easy Rider," Beverly Hills, Ca.

"Easy Rider." *Motion Picture Herald*, 16 July 1969.

"Easy Rider." *Variety* 254.13 (14 May 1969): 6.

"'Easy Rider' Honored." *Hollywood Reporter*, 30 Apr. 1970.

Ebert, Roger. "Carnal Knowledge." *Chicago Sun Times*, 6 July 1971.

_____. "Little Big Man Review." *Chicago Sun Times*, 1 Jan. 1970.

_____. "McCabe and Mrs. Miller." *The Chicago Sun Times*, 14 Nov. 1999.

_____. "Midnight Cowboy." *Chicago Sun Times*, 5 July 1969.

Edwards, Nadine M. "'The Graduate' Hilarious Romp Beautifully Done." *Hollywood Citizen-News*, 22 Dec. 1967.

Everett, Todd. "Hopper, Fonda Film Exceptionally Done." *Hollywood Citizen-News*.

Docksai, Ronald. "George S. Patton: A Magnificent Anachronism." *New Guard* 10.8 (Oct. 1970): 7.

Farber, Stephen. "End of the Road?" *Film Quarterly* 23.2 (Winter 1969–1970): 3–16.

Fisher, Craig. "Sound Snafu Didn't Dampen Foster's Faith in 'McCabe.'" *The Hollywood Reporter*, 5 Aug. 1971.

Fricke, David, and M. Seliger. "McGuinn, Roger." *Rolling Stone* 585 (23 Aug. 1990): 107.

Friedenberg, Edgar Z. "Calling Dr. Spock!" *The New York Book of Reviews* 10.6 (28 Mar. 1968): 25–26.

"From Method to Madness: Dennis Hopper." *Pacific Film Archive*, June 1988.

Gelatt, Roland. "SR Goes to the Movies, Arlo as Arlo." *Saturday Review* 52.35 (30 Aug. 1969): 35.

Gielberman, Owen. "Midnight Cowboy." *Entertainment Weekly* (4 Mar. 1994), http://www.ew.com/ew/article/0,,301325,00.html.

Gow, Gordon. "McCabe and Mrs. Miller." *Films and Filming*, Apr. 1972, n.p.

"The Graduate." *Time Magazine* (29 Dec. 1967).

Herndon, Venable. "Alice's Restaurant." *Hollywood Citizen-News*, 22 Aug. 1969.

Higham, Charles. "No Mash Note for McCabe." Letter to the Editor. *The New York Times*, 12 Sep. 1971.

"Hillard Elkins Plans Show, 'Real People' in 'Alice's.'" *Hollywood Reporter*, 6 Feb. 1969, p. 38.

Hollywood Reporter, 22 Jan. 1970. McCabe and Mrs. Miller Core Collection, Margaret Herrick Library of Arts and Sciences, Beverly Hills, Ca.

Hollywood Reporter, 28 Apr. 1970. McCabe and Mrs. Miller Core Collection, Margaret Herrick Library of Arts and Sciences, Beverly Hills, Ca.

Hollywood Reporter, 11 Dec. 1970. McCabe and Mrs. Miller Core Collection, Margaret Herrick Library of Arts and Sciences, Beverly Hills, Ca.

Howe, Desson. "Midnight Cowboy." *Washington Post*, 15 Apr. 1994.

Huzinec, Mary. "Passages." *People Magazine* (26 Sep. 1994): 75.

Johnson, William. "M*A*S*H." *Film Quarterly* 23.3 (Spring 1969): 38–41.

Kaufmann, Stanley. "Midnight Cowboy." *New Republic* 33 (7 June 1969).

_____. "On Films." *New Republic* (4 Sep. 1971): n.p.

_____. "Review." *New Republic* 161.5 (2 Aug. 1969): 22.

"Legal Briefs." *Hollywood Reporter*, 14 Mar. 1997.

Lipton, Edward. "Review of New Film." *The Film Daily Yearbook of Motion Pictures* 51 (1967).

"Little Big Man." *Motion Picture Herald*, 6 Jan. 1971.

"Little Big Man." *Variety*, 1 Jan. 1970.

Loynd, Ray. "'Wager' Robert Altman's Deep-Freeze Western." *Los Angeles Times Calendar*, 9 Mar. 1971.

Lydon, Susan. "The Graduate." *Rolling Stone*, 10 Feb. 1968.

"Maddow Scripts Foster's McCabe." *Hollywood Reporter*, 11 Oct. 1968.

Madsen, Axel. "Reaching the Tribes." *Sight and Sound* 39.1 (Winter 1969/1970): 33–35.

Mahoney, John. "'Easy Rider' Facing High Profits,

Critical Honors." *Hollywood Reporter*, 26 June 1969, p. 3.

Makeney, John. "'Graduate' Will Benefit from Word-of-Mouth Plugs." *Hollywood Reporter*, 18 Dec. 1967.

Mastoianni, Tony. "Sensationalism Obscures Point of 'Carnal Knowledge.'" *Cleveland Press*, 3 July 1971.

Mayerson, Donald J. "McCabe and Mrs. Miller." *Cue*, 3 Mar. 1971.

"McCabe and Mrs. Miller." *Variety*, 1 Jan. 1971.

"McCabe and Mrs. Miller." *Box Office*, 19 July 1971.

"*McCabe and Mrs. Miller*." *Postscript Heavy Spoilers*, 2 Feb. 2003.

McCormick, Sharon. "Alice's Restaurant," *Filmex* 3 (Apr. 1976): 55.

McGilligan, Patrick. "The Ballad of Easy Rider or How to Make a Drug Classic." *Los Angeles Magazine* (Mar. 2004): 61.

Milne, Tom. "Easy Rider." *Sight and Sound* 38.4 (Autumn 1969): 211.

_____. "Films." *The [London] Observer*, 11 Aug. 1968.

Morgenstern, Joseph. "A Boy's Best Friend." *Newsweek*, 1 Jan. 1968.

_____. "Movie: On the Road." *Newsweek* 74.3 (21 July 1969): 95.

Mortimer, Penelope. "A Lovable Satire." *The Observer Review*, 17 May 1970.

"Movies." *McCall's* 95.1 (Apr. 1968).

"Movies." *Playboy* 16.9 (Sep. 1969): 42.

"MPAA New Code and Ratings Rules." *Variety* 252.8 (9 Oct. 1968): 8.

Murf. "McCabe and Mrs. Miller." *Variety* 263.7 (30 June 1971): 22.

"New Films." *Cue*, 19 July 1969.

O'Connor, John J. "On Film: A Lonely Hustler." *The Wall Street Journal*, 27 May 1969.

"Patton." *Variety* 257.10 (21 Jan. 1970): 18.

P.D.Z. "Virgin Wood." *Newsweek*, 5 July 1971, p. 71.

Polt, Harriet R. "Easy Rider." *Film Quarterly* 23.1 (Fall 1969): 22–24.

"Precipitate, Unplanned N.Y. Preems; Kael: Distribs Damage Own Chances." *Variety* 263.12 (4 Aug. 1971): 18.

"Reviews, Alice's Restaurant." *Digest, Motion Picture Herald*, 13 Aug. 1969.

Rollin, Betty. "Of Wit." *Look* 32 (2 Apr. 1968): 74.

Rolling Stone 585 (23 Aug. 1990): 107.

Rossell, Deac. "Arlo Guthrie's 'Alice's Restaurant, ' Becomes Arthur Penn's Newest Movie." *Boston After Dark*, 11 Nov. 1968.

Sarris, Andrew. "Films." *Village Voice*, 26 Dec. 1967, p. 33.

_____. "Films." *Village Voice*, 14 Aug. 1969, p. 35.

Schickel, Richard. "Arlo's Off-the-record Movie, Alice's Restaurant." *Life* (29 Aug. 1969): 8.

_____. "Fine Debut for a Square Anti-Hero." *Life* (19 Jan. 1968).

_____. "A Lyric, Tragic Song of the Road, Easy Rider." *Life* (11 July 1969).

Schoeldahl, Peter. "'McCabe and Mrs. Miller': A Sneaky-Great Movie." *The New York Times*, 25 July 1971.

Schwarz, Helena. "Accurate." *The New York Times*, 7 Feb. 1971.

Seydor, Paul. "THE GRADUATE Flunks Out." Reprinted in *Film Society Review* 5–6.5 (Jan. 1969–1970): 36–44.

Shalit, Gene. "Look at the Movies: Beatty and Christie and 'McCabe and Mrs. Miller'—Stop!" *Look* (10 Aug. 1971): 44.

S. K. "Spiritual Disease." *Time* 98.1 (5 July 1971): 66–67.

Slattery, Daniel. Letter to the Editor. *The New York Times*, 14 Sep. 1969.

Smith, Liz. "Cosmo Goes to the Movies." *Cosmopolitan* 168.5 (May 1970): 10.

_____. "Cosmo Goes to the Movies." *Cosmopolitan* 169.3 (Sep. 1970): 6.

_____. "Cosmo Goes to the Movies." *Cosmopolitan* 169.4 (Oct. 1970): 12.

Sragow, Michael. "New Times, Los Angeles, Rebel Without a Clue." *Los Angeles Times*, 13 Mar. 1997, p. 26.

Thirkell, Arthur. "Sins and Lovers...." *Daily Mirror*, 17 Sep. 1971.

"Turman to Film 'Grad' for Levine; Ends Millar Tie." *Variety* (6 Oct. 1964).

Variety 262.8 (7 Apr. 1971).

Walker, John. "Cannes: The Prizewinners." *Arts Guardian London*, 18 May 1970.

Warshow, Paul. "Easy Rider." *Sight and Sound* 39.1 (Winter 1969–1970): 36–38.

"WB to Auction Its 'Church' Props Rather Than Ship Them Back Here." *Variety*, 6 June 1971, p. 10.

"West by Northwest." *Cosmopolitan*, Oct. 1971, n.p.

Wolf, William. "New Films." *Cue* 36, (23 Dec. 1967): 57.

_____. "New Films." *Cue* 38 (19 July 1969): 72.

Zimmerman, Paul D. "Alice's Restaurant's Children." *Newsweek* 74.13 (29 Sep. 1969): 101–106.

Cosmopolitan on Women's Liberation

"16 Men's Jobs You Can Do Now (Most of Which You Couldn't Do Before)." *Cosmopolitan* 168.5 (May 1970): 78–91.

"72 Ways to Jolt a Man into Loving You Again." *Cosmopolitan* 169.6 (Dec. 1970): 80, 82.

Allerton, Jane. "Help Bring Back the Seducer." *Cosmopolitan* 169.3 (July 1970): 26.

Brown, Helen Gurley. "Step into My Parlor." *Cosmopolitan* 168.4 (Apr. 1970): 6.

_____. "Step into My Parlor." *Cosmopolitan* 168.5 (May 1970): 6

_____. "Step into My Parlor." *Cosmopolitan* 168.6 (June 1970): 6.

_____. "Step into My Parlor." *Cosmopolitan* 169.3 (Sep. 1970): 2.

_____. "Step into My Parlor." *Cosmopolitan* 169.6 (Dec. 1970): 6, 40.

Collins, Hillary. "The New Puritanism." *Cosmopolitan* 168.3 (Mar. 1970): 50.

Dichter, Ernest. "How Well Do You Know Him? Test." *Cosmopolitan* 169.3 (Sep. 1970): 73–74.

"The Driven Girls Who Have to Make It." *Cosmopolitan* 169.3 (July 1970): 80–83, 135.

Fleming, Alice. "Girls Who Buy and Sell (in the Stock Market)." *Cosmopolitan* 169.6 (Dec. 1970): 130.

Fromme, Alan. "Masturbation, A Doctor's Report." *Cosmopolitan* 169.6 (Dec. 1970): 98–102.

Green, Gael. "Hardened: What Is It with Bachelors Like Maximilian Schell? Why Won't They Make Some Little Girl Happy?" *Cosmopolitan* 169.3 (July 1970): 84–89.

Houck, Catherine. "The Crisis at Thirty or Over the Hill and into the Trees." *Cosmopolitan* 169.4 (Oct. 1970): 84–90.

Millett, Kate. "Sexual Politics." *Cosmopolitan* 169.5 (Nov. 1970): 84–106.

Raffeld, Joan. "I Love the Establishment!" *Cosmopolitan* 169 (July 1970): 26, 78.

Schary, Joll. "How to Get married if You're Over Thirty." *Cosmopolitan* 168.5. (May 1970): 58–59, 116.

"The Sensuous Woman." *Cosmopolitan* 169.4 (Oct. 1970): 84–94, 105+, 114, 139–143.

Shaber, David. "The Military Male." *Cosmopolitan* 169.6 (Dec. 1970): 116–121.

Web sites and Internet

Altman, Robert. http://www.geocities.come/Hollywood/8200/altman.htm.

Curry, Andrew. "Custer's Bluster." *U. S. News and World Report.* http://www.usnews.com/usnews/doubleissue/mysteries/custer.htm.

Danks, Adrian. "Just Some Jesus Looking for a Manger: *McCabe and Mrs. Miller,*" Senses of Cinema, 2000. http://www.sensesofcinema.com/contents/00/9/cteq/...

http://lists.villiagep.

http://us.imdb.com.

http://www.AFI.com.

http://www.ambidextrouspics.com/html/francis_ford_coppola.html.

http://www.amctv.com/person/detail/0,,1136–1–EST,00.html.

http://www.canoe.ca/JamMoviesF/fonda_peter.html.

http://www.cinema.sfsu.edu/curricuframe.html.

http://www.emanuellevy.com/article.php?articlD=6782.

http://www.ezrider.co.uk/Easy-Rider/easy-rider-links.html. Accessed 14 Mar. 2003.

http://www.filmbug.com/db/1251.

http://www.filmsite.org/easy.html. Accessed 5 Nov. 2002.

http://www.filmsite.org/godf2.html.

http://www.indiatravelite.com/accommodations/monarchooty.htm.

http://www.lather.com/fsc/fsc1.html. Accessed 22 Nov. 2002.

http://www.moviediva.com/MD_root/reviewpages/....

http://www.onmag.com/ford.htm.

http://www.salon.com/people/bc/1999/10/19/coppola.

http://www.seeing-stars.com/Dine/ThunderRoadhouse.shtml. Accessed 26 Aug. 2003.

http://www.super70s.com/Super70s/Movies/1974/Godfather.

http://www.urbandecay.com/products/NailEnamel/MidnightCowboyNailpolish.cfm.

http://www.wm.edu/CAS/ASP/faculty/Lowry/Amst2000/....

Kael, Pauline. http://www.geocities.com/hollywood/8200/gradkael.htm.

Sarris, Andrew. http://www.geocities.com/hollyjwood/8200/dradsarr.htm.

Simon, John. http://www.geocities.com/hollywood/8200/gradfilm.htm.

sixties@list.com.

Films

Alice's Restaurant. Produced by Hillard Elkins and Joe Manduke, directed by Arthur Penn, 1 hr. 51 min. MGM/UA, 1969. Videocassette, 1988.

Carnal Knowledge. Produced by Joseph E. Levine, directed by Mike Nichols, 1 hr. 38 min. MGM, 1971. Videocassette, 1999.

"Coppola's Notebook." *The Godfather* DVD Collection. Produced by Paramount Pictures, 2001. DVD, 2001.

Easy Rider. Produced by Peter Fonda, directed by Dennis Hopper, 94 min. Columbia, Videocassette, 1985.

The Godfather. Produced by Albert S. Ruddy, directed by Francis Ford Coppola, 175 min. Paramount Pictures, 1972. DVD, 2001.

The Godfather: Part II. Produced and directed by Francis Ford Coppola, 200 min. Paramount Pictures, 1974. DVD, 2001.

The Graduate. Produced by Lawrence Turman, directed by Mike Nichols, 1 hr., 46 min. Embassy Pictures, 1967. Videocassette, 1999.

Little Big Man. Produced by Stuart Miller, directed by Arthur Penn, 139 min. Hillar Productions,

1970. Videocassette, Paramount Pictures, 2000.

M*A*S*H. Produced Ingo Preminger, directed by Robert Altman, 116 Minutes. Ingo Preminger Productions, 1970. DVD, Twentieth Century–Fox, 1997.

McCabe and Mrs. Miller. Produced by David Foster and Michael Brower, directed by Robert Altman, 121 min. Warner Brothers, 1971. Videocassette, 1999.

Midnight Cowboy. Produced by Jerome Hellman, directed by John Schlesinger, 113 min. MGM, 1969. DVD, 2006.

True Grit. Produced by Hal Wallis, directed by Henry Hathaway, 128 min. Paramount Pictures, 1969. Videocassette.

Television Series

All in the Family. Produced by Norman Lear, directed by John Rich. Tandem Productions, Inc., 1971. DVD, 2003.

Novels and Nonfiction

Puzo, Mario. *The Godfather*. New York: Putnam, 1969.

Webb, Charles. *The Graduate*. New York: New American Library, 1963.

Wolfe, Tom. *Electric Kool-Aid Acid Test*. New York: Quality Paperback Books, 1990.

_____. *The Pump House Gang*. New York: Farrar, Straus, and Giroux, 1963.

Theoretical Framework

Barta, Tony, ed. *Screening the Past: Film and the Representation of History*. Westport, CT, and London: Praeger, 1998.

Bhadha, Homi. *Location of Culture*. London and New York: Routledge, 1994.

_____. *Nation and Narration*. London: Routledge, 1990.

Bourdieu, Pierre. *Distinction: A Social Critique of the Judgement [sic] of Taste*. Richard Nice, trans. Cambridge: Harvard University Press, 1984.

_____. *In Other Words: Essays Towards a Reflexive Sociology*. Matthew Adamson, trans. Stanford: Stanford University Press, 1990.

Carnes, Mark C., ed. *Past Imperfect: History According to the Movies*. New York: Henry Holt and Company, 1995.

Chow, Rey. *Primitive Passions: Visuality, Sexuality, Ethnography, and Contemporary Chinese Cinema*. New York: Columbia University Press, 1995.

_____. *Writing Diaspora: Tactics of Intervention in Contemporary Cultural Studies*. Bloomington and Indianapolis: Indiana University Press, 1993.

Ciongoli, Kenneth, and Jay Purini, eds. *Beyond The Godfather: Italian American Writers on the Real Italian American Experience*. Hanover and London: University Press of New England, 1997.

de Lauretis, Teresa. *Technologies of Gender: Essays on Theory, Film, and Fiction*. Bloomington and Indianapolis: Indiana University Press, 1987.

Deloria, Philip J. *Playing Indian*. New Haven and London: Yale University Press, 1998.

During, Simon, ed. *The Cultural Studies Reader*. London and New York: Routledge, 1993.

Foucault, Michel. *The Archeology of Knowledge*. London: Tavistock, 1972.

_____. *The History of Sexuality: An Introduction*. Robert Hurley, trans. New York: Vintage Books, Inc., 1978, 1990.

Friedberg, Anne. "Cinema and the Postmodern Condition." In *Viewing Positions: Ways of Seeing Film*, edited by Linda Williams, 29–83. New Brunswick, NJ: Rutgers University Press, 1995.

_____. "The Mobilized and Virtual Gaze in Modernity: Flaneur/Laneuse." In *The Visual Culture Reader*, edited by Nicholas Mirzoeff, 253–262. London, New York: Routledge, 1998.

Gardaphe, Fred. *Dagoes Read: Tradition and the Italian/American Writer*. Guernica: Gurenica Editions, Inc., 1996.

Greenblatt, Stephen. "Culture." In *Critical Terms for Literary Study*, edited by Frank Lentricchia and Thomas McLaughlin, 225–232. Chicago and London: University of Chicago Press, 1990.

_____. *Shakespearean Negotiations*. Berkeley and California: University of California Press, 1988.

Hall, Stuart. *Representation: Cultural Representations and Signifying Practices*. London, Thousand Oaks, CA, New Delhi: Sage Publications, 1997.

_____, and Paul du Gay, eds. *Identity, Genealogy, History in Questions of Cultural Identity*. London, Thousand Oaks, CA, New Delhi: Sage Publications, 1996.

Hebdige, Dick. *Subculture: The Meaning of Style*. London and New York: Routledge, 1979, 2001.

Hunt, Lynn, ed. *The New Cultural History*. Berkeley, Los Angeles, and London: University of California Press at Berkeley, 1989.

Jacobson, Matthew Frye. *Whiteness of a Different Color: European Immigrants and the Alchemy of Race*. Cambridge, MA, and London: Harvard University Press, 1998.

Jameson, Frederic. *Geopolitical Aesthetic: Cinema and Space in the World System*. Bloomington: Indiana University Press, 1992.

_____. *Signatures of the Visible*. New York and London: Routledge, 1992.

Lears, T. J. Jackson. "The Concept of Cultural Hegemony: Problems and Possibilities." *American Historical Review* 90.3 (1985): 567–593.

Mannino, Mary Ann Vigilante. *Revisionary Identities: Strategies of Empowerment in the Writing of Italian American Women*. New York: Peter Lang Publishing, Inc., 2000.

Mast, Gerald, Marshal Cohen, and Leo Braudy. *Film Theory and Criticism: Introductory Readings*. 4th ed. New York and Oxford: Oxford University Press, 1992.

McDonald, Terrence J., ed. *The Historic Turn in the Human Sciences*. Ann Arbor: The University of Michigan Press, 1996.

Scott, Joan W. "The Evidence of Experience." *Critical Inquiry* 17 (Summer 1991): 773–797.

_____. *Feminism and History*. Oxford: Oxford University Press, 1996.

Seidler, Victor J. *Rediscovering Masculinity: Reason, Language and Sexuality*. New York and London: Routledge, 1989.

Staiger, Janet. *Interpreting Films: Studies in the Historical Reception of American Cinema*. Princeton: Princeton University Press, 1992.

Stam, Robert, and Toby Miller. *Film and Theory: An Anthology*. Malden, MA: Blackwell Publishers, Ltd., 2000.

Susman, Warren I. *Culture as History: The Transformation of American Society in the Twentieth Century*. New York: Pantheon Books, 1984.

Tamburri, Anthony. *A Semiotic of Ethnicity: In Recognition of the Italian/American Writer*. Albany: State University of New York Press, 1998.

Wallace, Joann. "Where the Body Is a Battleground: Materializing Gender in the Humanities." *Resources for Feminist Research* (22 Sep. 2001): http://www.encyclopedia.com/doc/1G1–9044 5821.html.

Press Books and Production Notes

AuWerter, Russ. "A Conversation with Robert Altman." Core Collection, Margaret Herrick Academy of Motion Picture Arts and Sciences Library, Beverly Hills, CA.

"Carnal Knowledge Hailed as a Picture Whose Time Has Come." Publicity Department Avco Embassy Pictures Corp. Core Collection, Margaret Herrick Academy of Motion Picture Arts and Sciences Library; Beverly Hills, CA.

"Easy Rider." Core Collection, Margaret Herrick Academy of Motion Picture Arts and Sciences Library, Beverly Hills, CA.

Fairbairn, John. "First Ever Round-the-Clock London Showing for Cannes Festival Winner." *A News Special, M*A*S*H*. Twentieth Century–Fox, Special Collections, Margaret Herrick Academy of Motion Picture Arts and Sciences Library, Beverly Hills, CA.

"The Graduate." Core Collection, Margaret Herrick Academy of Motion Picture Arts and Sciences Library, Beverly Hills, CA.

Harmetz, Aljean. "The 15th Man Who Was Asked to Direct 'M*A*S*H' (and Did) Makes a Peculiar Western." Core Collection, Margaret Herrick Academy of Motion Picture Arts and Sciences Library, Beverly Hills, CA.

"John Wayne Explains the Meaning of 'True Grit,'" press book, Margaret Herrick Academy of Motion Picture Arts and Sciences Library, Beverly Hills, CA.

Little Big Man. Core Collection, Margaret Herrick Academy of Motion Picture Arts and Sciences Library, Beverly Hills, CA.

"*M*A*S*H*." Core Collection, Margaret Herrick Academy of Motion Picture Arts and Sciences Library, Beverly Hills, CA.

"*M*A*S*H*." Press book. Core Collection, Margaret Herrick Academy of Motion Picture Arts and Sciences Library, Beverly Hills, CA.

"McCabe and Mrs. Miller." Core Collection, Margaret Herrick Academy of Motion Picture Arts and Sciences Library, Beverly Hills, CA.

Special Collections

California Historical Society at The North Baker Research Library, San Francisco, CA.

_____. Folder 1, MS3159, 1966–1969 and MS3159/1, "Diggers," Mar. 1967–3 Mar. 1969 and n.d.

_____. Folder 2 MS3159/3, Communication Company, 24 Jan. 1967 — 28 July 1967 and in folder MS3159/5.

_____. Folder 2 MS3159/4, Free City News Mar., June, July 1968 and n.d.

_____. Folder 2 MS3159/6.

_____. Folder 1, MS4008, The Friends of Perfection Collections, 3 July 1969–4 Sep. 1969.

_____. Folder 2 MS4008, issues of *Kaliflower*.

_____. Miscellaneous/n.d.

Jules Feiffer Collection. Library of Congress, Washington DC.

Marty Weiser Special Collections, Margaret Herrick Academy of Motion Picture Arts and Sciences Library, Beverly Hills, CA.

"The Mirth of a Nation," 17 Sep. 1976. Margaret Herrick Academy of Motion Picture Arts and Sciences Library, Beverly Hills, CA.

Lardner, Ring, Jr. Folders 21, 22, 25. Special Collections Margaret Herrick Academy of Motion Picture Arts and Sciences Library, Beverly Hills, CA.

Lardner, Ring, Jr. Script. Special Collections, Margaret Herrick Academy of Motion Picture Arts and Sciences Library, Beverly Hills, CA.

McCabe and Mrs. Miller. Script. Special Collections, Margaret Herrick Academy of Motion Picture Arts and Sciences Library, Beverly Hills, CA.

Publicity Folder for M*A*S*H. Core Collection, Margaret Herrick Academy of Motion Picture Arts and Sciences Library, Beverly Hills, CA.

"Script #27 for *Easy Rider*." In *Easy Rider* File. Special Collections, Margaret Herrick Academy of Motion Picture Arts and Sciences Library, Beverly Hills, CA.

Personal Interviews

Folias, Vickie. Interview by author, Feb. 2001, Salt Lake City, UT.

Parker, Susan. Interview, Feb. 2001, Salt Lake City, UT.

Sotiriou, Margo. Interview by author, Feb. 2001, Salt Lake City, UT.

Yeo, Rob. Chair Department of Film, University of Wisconsin — Milwaukee. Telephone interview by author, 3 Dec. 2002.

Index

Numbers in **bold italics** indicate pages with photographs.

Primitivism 174, 175, 194, 231*n*5, 231*n*5, 232*n*32, 33, 41
Puzo, Mario 181, 182, 205

Quigley, Martin, Jr. 23, 43, 216*nn*34, 45
Quinn, Patricia as Alice Brock 68, 73, 74

Rapf, Maurice 26, 27
Ratings system 23, 43, 204, 206, 217*n*51, 226*n*36; in *Midnight Cowboy* 111, 226*n*36
Representation 9, 124, 125, 139, 144, 155, 158, 166, 178, 206, 208, 222*n*4, 229*nn*38, 40, 230*n*49; *see also* Identity
Revisionism 132, 142, 170, 171, 232*nn*28, 29
Ross, Katharine 48, 53, 205

Schaffner, Franklin J. 114, 118, 127
Schlesinger, John 9, 95, 100, 102, 103, 109, 110
Scorsese, Martin 25, 33, 35, 203, 219*n*57
Scott, George C. 114, *116*, 117, 118, 127
Segal, George 22

Selznick, David O. 15, 24
Sexploitation 31, 153, 230*n*31
Sexual revolution 10, 130, 138, 228*n*9; in *Carnal Knowledge* 145, 151, 154, 155, 156, 231*n*58; in *McCabe and Mrs. Miller* 13, 138, 139
Sexuality 53, 60, 130, 138, 210, 228*n*6, 230*n*49; in *Carnal Knowledge* 145, 146, 154–156; see also *Alice's Restaurant*; Feiffer, Jules; *The Graduate*
Sixties as narrative 6–8
The Sound of Music 15, 25, 47, 201, 207
Spielberg, Steven 2, 10, 203, 204, 209
Student filmmaking and festivals 34–35, 219*nn*57, 63
Sutherland, Donald 113, 119, 120, 132
Swit, Loretta 126

Taylor, Elizabeth 18, 22, 99
True Grit (1969) 99 100, 102, 111, 143
Turman, Lawrence 36, 43, 48, 57, 235*n*21
Tusher, William 16, 24
20th-Century–Fox 15, 16, 114, 205

United Artists 112, 128, 216*n*50
University Film Producers Association 218*n*38

Vacarro, Brenda 106
Valenti, Jack 21, *22*, 23, 36, 111, 153, 205
Vietnam War 116, 120, 121, 127, 176, 200, 208
Voight, Jon 99, *103*, 105, 108

Warner Brothers 15, 21, 22, 131
Wayne, John 76, 79, 80, 94, 99, 100, *101*, 102–108, 114, 116; reference in *Midnight Cowboy* 104, 105, 107
Webb, Charles 49, 50, 55
Westerns 8, 79, 82, 84, 100, 101–108, 131, 132, 139, 142, 143, 165, 173, 224*nn*5, 6; women in 106; see also *Easy Rider*; *McCabe and Mrs. Miller*; *Midnight Cowboy*
Who's Afraid of Virginia Woolf? 5, 21–23, 26, 37, 216*nn*40, 41
Wild Angels 78
Women's liberation *see* Feminism

Zanuck, Darryl 15